Paul
& His World

ILLUSTRISSIMAE

UNIVERSITATE HUMBOLDTIANAE BEROLINENSI

OB SUMMUM IN SANCTA THEOLOGIA HONOREM SIBI OBLATUM

HUNC LIBRUM

GRATUS VENERABUNDUS

D. THEOL.

HELMUT KOESTER

Paul & His World

Interpreting the New Testament in Its Context

HELMUT KOESTER

Fortress Press
Minneapolis

PAUL AND HIS WORLD
Interpreting the New Testament in Its Context

Cover image: The Citadel of Acrocorinth. Photo from *The Cities of Paul,* Fortress Press, 2004 © The President and Fellows of Harvard College.
Cover design: Brad Norr Design
Book design and typesetting: H. K. Scriptorium

Library of Congress Cataloging-in-Publication Data
Koester, Helmut, 1926-
    Paul and his world : interpreting the New Testament in its context / Helmut Koester.
    p.   cm.
    Includes bibliographical references and index.
    ISBN-13: 978-0-8006-3890-0 (alk. paper)
    1. Paul, the Apostle, Saint. 2. Bible. N.T. Epistles of Paul—Theology. 3. Bible. N.T.—Criticism, interpretation, etc. I. Title.
    BS2506.3.K64 2007
    225.6—dc22
                                            2006026175

10 09 08 07 06 1 2 3 4 5 6 7 8 9 10

CONTENTS

ACKNOWLEDGMENTS

1. Paul's Proclamation of God's Justice for the Nations
   Cardinal Bellarmine Lecture, delivered at the University of St. Louis in October 2004, published in *Theology Digest* 51 (2004) 303–14; published here with slight revisions.

2. First Thessalonians: An Experiment in Christian Writing
   Published in F. Forrester Church and Timothy George, eds., *Continuity and Discontinuity: Essays Presented to George H. Williams* (Leiden: Brill, 1979) 33–44.

3. Apostle and Church in the Letters to the Thessalonians
   English translation of "Apostel und Gemeinde in den Briefen an die Thessalonicher," in Dieter Lührmann und Georg Strecker, eds., *Kirche: Festschrift für Günther Bornkamm zum 75. Geburtstag* (Tübingen: Mohr/Siebeck, 1980) 287–98.

4. The Text of 1 Thessalonians
   Published in Dennis E. Groh and Robert Jewett, eds., *The Living Text: Essays in Honor of Ernest W. Saunders* (Lanham, Md.: University Press of America, 1985) 219–27.

5. Archaeology and Paul in Thessalonike
   English translation of "Archäologie und Paulus in Thessalonike," published in Lukas Bormann, Kelly del Tredici, Angela Standhartinger, eds., *Religious Propaganda and Missionary Competition in the New Testament World: Essays Honoring Dieter Georgi* (Leiden: Brill, 1994) 393–404. The section on the Egyptian religion in Thessalonike in this essay has been expanded by the insertion of a lecture given at a later date by the author.

6. From Paul's Eschatology to the Apocalyptic Scheme of 2 Thessalonians
   Published in Raymond F. Collins, ed., *The Thessalonians Correspondence* (BETL 87; Leuven: Leuven University Press, 1990) 441–58.

7. Paul and Philippi: The Evidence from Early Christian Literature
   Published in Charalambos Bakirtzis and Helmut Koester, eds., *Philippi at the Time of Paul and After His Death* (Harrisburg: Trinity Press International, 1998) 49–66.

8. Wisdom and Folly in Corinth
   Translation from German of the review of Ulrich Wilckens, *Weisheit und Torheit: Eine exegetisch-religionsgeschichtliche Untersuchung zu 1. Kor. 1.18–2.16* (BhTh 26; Tübingen: Mohr/Siebeck, 1959), published in *Gnomon* 33 (1961) 590–95.

9. Hero Worship: Philostratos's *Heroikos* and Paul's Tomb in Philippi
   Published in slightly different form as "Epilogue" to Jennifer K. Berenson Maclean and Ellen Bradshaw Aitken, trans. and notes, *Flavius Philostratus: Heroikos* (SBL

Writings from the Greco-Roman World 1; Atlanta: Society of Biblical Literature, 2001) 257–64.

10. Suffering Servant and Royal Messiah: From Second Isaiah to Paul, Mark, and Matthew
    The lectures presented here were delivered as the Schmiechen Lectures at Eden Theological Seminary in October 2003. Published in *Theology Digest* 51 (2004) 102–24.

11. The Figure of the Divine Human Being
    Published under the title "The Divine Human Being" in *HTR* 78 (1985) 243–52.

12. Natural Law (Νόμος Φύσεως) in Greek Thought
    Published under the title "ΝΟΜΟΣ ΦΥΣΕΩΣ: The Concept of Natural Law in Greek Thought," in Jacob Neusner, ed., *Religions in Antiquity: Essays in Memory of Erwin Goodenough* (Studies in the History of Religion/Numen Sup 14; Leiden: Brill, 1968) 521–41.

13. The Cult of the Egyptian Deities in Asia Minor
    Published in Helmut Koester, ed., *Pergamon, Citadel of the Gods: Archaeological Record, Literary Description, and Religious Development* (HTS 46; Harrisburg: Trinity Press International, 1998) 111–35.

14. Associations of the Egyptian Cult in Asia Minor
    Published in Peter Scherrer, Hans Taeuber, and Hilke Thür, eds., *Steine und Wege: Festschrift für Dieter Knibbe zum 65. Geburtstag* (Österreichisches Archäologisches Institut, Sonderschriften Band 32; Vienna: 1999) 315–18.

15. The Red Hall in Pergamon
    Published in L. Michael White and O. Larry Yarbrough, eds., *The Social World of the Early Christians: Essays in Honor of Wayne A. Meeks* (Minneapolis: Fortress Press, 1995) 265–74.

16. Lefkopetra: Inscriptions from the Sanctuary of the Mother of the Gods
    This is a revised edition of a brief article published in *Numina Aegaea* 1 (1974) 1–3 (this journal was a private publication initiated by me; it is no longer in existence).

17. Melikertes at Isthmia: A Roman Mystery Cult
    Published in David L. Balch, Everett Ferguson, Wayne Meeks, eds., *Greeks, Romans, and Christians: Essays in Honor of Abraham J. Malherbe* (Minneapolis: Fortress Press, 1990) 355–66.

18. Thomas Jefferson, Ralph Waldo Emerson, the *Gospel of Thomas,* and the Apostle Paul
    English translation of an unpublished lecture delivered at the Humboldt University of Berlin, Germany, on June 28, 2006.

19. Writings and the Spirit: Authority and Politics in Ancient Christianity
    Published in *HTR* 84 (1991) 353–72.

20. The Apostolic Tradition and the Origins of Gnosticism
    Revised English version of a lecture presented at the Institut des Sciences Bibliques

in Lausanne on March 1, 1986. It was originally published as "La tradition apostolique et les origines du Gnosticisme," *RThPh* 119 (1987) 1–16. I am indebted to Margot Stevenson for the English translation.

21. The Theological Aspects of Early Christian Heresy
Originally published as "Häretiker im Urchristentum als theologisches Problem," in Erich Dinkler, ed., *Zeit und Geschichte: Dankesgabe an Rudolf Bultmann zum 80. Geburtstag* (Tübingen: Mohr/Siebeck, 1964) 61–76; after revision by the author, translated by Bentley Layton and published as "The Theological Aspects of Primitive Christian Heresy," in James M. Robinson, ed., *The Future of Our Religious Past: Essays in Honor of Rudolf Bultmann* (New York: Harper & Row, 1971) 65–83.

22. Ephesos in Early Christian Literature
Published in Helmut Koester, ed., *Ephesos: Metropolis of Asia* (HTS 41; Valley Forge, Pa.; Trinity Press International, 1995) 119–40.

23. The Designation of James as ὨΒΛΙΑΣ
English translation of a note published jointly with Klaus Baltzer as "Die Bezeichnung des Jakobus als ὨΒΛΙΑΣ," *ZNW* 46 (1955) 141–42. It is here republished with the permission of my coauthor.

24. Early Christianity from the Perspective of the History of Religions: Rudolf Bultmann's Contribution
Published in Edward C. Hobbs, ed., *Bultmann, Retrospect and Prospect* (HTS 35; Philadelphia: Fortress Press, 1985) 59–74.

ABBREVIATIONS

AB	Anchor Bible
ad loc.	*ad locum* = on the passage quoted
AJA	*American Journal of Archaeology*
ANRW	*Aufstieg und Niedergang der römischen Welt*
BAG	W. Bauer, W. F. Arndt, and F. W. Gingrich, *Greek-English Lexicon of the New Testament and Other Early Christian Literature.* Chicago: University of Chicago Press, 1957
BAR	*Biblical Archaeology Review*
BASOR	*Bulletin of the American Schools of Oriental Research*
BCH	*Bulletin de correspondance hellénique*
BDF	F. Blass, A. Debrunner, and R. W. Funk, *A Greek Grammar of the New Testament and Other Early Christian Literature.* Chicago: University of Chicago Press, 1961
BETL	Bibliotheca ephemeridum theologicarum Lovanensium
BevTh	Beiträge zur evangelischen Theologie
BFChTh	Beiträge zur Förderung der christlichen Theologie
BG	Berlin Gnostic Papyrus
BhTh	Beiträge zur historischen Theologie
Bib	*Biblica*
BKANT	Biblischer Kommentar zum Alten und Neuen Testament
BZNW	Beihefte zur Zeitschrift für die neutestamentliche Wissenschaft
CIG	*Corpus inscriptionum Graecarum*
Diels	Hermann Diels, *Die Fragmente der Vorsokratiker.* 10th ed.; Berlin: Weidmann, 1961
diss.	dissertation
EB	Études bibliques
ed(s).	editor(s)
EKKNT	Evangelisch-katholischer Kommentar zum Neuen Testament
EPRO	Études preliminaries aux religions orientales dans l'empire romain
ET	English translation
EthL	Ephemerides theologicae lovanienses
EvTh	*Evangelische Theologie*
FF	Foundations and Facets
frg(s).	fragment(s)
FRLANT	Forschungen zur Religion und Literatur des Alten und Neuen Testaments
GRBS	*Greek, Roman and Byzantine Studies*
HAW	Handbuch der Altertumswissenschaft

HDR   Harvard Dissertations in Religion
HNT   Handbuch zum Neuen Testament
HSCP   *Harvard Studies in Classical Philology*
HTR   *Harvard Theological Review*
HTS   Harvard Theological Studies
IG   *Inscriptiones graecae*
inv.   inventory
IvE   *Inschriften von Ephesos*
JbAC   Jahrbuch für Antike und Christentum
JBL   *Journal of Biblical Literature*
JETS   *Journal of the Evangelical Theological Society*
JHS   *Journal of Hellenic Studies*
JÖAI   *Jahreshefte des österreichischen archäologischen Instituts*
JR   *Journal of Religion*
JRomS   *Journal of Roman Studies*
JTS   *Journal of Theological Studies*
KEK   Kritisch-exegetischer Kommentar
LCL   Loeb Classical Library
LSJ   H. G. Liddell, R. Scott, and H. S. Jones, *Greek-English Lexicon*. 9th ed. Oxford: Clarendon, 1946
LXX   Septuagint
MS(S)   manuscript(s)
n(n).   note(s)
NA   Eberhard Nestle, Kurt Aland, et al., *Novum Testamentum Graece*. 25th ed. Stuttgart: Privilegierte Württembergische Bibelanstalt, 1963; 26th ed. 1979; repr. Stuttgart: Deutsche Bibelstiftung, 1981
NedTT   *Nederlands theologisch tijdschrift*
NF   Neue Folge
NHL   Nag Hammadi Library
NHS   Nag Hammadi Studies
NovT   *Novum Testamentum*
NovTSup   Supplements to *Novum Testamentum*
NRSV   New Revised Standard Version
n.s.   new series
NT   New Testament
NTA   Neutestamentliche Abhandlungen
NTS   *New Testament Studies*
OTP   *Old Testament Pseudepigrapha*. Ed. J. H. Charlesworth. 2 vols. New York: Doubleday, 1983–85
Pap.   Papyrus
par(s).   parallel(s)
PW   A. F. Pauly and Georg Wissowa, eds., *Real-Encyclopädie der classischen Altertumswissenschaft*. New edition G. Wissowa. 49 vols. Munich, 1980).
RAC   *Reallexikon für Antike und Christentum,* ed. Theodor Klauser. Stuttgart: Hieresemann, 1950–

RB	*Revue biblique*
RGG	*Die Religion in Geschichte und Gegenwart,* ed. Hans von Campenhausen, et al. 3d ed. 6 vols. Tübingen: Mohr/Siebeck, 1957–65
RThPh	*Revue de théologie et de philosophie*
RTL	*Revue théologique de Louvain*
RVV	Religionsgeschichtliche Versuche und Vorarbeiten
SBL	Society of Biblical Literature
SBLDS	Society of Biblical Literature Dissertation Series
SBT	Studies in Biblical Theology
SHAW.PH	Sitzungsberichte der Heildelberger Akademie der Wissensschaften. Philosophisch-historische Klasse
SNTSMS	Society of New Testament Studies Monograph Series
ST	*Studia theologica*
StUNT	Studien zur Umwelt des Neuen Testaments
Sup	supplement
s.v.	sub voce/verbo
TAPA	*Transactions of the American Philosophical Association*
TDNT	*Theological Dictionary of the New Testament.* Ed. G. Kittel and G. Friedrich. Trans. G. W. Bromiley. 10 vols. Grand Rapids: Eerdmans, 1964–76
ThLZ	*Theologische Literaturzeitung*
ThR	*Theologische Rundschau*
ThWNT	*Theologisches Wörterbuch zum Neuen Testament.* Ed. G. Kittel and G. Friedrich. 10 vols. Stuttgart: Kohlhammer, 1932–79
ThZ	*Theologische Zeitschrift*
TRE	*Theologische Realenzyklopädie,* ed. Gerhard Krause and Gerhard Müller. 36 vols. Berlin: de Gruyter, 1976–2004
TU	Texte und Untersuchungen
VC	*Vigiliae christianae*
vol(s).	volume(s)
v(v).	verse(s)
VuF	*Verkündigung und Forschung*
WMANT	Wissenschaftliche Monographien zum Alten und Neuen Testament
ZNW	*Zeitschrift für die neutestamentliche Wissenschaft*
ZRGG	*Zeitschrift für Religion und Geistesgeschichte*
ZSTh	*Zeitschrift für systematische Theologie*
ZThK	*Zeitschrift für Theologie und Kirche*

PLATES

PREFACE

This volume contains a selection of articles that I have published during the past fifty years of my work as a theologian and scholar in the study of the New Testament, early Christianity, and the world of antiquity. Only the essay on "Thomas Jefferson, Ralph Waldo Emerson, the *Gospel of Thomas,* and the Apostle Paul," and the last essay, "Insights from a Career of Interpretation," have not been published previously. The small note on "The Designation of James as 'ΩΒΛΙΑΣ" was written jointly by my friend Klaus Baltzer and myself; it was the first publication of our scholarly career and is here included with my coauthor's permission.

The essays do not appear in this volume in chronological order but are assembled according to their subject matter. Where they belong in the development of my scholarly career can be learned from the final essay of this volume, "Insights from a Career of Interpretation." There is, of course, no attempt to provide full coverage of all related subject matters. The articles in the first section, Reading Paul: His Letters and Their Interpretation, demonstrate that I have been working for some time on a critical commentary on the Letters to the Thessalonians, which I hope to complete in the near future. The second section will demonstrate my interest in the study of archaeological materials from the world of early Christianity. Several of the articles have been produced as public lectures and therefore do not include full bibliographical documentation and discussion of other scholars' work and arguments.

First of all, I have to express my thanks to Jörg Frey, Professor of New Testament Studies at the University of Munich, who originally suggested a publication of my collected articles. I am grateful to the editors at Fortress Press, Michael West and especially Dr. Neil Elliott, for encouraging this publication, proposing a division of the project into two volumes (a second volume with my articles on Gospel literature will follow soon), assisting in the selection of articles, and shaping the format of the publication. One of the articles ("The Apostolic Tradition and the Origins of Gnosticism"), first published in French, was translated by Margot Stevenson, doctoral candidate in New Testament Studies at Harvard University; I must thank her for her thoughtful and knowledgeable translation. I myself am responsible for the English translations of all articles originally published in German. Stephen Hebert and, in the final stages of the book, David Jorgensen, both graduate students at Harvard Divinity School, assisted me by scanning all older articles and in the meticulous work of bringing bibliographical references into a unified style; I am forever grateful for their tireless efforts and their care for every detail. Finally, I want to thank my wife Gisela, who has supported my work throughout these past five decades with love and patience.

HELMUT KOESTER

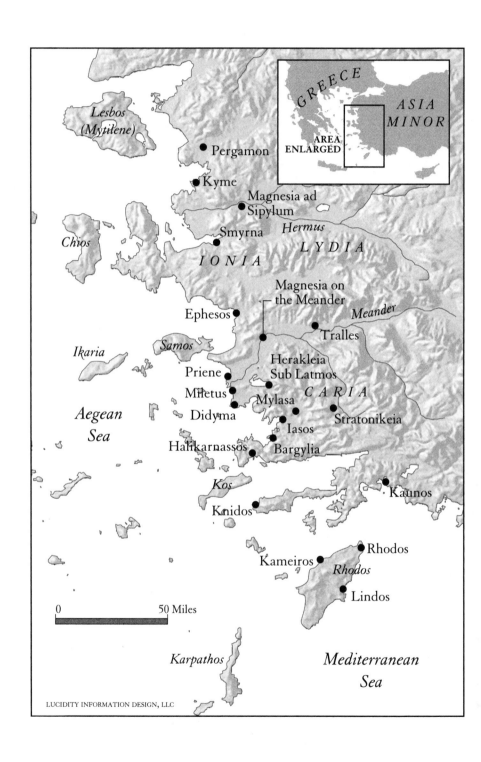

I

READING PAUL

His Letters and Their Interpretation

1

PAUL'S PROCLAMATION OF GOD'S JUSTICE FOR THE NATIONS

The Traditional Understanding of the "Righteousness of God"

Especially since the time of the Reformation, but already in the Middle Ages and in the Roman Catholic statements of the Council of Trent, "righteousness of God" has been primarily understood in anthropological and individualistic terms. Righteousness was something to be attained by the individual human being. Thus righteousness came to be identical with piety and obedience to the God-given moral standards of the society, reinforced through the institution of the Sacrament of Confession. During the centuries after the Reformation, the emphasis upon the righteousness of the individual was further enhanced by Pietism and the Enlightenment. Righteousness continued to mean piety and morality of the individual believer, often in the service of the maintenance of the fabric of the society and its structures. In nineteenth-century Romanticism it was understood to include also the attachment to God in the religious feeling of the soul. This understanding of righteousness still dominates today most of Christian thought in Roman Catholic as well as Protestant churches. Indeed, in today's religious and political scene of the United States, righteousness as piety and morality still functions as an important support for the structures of the state, especially among Christians of the religious right. Unfortunately, it also implies a good degree of boasting, self-righteousness, hypocrisy, and judgmental attitudes over against those who do not seem to share the same values and moral commitments and whom one therefore considers as impious or immoral and thus a danger to the well-being of the entire state and its order. It can also take the form of the claim of moral superiority of our entire country and thus establishing our own country as better than other nations.

According to such interpretation, individuals, with the help of God's gifts, are challenged to achieve this righteousness for themselves and to follow all rituals and all required moral precepts. The gifts of grace administered by the church and the striving for holiness by the efforts of the individual should combine to result in the creation of the perfect religious person, and at the same time in the building of a just and moral

I owe much to my friend and colleague Krister Stendahl, especially to his essay on "Paul and the Introspective Conscience of the West" (*HTR* 56 [1963] 199–215), and to Richard Hays's book on *The Faith of Jesus Christ* (Grand Rapids: Eerdmans, 2002), and want to express my gratitude to their pioneering discussions of Paul's theology.

society. To be sure, the Reformation protested: righteousness of the individual is a pure gift of divine grace, involving no human effort and therefore, as Paul formulates, making it impossible for human beings to boast of their achievements. But in the end it makes not much difference whether an individual believer claims to have achieved that righteousness by his or her effort or by accepting personal righteousness as a pure gift from God.

This individualistic and pietistic interpretation still persists. When Paul says in Rom 5:1 that "we, being justified by faith, now have peace with God through our Lord Jesus Christ," the common interpretation is that each individual believer on the basis of his or her faith is now at peace with God. Interpreters overlook that Paul is here using the plural "we" and that "by faith" may not denote the faith that every individual provides but rather means "by the faithfulness of Jesus"—not your personal faith and my personal faith. Only more recently some scholars argued that "justified by Jesus Christ's faith" (Gal 2:16) really speaks about Jesus' faithfulness by giving his life for the sake of all of humankind; Paul does not speak of the belief *in* Jesus on the side of the believer. Rather, Jesus is here the subject of "faith"—"Jesus' faith." Jesus is the one who was faithful to God. That is what justifies us—not that Jesus is the object of our faith so that we are justified because we believe in Jesus. Moreover, "we" in Rom 5:1 does not point to a cluster of individuals who happen to share the same religious convictions, but rather to a new community, the new people of God. Examples of mistaken individualistic interpretations of the text of Paul's letters could be easily multiplied. But it seems to me that a thorough reconsideration of this interpretation is now called for. Is it really our individual offering of faith that matters? And is it really our individual righteousness (i.e., our piety and morality) that matters?

It is important to observe that in the early Christian period the terms that could be translated with "piety" or "morality" (Greek *eusebeia* and *hosiotēs,* Latin *pietas*) are completely missing in the genuine letters of Paul, although they occur in the later letters to Timothy and Titus and in 1 and 2 Peter. In fact, Paul never equates righteousness with piety and morality. What was meant in the Roman imperial period by "piety" is the proper worship of the gods and of the emperor; respect of the structures of the family, especially the respect that wife and children owed to their husband and father; and the obedience of slaves to their masters. "Piety" had nothing to do with religious feelings—that is an invention of the modern age. But "piety" signified the appropriate reverence of the religious observances and the fitting social behavior within the hierarchical structures that guaranteed the well-being of the empire and the peace that was ultimately guaranteed by the very piety of the emperor himself. Peace and welfare of the empire were established by the gods as a reward for human piety and morality.

Paul had no interest whatsoever in the preservation of an imperial hierarchical system and in the piety and moral values it demanded; nor would he argue for any society that was upheld by the righteousness of the individual. It is therefore not possible to understand Paul's proclamation of the righteousness of God as aimed at the establishment of a society of righteous and moral individuals, who expected divine rewards for their piety. A reconsideration of Paul's concepts of righteousness and justice requires a brief recourse to the prophetic tradition of Israel's Bible.

The Prophetic Proclamation of Justice
for Israel and for the Nations

The tradition of Israel's Scriptures, what we now call the Hebrew Bible or Old Testament, is deeply divided by two fundamentally different expectations of the future of the people of Israel. On the one hand, there is the belief that God is the God of Israel, and of Israel alone, and that the salvation of Israel would come through the appointment of a new king, the Messiah, as the heir of David. This expectation is most clearly expressed in the oracle of Nathan to King David that his heir would sit on his throne forever:

> Thus says the Lord of hosts: I took you from the pasture, from following the sheep to be prince over my people Israel; and I have been with you wherever you went. ... When your days are fulfilled and you lie down with your ancestors, I will raise up your offspring after you, who shall come forth from your body, and I will establish his kingdom. He shall build a house for my name, and I will establish the throne of his kingdom forever. I will be a father to him and he shall be a son to me. ... Your house and your kingdom shall be made sure forever before me. Your throne shall be established forever. (2 Sam 7:8–16)

This belief has dominated the expectation of a divinely legitimized "Messiah," who would, as a king, liberate the people from oppression and lead Israel to victory over the nations. Justice in the land would be upheld by the proper obedience to the king, the power of his army, and the moral behavior of the subjects, guided by the law. The term "Messiah" became the technical term for the king of Israel, the messianic Davidic heir to the promise of Nathan. This messianic expectation is decidedly nationalistic. The Davidic Messiah is the king of Israel, and only of Israel. This messianic king would rule over the entire land that God had promised to his people Israel. As far as other nations are concerned, they are seen as the enemies of Israel, vanquished and subdued, or even completely annihilated, by the power of the God of Israel and his royal agent.

On the other hand, over against this Davidic expectation of the messianic king, there is the fundamentally different insistence of some of the prophetic tradition that not David and his heir but God himself is the king of Israel. This lies at the heart of the conflict between the prophets and the royal establishment that lasted for centuries, beginning as early as the time of the prophets Amos and Hosea, dominating the book of Deuteronomy, reaching a high point in Jeremiah's conflict with the royal establishment, and finally culminating in the prophetic book that we now know as Second Isaiah, comprising chapters 40–55 of the book of Isaiah. The one who will remind Israel of its covenant and calling for justice is God himself working through his agents, the prophets. Indeed, prophets repeatedly confront the king in the name of God, accusing him of having broken the covenant and of having increased the injustice in Israel. Israel's prophets had a very low and pessimistic opinion regarding the piety and justice of the ruler. They suspected that whoever ruled the country was most likely to be unjust and greedy. For the prophets, God is the undisputed king of Israel, and the prophets are God's legitimate representatives on earth. Thus, on the basis of the authority granted to them by God, they can claim to have rights that supersede any royal authority.

The prophetic call for justice is always a call for the creation of a just society, in which the poor are not suppressed and exploited and all people have equal standing in the court of judgment. There is never any emphasis upon the establishment of the morally righteous and pious individual. To do right is in the interest of justice for the entire community. If individuals, especially those in government and in the upper classes, sin and do wrong, they jeopardize the entire community and thus, violating the covenant, call down God's wrath upon the community of Israel as a whole. It is the covenantal obligation of the people to maintain justice for all. If these obligations are violated, punishment will condemn not only the individual sinner but the entire nation.

The pronouncement of God's rights as the sovereign king of Israel was not limited to God as the king of Israel only. The proclamation of God as the king of not only Israel but as God of all nations appears as early as the ninth century BCE in the prophet Amos, who pronounced oracles not only for Israel but also for the nations. The view of the God of Israel as the God who created the universe and the earth was reinforced in the fifth century BCE, that is, in the early Persian period. It is clearly evident in the creation story of Genesis 1: God created the entire world, the firm earth, the sun, the moon, and all living creatures, including all human beings on the face of the earth. Greek influences are perhaps at work here. Greek philosophy had developed at that time the concept that the primary god of the Greek nation, Zeus, was not only the god of the Hellenes but the creator of the entire world and of all humankind.

The book of Second Isaiah,[1] written in the Persian period, probably early in the fifth century BCE, emphasizes throughout that Yahweh, the God and king of Israel, is also the God of the entire earth and of all its nations. At the same time, Second Isaiah also rejects the Davidic messianic claim to royalty in Israel and the idea that Israel had a God-given right to the promised land. The earthly ruler and king appointed by God is no longer the descendant of David but the Persian king Cyrus. God has anointed Cyrus to rule the known world and all the lands on the earth, and although Cyrus does not know him, it is God who has put the nations under his feet and forced them into obedience. There is no longer a Davidic messianic king. The Persian king Cyrus is the "Messiah":

> Thus says the Lord to his Messiah, to Cyrus, whom I have taken by his right hand to subdue peoples before him—and he will ungird the hips of kings, to open doors before him—and gates will not be closed. . . . Who calls you by your name? The God of Israel. . . . I am the Lord and there is no other. Besides me there are no gods. I gird you although you have not known me, so that they may know in the east and the west that besides me there is no other. (Isa 45:1–6, trans. Baltzer, mod.)

The parochialism of the expectation of a Davidic offspring as the Messiah of Israel together with the concept of a God who cares only for his own people of Israel, to whom he owes the promised land, is rejected. At the same time the appointment of a

---

1. For my understanding of Second Isaiah I am grateful to what I have learned from Klaus Baltzer, *Deutero-Isaiah: A Commentary on Isaiah 40–55* (Hermeneia; Minneapolis: Fortress Press, 2001).

universal ruler by a God who is not only the God of Israel but also the God of creation and of all nations is closely connected with the idea of God fashioning righteousness and justice for all nations in the world that God created:

I am the Lord, and there is no other, who forms light and creates darkness, who makes peace and creates disaster. I am the Lord who does all this. Drop, heavens, from above! And let clouds rain down salvation. Let the earth open itself so that help may ripen and let righteousness spring up with it. I am the Lord who created it. (Isa 45:6–8)

Accordingly, also the task of the Servant of God is directed not only to Israel but to all nations. The prophet is not just God's servant for Israel but has a universal task as the representative of God on earth for all the nations of the world:

The Lord said: it is too little that you should belong to me as servant to raise up the tribe of Jacob and to bring back those who have been preserved in Israel. Thus I shall make you a light to the nations, so that my help may reach to the end of the earth. (Isa 49:6).

The term "light" is closely associated in the Hebrew Bible with justice and can serve as its synonym. The task of the Servant of God is thus the call for justice in the entire world. Also the suffering of the Servant of God in behalf of the sins of all people is seen in this prophetic book as an event that concerns not just Israel but the entire world. In the famous Servant of God text in Isa 52:13–53:12, Israel is never mentioned as the specific beneficiary of his suffering. Instead the text speaks of "kings who will shut their mouths, when they see his suffering," and his sacrifice will benefit "the many," that is, all people of the world.

These references in the prophetic tradition of the Hebrew Bible to the universal understanding of God and of the role of his Servant in the proclamation of justice to all nations must suffice in this context.[2] The apostle Paul belongs to this prophetic tradition of Israel. Jesus is for Paul not the Messiah of Israel but the Servant of God, who gives his life for the establishment of justice for all.

All Are Guilty, but God Creates a Realm of Righteousness for All Nations

That Paul stands fully in the prophetic tradition of Israel is evident in the account of his own calling. It is not an account of Paul's "conversion" to the Christian faith but of his calling to an office that he understood in terms of a prophetic call. Paul never was "converted." Rather, unworthy as he was because he had persecuted the church of God,

---

2. See also "Suffering Servant and Royal Messiah: From Second Isaiah to Paul, Mark, and Matthew," chapter 10 in this volume.

he was called to an office that he understood in analogy to the office of Israel's prophets. In the recollection of his call he speaks with words that echo the words in which the prophets Jeremiah and Second Isaiah describe their calls: "When God, who had set me apart before I was born and called me through his grace, was pleased to reveal his Son to me, so that I might proclaim him among the Gentiles, I did not confer with any human being, nor did I go up to Jerusalem" (Gal 1:15–17).

As this description of his call evokes the words in which Jeremiah (1:5) and Second Isaiah (49:1–6) describe their calls, it is evident how Paul understood his mission. That Paul experienced this as a prophetic call is also evident in his emphasis upon his independence from any human agency, especially his independence from the Jerusalem leaders. It was God who gave him his commission. No human agency was involved. Moreover, the Jerusalem leaders were the representatives of a particularistic position that wanted to limit the Christian community to those who legitimately belonged to law-abiding Israel and demanded circumcision from new members of the community of Jesus. Paul's call was a prophetic call for the proclamation of the gospel to all people and all nations, to the Gentiles, and his mission could not possibly be subject to, or authorized by, the leaders of the Jerusalem community.

Proclamation of God's gift of righteousness to all nations implied that the law had lost its power in that it was the dividing line between Israel and the nations. There is another element that made it necessary for Paul to draw a sharp line between himself and the tradition of law-abiding Jews: peace-loving Jews like Philo and Josephus and many other leaders of the Jewish community were trying to demonstrate that precisely their obedience to the law included respect for the Roman order of justice and peace guaranteed by the Roman emperor. Moreover, if the law was understood also as an opportunity for the individual to acquire one's own righteousness by fulfilling it and thus claiming to have become righteous through one's own efforts, the concept of righteousness and justice was perverted because for Paul righteousness and justice belonged to God and to God alone. God's righteous actions are not addressed to individuals but to all people, to Israel as well as to the nations. God is not interested in pious individuals but in calling peoples and nations into a new society in which justice, righteousness, and equality reign supreme. The problem is not that the demands of the law were so difficult and so complex that human beings could not fulfill them and therefore needed God's grace and forgiveness. On the contrary, Paul assumes that it is perfectly possible to fulfill the law, and he says of himself that he has in his previous life under the law achieved that fulfillment, but he calls it "confidence in the flesh," that is, confidence in oneself rather than in God: "If anyone else has confidence in the flesh, I have more: circumcised on the eighth day, a member of the people of Israel, of the tribe of Benjamin, a Hebrew born of Hebrews; as to the law, a Pharisee; as to zeal, a persecutor of the church; as to righteousness under the law, blameless" (Phil 3:4–6). The problem is that righteousness is something that God has to grant regardless of anything that human beings are and do, and regardless of any political order that human beings try to establish through pious and moral actions. Righteousness is not something that is awarded to the individual believer, Jew or Gentile. Rather, God is not interested in righteous individuals but God wants to create righteousness and justice for people, for communities, and for nations. Paul is a radical monotheist in the postexilic tradition of

Israel. For him God is not just the God of Israel but of the entire world that God created with all its people. It must therefore be God's will that his justice goes out to all people and all nations, to Jews and Gentiles alike.

How Paul's proclamation of the gospel refers to the salvation of, and justice for, all nations is spelled out in the first chapters of the Epistle to the Romans. Paul begins his exposition with a description of the sinfulness of the world seen as the result of the failure of human beings to worship God, although God's eternal power was visible in the works of creation from the beginning: "Ever since the creation of the world God's eternal power and divine nature, invisible though they are, have been understood and seen through the things God has made. So they are without excuse; for though they knew God, they did not honor him as God or give thanks to him. . . . Therefore God gave them up in the lusts of their heart to impurity" (Rom 1:18–24). A long list of vices and sinful actions follows, beginning with idol worship, then homosexuality and an entire catalogue of vices, including covetousness, envy, murder, strife, and many others (1:25–31).

Paul here reproduces the chastising of the Gentile world in the tradition of the typical Jewish apology, in which the Gentiles are condemned for their unlawful behavior. The point is not, as many have argued, that Paul wants to condemn specifically homosexuality; rather, his argument is that *all* are guilty and worthy of death because all people do those things (1:32). Sexual sins and especially homosexuality were favorite topics in the traditional Jewish apology, and Paul singles these out in order to invite the Jewish reader, who is proud to possess the divine law and is not engaging in sexual actions forbidden by the law, to agree with him and approve what he says. So far any law-abiding Jew would be in accord with everything Paul has written. They would have applauded because they were convinced that these kinds of perversion are typical of the Gentiles, who do not have the law.

The Jewish reader, however, is disappointed in the following chapter (Romans 2), which argues that the Jews are equally guilty because, although they have the law of God, they are not fulfilling the law. This criticism of the Jews is nothing new in the tradition of Israel's prophetic tradition. The question then, "Are we Jews any better off?" is answered: "No, not at all; for we have already charged that all, both Jews and Greeks, are under the power of sin" (3:9). The concept of "sin" is radically redefined in these chapters of Romans. "Sin" is no longer the individual deed of transgressing a commandment. Rather, "sin" is for Paul a realm into which God has condemned the entire human race, Jews and Gentiles alike, because they had not acknowledged that God is the sole owner of righteousness and had instead tried to establish a just society on the basis of their own piety and morality. The Jews, who are seeking to establish their righteousness by fulfilling the law, are also caught in the realm of sin. Establishing one's own righteousness violates God's right as the sole giver of righteousness and justice. Righteousness therefore cannot come through the law, because the law is thus abused as an instrument to take the sole right to justice away from God. By doing so, the Jews also established a dividing line between themselves, the only law-abiding nation, and the Gentile nations, insisting that Gentiles could be saved only by conversion to Judaism, the only righteous nation in the world. What is at stake here should sound familiar to us today: we have been hearing a lot these days about ourselves as a righteous nation and others as at least deficient if not part of an axis of evil; other nations therefore must be converted to the American way.

All that human beings can do, even in their best efforts to obey the law, cannot bring about righteousness and justice. Individual human efforts striving to achieve their own righteousness can bring about only what Reinhold Niebuhr once characterized as "righteous people and an unjust society." That the United States may have more pious people than, for example, France does not mean that the poor people are better off here than there. And it does not mean that France was wrong in its opposition to the Iraq War and that the United States was right in going to war. The Roman Empire had a lot of righteous people—indeed, the Romans were boasting that they were the most pious people on earth—but Rome's empire was no doubt an unjust society. How then can humankind share in God's righteousness?

This question is answered by Paul in Rom 3:21: "But now, apart from the law, the righteousness of God has been revealed, attested by the law and the prophets, the righteousness of God through the faith *of* Jesus Christ for all those who believe." Most modern versions translate here "through faith *in* Jesus Christ." There is, however, no reason to translate the Greek genitive as an objective genitive. It is not the faith of the believer through which God's righteousness has been revealed; rather, God's righteous action became manifest through the faithfulness of Jesus, who gave his life for the salvation of the world through his faithful and obedient suffering and death. Only Jesus' faithfulness breaks down the power of the realm of sin, in which all human beings, Jews and Gentiles alike, have been caught. God has enacted this in order to make evident that God is righteous and makes righteous everyone who accepts the faithfulness of Jesus (3:26). Here again I would argue that the translation "makes righteous everyone who believes in Jesus" is a wrong interpretation of the Greek genitive case. It is not the believing in Jesus that makes everyone righteous. Rather, it is that Jesus was obedient and faithful to God's command through which justice and righteousness were revealed. God's justice does not come through people acting righteously and not through a righteous nation but, as God has acted by giving his Son's life as a redemption for all, through the giving of one's life in behalf of others.

Nothing is said here about repentance, contrition, confession, forgiving, and absolution of individual sinfulness. Paul has no interest whatsoever in these performances of individuals who seek to gain affirmation of their own goodness and acceptability to God through such ritual actions. There is no emphasis upon anything that any individual could possibly do through pious behavior in order to obtain this righteousness of God for himself or herself. Rather, it is Jesus' faithfulness and obedience to the will of God through which the wall of imprisonment in the realm of sin is removed for all people, Jews and Gentiles alike—no matter whether some individuals may have become morally good through obeying God's law, while others committed acts that could be called sinful. One looks in vain in Paul's genuine letters for repentance and forgiving of sin as entrance acts into the new community of Christ. Paul only once (2 Cor 12:21) speaks about repentance, referring to some members who had violated the integrity of the community; the concept of the forgiving of individual sins is at best marginal in the letters of Paul. Not through repentance does one become a member of the new community, but through the faithfulness of Jesus. One enters the new community through baptism and confessing one's faith in Jesus as Lord because of Jesus' faithfulness in his suffering and death—Paul never mentions repentance and confession of sins in this context. Even of himself Paul never says that he repented his previous persecution of the church. He simply states that he has been called to proclaim the gospel, because he was chosen from his mother's womb to fulfill this task, in spite of the fact that he had persecuted the church.

Proclamation of the righteousness of God has therefore nothing to do with individual repentance or personal sinfulness and forgiveness. It is a global and universal act of God, which has been accomplished through Jesus' obedient and faithful suffering and death at the hands of an unjust political system. But God had vindicated Jesus by raising him from the dead. In this way God's righteousness has been revealed as God's will to bring justice to the nations through the one who gave himself for the sake of those who were under the power of sin. Sin is overcome by giving oneself up for the sake of others. Human beings can emerge from the realm of sin only by following Jesus' footsteps in building up a new national and international community of justice through giving themselves up for the sake of others. This applies to individuals as well as to nations. As sin is seen as the result of God's acting universally, also God's righteousness and justice apply universally to all people and all nations.

The Vision of the New Community of Justice for All

Making this revealed righteousness of God visible in this world is accordingly not a task assigned to individual moral action, as if the awarding of righteousness to the believer and the maintaining of this personal righteousness through obedience to the law or to any moral code were the documentation of God's revelation in this world. Rather, the documentation of God's righteous action is the new community. In this new community, individuals are no longer measured according to what they do to build up their own moral and righteous stature or religious piety. The only measurement for their behavior is their role in the building of the community of the new age. This is where God's justice becomes a reality. To be sure, there is in Paul's writings no call for a new political party supporting the general abolition of slavery and the demolition of the patronage system of the hierarchically organized Roman society. Members of the new community are instead requested to establish equality and justice in their own midst and to spread the message, the gospel, to as many people as they can, inviting them to join the new community of justice and love. This will make a reality already at the present time of what Christ will bring in the future to all people, when he returns.

All those who accept the message of the gospel, that is, "believe" in the gospel, are "in Christ." It was formerly thought that "in Christ" designated a kind of personal mystical relationship to Christ. Most scholars today, however, agree that "in Christ" is a sociological term designating the inclusion into the new community of believers. The term "Christian" for a person believing in Christ and thus belonging to a new religion as distinct from a pagan religion or Judaism was not yet known in Paul's time. It appears in Christian writings, and soon also in non-Christian literature, only half a century after Paul's time, when the believers had to draw a line of distinction between themselves and the nonbelieving Gentiles on the one hand and the nonbelieving Jews on the other hand. At the time of Paul, in the middle of the first century, "being in Christ" meant to be a part of the new community of believers, the body of Christ, that was meant to include all people, Jews and Gentiles alike.

The new community is called the *ekklēsia,* a term that we translate today as "church." This is highly misleading because the term "church" invokes the image of a religious community and its identity and even a building used as a sanctuary or assembly hall. The term *ekklēsia,* however, is drawn from the political, not the religious, world. Words commonly used for religious societies in the ancient world (*koinon, thiasos*) never appear in Paul's writings. In the Greek translation of the Hebrew Bible *ekklēsia* designates the political assembly of all Israel, and in the Greco-Roman world it is the term for the political meeting of all free citizens of a city. The latter is the more likely background for Paul's usage because he never uses the term for the church at large but always for the local assembly of believers: the *ekklēsia* that is in Corinth, or the *ekklēsia* in Christ that is in Philippi.

Hand in hand with this designation of the new community goes its description as "the body of Christ." This body of Christ is present in the celebration of the Eucharist, the central ritual of the new community (see especially 1 Cor 11), in which the unity of the community is documented. "Not discerning the body of Christ" (11:29) does not mean not realizing that the bread of the Eucharist is Christ's body mysteriously present for the individual in the bread, but it means not recognizing that the shared bread establishes and maintains a new community of equality and mutual care and respect; all its members are part of the body of Christ. Disregarding the poor violates the principles of love and equality in the assembly. In the following chapter (1 Cor 12) Paul continues to spell out the relationships of all the members of the body of Christ in sociological terms drawn from the Greek depictions of the ideal society of the city.

That the designation for the new community is drawn from the realm of politics implies that Paul envisages this new community not as a new religion but as a functioning social and political entity in its own right, distinct from such organizations as the Roman society and its imperial hierarchy. The vision, to be sure, is utopian. The ideals for this vision are mostly drawn from the utopian literature of the Greco-Roman world, which deals especially with the issue of the society of the ideal city, in which all inhabitants have equal rights and enjoy mutual respect for one another. This will be the new order of the society under Christ's rule. To be sure, Christ's rule and its new order have not yet arrived; they will be fully realized only in the coming of Christ in the near future. But the new community of the last ages in Christ, indeed the body of Christ, is challenged to make real the vision of the future already here and now in the way in which its members order their own lives with each other. God's justice that will eventually be revealed in a new order of the world should already now become a reality in the new community.

What then are the criteria of ethics and morality in this new community? All those things that any society and its legal code would condemn, like murder, theft, and prostitution, are presupposed as unacceptable. The laws of a society or nation are to be respected unless they are immoral and discriminatory. That is evident in the discussion of the man who had sexual relations with his father's wife (1 Cor 5); even pagans would not tolerate such things! With respect to these things, however, the discussion of ethical standards for the new community has not even begun. These are nonissues for the ethical criteria that instruct the conduct of the new community.

What matters—and all that matters—is the question how one relates to one's brothers and sisters in the community of the new age that endeavors to make God's justice a reality already now in this world. Here only one principle determines what its members have to do: to follow the commandment of love regardless of all distinctions of ethnic, social, and gender identity. Mutual respect is required of all. "In Christ there is no Jew or Greek, no slave or master, not male and female" (Gal 3:28). This sentence is a baptismal formula that defines the status "in Christ" for all who join the new community. There must be total equality. The documentation of inclusion regardless of national identity, social status, or gender is the celebration of the Eucharist, in which all share the same bread and drink from the same cup as a demonstration of their belonging to the body of Christ. No commitment of faith, no definition of one's belief, no religious posture is required. Paul does not criticize the community in Corinth because their religious devotion is too shallow, or because they do not honor the sacredness of the eucharistic elements of bread and wine (1 Cor 11). Rather, he chastises them because they dishonor the poor in their common meals; thus they do not discern the body of Christ, the community in which total equality, mutual respect, and caring for one another's needs are constitutive.

Total equality, regardless of any inherited differentiations, is the basis for ethical conduct. This cuts across any and all of our commonly established boundary lines. Whether someone is a Jew or an Arab or a Hindu does not matter. Whether someone is a heterosexual or homosexual is totally irrelevant. Whether one is poor and the other is rich—who cares? All are welcome in the community of the new age, as long as they respect their differences and love and serve each other; as long as the rich share with the poor; as long as you love your gay brother or lesbian sister, although you for yourself reject such sexual practices; as long as you visit an inmate known to you, although you know that he or she has done something terribly wrong. Paul demands a new definition of ethics that is fundamentally different from generally accepted moral values and piety. It grows out of the statement that Christ has freed us for freedom (Gal 5:13), which is summarized in the commandment of love, in which the entire law is condensed (5:14). This freedom leads to a new community that is no longer under the law but guided by the Spirit: "If you are led by the Spirit, you are not subject to the law" (5:18). This means that not only the rituals prescribed by the law are no longer valid. It also implies that all ancient culturally conditioned commandments and traditional prejudices found in the law have become irrelevant. The commandment of love alone determines the works of the Spirit, which Paul defines as "love, joy, peace, patience, kindness, generosity, faithfulness, gentleness, and self-control" (5:22–24). Judging others on the basis of traditional legal and cultural prejudices, like color, ethnicity, gender orientation, or religious affiliation is by all means excluded.

It is not a new religion that Paul wants to establish—a new religion with all its boundary definitions and rules of exclusion. Nor is there any interest in the building up of personal piety (this term never appears in the genuine Pauline letters) or in the creation of righteous and moral personalities banding together in their pride of religious devotion, in their self-righteousness that makes them superior to others, in their assurance of having their personal sins forgiven, and sure that they have the right to judge others. People who understand the gospel in this way are several times attacked and severely criticized in Paul's letters: the Galatians, who want to demonstrate their newly found faith by fulfilling the Jewish law, thus erecting walls for their own security that excludes others; the Corinthians, who boast of their piety and devotion but dishonor the poor and their weak brothers and sisters; the Philippians, who want to be perfect but compete with one another with respect to the status of the achievement of perfection.

It is a new just society that the apostle envisages. Personal righteousness, piety, and moral achievements no longer matter. Justice and righteousness belong to God. Jesus' faithful and obedient giving of his own life is God's risky adventure of offering forgiveness of sins to all people and all nations, to the unrepentant sinners and to the boastful righteous alike. God is love, and his justice becomes a reality among all those who venture to accept this offer by becoming members of the new worldwide community of those who love each other and care for each other regardless of any racial, ethnic, gender, sexuality, and social-status distinctions. Righteousness as personal piety and morality only creates divisions within a society and among nations. The justice of God cannot be realized in this way. It can become real already here and now in a society without hierarchs who try to enforce divisive moral obligations, and without the borderlines of traditions that are reinforced by pious self-righteousness. God's righteousness is the gift of freedom—even freedom from piety and particularly from moral self-righteousness. It requires the establishment of justice among people who are free to abide by the standards of mutual respect, equality, and carrying one another's burdens. To be sure, this society will become a full reality only when Christ returns to establish his rule. But that only reinforces the demand that the new community should make God's justice a reality already now in its political and social organization. All nations, all religions, all sexual orientations, all rich and all poor are invited to come to the thanksgiving meal of God, in which the body of Christ becomes a reality in anticipation of the new world to come.

2

FIRST THESSALONIANS

An Experiment in Christian Writing

The First Letter of Paul to the Thessalonians appears as one of the minor letters of Paul, albeit his first. It is short and relatively insignificant, dwarfed by such giants as the letters to the Romans, Corinthians, and Galatians. This is the general opinion.

However, this carefully composed writing is actually an experiment in the composition of literature that signals the momentous entry of Christianity into the literary world of antiquity. The consequences of this experiment cannot be underestimated. With the creation of the letter, Paul had forged for himself a powerful political weapon in his struggle to organize and sustain the churches he had founded; the first collection of his letters spawned the composition of more letters written in his name; numerous endeavors followed in the use of this literary genre as a political and theological agency—from 1 Peter, *1 Clement,* and Ignatius to Dionysios of Corinth, Irenaeus, Cyprian, and many others. First Thessalonians testifies to the creative moment, it is "the Christian letter in the making."[1]

The analysis of established genres in art, literature, and architecture has provided most of our critical canons. Scientific research and its methods have taught us to consider each individual phenomenon as an instance of a group or species. But when 1 Thessalonians was composed, no species or genre of the Christian letter existed; there was no pattern for the incorporation of particular subgenres and forms, nor had the literary vocabulary and terminology for this type of writing been established.

To be sure, a treatment of 1 Thessalonians can draw on the wealth of information that is available to us from the rest of the Pauline corpus and from other Christian literature, and thus treat this letter as an instance of the genre "Pauline letter." The most detailed and comprehensive recent commentary, that of Béda Rigaux,[2] utilizes these resources extensively and with great erudition. But precisely this approach obscures the real task, because all the other Pauline letters are continuations and results of the experiment that began with 1 Thessalonians. They reveal its direction, further development, and success, but cannot explain the creative process itself.

---

1. This formulation is an adaptation of the title of the recent book of Ernst Kitzinger, *Byzantine Art in the Making* (Cambridge: Harvard University Press, 1977). I gratefully acknowledge my great indebtedness to this rich and instructive work. It has provided important intellectual stimulus for my work on 1 Thessalonians. It seems to me a fitting tribute to my colleague and friend, George H. Williams, if this essay can demonstrate that the historian of literature can learn much from the historian of art.

2. Béda Rigaux, O.F.M., *Saint Paul: Les Épitres aux Thessaloniciens* (EB; Paris: Gabalda, 1956).

On the other hand, studies of non-Christian analogies for the genre of the letter can explain only some aspects of the formal composition and the material resources for the creation of the Pauline letter.[3] Such studies, however successful, do not provide a model for the first experiment, nor are they capable of explaining its success.[4] A new message and a new community that is utilizing old forms and traditions remains indebted to the language of its culture, but is also faced with the need to make explicit its departure for new shores. I will try to demonstrate the resulting *concordia discors* in the consideration of two aspects of the creation of the first Christian letter: (1) the genre of the letter, and (2) the use of traditional materials.

The Genre of the Letter

Numerous letters and epistles from antiquity, particularly from the late Hellenistic and Roman imperial period, are extant. They have been analyzed and classified repeatedly: private communications, official letters, treatises in letter form, and so on, not to speak of the pseudepigraphical letters and letter collections.

It is difficult to classify 1 Thessalonians according to any of the known genres of ancient letters.[5] Paul seems to use the form of the private letter: prescript with sender introduced by name (no title), proem with personal remembrance and thanksgiving, personal greeting in the conclusion. But one looks in vain for analogies among private letters that have such extensive and elaborate thanksgiving sections, let alone the lengthy moral and eschatological instructions.

That 1 Thessalonians as a letter substitutes for the personal presence of the apostle is also paralleled in private letters.[6] But Paul's presence has an official function and is not simply serving a personal relationship, although signs of the genre of the official letter are otherwise absent. Only in later letters does Paul introduce himself with his title (apostle) or an equivalent designation.[7] Instructions appear also in the official letter; yet

---

3. Great progress has indeed been made in recent years in analyzing formal structures and literary genres that must be presupposed for the Pauline letters. For a survey of such studies see William G. Doty, *Letters in Primitive Christianity* (Philadelphia: Fortress Press, 1973). Most influential was the work of Robert W. Funk, *Language, Hermeneutic, and the Word of God* (New York: Harper & Row, 1966); idem, "The Apostolic *Parousia*: Form and Significance," in William R. Farmer, C. F. D. Moule, and R. Richard Niebuhr, eds., *Christian History and Interpretation: Studies Presented to John Knox* (Cambridge: Cambridge University Press, 1967) 249–68.

4. This is most clearly evident in the otherwise most instructive essay of Hendrikus Boers, "The Form-Critical Study of Paul's Letters: I Thessalonians as a Case Study," *NTS* 22 (1976) 140–58. Characteristically, Boers concludes his investigation with the statement: "The letter [i.e., 1 Thessalonians] has a completely normal form" (p. 158)—a statement that is quite correct, but misses the excitement of the analysis of the "Christian letter in the making."

5. Boers's definition, "a paraenetic letter with two characteristic main parts, philophronesis and paraenesis" ("Form-Critical Study," 158, referring to an unpublished SBL seminar paper of 1972 by Abraham Malherbe, "I Thessalonians as a Paraenetic Letter") points to the constituent parts of 1 Thessalonians; but there is no extant example of such a parenetic letter with the same formal characteristics, i.e., those of a personal and private letter.

6. On this aspect of the Pauline letter see Funk, "Apostolic *Parousia*."

7. Δοῦλος as a title appears even in the otherwise deceptively "private" letter to Philemon.

such instructions as given in 1 Thessalonians, coupled with eschatological exhortations, rather resemble the protreptic letter, which invites the reader to the true way of philosophy and moral life. This observation, however, should not mislead us to assume that Paul composed a philosophical or religious treatise, or used the letter form simply in order to expound his theology and his invitation to a moral life.

Faced with such difficulties, one is tempted to describe the literary form and dynamics of composition of this letter as sui generis. That explanation, however, disregards the indispensable presuppositions for the identification of a "genre." Any production of literature implies cultural establishment, convention, and continuity—or at least development along set lines. Development, however, can be continuous or discontinuous; it may be defined in terms of utilization or alteration, old forms in a new frame or old frames for new images. If a letter does not fit the established conventions, although it is still dependent upon them, how are traditional elements used, altered, bent, reshaped? What is the new message or experience that reveals the motivation for the transforming of traditional patterns?

The thanksgiving section (proem; 1 Thess 1:2–3:13) may serve as an example. The disproportionate length of this section is striking[8] if one compares 1 Thessalonians with other Pauline letters. But the proem of 1 Thess 1:2–3:13 corresponds more closely to the conventions of the private letter than the proem of any other letter of Paul. Its three major sections—remembrance of the relationship in the past (1:2–10), explanation of and apology for one's past behavior (2:1–12), and discussion of the present situation (2:17–3:13)—are standard features of proems in private correspondence. Thus the general form of a traditional genre is very clearly visible. In each instance, however, Paul forces the traditional topos to convey a message that cannot be contained in the conventional frame. The unusual length of Paul's proem is only the external documentation of a clear break with a traditional form.

The first topos of the thanksgiving section—remembrance of past relationships between sender and addressee—breaks out of the description of a personal relationship for which the deity (if mentioned at all) functions simply as benign protector. In contradistinction, 1:2–10 describes this relationship with the church not as a private matter, but as an event before God in which the Holy Spirit is the primary agent. Repeatedly Paul introduces "God" as the reference point of this relationship in an almost importunate fashion: "faith . . . love . . . and hope before God" (1:3); "brothers and sisters beloved by God" (1:4); "your faith, which is faith toward God" (1:8); "how you turned to God . . . to serve the living God" (1:9). Furthermore, the characterization of the church moves this church out of the realm of personal relationship with the apostle into a universal horizon of participation in an eschatological event ("From you the word of the Lord has sounded forth not only in Macedonia and Greece, but your faith in God has gone out everywhere," 1:8). This also implies that the addressees are released from their dependence upon the writer: "there is no need for us to say anything (about you)" (1:8). In this way, the thanksgiving section of the letter radically departs from its conventional purpose. Rather than binding writer and addressee more closely together

---

8. This long thanksgiving section has been in the center of attention ever since the classic monograph of Paul Schubert, *Form and Function of the Pauline Thanksgiving* (BZNW 20; Berlin: Töpelmann, 1939).

in their personal relationship, it establishes a situation for the addressee that is independent of the writer and seen within the context of a universal eschatological event.

The second topos of the proem (2:1–12), explanation of the writer's behavior and actions, similarly transcends the conventional concentration upon the writer's motivations, one's fortune or misfortune, and one's justified actions or deplorable failures. To be sure, the elements of this topos are clearly present. But what the author has done in the past is justified as a behavior that does not want "to please people, but to please God" (2:4), and his actions are not just explained as contributions to a personal relationship; rather, they seek to strengthen the addressees' relationship to God's coming kingdom (2:12). I will return to this section below.

Elements of the private letter are clearly visible in the third topos of the proem, the discussion of the present situation (2:17–3:13). The emphasis upon the physical separation and the desire to communicate (2:17, 18; 3:1–2, 5–6, 10–11) are almost pathetic and quite in style. But Robert Funk has already demonstrated that these familiar items of the common letter have been gathered into a discrete section in which Paul discusses the media through which "his apostolic authority and power are made effective."[9] The traditional topic "friendship" (*philophronēsis*) has been transformed into a new topic of the genre of the Christian letter, namely "apostolic *parousia*." However, Paul goes even further in his transformation of the *philophronēsis:* even the apostle's presence is transcended by the coming (*parousia*) of Christ. In 1 Thessalonians Paul never uses the term *parousia* of his own anticipated or prevented personal presence, but always for the "coming of the Lord" (4:15; 5:23; and twice in this third section of the proem, that is, in its first and last paragraph, 2:19; 3:13). Outside 1 Thessalonians, 1 Cor 15:23 is the only passage in which Paul speaks of Christ's *parousia*.[10] The sorrow and concern caused by the absence of the apostle is therefore not overcome by the joy that will be brought with Paul's presence (be it in his personal arrival or through an emissary or through his letter), but by the outlook to the expected coming of the Lord (see especially 1 Thess 2:19). Paul thus relativizes the theme of friendship. No longer is the letter a substitute for physical presence for friendship's sake, but a medium through which both writer and addressees are bound together in the eschatological perspective of a new message. Closely related to this new Christian view of the traditional theme is the reinterpretation of the sorrows and tribulations (θλίψεις). They are no longer caused by temporary physical separation, but are seen as the fundamental condition of Christian existence (3:3–4; cf. 1:6), which can be remedied neither by the letter nor by the personal presence, although personal communications bring consolation (παράκλησις, 3:2, 7).

A brief discussion of 2:13–16 is in order here. If the whole proem of 1 Thessalonians (1:2–3:13) is a conscious and careful creation of a part of a Christian letter, this section is obviously a foreign element. The arguments against the Pauline authorship of this anti-Jewish polemic seem to me fully convincing:[11] unnecessary resumption of the

---

9. Cf. Funk, "Apostolic *Parousia*," 266.

10. Elsewhere in Paul's letters the term *parousia* always refers to the arrival of a human being; cf. 1 Cor 16:17; 2 Cor 7:6; 10:10; Phil 1:26; 2:12—in the last three passages to Paul himself.

11. Arguments against Pauline authorship were brought forth first by Ferdinand Christian Baur in his *Paulus, der Apostel Jesu Christi* in 1845; several scholars of the 19th century accepted Baur's judgment. But a conclusive case was made only recently by Birger A. Pearson, "1 Thessalonians 2:13-16: A Deutero-Pauline Interpolation," *HTR* 64 (1971) 79–94. See also Boers, "Form-Critical Study," 151–52.

"thanksgiving," interruption of the close connection between 2:12 and 2:17, non-Pauline use of Pauline terms (especially μιμηταί, 2:14), characterization of the Jews that conflicts with Romans 9–11, lack of a historical point of reference for the last phrase ("the wrath to the end has come upon them," 1 Thess 2:16) before 70 CE, absence of any allusion to 2:13–16 in 2 Thessalonians. But also as part of Paul's effort to create a Christian form of the conventional proem, this section makes no sense whatsoever. A polemic against the Jews, consisting of statements from a traditional topos, is completely unwarranted in a proem that makes every effort to reshape the theme of the writer-recipient relation in the conventional proem of the private letter. A polemic against a third party would destroy the very result that Paul wants to accomplish.[12]

The instructions that follow upon the proem, 1 Thess 4:1–12, appear in the appropriate position according to the usual conventions of letter writing. However, they differ in that they are not specific but general. They are not occasioned by the situation; rather they elaborate a tradition. The basis for part of the instruction seems to be a catalogue; the vices of this catalogue are common enough, but Col 3:5 has independently preserved the same brief catalogue that is used in 1 Thess 4:3–7: πορνεία, πάθος, ἐπιθυμία, πλεονεξία, ἀκαθαρσία (only εἰδωλολατρία is missing in 1 Thess 4). The generalizing tendency of these instructions is even more patent in the positive admonitions (4:9–12); no specific advice is given.[13] On the contrary, in 4:9 Paul coins a new term, θεοδίδακτοι,[14] in order to characterize a relationship between writer and recipients that differs fundamentally from the common letter. "Taught by God" emphasizes that the recipients are not dependent upon the writer's instructions. An analogy may be found in the philosophical parenesis, which stresses the independence of moral action, and in Philo's use of αὐτοδίδακτος: the truly wise man is a "self-learner" (αὐτομαθή) and "self-taught" (αὐτοδίδακτος) and "finds wisdom readily prepared, rained down from heaven above" (*De fuga et inventione* 166).[15]

Paul has thus accomplished two things: he has made room for the use of traditional parenetic materials in the frame of the Christian letter—this became very important in the composition of letters dependent upon Paul[16]—and he has liberated the addressees

---

12. With the elimination of 1 Thess 2:13–16 one significant argument for the division hypothesis of 1 Thessalonians as proposed by Walter Schmithals disappears ("Die Thessalonicherbriefe als Briefkomposition," in Erich Dinkler, ed., *Zeit und Geschichte: Dankesgabe an Rudolf Bultmann zum 80. Geburtstag* [Tübingen: Mohr/Siebeck, 1964] 295–315). Other arguments for this hypothesis are less weighty. Any attempt to assign parts of 1 Thess 1:2–3 to two different letters (see also Karl-Gottfried Eckart, "Der zweite echte Brief des Apostels Paulus an die Thessalonicher," *ZThK* 58 [1961] 30–44) disregards the careful composition that elaborates and transforms an established literary genre.

13. Even the admonitions to lead a quiet life and work with one's own hands are general, albeit concrete, requests to insure the moral and economic independence of the church, not attacks upon some lazy church members; cf. Martin Dibelius, *An die Thessalonicher I, II, An die Philipper* (3d ed.; HNT 2; Tübingen: Mohr/Siebeck, 1937) 23.

14. There is no evidence for the use of this term in pre-Christian literature. The only non-Christian use I am aware of is θεοδίδακτος ἡ ῥητορική in *Prolegomenon Sylloge,* ed. Hugo Rabe (*Rhet. graeci* 15; Leipzig, 1931) 91, line 14. This is apparently a phrase from a late introduction to one of the rhetorical theorists. But since I was unable to get access to this book, I cannot say more about the exact date. That the word was coined on the basis of such passages as Isa 54:13 and Jer 31(38):33–34, as is usually assumed (cf. Rigaux, *Thessaloniciens,* 517), is not impossible. See below, however.

15. This term occurs more frequently in Philo, especially of Isaac (*De somnis* 159).

16. Cf., e.g., Eph 4–5; 1 Pet 2:11–4:6; *1 Clement* passim; etc.

from the dependence upon the writer's demands; their responsible action is bound to their relationship to God.

In the case of the "instructions" it is still possible to cite the philosophical moral epistle as an analogy or parallel; but no analogies exist in letters of any kind for the eschatological admonitions that are found in 1 Thess 4:13–5:11. The reason for writing 4:13–18 has been sought in a specific problem of the church, that is, that members had died and that Paul felt compelled to address this problem. But for 5:1–11 no such immediate and urgent problem that called for an answer can be identified. For this entire eschatological section, the search for a specific problem in the church of Thessalonike as cause for Paul's writing is awkward in any case: Had Paul, during his stay in Thessalonike, forgotten to speak about the possibility that some Christians might die before the parousia? Or had he failed to tell them that the parousia would happen suddenly?

The cause for this eschatological section can be more easily found if one considers Paul's effort to transform the conventional genre of the letter into a Christian medium of communication. It was the message of the Christian gospel that demanded this drastic expansion of the traditional genre. The gospel did not endeavor to add another, albeit better, religious movement to the religions of the world. In that case the letter could have been satisfied with responses to problems in the ongoing life of the churches. Rather, the gospel announced the end of the world, the coming of a new age, an expectation that the future of God, which was at hand, would make everything new, including the role of those who had died, in the events of the parousia. The "letter" could become a Christian medium only by expressing this perspective. How traditional apocalyptic materials, drawn from a genre that has no relationship to the common form of the letter, are utilized and interpreted for his purpose will be discussed below. In 1 Thessalonians, as well as in later Christian letters, the eschatological section became the most distinctive mark of the new genre, be it as the typical final paragraph as in 1 Corinthians 15 or 2 Peter 3, or as the primary corpus of a letter as in Rom 3:21–11:36.

The Use of Traditional Materials

No work of art or literary creation can be fashioned without the use of traditional forms and materials. Its message is conveyed not through forms and materials themselves, but through the reshaping of the form and the interpretation of the material.

The writing of the first Christian letter could not rely on established Christian conventions for the use and interpretation of traditional materials in the form of literary communications. There were no precedents. Moreover, very few of whatever traditions there were could be termed specifically "Christian." An alternative might have existed in the cultivation of traditions that could claim to derive directly from the originator of the Christian movement, that is, Jesus of Nazareth. But the tradition of the words and works of Jesus, at the time of the writing of 1 Thessalonians, was still in the process of being formed and had certainly not yet reached the stage of literary production. In any case, Paul exhibits very little knowledge of this tradition. It is characteristic that the only "word of the Lord" that he quotes in 1 Thessalonians (4:15–17) is the word of a

Christian prophet, and it uses traditional Jewish apocalyptic imagery.[17] One may also point to a few kerygmatic or baptismal formulae as parts of a specifically Christian tradition. Both 1:10 and 4:14 seem to utilize such formulae. But these are very small portions of the total writing, and even if such formulae may have been stable in their ecclesiastical usage (which I doubt), Paul's letters demonstrate that, in their literary usage, their wording is not yet fixed (not a single formula is ever repeated by Paul).

When Paul wrote 1 Thessalonians he could not rely to any major extent upon traditional materials that were clearly shaped by the new departure and the message of the Christian movement. Almost all traditions used here were not yet very far removed from their non-Christian origin. Three examples must suffice here.

The second section of the proem explains the writer's behavior and actions, and thus in 2:1–12 Paul uses the traditional topos and vocabulary of the description of the "philosopher." Applied to himself, he seeks to respond to the standard criticism of the wandering philosopher, preacher, or magician[18]—not, however, to specific attacks directed at his own behavior. Was anything accomplished? Did the philosopher stand the test of a public appearance? Did he use dirty tricks and deceit? Did he simply try to please the audience? Did he just play games in order to make money and gain honor? These and similar questions are all part of the conventional polemic and apology. So are the answers: he stood the test of public appearance, he had no deceit, he was following a divine call, he had no desire for money, he was gentle and kind. Except for the quotation of Jer 11:12 in 1 Thess 2:4, all the answers Paul gives belong to the general requirements of behavior for the philosopher, in particular the Cynic preacher. Had Paul said no more than this, his image of himself would have fitted perfectly into the accepted image of the morally respectable, honest, and skilled preacher. But in 1 Thess 2:7–11 Paul expands a specific argument for the good philosopher in a nonconventional way. Gentleness, for the Cynic philosopher, was a rhetorical device, used in order to be more effective, because human nature does not always respond well to harshness; thus one should be careful to choose either harshness or gentleness, depending upon the situation.[19] For Paul, however, gentleness is not a device, but the first step in the direction of establishing a new relationship between apostle and church. Therefore, the traditional image of the nurse is further expanded. Unfortunately, one word used in this context, ὀμειρόμενοι (2:8), has so far withstood all attempts at translation.[20] It seems

---

17. To be sure, such sayings of revelation, circulating as "words of the Lord," were later incorporated into the gospel tradition (cf. Mark 13 and similar materials), but they have no claim to derive from Jesus of Nazareth.

18. On the general philosophical background of this "apology" of Paul see the illuminating discussion by Abraham J. Malherbe, "'Gentle as a Nurse': The Cynic Background to I Thess ii," *NovT* 12 (1970) 203–17.

19. Ibid., 212–13.

20. This word is attested elsewhere only in a 4th-century CE tomb inscription from Lycaonia: ὀμειρό-μενοι περὶ παιδός (*CIG* 3.4000.7). Job 3:21, οἱ ὀμείρονται τοῦ θανάτου ("those who long for death"), is probably a scribal error for ἱμείρονται ("to be desirous of"). It is on the basis of this passage that the translation "desirous" arose, which is, however, complete nonsense because Paul speaks of the time when he was right there and had no reason to "long for" the Thessalonians. Etymologically there is no relation of ὀμείρεσθαι to either ἱμείρεσθαι or μείρεσθαι ("to receive one's portion").

to be a vernacular term from the nursery.[21] The use of such terms as well as the following statements ("I gave myself to you," "I worked day and night") demonstrate that Paul understands gentleness not as a device, but as a commitment. That would not be required from the professional philosopher, indeed it would violate his freedom. The people in Thessalonike have become Paul's "beloved" (2:8) to whom he has committed his own being and status as an apostle. This undercuts the authority structure implied in the tradition of the true philosopher used here. No longer is the apology of the philosopher used to establish his dignity and integrity. Instead, it establishes a relationship between partners who are tied together by an almost embarrassingly intimate bond of affection.

As already stated, in 4:1–12 Paul uses and interprets a catalogue of vices. The catalogue derives from Hellenistic Judaism, and it may have been used in Christian baptismal instruction. There is nothing new about the use of such catalogues in order to construct moral teachings, which make explicit what one should avoid and what one should do. Paul brackets his interpretation by the traditional term ἁγιασμός, "sanctification" (4:3 and 4:7).[22] But his use of this term neither points to ritual purification, nor does it indicate personal moral perfection. The two exhortations that are given speak about mutual behavior in matters of sex (4:3b–5) and of business (4:6): "treat your marriage partner with respect, not in blind passion"—that seems the best way to understand the difficult term σκεῦος[23]—and "don't rip off your brother in a business deal." The exhortations are obviously concerned with relationships. That is underlined in the sentence of "sacred law" in 4:8:[24] disregard for one's brother or sister is disregard for God, because all members of the church have received the Holy Spirit. "Sanctification," therefore, cannot be understood as a task of moral perfection for the individual, as the traditional use of such catalogue instruction in Hellenistic Judaism suggests. Rather, "sanctification" involves a reassessment of the values for dealing with each other in everyday life.

A final comment regarding the use of traditional material concerns the "eschatological" section, specifically 5:1–11: these verses are full of traditional eschatological metaphors and clichés. But Paul has used a method of interpretation that is particularly applicable in a literary composition: the play with words and their different connotations. The traditional saying about the day of the Lord coming like a thief in the night (5:2) conventionally connotes unexpectedness;[25] but "night" also connotes "darkness"

---

21. This would fit the other words used here: τροφός "nurse" or "mother breastfeeding the children"; θάλπειν "to cuddle," "to pet"; cf. *Pap. Rainer* 30.20 of the husband's behavior towards his wife: ἀγαπᾶν καὶ θάλπειν καὶ θεραπεύειν. Like these words also ὁμείρεσθαι must belong to the nursery or bedroom slang.

22. This term, not used outside biblical and Christian literature, specifically designates cultic sanctification (cf. Judg 17:3; Ezek 45:4); in *1 Clem.* 30.1 it is used together with ἐγκράτεια "self-control."

23. This term has been discussed extensively; cf. Christian Maurer, "σκεῦος," *TDNT* 7 (1971) 359–68, for literature. In the space of this article it is impossible to debate the suggestions for translation, which range from *membrum virile* to "woman." The phrase σκεῦος κτᾶσθαι seems to resist any rational attempt of translation. I would suggest that Paul uses this formulation because he does not want to say γυνή ("wife"). The choice of the neuter term σκεῦος emphasizes mutuality of sexual control.

24. Cf. Ernst Käsemann, "Sentences of Holy Law in the New Testament," in *New Testament Questions of Today* (Philadelphia: Fortress Press, 1969) 66–81.

25. Rev 3:3 makes this quite clear; cf. also Luke 12:39 (Matt 24:43).

(5:4). This allows Paul to conclude that the "day" cannot surprise us, since we are already living as "children of the day" (5:5). Thus the significance of the future day of the Lord is relativized for the believer. A second connotation of the contrast of "night" and "day," that is, "to sleep" and "to be awake," leads to a new set of metaphors for Christian life in the present: "to be awake" and "to be sober" (5:6–8). The latter term is associated with another set of traditional imagery: the armor of God, which, in turn, is interpreted as faith, love, and hope (5:8–9). What started as apocalyptic instruction has thus become demythologized eschatology, describing faith, love, and hope as the presence of eternity. A final daring play on the terms "death" (of Jesus), "being awake" and "being asleep" (of Christians), and "life" (with Jesus) seems to relativize also the problem of being alive or dead at the parousia. The timetable of the eschatological expectation has been rendered meaningless.

Here and elsewhere in this first Christian piece of literature, Paul has set the stage for the incorporation of traditional materials and their critical reinterpretation: never are such materials simply repeated or only expanded and further elaborated. That this genre of literature demands critical assessment of tradition, imitators of Paul—including the author of 2 Thessalonians—have sometimes overlooked to their own detriment.

What I can present here is only a suggestion, not a set of solutions. All that is to be learned is that this earliest Christian letter is neither a reflection of a fixed form nor a quarry of information for pieces of a genre or established traditions. Rather, it is a composition using inherited themes in the context of a new counterpoint. In the formation of the Christian letter, some laws of this counterpoint that Paul introduced were forgotten, or the inherited themes simply prevailed; but more often than not attempts were made by Paul himself and by his successors to write new fugues using Paul's rules of counterpoint—or, to use another image, Christian artisans tried to present individual figures in their reliefs in such a way that they faced the experience of a new message.

3

APOSTLE AND CHURCH IN THE LETTERS TO THE THESSALONIANS

I

First Thessalonians in particular resists all attempts to highlight the special apostolic character of Paul's experience of existence.[1] The reason may be that Paul is here not dealing with opponents who question his apostolic qualifications. But perhaps this first letter of Paul shows more clearly than the later letters that life under the eschatological actions of God does not permit any differences in the theological definitions of the human situation. That is especially evident in 1 Thessalonians with respect to the experience of tribulation (θλῖψις). It certainly is not the case in this letter that "the christological function of epiphany and proclamation is the specific property of the apostolic suffering."[2] Rather, especially the experience of tribulation by the congregation is a sign of the presence of the gospel. The congregation shares therefore fully the experience of the apostle's existence. In this respect 1 Thessalonians differs from 2 Thessalonians, where the relationship between apostle and congregation is not understood as a unity of faithful experience of the present salvation but as a contrast between the holder of the apostolic office and the members of the community, who owe him their obedience. This difference between the two letters to the Thessalonians in their presentation of the relationship between apostle and congregation should be weighted more strongly in the discussion of the problem of the authenticity of 2 Thessalonians.[3]

---

1. Ehrhardt Güttgemanns (*Der leidende Apostel und sein Herr: Studien zur paulinischen Christologie* [FRLANT 90; Göttingen: Vandenhoeck & Ruprecht, 1966]) has carried through this attempt in a most radical fashion and with great consistency. Cf. p. 323: "Although Paul also speaks of the sufferings of the community, the result of this investigation differs from the majority of all other publications in so far as it distinguishes the 'sufferings' of the apostle thematically from the 'sufferings' of the community." Also p. 327: "Because of their function as proclamation the sufferings of the apostle have to be distinguished clearly from the sufferings of the community." On the other hand, it has been especially Rudolf Bultmann who has used emphatically and with almost pastoral care all statements of Paul about his sufferings and tribulations in order to tell how faith can overcome all sufferings and gain freedom from the threat of death; see his *Theology of the New Testament,* trans. Kendrick Grobel (2 vols.; New York: Scribner's, 1951–55) 1.349–50. Günther Bornkamm (*Paul,* trans. D. M. G. Stalker [1975; repr. Minneapolis: Fortress Press, 1995] 172) understood Paul's statements about the sufferings of the apostle in a similar way: "Paul's presenting of Christ by means of his own fortunes and sufferings as well as by his preaching certainly meant more to his churches than anything else. His fate was not, however, to be thought of as exceptional, but exemplifying what being a Christian meant: dying and rising with Christ."

2. Güttgemanns, *Leidende Apostel,* 324–25.

3. This fundamental difference between the two letters is almost totally missing from the discussion of

Paul states in 1 Thess 1:5 that his proclamation came "not only through the spoken word, but also through power, the Holy Spirit, and with great certainty." At first glance this seems to suggest accompanying demonstrations of power and miracles of the apostle, especially since "power and Holy Spirit" are clearly juxtaposed to the spoken word. Acts 2:22 describes Jesus as a "divine man," attested in a similar way ("through powerful deeds, signs, and miracles")—actions that are repeated by the apostles. In this case, Paul would indeed, according to 1 Thess 1:5, be an apostle who was clearly distinguished from the congregation through the demonstration of a special authority. But already the choice of terminology in 1:5 does not invite such an understanding. "Through power" (δυνάμει)[4] and perhaps also "through the Holy Spirit" (ἐν πνεύματι ἁγίῳ) may still permit such an understanding.[5] But "with great certainty" (ἐν πληροφορίᾳ πολλῇ)[6] argues against such an understanding. The continuation "as you know what kind of people we were among you" makes such an understanding completely doubtful. What kind of people were Paul and his associates among the Thessalonians? Miracle-working itinerant preachers?

Verse 6 excludes that interpretation: the Thessalonians have become "imitators" (μιμηταί) of Paul and his associates. But if the Christians in Thessalonike are "imitators," Paul cannot remind them in this context that he and Timothy and Silvanus performed miracles in Thessalonike. "Imitators of the apostles and the Lord" in Paul always implies that one is nothing oneself and can therefore be everything for others.[7] As imitators of the apostle and of the Lord, the Thessalonians have "accepted the proclamation in much tribulation and in the joy of the Holy Spirit." Thus the preceding description of the apostle's appearance in Thessalonike must be understood accordingly: "through the Holy Spirit" and "with great certainty" do not describe the miraculous works of the apostle but joy and confidence in adverse circumstances. In this respect, apostle and congregation

---

the authenticity of 2 Thessalonians; for an overview of the question of the authenticity of this letter, see Werner-Georg Kümmel, *Introduction to the New Testament,* trans. Howard Clark Kee (rev. ed.; Nashville: Abingdon, 1975), 264–69; Martin Dibelius, *An die Thessalonicher I, II; An die Philipper* (3d ed.; HNT 11; Tübingen: Mohr/Siebeck, 1937) 57–58; Béda Rigaux, O.F.M., *Saint Paul: Les Épitres aux Thessaloniciens* (EB; Paris: Gabalda, 1956) 124–44.

4. For a rich documentation of the use of this term see Rigaux, *Thessaloniciens,* 375–76. But Rigaux wants to understand this term here as a designation of "the power of God, which accompanies the proclamation of the apostle" (p. 376). For more literature, see Walter Grundmann, "δύναμις," *TDNT* 2 (1964) 311–12 and passim.

5. Rom 15:19 (ἐν δυνάμει σημείων καὶ τεράτων) demonstrates that Paul could speak of the apostolic activity in this manner.

6. Πληροφορία πολλή must be translated with "in full conviction" or "with great certainty." The meaning "highest fullness" is not impossible but there is no evidence for this meaning in the few non-Christian occurrences (cf. Delling, *TDNT* 5 [1967] 310–11). This meaning appears only later in post-Pauline usage (Col 2:2). Paul himself employs the noun only here, but uses the verb πληροφορεῖν in Rom 4:21 and 14:5 with the meaning "to gain certainty." Πληροφορία is later resumed by the term παρρησία (see the correspondence of the two terms in Heb 10:19 and 22).

7. See especially 1 Cor 10:33–11:1. The concept of imitation in Paul must be understood in a most radical way. Nothing is said here about following a moral example. It is also not indicated that "they [the congregations] should be obedient to him [Paul] and act according to his instructions" (Wilhelm Michaelis, "μιμέομαι κτλ.," *TDNT* 4 [1967], 679ff., etc.). Even in Phil 3:17 Paul does not speak about obedience to him but about the surrender of the assumed possession of perfection.

have become equals. Neither with regard to the greatness of his actions nor in the experience of tribulations is the apostle superior to the congregation.

The congregation therefore also enters into the apostolic function of proclamation in the public documentation of its faith: "Thus you have become a model for all believers in Macedonia and Achaia because the word of the Lord has sounded forth from you" (1:7–8). This, of course, does not mean that all members of the congregation have now become apostles.[8] It is the faith of the newly converted which is active as "the word of the Lord" (1:8–9). But if indeed the proclamation of the apostle is part of the event of salvation, the same can be said about the faith of the congregation. Nothing can be found here about a theological preeminence of the apostle.

The same commonality and identity of the experience of tribulation appears again in the last part of the proem (3:1–5): ". . . these tribulations. Indeed you yourselves know that this is what we are destined for" (3:3)—these are the eschatological afflictions, which cannot be avoided.[9] Paul is here referring to a traditional topic of the eschatological expectations and includes himself as well as the congregation in the "we" of the statement, although the experience of such afflictions is not in itself a sign of the beginning of the end. One cannot conclude from such experiences that God is acting. On the contrary, it could well be that the tempter will be successful (3:5). The presence of God's action is rather evident in the mutual assurance of consolation and in the joy that is thus experienced—an opportunity that has been created through the proclamation of the gospel. Thus the eschatological event of salvation extends from the proclamation into the experience of consolation and joy. Timothy, whom Paul has sent to Thessalonike for the strengthening of the congregation, is in this context not just accidentally designated as "coworker of God in the gospel" (σύνεργος τοῦ θεοῦ).[10] The returning Timothy is accordingly a "messenger of the gospel" (3:6). The choice of the terms εὐαγγέλιον and εὐαγγελίζεσθαι is striking. The bond that has been established between apostle and congregation is in the experience of mutual consolation of the same theological quality as the proclamation that has created the faith of the congregation.

---

8. It is correct that not all members of the congregation become apostles or even suffering apostles (Güttgemanns, *Leidende Apostel*, 324–25, etc.). But that does not justify speaking of "the unique position of the apostle between God and Christ on the one hand and the congregation on the other" (ibid., 325). One cannot appeal to Hans von Campenhausen for such a statement, because von Campenhausen was primarily concerned to demonstrate that Paul meticulously avoided putting himself in a position of superiority over against his congregation (*Ecclesiastical Office and Spiritual Authority* [Stanford: Stanford University Press, 1969] 49). To be sure, Paul distinguishes between different types of charismata. But that the apostles appear in first position in 1 Cor 12:28 has a practical rather than a theological reason (cf. Rom 10:14–16).

9. Cf. Heinrich Schlier, "θλίβω, θλῖψις," *TDNT* 3 (1965) 143; Dibelius, *Thessalonicher/Philipper*, 17.

10. This is certainly the most original text (D* 33 b m* Ambst). To be sure, διάκονος τοῦ θεοῦ has a much stronger attestation (ℵ A P Ψ et al.) but must be considered, just as some other readings here, to be a secondary correction of the older *lectio difficilior*. Cf. on this text-critical question also Rigaux, *Thessaloniciens*, 466–68. This designation of Timothy does not, of course, speak about "a cooperation of God with the apostle but emphasizes the rank and dignity of Paul's coworker Timothy, especially in view of all that he has done in behalf of the relationship of apostle and congregation. On this topic, see 2 Cor 5:20–6:1; on the question of Paul's coworkers, see Bornkamm, *Paul,* 166–67.

The apostle can therefore not be satisfied to distinguish his own missionary actions from the charlatan activity with respect to integrity and sincerity. This traditional justification also appears, to be sure, in 2:3–6. One could even include here the emphasis upon the apostle's "gentleness" (ἤπιοι, 2:7).[11] By all means, gentleness and mildness for the Cynic is not more than a means to an end; severity and censure could be used instead if circumstances called for it. Paul, however, uses this traditional topic differently. Not only in the image of the nurse but also in the following description of his loving surrender (2:8) Paul points to the founding of his relationship to the congregation, which relationship can no longer be compared to that of the most sincere Cynic preacher and his audience. The Christians in Thessalonike have become "the beloved" of Paul and his coworkers.[12] A Cynic philosopher would have called such behavior unwise, just as a modern psychologist would strongly argue against it. Such surrender violates the self-sufficiency of the hearer and undercuts the authority of the preacher. Paul himself was not spared that experience; the opponents in 2 Corinthians were able to call into doubt his authority, and they apparently found willing listeners among the members of the congregation. That Paul also waived his right to claim financial support, not for opportunistic reasons but for the sake of a loving relationship to the church (1 Thess 2:9), would further arouse the suspicion of his opponents (cf. the accusations in 2 Cor 12:13). It is, however, an intrinsic part of the gospel to require such a relationship of love. Paul explicitly parallels his surrender to the gospel, which is in this context especially and, it seems, unnecessarily called "the gospel of God" (1 Thess 2:8).[13]

Paul's description of the apostles' conduct as "pure, upright, and blameless" (1 Thess 2:10), which at first seems to have moral connotations, is immediately illustrated by an image: "We dealt with each one of you like a father with his children" (2:11). The image of the father is by no means used in order to point to a relationship of authority. That becomes clear in the continuation, where Paul portrays himself and his coworkers, now separated from the congregation, as "orphans" (ἀπορφανισθέντες, 2 Thess 2:17). The image "father" can be exchanged by the image "orphan," which would not be possible if "father" described a position of authority.[14] Moreover, the conclusion of the proem

---

11. Cf. here the instructive essay of Abraham Malherbe, "'Gentle as a Nurse': The Cynic Background to 1 Thess ii," *NovT* 12 (1970) 203–17; also Günther Bornkamm, "Glaube und Vernunft bei Paulus," in *Studien zu Antike und Christentum* (BevTh 28; Munich: Kaiser, 1963) especially 128ff.

12. See Helmut Koester, "First Thessalonians—An Experiment in Christian Writing," chapter 2 in this volume. See ibid., pp. 20–21, on the still untranslatable term ὁμειρόμενοι. It is probably a term of the vernacular that characterizes a cordial and personal relationship of love.

13. "Gospel of God" appears three times in 1 Thessalonians 2 (vv. 2, 8, and 9), elsewhere in Paul only when he emphasizes his worldwide commission of preaching to the Gentiles (Rom 1:1; 15:16; and once in 2 Cor 11:7). To be sure there is no fundamental difference between this designation and the more frequently used "gospel of Christ"; but the special nuance of the usage in 1 Thess 2 is worth noting.

14. This remaining mutual relationship, which reaches perfection only in the future coming of Christ, has been comprehensively described by von Campenhausen (*Ecclesiastical Office*, 44ff.). But this relationship does not need to have reached "maturity" in order to permit a description of the intimacy of this relationship (ibid., 44). Paul is talking to the recently established church of the Thessalonians as warmly, cordially, and lovingly as he later does in his letter to the Philippians, with whom he had been connected for many years. Paul's comparison of himself with the conduct of a father is not based on the use of the title "father" as a title of honor in rabbinic use of language (cf. Gottlob Schrenk, "πατήρ," *TDNT* 5 [1967] 977–78, also 1006), nor

repeats that mutual love is at stake here (1 Thess 3:12). Love is the realm in which apostle and congregation grow together toward the return of Christ. In the increase of the documentation of love the event of salvation proceeds to its climax in Christ's return (2:19; 3:12–13).

It is therefore not possible to explain the question of the apostolic presence, which is the central feature of the Pauline letter, as something that is superior to the status of the community.[15] Paul does not write because—unfortunately absent—he is now forced to give full weight to his authority through letters. Rather, the desire to visit the Thessalonians results from his description of the relationship of love and surrender (2:7–12 and 17–20).[16] This relationship is again seen in an eschatological perspective. Satan, the eschatological enemy of God, prevents the visit of Paul because he wants to destroy God's work, that is, the increase of love and joy (2:18–20). This increase of love and joy is especially promoted by Paul's personal presence. If the letter instead has to be used, it is as good and as insufficient as a letter of love serving as a substitute for the personal being together of two lovers.

II

The first segment of 2 Thessalonians is devoted to the topic of tribulation. But it only seems that the corresponding topic of 1 Thessalonians is thus treated once more. What is missing in the second letter is the connection of this topic to the situation of the acceptance of the gospel (cf. 1 Thess 1:6). Tribulation is here paralleled with "persecutions" (διωγμοί), while the first letter does not speak of persecutions in the understanding of the second letter.[17] The term πίστις in the second letter does not mean "faith" but rather "constancy."[18] The "Paul" of 2 Thessalonians thus boasts of the steadfastness and constancy of the Thessalonians in persecutions and tribulations, which they have to endure. In the first letter, on the other hand, the question was tribulation connected to the acceptance of the gospel, over which faith and joy triumphed; and it was

---

is it derived from the use of this title in the mysteries (ibid., 953). Its background is rather the common vernacular language, from which also the metaphors in 1 Thess 2:7–8 are derived.

15. Robert W. Funk, "The Apostolic *Parousia*: Form and Significance," in William R. Farmer, C. F. D. Moule, and R. Richard Niebuhr, eds., *Christian History and Interpretation: Studies Presented to John Knox* (Cambridge: Cambridge University Press, 1967) 249–68.

16. Unfortunately, the close connection between these two passages has been masked by the interpolation of 1 Thess 2:13–16. Doubts regarding the originality of this section were raised for the first time by Ferdinand Christian Baur in 1845 (*Paulus der Apostel Jesu Christi*; ET *Paul the Apostle of Jesus Christ*, 2 vols., trans. Eduard Zeller [London and Edinburgh: Williams and Norgate, 1876]) and were repeated several times during the 19th century. More recently, Birger A. Pearson ("1 Thessalonians 2:13–16: A Deutero-Pauline Interpretation," *HTR* 64 [1971] 79–94) has brought forward convincing arguments for the assumption of an interpolation; see my article "First Thessalonians—An Experiment in Christian Writing," chapter 2 in this volume, for further arguments. See also Hendrikus Boers, "The Form-Critical Study of Paul's Letters: I Thessalonians as a Case Study," *NTS* 22 (1975/76) 151–52.

17. 1 Thess 2:13–16 cannot be used as evidence; see the preceding note.

18. Rudolf Bultmann ("πιστεύω κτλ.," *TDNT* 6 [1968] 208) has demonstrated that the use of πίστις here corresponds neither to the specific Christian use of the term nor to that of the genuine Pauline letters.

not necessary for Paul to boast about that because it sounded forth loud and clear by itself as part of the event of salvation (1 Thess 1:8–10).

Altogether missing in the second letter is any attempt to connect the tribulations experienced by the congregation to the experience of the apostle; nor is anything said about mutual consolation or about the joy through which the power of the gospel is demonstrated. To be sure, there is a reference to the gospel (2 Thess 1:8), but it is understood very differently (see below). Tribulations are not compensated for by joy but by a reference to the eschatological punishment that will meet the persecutors in the court of God (1:5–6), while the persecuted congregation can be sure of their participation in the coming rule of God. Only at this point is a community with the apostle established: the community will then receive "relief" (ἄνεσις, 1:6) together with the apostle. And only at this point does the letter speak about the gospel: the unbelievers and those who did not obey the gospel of our Lord Jesus will then be punished (1:8). The original purpose of the gospel was, of course, to create faith; the author of this letter is finally mentioning that point somewhat ill at ease (1:10).

It is not accidental that the author awkwardly appends the mention of the gospel to the description of the divine judgment of the persecutors as a revenge for the tribulations they have caused for the congregation. The author of 2 Thessalonians knew quite well that Paul had spoken about tribulation in relation to the gospel. But he did not know what to do with the concept of the community of apostle and congregation, the identity of their experiences, and the mutuality of consolation, because for him the apostle was an authority, not dependent upon the congregation, and clearly its superior. That is shown in the way in which he presents the apostle as admonisher and example for the congregation.

Of course, the congregation came to faith through the apostle (2:14), but the congregation no longer enters into the eschatological task of the proclamation. The gospel remains an authoritative word that is set above the congregation (2:13–17). At first something is still said about the gospel's call to the attainment of the glory of our Lord Jesus Christ (2:14), but the congregation is admonished not to "steadfastness in faith" (1 Cor 16:13) or to "standing firm in the Lord" (Phil 4:1; 1 Thess 3:8)[19] but "to stand firm and hold fast to the traditions" (2 Thess 2:15).[20] In view of these traditions, "every good work and word" is demanded from the congregation so that it may be able to obtain the promise (2:17; compare the reference to the "work of faith" in 1:11). As Paul was once the preacher of the gospel, his commandment is now present as tradition in word and letter (2:15). The wish that the Lord may strengthen the congregation in this

---

19. The absolute use of στήκειν in 2 Thess 2:15 is striking and awkward (Gal 5:1, στήκετε οὖν καὶ μή . . . , is not a true analogy) and raises the question whether the admonition στήκετε has been inserted deliberately as a reminiscence of 1 Thess 3:8, although it no longer has a specific meaning in the context of 2 Thess 2:15.

20. Klaus Wegenast (*Das Verständnis der Tradition bei Paulus und in den Deuteropaulinen* [WMANT 8; Tübingen: Mohr/Siebeck, 1962] 116–18) demonstrates correctly that 2 Thess 2:15 does not differ terminologically from the understanding of tradition in the genuine Pauline letters. The reason for this, however, is the direct literary dependence of this letter upon 1 Thess 4:1! It must be added that Paul never connects the admonition to adhere to the tradition with a reference to the gospel. In this respect, the concept of tradition in 2 Thessalonians is not Pauline.

tradition is identical with the admonition to be obedient and to perform good works (2:16–17).

With respect to the prayer for the success of the gospel, however, the congregation participates in the work of proclamation (3:1).[21] But it is exactly here that, compared with the first letter, the quite differently defined relationship between apostle and church emerges: *only* its prayers but not its actions are related to the apostle's office of proclamation (3:3–4).[22] The apostle therefore stands at a peculiar distance from the congregation. He has been removed to a far place. According to 1 Thessalonians 2, it was in Paul's activity of proclamation that he had surrendered himself to the congregation in love. All his hope was directed to the wish that the Lord might prepare a path for him (κατευθῦναι τὴν ὁδὸν ἡμῶν) to be united again with the congregation that had grown in mutual love (1 Thess 3:11–12). In 2 Thessalonians the apostle is not interested in seeing the congregation again: 2 Thess 3:5 says only in a formal way that the Lord "may direct your hearts" (κατευθῦναι ὑμῶν τὰς καρδίας) to the love of God and steadfastness of Christ. What Paul as the preacher of the gospel had offered to the congregation, namely his exhausting work with his hands that was motivated by his love for the congregation (1 Thess 2:9), is mentioned, but not because the apostle wanted to strengthen and renew the mutual relationship of consolation and love; rather, this now becomes an example for a Christian order of life (2 Thess 3:7–10).

The apostle, toiling day and night, no longer is thought to love those who had become his beloved. On the contrary, he is now very concerned that laziness might spread in the congregation, and thus he works so hard in order to be an example: everyone is obligated to earn their bread through the work of their hands. The terms "example" (τύπος) and "imitation" (μιμεῖσθαι) from 1 Thess 1:6–7 appear again in this context. In the first letter, however, Paul had spoken about the way in which the church had become an example for others; in the second letter they have been connected to the concept of tradition and have been understood in a moralistic fashion (2 Thess 3:6). In this respect, 2 Thessalonians moves into the neighborhood of the Pastoral Epistles, where the leader of the community is admonished to be an example in words and in works (1 Tim 4:12; cf. Titus 2:7). In 1 Thessalonians, however, the concepts of example and imitation were not connected to apostolic instructions for an orderly and hardworking life (1 Thess 4:11). In that letter, the concept of imitation rather placed the entire congregation into a position of equality with the apostle and enabled it to continue the proclamation of the apostle. In the second letter, the congregation is subordinated to the apostle and to his command and example. Only in this letter one finds

---

21. This sentence is drawn from the concluding words of 1 Thess 5:25, where it serves to strengthen the personal relationship with the congregation.

22. It corresponds to the genuine Pauline letters that the congregation is connected with the apostle and his work through its prayers of intercession (Rom 15:30; 2 Cor 1:11; Phil 1:19–20; Phlm 22). But it is not true in the genuine letters of Paul that it participates in the work of the apostle only through intercession and—in the case of Paul as an exception—through material support (von Campenhausen, *Ecclesiastical Office*, 41–42); see above on 1 Thess 1:7–8. Also with respect to the collection the question was not "material support," certainly not of the apostle, but the essential documentation of the right and the fruits of the Gentile mission.

the understanding of the word and work of the apostle as superior to the congregation; participation is possible only in an obedient moral conduct.

III

It should not come as a surprise that the notion of apostolic suffering as part of Paul's office of proclamation is absent from 2 Thessalonians. It was not until the writing of the deutero-Pauline letter to the Colossians (1:24) that the preeminent position of the apostle would be grounded in the concept of his suffering.[23] What the apostle is suffering as a prisoner receives a special position in the economy of the salvation of God and is accomplished in behalf of the church, which does not share this experience of suffering. Office and mission of the apostle are clearly distinguished from the congregation and its mission and contrasted to it. The suffering of the apostle is an objective fact of salvation; its result is benefiting the church. The further development of this concept in the Pastoral Epistles (see also Eph 3:1; Acts 9:16), in Ignatius of Antioch, and in *1 Clement* into an ideology of the martyr is well known.[24]

First Thessalonians thus does not provide any points of departure for this development. But it is necessary to ask whether other genuine letters of Paul do not already speak about a special function of the apostle's suffering, that is, a suffering that the congregation does not share and, in principle, is not able to share. To be sure, Paul speaks several times about his sufferings, opposition, dangers, and tribulations and connects them closely to his apostolic mandate (2 Cor 1:4–11; 4:7–12; 1 Cor 4:9–13).[25] Striking is first of all the realism in the description of the experience of tribulation (e.g., 2 Cor 1:8). There is no romanticism and no pride of the martyr.[26] Whenever Paul boasts of his sufferings and persecutions, he speaks in the style of a telegram, uses the style of the catalogues of tribulations, and avoids novelistic embellishments (2 Cor 11:23–32). The only more detailed report here does not lack a note of irony (1 Cor 11:31–32).

Where Paul explores the theological dimensions of the apostolic suffering, he emphasizes the community of the experience with his congregations. Through their financial support for Paul, the Philippians have become people who share his tribulations (συγκοινωνήσαντές μου τῇ θλίψει, Phil 4:14). Paul and Timothy received

---

23. See Eduard Lohse, *Colossians and Philemon: A Commentary on the Epistles to the Colossians and to Philemon,* trans. William R. Poehlmann and Robert J. Karris (Hermeneia; Philadelphia: Fortress Press, 1971), on Col 1:24.

24. In Ignatius, in the Epistle to Titus, and in the *Acts of Paul,* the fate of the suffering of Paul is a fate of the martyr that is clearly distinguished from the general experience of the congregation and contrasted to it. It becomes, however, also an example that might be imitated, but only for those Christians who are destined to become martyrs and are thus distinguished from the congregation.

25. Bornkamm, *Paul,* 169–72; von Campenhausen, *Ecclesiastical Office,* 41ff.

26. Paul is never concerned with tribulations that came to him as occurrences that were special and lay outside of the normal human experience. Rather, what is here coming to expression is that "apostolic existence is tied to the earthly past of Jesus, and this tie is brought about by the exalted one. As a result, the apostle must not flee the workaday world, the realm of human frailty, but turn to it" (Dieter Georgi, *The Opponents of Paul in Second Corinthians* [Philadelphia: Fortress Press, 1986] 274).

consolation in their tribulation so that they can now on their part console the Corinthians in their tribulations (2 Cor 1:3–7). There is no indication that Paul is thinking here
of a mysterious effect of the sufferings of the apostle upon the congregation. Rather,
Paul thinks here of the tangible worldly wisdom that the experience of consolation in
tribulations enables one to give consolation to others. This is what Paul has in mind
when he speaks of the "sufferings of Christ" and the "consolation through Christ"
(2 Cor 1:5). Paul does not develop here a theory about apostolic sufferings but speaks
as a pastor.

Even in 2 Cor 4:7–18, the presentation of the suffering of Christ in the apostle does
not establish a special apostolic privilege. The "we" style of this section is not readily the
apostolic "we." Paul distances himself here from his opponents but not necessarily also
from the congregation (compare on the other hand 2 Cor 10–11). 2 Cor 4:7–18 and
5:1–10 certainly speak in the "we" style inclusively about all Christians. What matters
here is not the difference between the apostle and the congregation but what separates
the apostle from his opponents. Thus this section wants to clarify at the same time why
the congregation should not have any business with these opponents. If the congregation stands firm in its faith, even the suffering apostle enjoys no distinctive dignity. The
proclamation of the apostle as also the realization of the suffering of Jesus in his mortal body do not have any other purpose than to present the whole congregation
together with the apostle in the same faith before Christ (4:13–14). The rhetorical
phrase "the dying of Christ in our bodies—the life in you" should not mislead one to
an interpretation of Paul's understanding of suffering in the way it is understood in the
Epistle to the Colossians.

This confirms that the eschatological experience of the unity and equality of apostle and congregation, which is clearly expressed in 1 Thessalonians, is maintained also
in Paul's later letters, especially in view of the office entrusted to him, namely the proclamation of the gospel. According to the statement of Phil 1:7–8, Paul is able in his last
letter to confirm to the Philippians that they can be certain of the same participation
in the gospel. In 1:3–8 Paul explicitly addresses the entire community.[27] All Christians
in Philippi have a share in his χάρις[28] with Paul in his chains in the defense and attestation of the gospel (1:7). "Through their support, the Philippians participate in the
grace of Paul's apostolic service."[29] It is no accident that Paul here underlines his yearn-
ing for the congregation by an oath (1:8). The distance between apostle and congregation is cancelled especially in the experience of tribulations.

---

27. Note the repeated occurrence of πάντες in Phil 1:3–8.

28. Χάρις here cannot simply be translated with "grace" in its normal meaning. It does not mean that
Paul experiences his imprisonment as "grace" (*pace* Dibelius, *Thessalonicher/Philipper*, 63). There is also nothing said about the Philippians themselves as suffering persecution (*pace* Ernst Lohmeyer, *Die Briefe an die
Philipper, an die Kolosser und an Philemon* [2d ed.; KEK 9; Göttingen:Vandenhoeck & Ruprecht, 1953] 26–27).
A. Satake ("Apostolat und Gnade bei Paulus," *NTS* 15 [1968/69] 99) has aptly explained the term: "the
'grace' about which Paul speaks in this context can only be the grace that even in his chains he is concerned
with the proclamation and thus continues his apostolic service." See also Hans Conzelmann, "χάρις κτλ.,"
TDNT 9 (1974) 395–96.

29. Satake, "Apostolat," 100.

4

THE TEXT OF 1 THESSALONIANS

In the new *Novum Testamentum Graece* (NA²⁶)[1] the text of 1 Thessalonians has been changed from its predecessor, NA²⁵,[2] in thirteen instances. To be sure, a comprehensive review of the text of the entire Corpus Paulinum is required in order to evaluate this new text of one of the Pauline Epistles.[3] But it may be permitted to raise some questions with regard to 1 Thessalonians, voiced not by a specialist in textual criticism but by an exegete who would like to settle the textual problems of this Pauline letter in order to complete a commentary on this writing.

The most striking feature in the changes introduced by Aland is the increase in the use of brackets.[4] In NA²⁵ brackets were used three times: 1 Thess 1:4; 4:10; and 5:25. NA²⁶ uses brackets in these three instances, adds brackets in three other cases (1:5, 10; 4:8), and adds words in brackets in five more passages (1:5, 8; 3:13; 4:11; 5:15). Apart from this increased use of brackets, the text has been changed in five other instances (2:7, 8, 13; 5:10, 13). I shall first discuss the cases in which words in brackets have been added.

1 Thess 1:5 NA²⁶: ἐν δυνάμει καὶ ἐν πνεύματι ἁγίῳ καὶ [ἐν] πληροφορίᾳ πολλῇ = A C D F G Ψ l r vg^mss. The bracketed ἐν is missing in ℵ B 33 lat. Tischendorf, Westcott-Hort, and Nestle did not admit ἐν into their text. It is easily understood why scribes would have added the preposition here: both preceding nouns have the same preposition.[5] On the other hand, its omission is not motivated. That ἐν is also missing in most of the Latin tradition confirms the age of this reading. It is *lectio difficilior* and should be preferred.

1 Thess 1:8 NA²⁶: ἐν τῇ Μακεδονίᾳ καὶ [ἐν τῇ] Ἀχαΐᾳ = ℵ C D F G P Ψ l lat. The bracketed words are missing in B K 6. 33. 365. 614. 629. 630. 1739. (1881) *al* r vg^mss.

---

1. Kurt Aland, et al., eds., post Eberhard and Erwin Nestle, *Novum Testamentum Graece* (26th ed.; 1979; repr. Stuttgart: Deutsche Bibelstiftung, 1981).

2. Eberhard Nestle, Erwin Nestle, and Kurt Aland, eds., *Novum Testamentum Graece* (25th ed.; Stuttgart: Privilegierte Württembergische Bibelanstalt, 1963).

3. No comprehensive study of these changes has yet appeared to my knowledge, although there are a number of brief reviews, e.g., Frans Neirynck, "The New Nestle-Aland: The Text of Mark in N²⁶," *EThL* 55 (1979) 331–56; J. Duplacy, "Une nouvelle edition du Nouveau Testament grec," *RTL* 11 (1980) 229–32; Johannes Karavidopoulos, "Nestle-Aland, *Novum Testamentum Graece*, 26th ed., 1979," *Deltion Biblikon Meleton* 9 (1980) 82–87; J. K. Elliott, "An Examination of the Twenty-sixth Edition of Nestle-Aland *Novum Testamentum Graece*," *JTS* 32 (1981) 19–49; Hans-Werner Bartsch, "Ein neuer Textus Receptus für das griechische Neue Testament?" *NTS* 27 (1981) 585–92; H. J. de Jonge, "De nieuwe Nestle: N26," *NedTT* 34 (1980) 307–22.

4. The extensive use of brackets had already been criticized with respect to the United Bible Societies' Greek text by J. K. Elliott, "The Use of Brackets in the Text of the United Bible Societies' Greek New Testament," *Bib* 60 (1979) 575–77.

5. Béda Rigaux, *Saint Paul: Les Épitres aux Thessaloniciens* (EB; Paris: Gabalda, 1956) ad loc.

Only Tischendorf admitted ἐν τῇ into his text, revealing his well-known preference for ℵ; von Soden bracketed the words; but Westcott-Hort and all other editors (including Nestle) rejected them. This secondary addition is motivated by 1:7: ἐν τῇ Μακεδονίᾳ καὶ ἐν τῇ Ἀχαΐᾳ.[6] The tradition that does not contain these words is old; though ℵ does not support the reading, B is backed by 1739, the important companion of 𝔓46.[7]

3:13 NA[26]: μετὰ πάντων τῶν ἁγίων αὐτοῦ, [ἀμήν] = ℵ*.2 A D* 81. 629 *pc* a m vg bo. The bracketed word is missing in ℵ1 B D2 F G Ψ 1 it sy sa bo[mss]. Editors are almost unanimous in rejecting this later liturgical addition.[8] Examples for the secondary addition of "Amen" are numerous (especially at the end of letters and after liturgical formulae). The textual basis for the omission is very good. It includes all older translations (it sy sa), whereas only the later translations (vg bo) are witnesses of this secondary expansion.

4:11 NA[26]: ταῖς [ἰδίαις] χερσὶν ὑμῶν = ℵ* A D1 l. The word ἰδίαις is missing in ℵ2 B D* F G Ψ 6. 104. 365. 1175. 1739. 1881 *pc* sy[h]. Tischendorf, Westcott-Hort, Merk, Bover, and Nestle do not include the word in their editions. ἰδίαις is a redundant addition that wants to harmonize this passage with 1 Cor 4:12 and Eph 4:8 (ταῖς ἰδίαις χερσίν). In those two passages there is no following possessive pronoun, whereas ἰδίαις in 1 Thess 4:11 conflicts with the following ὑμῶν.[9] As in the case of 1:5, the minuscule 1739, frequent companion of 𝔓46, supports B, whereas ℵ joins the secondary "Majority Text."

5:15 NA[26]: τὸ ἀγαθὸν διώκετε [καὶ] εἰς ἀλλήλους καὶ εἰς πάντας = 𝔓30 ℵ2 B l vg[st] sy[h]; καί is missing in ℵ* A D F G 6. 33. 1739. 1881. 2426 *pc* it vg[cl] sy[p]; Ambst Spec. Tischendorf, Westcott-Hort, Merk, and Nestle do not include καί in their text, though Westcott-Hort list it as a marginal reading. Von Soden includes καί in brackets. The evidence for the inclusion of καί is not very strong, whereas 1739 (thus probably also 𝔓46) together with ℵ and the Western witnesses strongly support a text without καί. Zuntz has investigated the instances of "the interpolation of καί to correspond with a second καί later on"[10] and observes with respect to 1 Thess 5: 15 that the addition of καί is "so evidently spurious as to require no discussion."[11] It is hard to understand the addition of καί in NA[26] (even in brackets).[12]

In three instances NA[26] brackets words of the text of NA[25].

---

6. For similar instances of the secondary addition of ἐν, cf. Rom 13:9; Col 2:7.

7. The text of 𝔓46 is not extant in any instance discussed in this paper. But its text or *Vorlage* survives in 1739; cf. Günther Zuntz, *The Text of the Epistles* (London: Oxford University Press, 1953) 68–84.

8. Only von Soden adds the word in brackets. Tischendorf again follows the original reading of ℵ.

9. The word ἴδιος is frequently used as a possessive pronoun; cf. BAG s.v. 2. See also Rigaux, *Thessaloniciens*, ad loc.

10. *Text of the Epistles*, 199–200.

11. Ibid., 199. Zuntz (200–201) has made some very important observations with regard to the value of the preservation of original asyndeta in 𝔓46, "almost always joined by one, or a few, members of the 'Alexandrian' group; most often B and/or 1739; while the larger part of this group . . . is in opposition and wrong" (201).

12. While in this new edition a superfluous connecting particle was added to the text, no attempt has been made to eliminate other secondary particles from the text, e.g., the second δέ in 1 Cor 12:10 (missing in 𝔓46 B 1739); δέ after ἄλλος in 1 Cor 3:10 (missing in 𝔓46 D and others—the variant is not listed in NA[26]); δέ after οὐ πολύ in Heb 12:9 (not in NA[25], but added in brackets in NA[26]); οὖν in 1 Cor 6:7 (miss-

1:5 NA[26]: ἐγενήθημεν [ἐν] ὑμῖν. The bracketed word appears in B D F G Ψ it sy[(p)], and all editors include it in their text. It is missing in ℵ A C P 048. 33. 81. 104. 326★. 945. 1739. *pc* vg[st]. The cause for this omission is an obvious haplography after ἐγενή-θημεν. ἐν before ὑμῖν is required by the context: "among you" (not: "through you" or "for you"). It is difficult to understand why brackets were introduced here.

1:10 NA[26]: ἐκ [τῶν] νεκρῶν. The evidence for the omission of the article is very narrow: A C K 323. 629. 945. 2464. 2495 *al*, whereas the article is well attested: ℵ B D F G I Ψ 1 Eus. Only Westcott-Hort put the word in brackets; all other editors judge it to be an original part of the text. In all other instances Paul does not use the article before νεκρῶν when speaking of Christ's resurrection.[13] This explains why a scribe would delete the article here. Moreover, Paul seems to quote a formula in 1 Thess 1:10.[14] There is no reason to doubt that the article is part of the original text.

4:8 NA[26]: τὸν θεὸν τὸν [καὶ] διδόντα τὸ πνεῦμα αὐτοῦ. The καί is missing in A B D[1] I 33. 365. 614. 1739★. 2464 *al* b sy[p] bo; Ambst Spec. Witnesses for the text are ℵ D★.[2] F G Ψ 1 lat sy[h] sa[mss]; C1. Of the editors only Westcott-Hort do not admit καί into the text. The evidence for the omission is indeed strong. But bracketing the word is no solution because this variant is closely related to the following: διδόντα (ℵ* B D F G I 365. 2464. *pc*) and δόντα (ℵ[2] A Ψ 1 sy co; Cl). Bernhard Weiss has shown that ΔΙΔΟΝΤΑ is the result of a faulty copying of ΚΑΙΔΟΝΤΑ, because of the similarity of ΑΙ and ΔΙ.[15] The aorist δόντα is also required by the context: "God has called you" (ἐκάλεσεν, 4:7)—"who *gave* you his Holy Spirit."[16] Thus καί should stay in the text (without brackets), but δόντα (not διδόντα) must be read following the καί. In this case, only the "Majority Text" has preserved the original reading.[17]

Of the five other changes in NA[26], two are certainly correct.

5:10: τοῦ ἀποθανόντος ὑπὲρ ἡμῶν (𝔓30 ℵ[2] A D F G Ψ 1) for περὶ ἡμῶν (ℵ* B 33 = Tischendorf, Merk, Nestle). Although ὑπέρ and περί are used synonymously in Hellenistic Greek, ὑπὲρ ἡμῶν is overwhelmingly attested in Pauline usage.[18]

5:13: ὑπερεκπερισσοῦ (ℵ A D[2] Ψ 1) for ὑπερεκπερισσῶς (B D★ F G *pc* = Tischendorf, Nestle). Both adverbs are possible, but Paul uses the form ὑπερεκπερισσοῦ also in 3:10.

---

ing in 𝔓46 N D 1739 and others; cf. Zuntz, *Text of the Epistles*, 188–93). A most striking case is 1 Cor 7:34: the reading of 𝔓46 A D P 33. (629). 1175. 2495. *pc* a t vg[cl] sy[p]; Epiph is τῷ σώματι καὶ τῷ πνεύματι. NA[26] with all other previous editions adds καί before τῷ σώματι (Westcott-Hort are uncertain). But Zuntz (*Text of the Epistles*, 199) rightly argues that this καί is an intrusion from an old variant without articles, καὶ σώματι καὶ πνεύματι (𝔓15 F G and others—not listed in NA[26]), thus creating the reading καὶ τῷ σώματι καὶ τῷ πνεύματι that "is bad from every point of view. It is overlong and rhythmically clumsy; the twofold καί gives undue weight to the plain phrase 'in body and soul,' and the evidence for this reading is small and narrowly confined" (Zuntz, *Text of the Epistles*, 199). NA[26] is here still so much under the spell of ℵ and B (both have the additional καί) that 𝔓46 is not permitted to outweigh their combined witness.

13. Rom 4:24; 6:4, 9; 7:4; 8:11; 10:9; 1 Cor 15:12, 20; Gal 1:1.

14. Cf. πρωτότοκος ἐκ τῶν νεκρῶν in the hymn quoted in Col 1:10.

15. *Textkritik der paulinischen Briefe* (TU 14.3; Leipzig: Hinrichs, 1896) 112. See also Rigaux, *Thessaloniciens*, ad loc.

16. Cf. Rigaux, *Thessaloniciens*, ad loc.; see the use of the aorist δόντα in Gal 1:4.

17. Of the modern editors, only von Soden reads καὶ δόντα.

18. Zuntz, *Text of the Epistles*, 87. Westcott-Hort, von Soden, and Vogels read ὑπέρ. Cf. also Rigaux, *Thessaloniciens*, ad loc.

Doubts can be raised in 2:13 with respect to the word order ἐστιν ἀληθῶς (ℵ A D F G H Ψ 0208^vid l lat sy), changed from ἀληθῶς ἐστιν (B 33. 326. 1739. 1881. *pc* = Westcott-Hort, Nestle). ℵ must be added to the latter, because the *Vorlage* of ℵ certainly read ἀληθῶς ἐστιν: the scribe omitted ἀληθῶς because of homoioteleuton with the preceding καθώς, the first corrector of ℵ then added the omitted word after ἐστιν.[19] Thus the evidence for the word order ἀληθῶς ἐστιν is stronger than it appears at first glance, especially in view of the support of 1739, which may indicate that also 𝔓46 would support this reading if its text were preserved here.[20]

In the problematic passage 2:7–8, Aland has changed the traditional text of Nestle in two instances. In 2:7 NA^26 νήπιοι (𝔓65 ℵ* B C* D* F G I Ψ* 104*. 326^c. 2495 *pc* it vg^ww sa^ms bo; C1 = Westcott-Hort) for ἤπιοι of the earlier editions (ℵ^c A C^2 D^2 Ψ^c l vg^st (sy) sa^mss = Tischendorf, von Soden, Vogels, Nestle). On the basis of the manuscript evidence alone, this decision may be justified. But the variant is caused by either haplography or dittography after ἐγενήθημεν—both mistakes could occur repeatedly even in the same family of manuscripts. Other criteria are therefore needed. Considering context and subject matter, there cannot be the slightest doubt that νήπιοι is wrong. To be sure, this word is used elsewhere in Paul's letters, but always with the meaning "babe," "immature" (Rom 2:20; 1 Cor 3:1; 13:11; Gal 4:1, 3; cf. Eph 4:14). The contrast is always "mature," "perfect." The possible meaning "innocent," contrasted with "learned" (σοφός, συνετός)[21] does not occur in Paul. But even in this latter meaning, νήπιος would be awkward in 1 Thess 2:7, because Paul here emphasizes his loving care for the Thessalonians: "like a mother comforts her children" (2:7), "ready to share . . . our own selves" (2:8).[22] Only the term ἤπιος, "gentle," "kind,"[23] fits this context and contrasts well with the preceding "although we could have wielded authority as apostles of Christ" (2:7a).

In 2:8 NA^26 has correctly changed the Atticistic imperfect ηὐδοκοῦμεν (B = Westcott-Hort, Nestle) to the customary nonaugmented Koine imperfect εὐδοκοῦμεν.[24] This may be the best possible text, but questions remain. Why would Paul choose the imperfect tense—which could be misread as a present[25]—rather than the aorist?[26] The preceding and following finite verbs are all aorists: ἐγενήθημεν (2:7), ἐκηρύξαμεν (2:9), ἐγενήθημεν (2:10). Moreover, the aorist of εὐδοκεῖν occurs in the next chapter of 1 Thessalonians (3:1) and frequently elsewhere in Paul's letters,[27] while there is no

---

19. Rigaux, *Thessaloniciens*, ad loc.

20. Rigaux, *Thessaloniciens*, ad loc., prefers the reading now printed in NA^26.

21. Cf. Matt 11:25; Luke 10:21.

22. See also below on 2:8.

23. The term ἤπιος is used in the NT only here and in 2 Tim 2:24. In 1 Thess 2 it belongs to the standard concepts that describe the behavior of the Cynic philosopher. Paul's apology of his own ministry in 1 Thess 2 draws on this model; cf. Abraham J. Malherbe, "'Gentle as a Nurse': The Cynic Background to 1 Thess ii," *NovT* 12 (1970) 201–17.

24. Cf. J. K. Elliot, "Temporal Augment in Verbs with Initial Diphthong in the New Testament," *NovT* 22 (1980) 5; BDF §66; Rigaux, *Thessaloniciens*, ad loc.

25. In 2 Cor 5:8 εὐδοκοῦμεν is present tense.

26. The aorist εὐδοκήσαμεν is read here by 33. 31 *pc* f vg—too narrow a basis for textual emendation.

27. Rom 15:26, 27; 1 Cor 1:21; 10:5; Gal 1:15; cf. Col 1:19; Heb 10:6.

instance of the imperfect of this verb in the New Testament. One must ask, therefore, whether εὐδοκοῦμεν in 2:8 is not actually a present tense, caused by the misreading of the preceding ὁμειρόμενοι as "to be desirous of," "to long for." This is apparently an ancient misunderstanding of this rare word as a synonym of ἱμείρομαι.[28] If ἱμείρομαι ὑμῶν really meant that Paul "longed for" the Thessalonians (i.e., in a situation in which he was absent and not present) the present tense of εὐδοκοῦμεν would be called for: "(Now absent) longing for you, we are ready to share with you not only the gospel but our own selves." Such misunderstanding of ὁμείρομαι at a very early stage of the transmission of the letter could have caused the change of an original εὐδοκήσαμεν into εὐδοκοῦμεν (present, not imperfect). However, in view of the context and in view of the impossibility of translating ὁμείρομαι with "to long for," "to be desirous of,"[29] εὐδοκήσαμεν is most likely the original reading: it was then, when Paul, Timothy, and Sylvanus were in Thessalonike, that they gave the Thessalonians their own selves. In this context, ὁμειρόμενοι—probably a term from the vernacular language—must express a loving behavior among members of the family, analogous to "gentle" and "as a mother comforts."[30]

Did NA[26] improve the Greek text of 1 Thessalonians? In the five instances where words in brackets were added (1:5, 8; 3:13; 4:11; 5:15), we can say with great certainty that these words are not part of the original text. Of the three instances in which words of NA[26] were bracketed, two are not justified (1:5, 10); in the third case (4:8) the brackets do not solve the textual problem. Of the five other changes, two are a definite improvement (5:10, 13); one can be disputed (2:13); one is justified, but does not bring us closer to the original text (2:8); and one is clearly wrong (2:7). Thus, though the text has been improved in three cases, it is still problematic in two cases (2:8; 4:8), and it is inferior to its predecessor in eight instances. Most problematic is the greater degree of uncertainty (addition of brackets), the disregard of Zuntz's insights in his masterwork on *The Text of the Epistles*, and a failure to consider the context and subject matter (especially evident in 2:7).

---

28. Job 3:21 translates Hebrew מחכה, "to wait for," "to long for," with ὁμείρομαι. Hesychius explains ὁμείρομαι as ἐπιθυμεῖν.

29. There is general agreement now that ὁμείρομαι cannot be equated with ἱμείρομαι / μείρομαι; cf. BDF §101 s.v.; Rigaux, *Thessaloniciens*, ad loc. (with extensive literature, p. 421). The 3d-century CE inscription on a tomb from Lycaonia, ὁ[μει]ρόμενοι περὶ παιδός (*CIG* III 4000), is the only other evidence, and it remains enigmatic.

30. But the term remains untranslatable, though it can be said with confidence that all extant translations are either wrong or ambiguous.

5

ARCHAEOLOGY AND PAUL
IN THESSALONIKE

Archaeology that is occupied with the cities of the Pauline missionary activity appears to promise more than the attempt to follow step by step the footprints of Jesus in the Holy Land. The latter attempt can escape only with difficulties from the suspicion of being archaeology in the traditional sense of what my teacher Ernst Fuchs once in a lecture characterized as "archaeology of the empty tomb." But even in the search for archaeological materials from the places of activity of the great apostle to the Gentiles there remains the temptation to search for materials that illustrate the immediate context of Paul and may illustrate possible references, for example, from the book of Acts, to places of his activity.

Some archaeological discoveries may be tempting, such as the poorly preserved inscription [ΣΥΝΑ]ΓΩΓΗ ΕΒΡ[ΑΙΩΝ] ("Synagogue of the Hebrews") that was found in Corinth.[1] But this inscription must be dated much later and says nothing about the Jewish congregation in Corinth at the time of Paul. It may be more rewarding to point to the inscription of the high priest Iouventianus from Isthmia (2nd century CE), who boasts that he was the first to build permanent housing for the athletes of the Isthmian Games.[2] This implies that the athletes as well as the visitors at the games were still living in tents at the time of Paul. This may have given Paul, who was a tentmaker, ample opportunity for employment. One learns, however, from this inscription more about the considerable building activity of the second century CE than about the missionary activity of the apostle.

As far as Thessalonike is concerned, things are even worse.[3] To be sure, the often-quoted inscription about the politarchs of Thessalonike[4] demonstrates that the author of the Acts of the Apostles had a good knowledge of the structure of the local admin-

---

1. Cf. Hans Conzelmann, *1 Corinthians: A Commmenary to the First Epistle to the Corinthians,* trans. James W. Leitch (Hermeneia; Philadelphia: Fortress Press, 1975) 12.

2. *IG* IV, 203. See on this inscription Helmut Koester and Eric Sorensen "Isthmia," in Helmut Koester, ed., *Archaeological Resources for New Testament Studies* (Philadelphia: Trinity Press International, 1994) 2, nos. 39 and 40; now also in Helmut Koester, ed., *Cities of Paul: Images and Interpretations from the Harvard New Testament Archaeology Project* (CD-ROM; Minneapolis: Fortress Press, 2004). References in the following will be to this latter publication.

3. For a more detailed discussion see "From Paul's Eschatology to the Apocalyptic Scheme of 2 Thessalonians," chapter 6 in this volume.

4. Charles Edson, *Inscriptiones graecae Epiri, Macedoniae, Thraciae, Scythiae,* Pars 1: *Inscriptiones Macedonia,* Fasciculum 1: *Inscriptiones Thessalonicae et viciniae* (Berlin: de Gruyter, 1972) 126; Koester, *Cities of Paul: Thessalonike: General.* The date of this inscription is debated (1st century BCE to 2d century CE).

PLATE 2. Herm of Dionysus with hole for the insertion of a phallus; from Thessalonike

istration,[5] but it says nothing about the missionary activity of Paul. The earliest archaeological evidence for the presence of a religious community from Israel is a Greek inscription with two lines in Hebrew,[6] which can be dated at the earliest in the fourth century CE and is not Jewish but Samaritan.[7] The inscription is important as evidence for the continuation of a Samaritan diaspora in the time of ancient Christianity, though it can hardly be used in order to argue that Paul once preached in a Samaritan synagogue.

Not much more is known about pagan religions at the time of Paul. One may, of course, assume that the traditional Greek religions were present, even if archaeological finds are rare. That Dionysus was worshiped is evident from a number of inscriptions.[8] But it is hardly possible to conclude from a small herm of Dionysus with a hole for the insertion of a phallus[9] that a rite existed in which the phallus was solemnly inserted, nor

---

5. *Politarchs* as the highest officials in the administration of a city existed only in Thessalonike and in a few other Macedonian cities; see the commentaries on Acts 17:6; e.g., Ernst Haenchen, *The Acts of the Apostles,* trans. and ed. R. McL. Wilson (Philadelphia: Westminster, 1971) 507–8.

6. *Inscriptiones Thessalonicae et viciniae,* 789; Koester, *Cities of Paul: Thessalonike: Samaritan Inscription.* The inscription quotes the text Num 6:22–27 in a Greek translation that is different from the LXX but is closely related to the Hebrew text of the Samaritan Bible.

7. Cf. B. Lifshitz and J. Schiby, "Une synagogue samaritaine à Thessalonique," *RB* 75 (1968) 368–78; Emmanuel Tov, "Une inscription grecque d'origine samaraitaine trouvée à Thessalonique," *RB* 81 (1974) 394–99; James Purvis, "Paleography of the Samaritan Inscription from Thessalonica," *BASOR* 221 (1976) 121–23.

8. *Inscriptiones Thessalonicae et viciniae,* 28, 59, 259, 503, 506.

9. See plate 2.

is it plausible to use this as an explanation for the difficult and debated phrase τὸ ἑαυτοῦ σκεῦος κτᾶσθαι ἐν ἁγιασμῷ καὶ τιμῇ ("to control their own 'vessel' in holiness and honor") from 1 Thess 4:4.[10] Finally, that the god of wine was worshiped in Thessalonike is a poor explanation for Paul's warning of drunkenness in 5:7.[11]

Similarly unconvincing is the attempt of Robert Jewett to demonstrate on the basis of the combination of sundry materials about the Kabiroi the existence of a chiliastic movement in Thessalonike at the time of Paul.[12] A drinking cup from Thebes from the fifth century BCE showing ithyphallic satyrs and the inscription ΚΑΒΙΡΟΣ is too far removed in locale and time and can therefore not tell anything about the enthusiasm of the cult of the Kabiros in Thessalonike at the time of Paul. That a priest from Thessalonike traveled to Samothrake and was in the third century CE president of the cult of the Kabiros[13] is no plausible evidence that the cult of the Kabiros had been alienated from the broad class of the working population at the time of Paul (or at any other time). On the other hand, the significance of the cult of the Kabiros for Thessalonike and its population is indisputable, although little is known about the ritual.[14] Together with Tyche, the Kabiros was the protector of the city and of its walls, and with Tyche he often appears on bronze coins of Thessalonike.[15] It also seems likely that the later Saint Demetrius inherited the Kabiros's function as protector of the city.[16] But one

---

10. Karl Paul Donfried, "The Cults of Thessalonica and the Thessalonian Correspondence," *NTS* 31 (1985) 338.

11. Ibid.; Robert Jewett, *The Thessalonian Correspondence: Pauline Rhetoric and Millenarian Piety* (FF; Philadelphia: Fortress Press, 1986) 127. For the controversy with Donfried and Jewett, see also "From Paul's Eschatology to the Apocalyptic Scheme of 2 Thessalonians," chapter 6 in this volume.

12. Jewett, *Thessalonian Correspondence,* 161–78.

13. For the relevant inscriptions, see Louis Robert, "Inscriptions de Thessalonique," *Revue philologique* 48 (1974) 180–246.

14. Cf. Koester, *Cities of Paul: Thessalonike: General.*

15. See plate 3.

16. See the early Byzantine mosaic in the Basilica of Saint Demetrius; Ernst Kitzinger, *Byzantine Art in the Making* (Cambridge: Harvard University Press, 1977) 105–6 and plate 189. Saint Demetrius is here depicted in front of the city walls as the protector of the city; see plate 4.

PLATE 4. Mosaic of St. Demetrius from the Basilica of St. Demetrius in Thessalonike (with city walls)

looks in vain in the surviving archaeological record for proof of a religious enthusiasm and fanaticism of this cult. Thus Jewett's hypothesis about Paul's reaction against such a movement in his letters to the Thessalonians must remain pure speculation.[17]

All attempts to draw direct lines from archaeological materials to the New Testament or other early Christian writings suffer from three fatal mistakes: (1) They want to use archaeological data in order to anchor texts from the New Testament in a particular historical situation and in a specific location; thus they are nothing but a continuation of "biblical archaeology." (2) They neglect the necessary task of interpreting archaeological data first of all with respect to the general framework of the history of religions and culture of the Greco-Roman world. (3) They cannot clarify under which statement of the problems early Christian texts as well as archaeological data should be interpreted.

---

17. Jewett assumes that both letters are authentic and finds in the warnings regarding an immediate expectation of the parousia a Pauline reaction against the chiliasm of the cult of the Kabiros.

In that New Testament scholarship for many decades had been preoccupied with the theology of the New Testament, insights into non-Christian religions of that period were often used as a negative foil for the elaboration of the superiority of early Christian theological insights. In general, "theology" was the slogan that implied in itself the superiority of Christianity over paganism, because the non-Christian had merely "religions." Christianity was presented as "the end of religions." It might perhaps help if also paganism and Judaism of that time were interpreted theologically in order to establish a base for an unbiased comparison. But in that case, nonliterary materials would still receive short shrift. At the same time, it is no solution to replace the theological formulation of the question by a sociological one. To be sure, archaeological materials could thus be included more felicitously. But in that case, one is either tempted to characterize subject matters and persons with respect to their social origin and background—it would remain unclear, however, how this sociological categorization is related to the history of religion and theology—or one abstracts a sociological ideology from nonliterary materials and confronts it with a Christian ideology, as it happens in Jewett's thesis.

It seems much better to me to reinstate the concepts of religion and history of religions into their genuine right and to bring them to bear upon the Christian as well as the non-Christian world. This would provide a handle for all subject matters of the history of religion, including also the nonliterary materials. Cultural and religious phenomena would thus be included in the quest for an understanding of the history of religions, which would include the care for all matters that emerge only from archaeological investigations and are not readily apparent in literature.

A history-of-religions approach will be unwilling to accept a fundamental distinction among Christian theology, Judaism, and pagan cults. As parts of the history of religion, Christianity, paganism, and Judaism belong together as phenomena of religious life of antiquity and late antiquity. Individual forms of organization, of religious rituals, and of literary and architectural expressions may differ in many instances. But it still remains one and the same Greco-Roman world and one and the same development of the history of religions and culture, to which all these religions belong. For the work with archaeological data this implies first of all that it will not do to employ pagan materials as illustrations for the world of early Christianity. Christian as well as non-Christian materials, whether they are in literary or nonliterary form, must be interpreted in order to gain a better understanding of the whole phenomenon of the history of religions of the Greco-Roman world. Only then will it be possible to discuss special features of Christian texts.

A number of difficulties have to be overcome. Most of all, it is necessary to intensify the collaboration of the various scholarly special disciplines. Among us New Testament scholars who are interested in archaeology of the Pauline cities, there are precious few archaeologists, art historians, and epigraphers. Scholars in these disciplines are often also guided by questions that differ greatly from our questions. It is necessary therefore that New Testament scholars learn to listen to their questions. On the other hand, it is equally necessary to bring our own questions into the discussion in order to arrive together at an interpretation of archaeological materials.

Another difficulty can best be illustrated with regard to the question of archaeology and the Pauline congregation in Thessalonike. On the one hand, it is important to respect regional differences; on the other hand, such differences should not be overestimated. It is without question that the development of early Christianity in Palestine took place under social and cultural conditions that were by no means identical with those of the realm of the Aegean world. Archaeological discoveries from different realms of the Roman world demonstrate sufficiently considerable differences in social structure, political organization, commerce, and trade. Yet there were many common things through which the people in the East and the West were bound together. Wherever the Greeks went, they built theaters; wherever the Romans went, they built baths and aqueducts. With respect to the history of religions, one can observe, for example, that statues of Sarapis follow the same canon everywhere, no matter whether such statues come from Colon or Rome or Ephesus. And as far as early Christianity is concerned, all congregations up to the time of Marcion used the Bible of Israel as their Holy Scripture.

With respect to archaeological finds one must therefore ask whether they belong to a specific regional phenomenon or relate to generally observable patterns. But even if striking special religious features emerge from Thessalonian archaeological finds from the time of Paul, it remains an open question whether Paul in his letter to the Thessalonians refers to them or rather speaks in a language that has nothing to do with them because it derives from general conventions, for example, from Holy Scripture or from Roman political propaganda.

In the case of Thessalonike this question is especially important because archaeological discoveries here are accidental and incoherent to such a degree that they allow only very limited conclusions for a specific time and only rarely suffice to draw conclusions for a continuing religious development. For the first two centuries BCE, a worship for the Roman benefactors can be reconstructed that bears clear signs of local tradition.[18] But upon this time follows a period of three hundred years of silence with respect to the cult of the Roman emperors until the monuments from the time of the emperor Galerius. Then, however, we are no longer dealing with a special Thessalonian local cult as in the pre-Christian period, but with an appearance of generally used symbols of imperial worship.

The transition from the local Thessalonian cult for the Roman benefactors to the generally valid late form of the imperial cult is demonstrated by the bronze coins minted in Thessalonike in the third century CE. Bronze coins from the early imperial period present the head of the divinized Caesar (*divus Iulius*) with the legend ΘΕΟΣ,[19] but neither Augustus nor any of his successors (with the exception of Nero) is ever designated in this way.[20] The normative type used by the mint produced coins with Tyche on the obverse and the Kabiros on the reverse. At the beginning of the third century CE, the portrait of Julia Domna (wife of Emperor Septimius Severus) replaced the Tyche on these local coins.[21] A little later, the head of the Roman emperor with the solar halo replaced

---

18. This has been demonstrated by Holland L. Hendrix, "Thessalonicans Honor Romans" (Th.D. diss., Harvard University, 1984).

19. Barcley Head, *A Catalogue of Greek Coins in the British Museum,* vol. 5: *Macedonia* (London: Longmans, 1879) no. 58; Koester, *Cities of Paul: Thessalonike: General.* See plate 5.

20. Hendrix, "Thessalonicans Honor Romans," 170–77; Charles Edson, "Macedonia: State Cults of Thessalonike," *HSCP* 51 (1940) 125–36.

21. See plate 6.

PLATE 5. Coin with head of Caesar and the legend
ΘΕΟΣ; from Thessalonike

PLATE 6. Coin with Julia Domna on the obverse;
from Thessalonike

PLATE 7. Coin with a Roman emperor radiate on
the reverse

Plate 8. Marble Arch of Galerius from Palace of Galerius in Thessalonike

the Kabiros on the reverse,[22] while Tyche received again her traditional place on the obverse. On the marble arch that was discovered in the palace of Galerius, Tyche with mural crown appears again in the medallion on the left, while the head of the emperor Galerius is set into the medallion on the right, thus replacing the Kabiros.[23] The emperor has assumed here the function of the Kabiros as the protector of the city. Thus far, the propaganda for the imperial cult still remains within the traditional local patterns.

But this is no longer the case in the Arch of Galerius in Thessalonike. The imagery here alludes to religious and political topics that have no relationship to the local traditions of the city. They are rather serving the propaganda of the universal ideology of the Tetrarchs. The relief of the third register on the northern side of the south pillar[24] shows the four Tetrarchs enthroned in the heavenly realms (ἐν τοῖς ἐπουρανίοις): Diocletian, Augustus of the East, seated to the left—on the eastern side; his Caesar Galerius standing on his left; Maximian, Augustus of the West, seated on the right of Diocletian; on his right standing his Caesar Constantius Chlorus. Kneeling female figures next to the two Caesars represent the two pacified provinces Mesopotamia and Britannia. The Tetrarchs are surrounded by deities on both sides. On the eastern side first Sarapis, clearly recognizable from the calathus on his head. Of Isis on the far left, only her sistrum has survived. Corresponding on the western side are two deities, probably Jupiter and Fortuna. Oceanus and Tellus in the two lower corners emphasize that the Tetrarchs are indeed represented as rulers of the world.[25] As much as the religious propaganda of the Tetrarchs is expressed, as little does this relief tell about the specific forms of the imperial cult of the Thessalonians.

---

22. See plate 7.

23. Cf. Koester, *Cities of Paul: Thessalonike: Galerius;* see plate 8.

24. For the interpetation of these registers, see ibid.; see plate 9.

25. The other figures standing between the deities are probably the Dioscouri and Virtus and Honos; see Holland Hendrix, "Imperial *Apotheosis* on the Arch of Galerius at Thessalonica," *Numina Aegea* 3 (1980) 25–33; Margaret Rothman, "The Panel of the Emperors Enthroned," *GRBS* 2 (1975) 19–40.

Plate 9. Arch of Galerius in Thessalonike: enthronization of the tetrarchs

Of course, the inquisitive New Testament scholar would like to know something also about the places where the apostle might have delivered his speeches, especially about the agora of the city. The great forum, however, a rectangular Roman market, was built in the second century CE. At this time, the major part of the upper section has been excavated.[26] To the south, a lower area was attached. The southern colonnade of the northern forum stood on a cryptoporticus, which formed at the same time the northern border of the lower forum, which remains unexcavated. The transformation of an older market into two fora that were surrounded by porticos is again no typical Thessalonian phenomenon. Rather, it mirrors the widespread tendency of the Roman imperial period to transform the older open agora of the Greek city into the shape of an enclosed forum. Otherwise, nothing has come to light in the excavations of Thessalonike that could be dated with certainty to the first century CE.

The Egyptian Religion in Thessalonike: Regulations for the Cult

With respect to the religions of Thessalonike, the Egyptian religion is the only one that is attested by finds from several centuries.[27] A total of 69 inscriptions found in Thessa-

26. Charalambos Bakirtzis, "The Thessalonian Agora Complex," in *Ancient Macedonia,* vol. 2 (Thessaloniki: Institute for Balkan Studies, 1977) 257–69 (in Greek); cf. Koester, *Cities of Paul: Thessalonike: Forum.*

27. The following discussion of the Egyptian religion in Thessalonike replaces the respective discussion in the original German essay by an unpublished lecture, "The Egyptian Religion in Thessalonike," which was

lonike refer to the worship of the Egyptian deities.[28] The worship of the Egyptian gods must have been introduced to Thessalonike before 200 BCE. This is attested in an inscription that records a letter of King Philip V of Macedonia, dated to 187 BCE.[29] Among other regulations, this letter prohibits the use of the Sarapeion's funds for extracultic purposes and declares specific penalties for contraventions of the regulations. This inscription is the only tangible evidence for the existence of this cult in Thessalonike at the early Hellenistic period. Rich evidence, witnessing to a later period of this religion, came from a discovery early in the twentieth century.

The Sarapeion

At the end of World War I, the Greek scholar Professor S. Pelekides found a small temple, parts of a stoa, and ruinous remains of some other structures in the eastern part of Thessalonike during excavations in the middle of a street.[30] These findings were reported in the *Bulletin de correspondance hellénique* in 1921. In the beginning of 1939, other structures were found a few meters away from that site, as the ground was excavated for a new building. Charalambos Makarona reported these later finds in an article published in the first volume of the journal *Makedonika* in 1940.[31] But the fact that this publication appeared just at the beginning of World War II and that it was written in Greek resulted in it being barely noticed in the scholarly world. In the following, I want to give a description of some of the more important finds.[32]

The most significant part of the 1939 discovery was a small temple-like structure, measuring approximately 11 by 8 meters, with a crypt under its entrance hall.[33] Especially this crypt yielded a number of significant artifacts, which leave no doubt that this structure belonged to the cult of the Egyptian gods. Although it is not known to which Egyptian god the temple was dedicated, it is simply a matter of convenience to call it a Sarapeion. The structure itself is no longer accessible. But a scale model was made at the time of the excavation, which is now housed, together with the other finds, in the Archaeological Museum of Thessaloniki.

I shall quote here parts of the description of that temple-like structure from the article of Makarona.

---

presented at the meeting of the Society of Biblical Literature 2001. For this presentation I owe much to Daniel Fraikin's publication about the excavation of the Sarapis temple in *Numina Aegaea* and to Holland Hendrix's descriptions of various finds in *Archaeological Resources for New Testament Studies*. My thanks also go to Dr. Katerina Romiopoulou, then-director of the Archaeological Museum in Thessalonike, who helpfully granted access to the relevant materials in the early seventies, when all finds were still housed in the basement of the museum.

28. Edson, *Inscriptiones Thessalonicae et viciniae*, nos. 3, 5, 16, 37, 51, 53, 59, 75–123, 221, 222, 254–259.
29. Ibid., no. 3.
30. Charles Edson, "Cults of Thessalonica (Macedonia III)," *HTR* 41 (1948) 181–88.
31. Charalambos Makaronas, "Excavations at the Serapeion," *Makedonika* 1 (1940) 464–65 (in Greek).
32. I am mostly following here Daniel Fraikin, "Note on the Egyptian Gods in Thessaloniki," *Numina Aegaea* 1 (1974) 1–6. For this and other items of the Egyptian Gods discussed in the following see Koester, *Cities of Paul: Thessalonike: Egyptian Gods*.
33. See plate 10.

Plate 10. Model of the Sarapeion in Thessalonike with open underground passage

The building consists of a small fore hall (πρόδομος) or narthex, and a hall (αἴθουσα) ending to the north with a small niche (κόγχη). The walls, of simple Roman construction, were made of rough stones and lime-mortar interrupted by successive horizontal belts of three layers of baked brick. The floor was decorated with a marble pavement made of small irregular pieces of multi-colored plaques forming a decoration of simple geometric design. Inside and in front of the niche, which was filled to a height of about two meters, stood a stone bench, which probably served as a sacred table.

The crypt, which seems to have been a place for a mystery cult, consisted of an elongated vaulted room lying exactly under and along the length of the hall of this aedicule and of a tunnel-like corridor about 1 m wide and 10 m long. This corridor communicated with the vaulted room by an arched opening at the western extremity of the north wall of the room. The corridor ran parallel to the west wall of the building above and terminated in an exit staircase located beside the niche. The vaulted room, that is, the crypt proper, measured about 4 m by 1,60 m. In the middle of the east side, on the wall, was a niche, in which a small herm of a bearded god stood on a marble base. The floor of the crypt had no special covering. . . . The difference of construction technique between the crypt proper (simple mortar without lime) and the rest offers clear evidence that the temple and the corridor are of a later date. It seems, that is, that at an earlier period only the crypt existed and that later on the temple was built on top of it along with an exit corridor.[34]

As the entrance to the crypt had been sealed in late antiquity with marble slabs, inscriptions and various statues and statue fragments hidden in the underground struc-

---

34. The translation is by Fraikin, "Note on the Egyptian Gods," 2–4.

ture were found in relatively good condition. The latter have been published in various publications. All 69 inscriptions relating to the Egyptian cult in Thessalonike, 35 of these found in the context of the excavations described above, are now published.[35]

The discovery of this structure is important not only because of the underground crypt, which gives rise to speculations about secret initiation rites celebrated there, but also because this structure is not a "temple" in the traditional form, that is, a house for the gods. Rather, it is a small assembly hall, in which the place for the deity has been moved into a niche at the northern end of the room, leaving space for the assembly of a worshiping congregation. This parallels, on a smaller scale, the Sarapis temples in Pergamon,[36] Ephesus,[37] and Miletus.

The Herm from the Crypt of the Sarapeion

This small herm of Dionysos was discovered in the crypt of the Sarapeion.[38] This may indicate that this popular Macedonian deity was somehow involved in the mystery celebrations of the Egyptian cult. It is also possible that Dionysus was identified with the Egyptian god Osiris. Some mythical traditions tell that Dionysus, like Osiris, suffered dismemberment. It can hardly be argued, however, that the absence of the phallus in the statue of the herm would suggest a ritually enacted restitution, symbolizing the god's powers of renewal and regeneration. The sculptor may have simply found it convenient to sculpt the phallus as a separate piece.

Votive Relief of Demetrios for Osiris

This inscribed relief, executed in thoroughly Hellenistic style, has been dated to the late second century BCE.[39] According to the inscription,[40] it was given by one Demetrios, standing behind the altar, to his father Alexander, on the right of the altar pouring a libation, and his mother Nikaia on the left. The money purse, hanging from the father's wrist, designates him as a benefactor of the sanctuary.

The inscription reads:

Ὀσείριδι μύστει Ἀλέξανδρον Δημητρίου καὶ Νικαίαν
Χαριξένου Δημήτριος τοὺς αὐτοῦ γονεῖς

To the initiate Osiris, Demetrios, for his parents Alexander, son of Demetrios, and Nikaia, Daughter of Charixenos.

---

35. Edson, *Inscriptiones Thessalonicae et viciniae*; *IG* X 2.1.
36. See Koester, *Cities of Paul: Pergamon: Red Hall*; also idem, "The Red Hall in Pergamon," chapter 15 in this volume.
37. Ibid., *Ephesus: Sarapeion*.
38. Ibid., *Thessalonike: Egyptian Cult*; see plate 11.
39. See plate 11.
40. Edson, *Inscriptiones Thessalonicae et viciniae*, no. 107; see plate 11.

PLATE 11. Dedication of Demetrios to his parents from Sarapeion; in Thessalonike

It is striking that it is not Demetrios, the devotee, who is called "initiate" but rather the god Osiris. Holland Hendrix explain this as follows: "If Demetrios' dedication was intended to honor his deceased parents, as seems likely, the implication of the inscribed relief is that Osiris as 'initiate' oversees the continuing devotions of his deceased followers."[41]

Introduction of Sarapis to Opus

This inscription, found in the Sarapeion excavations,[42] is a fragment of a larger inscription that seems to have recorded several deeds of the god Sarapis,[43] in other words, of an aretalogy. Most of the well-preserved text reports about the introduction of Sarapis and Isis to the city of Opus. I quote in translation part of the inscription:

> Xenainetos . . . thought that Sarapis stood beside him while asleep and ordered that on his return to Opus he should tell Euronymos, son of Teimasitheos, to receive both him and his sister Isis and to deliver to him the letter which was

41. In Koester, *Thessalonike: Egyptian Cult.*
42. See plate 12.
43. Edson, *Inscriptiones Thessalonicae et viciniae,* no. 225; Koester, *Cities of Paul: Thessalonike: Egyptian Cult.*

PLATE 12. Inscription of Introduction of Sarapis to Opus; from Thessalonike

under his pillow. When he woke up he marveled at the dream and was uncertain as to what should be done, because there was political rivalry between him and Euronymos. But when he fell asleep again he saw the same things, and when he awoke he found the letter under his pillow, just as had been indicated to him. On his return he delivered the letter to Euronymos and reported what the god had prescribed. But Euronymos was perplexed for a time after taking the letter and hearing the things said by Xenainetos to him because, as was explained above, there was political opposition between them. But when he had read the letter and had seen that the things written agreed with what had been said by Xenainetos, he received Sarapis and Isis.[44]

That this story was found copied in an inscription from the first century CE is rather remarkable. The dialect of the inscription is not Macedonian or Attic but belongs to the Koine Greek spoken in the area of the Aetolian league, including Lokris and its city Opus. Moreover, according to linguistic evidence, the story must have been produced in the third or second century BCE. It has been preserved in Thessalonike probably because Xenainetos received this dream vision in the Sarapeion of Thessalonike.

The story is a typical example for the missionary style of the Egyptian religion, where the god himself initiates the movement of his cult to new areas. Such dream

---

44. Translation by Philip Sellew, "Religious Propaganda in Antiquity: A Case from the Sarapeum at Thessalonike," *Numina Aegaea* 3 (1980) 15–20.

PLATE 13. Isis with ears of Phouphikia from Thessalonike

vision reports, however, can also be found in Christian propaganda; see Peter's vision in the book of Acts of the unclean animals that moves him to bring the gospel to a new city (Acts 10).

Phouphikia to Isis with Relief of Ears

The inscription on this stone is dated to the second or third century CE.[45] It reads:

Κατ᾽ εὐχὴν Φυφικία Ἴσιδι ἀκοήν

According to a vow, Phouphikia to Isis for hearing.

This ex-voto of a woman, who thanks the goddess for hearing her prayer, is probably a testimony that also healing activities were connected with the Egyptian sanctuary in Thessalonike. This does not come as a surprise. Financial records from the island of Delos demonstrate that the income of the once flourishing sanctuary of Asklepios declined dramatically as the income of the major Egyptian sanctuary on the island (Sarapeion C) increased sharply.

---

45. Edson, *Inscriptiones Thessalonicae et viciniae*, no. 100; see plate 13.

PLATE 14. Stele of dining association of Anubis from Thessalonike

Votive Inscription with Feet

This plaque measures 58 by 68 cm. Its inscription is dated to the same time as the preceding one[46] and may also be evidence for healing activities at the Egyptian cult center. The name of this female devotee, Venetia Prima, is Latin. The feet, probably those of Isis, indicate that the goddess had been present in the sanctuary.

Dining Association Stele with Relief of Anubis

This stele with a relief of the Egyptian god Anubis, measuring 89 by 25 cm., was found in the Eliades district of Thessalonike.[47] The inscription begins with a dedication to "Aulus Papius Chilon, who provided the meeting place."[48] The dedicators call themselves "the bearers of holy objects (ἱεραφόροι) and table companions (συγκλῖται)." More than a dozen names follow. At the end of the inscription stands the name of

---

46. Ibid., no. 120.

47. See plate 14.

48. Edson, *Inscriptiones Thessalonicae et viciniae*, no. 58.

Kallistratos, the leader (ἄρχων) of the dining association. Remarkable is the frequency of typical names of slaves and freedman, such as Felix, Primus, and Secundus. The inscription demonstrates that persons of lower social status belonging to the Egyptian religion were organized in a separate dining club under the protection of the Egyptian god Anubis—a practice that the apostle Paul would have criticized as sharply as he criticizes the Corinthians' neglect of the poor at their common meals (1 Cor 11:20–22).

Other finds that are testimonies for the religions of Thessalonike in the Hellenistic and Roman period[49] attest the presence of several typical Hellenistic religions but do not allow conclusions with respect to their rituals and their popularity. It is certain that the worship of Dionysus played a role, as the Dionysus herm from the Egyptian sanctuary demonstrates.[50] But most of these finds belong the period before the rise of Christianity.

In all cases, conclusions regarding typical local features of these religions must be very cautious. In most instances, such finds need to be interpreted in the context of other materials from Macedonia, Greece, and Asia Minor as well as from other areas of the Greco-Roman world. This judgment must be valid for archaeological finds from the world of early Christianity in general. It is necessary, both geographically and chronologically, that such finds be considered within a larger context. To be sure, occasionally special features of such discoveries from a limited area may yield information about religious circumstances of a particular time and place. A careful examination of the materials must therefore take account of the peculiarities of a particular city or a limited area. But the relationship to culture and religion of the larger areas, such as Palestine/Syria, the realm of the Aegean, Rome and the West, and Egypt, must be taken into account. At the same time, also with respect to early Christian writings one must face the possibility that they are not directed to a special local situation but are dependent upon more universally valid conventions, ideologies, and realms of languages, for example, apocalypticism or the political propaganda of the Roman Empire.

---

49. E.g., a bronze hand of Sabazios, two inscriptions for Zeus Hypsistos, and a mold for a terra-cotta of Kybele.

50. Rather famous is the guilded bronze funerary urn with scenes from the cult of Dionysus from Derveni near Thessalonike; it dates to the 4th century BCE.

6

FROM PAUL'S ESCHATOLOGY TO THE APOCALYPTIC SCHEME OF 2 THESSALONIANS

Christian Eschatology and the Religions of Thessalonike

The church in Thessalonike stands out as the first Christian church about which we possess direct information through the letter that Paul wrote to them. Throughout the history of scholarship, numerous suggestions have been made with respect to the religious thoughts and attitudes of the Christians in Thessalonike.[1] Traditionally, such statements have been based upon the information provided by the Thessalonian letters themselves. More recently, however, several studies have tried to reconstruct the peculiar pagan religions of this city and to draw conclusions from such observations about the religion of the first Christians in Thessalonike.[2]

The study of materials about the religions of any particular Pauline city is certainly important. Results are intriguing, and the emerging diversity of pagan religions is amazing.[3] To restrict the study to the religions of *one* city or area should be encouraged in order to avoid the pitfalls of combining information gathered from geographically and culturally diverse regions. The scrutiny of archaeological materials will open up insights also into the cultural and religious milieu of all classes of the population.

But to move from geographically restricted archaeological information to the interpretation of a New Testament writing is a complex and difficult, perhaps even impossible, venture. Let me comment specifically on Thessalonike.[4]

---

1. For a review of the history of recent scholarship on this and other questions, see Raymond F. Collins, *Studies on the First Letter to the Thessalonians* (BETL 66; Leuven: Leuven University Press, 1984) 3–75.

2. Holland L. Hendrix, "Thessalonicans Honor Romans" (Th.D. diss., Harvard University, 1984); Karl P. Donfried, "The Cults of Thessalonica and the Thessalonian Correspondence," *NTS* 31 (1985) 336–56; Robert Jewett, *The Thessalonian Correspondence: Pauline Rhetoric and Millenarian Piety* (FF; Philadelphia: Fortress Press, 1986).

3. For a general survey, see Wonfried Elliger, *Paulus in Griechenland: Philippi. Thessaloniki. Athen. Korinth* (Stuttgart: Katholisches Bibelwerk, 1978); Helmut Koester and Holland L. Hendrix, *Archaeological Resources for New Testament Studies,* vol. 1: *Athens. Corinth. Olympia. Thessalonike* (Philadelphia: Fortress Press, 1987); republished in Helmut Koester, ed., *The Cities of Paul: Images and Interpretations from the Harvard Archaeology Project* (Minneapolis: Fortress Press, 2004) (CD-ROM).

4. For a survey of some available materials, see Hendrix, *Thessalonike*; Michael Vickers, "Hellenistic Thessaloniki," *JHS* 92 (1972) 156–70; idem, "The Town Planning of Roman Thessaloniki," in *Ancient Macedonia,* vol. 1 (Thessaloniki: Institute for Balkan Studies, 1970) 239–51. In general, a still very useful detailed account

1. In Thessalonike a major city has occupied the same site from antiquity to our century. The archaeological record is extremely spotty; most of the archaeological data come from the few monuments that miraculously survived the ravages of time, like the Rotunda and the Arch of Galerius, and from emergency excavations of the archaeological service. Only two locations in Thessalonike have been excavated more thoroughly: the Roman Forum from the second century CE[5] and the Palace and Octagon of Galerius,[6] Arch of Galerius,[7] and Rotunda, all built around 300 CE. Beyond these, some chance finds have been very exciting, especially the discovery of a Sarapis temple[8] and numerous inscriptions and some sculpture relating to the Egyptian cult that were unearthed during the construction of a street sixty years ago.[9]

2. There is very little chance that a complete history of the religions of Thessalonike will ever be written. There was enough material for Holland Hendrix to study the cult of the Roman benefactors in the late Republican and early Imperial periods.[10] But for the following two hundred years, information about the Roman Caesars in Thessalonike is spotty[11] (only at the time of Galerius do we find some more solid data).

With respect to other religions at the time of early Christianity, the information is even more fragmentary. The archaeological record is silent about "Judaism" in Thessalonike.[12] The fifth-century Samaritan inscription is an amazing document;[13] but this inscription and Jason of Acts 17:5–9[14]—not mentioned by Paul—are not enough material for the reconstruction of the history of Jews in Thessalonike over the period of half

---

can be found in Béda Rigaux, *Saint Paul: Les Épitres aux Thessaloniciens* (EB; Paris: Gabalda, 1956) 11–20. See further Charles Edson, "Cults of Thessalonica (Macedonia III)," *HTR* 41 (1948) 153–204.

5. Charalambos Bakirtzis, "On the Thessalonian Agora Complex," in Basil Laourdas and Charalambos Makaronas, eds., *Ancient Macedonia*, vol. 2: *Thessaloniki* (Thessaloniki: Institute for Balkan Studies, 1977) 257–69 (in Greek).

6. Ejnar Dyggve, "La region palatiale de Thessalonique," in *Acta Congressus Madvigiani* (Copenhagen: 1958) 353–65; Michael Vickers, "Observations on the Octagon at Thessaloniki," *JRomS* 63 (1973) 111–20.

7. Margaret Rothman, "The Arch of Galerius: A Sculptural Record of the Age of the Tetrarchies" (Ph.D. diss., University of Michigan, 1970).

8. Charalambos Makaronas, "Excavations at the Serapeion," *Makedonika* 1 (1940) 464–65; Daniel Fraikin, "Note on the Sanctuary of the Egyptian Gods in Thessaloniki," *Numina Aegaea* 1 (1974).

9. Reginald E. Witt, "The Egyptian Cults in Ancient Macedonia," in Laourdas and Makaronas, eds., *Ancient Macedonia*, 2.324–33. For the inscriptions see Charles Edson, ed., *Inscriptiones graecae Epiri. Macedoniae. Thracae. Scythiae. Pars II/I: Inscriptiones Thessalonicae et viciniae* (Berlin: de Gruyter, 1972).

10. Hendrix, "Thessalonicans Honor Romans."

11. Charles Edson, "Macedonia: State Cults of Thessaloniki," *HSCP* 51 (1940) 125–36.

12. It is characteristic that Rigaux *(Thessaloniciens,* 20) barely manages to write one single paragraph on the Jews in Thessalonike, for which he draws most of the information from Acts 17:5–9.

13. See B. Lifshitz and J. Schiby, "Une synagogue samaritaine à Thessalonique," *RB* 75 (1968) 368–78; James Purvis, "Palaeography of the Samaritan Inscription from Thessalonica," *BASOR* 221 (1976) 121–23; Emmanuel Tov, "Une inscription grecque d'origine samaritaine trouvée à Thessalonique," *RB* 81 (1974) 394–99.

14. The name Jason was used in Macedonia in general by Greeks, occasionally also by Jews (= Joshua); cf. F. J. Foakes-Jackson and Kirsopp Lake, eds., *The Beginnings of Christianity* (5 vols.; London: MacMillan, 1920–33) 4.205. It may be correct that "there has always been a significant Jewish community in Thessalonica" (Donfried, "Cults," 356, n. 93), but there is no evidence to substantiate this statement.

a millennium. Nor would one dare to reconstruct the development of Christian religious thought in Thessalonike in the second and third centuries on the basis of the Thessalonian correspondence from the first century and the cult of Agios Demetrios in the fourth century.

If it is, therefore, impossible to reconstruct the history of any of the religions of this city on the basis of archaeological data, how can those data be used for a better understanding of the religious milieu of the Thessalonian Christians and of respective statements of the Thessalonian correspondence? Let me give a few examples from recent publications, in particular from Robert Jewett's book.[15]

Nobody can doubt the importance of the cult of the Kabiros for Thessalonike and its connection with the cult of the Caesars.[16] We also know from an inscription that a priest of Augustus from Thessalonike visited the Kabiros sanctuary on Samothrake.[17] Another inscription from the third century CE names a member of the aristocracy and politarch who was also the leader of the cult of the Kabiros.[18] First conclusion: the cult of the Kabiros was taken away from the common people.[19] "The cooptation of the figure of the Cabirus, whose primary role had been to provide equality, aid, and succor for Greeks whose livelihood came from manual labor, left the craftsmen and laborers of Thessalonica without a viable benefactor."[20] As the reader really must feel sorry for the deplorable situation of the Thessalonians who were deprived of their god and had become the victims of "propagandistic cooptation," "moralistic domestication," and "exploitation . . . by the ruling class,"[21] the second conclusion is no longer surprising: all this must have triggered millenarian unrest.[22] Thus the apocalyptic milieu of the Thessalonian correspondence!

Whatever else Jewett knows about the cult of the Kabiros and its orgies is all drawn from R. E. Witt's sometimes uncritical gathering of evidence that often has nothing to do with Thessalonike.[23] Archaeological data from Thebes are suddenly more important for the understanding of 1 Thessalonians 5 than an honest reference to Isaiah 59. It is

---

15. *Thessalonian Correspondence* (see n. 2 above).

16. Cf. Edson, "Cults of Thessalonica," passim; Hendrix, "Thessalonicans Honor Romans."

17. Jewett, *Thessalonian Correspondence,* 131, with reference to Edson, "Cults of Thessalonica," 189–90. For the inscriptions see Louis Robert, "Inscriptions de Thessalonique," in *Revue philologique* 48 (1974) 180–246.

18. Jewett, *Thessalonian Correspondence,* 131, with reference to Edson, "Cults of Thessalonica," 192–94. For the inscription, see the preceding note.

19. Jewett (*Thessalonian Correspondence,* 131), quoting Robert M. Evans ("Eschatology and Ethics: A Study of Thessalonica and Paul's Letters to the Thessalonians" [Princeton: McMahon, 1968] 71): "The cabiri rose to be identified with the city god of Thessalonike, but in so doing lost their religious value and contact with the lower classes." The reader is left wondering why a plural of "cabiri" appears here—Thessalonike traditionally only had one Kabiros—and who is meant by "the city god of Thessalonike" other than the Kabiros.

20. Jewett, *Thessalonian Correspondence,* 131.

21. Ibid.

22. Ibid., 161–78.

23. Reginald E. Witt, "The Kabeiroi in Ancient Macedonia," in Laourdas and Makaronas, eds., *Ancient Macedonia,* 2.67–80. Jewett also uses extensively Bengt Hemberg, *Die Kabiren* (Uppsala: Almqvist and Wiksells, 1950); and Phyllis Williams Lehmann and Denys Spittle, *Samothrace: The Temenos* (Princeton: Princeton University Press, 1982).

necessary to quote in full what Holland Hendrix, who has studied the relevant materials in detail, says about the cult of the Kabiros in Thessalonike:

> Little is known of the actual cult of the Kabiros at Thessalonica. The most that can be drawn from Firmicus' (4th century CE) references to the cult at Thessalonica is that rituals involved sacrifice which may have included some sort of communion with the blood of the animal. The Kabiros Temple at Thessalonica has not been found, and until new material or literary evidence is discovered, the nature of the Thessalonian cult ritual and its "legend" cannot be determined more precisely.[24]

It is instructive to compare this sober assessment of the available evidence with the conclusions drawn by Jewett: "If the experience of initiation involved identification with the god, the gift of apotheosis, the achievement of equality, the relief of guilt, and the promise of the elimination of threats, a raucous celebration would seem as appropriate as it appeared for Pauline Christians whose violent, apocalyptic theology evoked repentance, regeneration, and joy."[25] No wonder, then, that general references to "Dionysiac sexuality" must explain Paul's insistence upon marital purity in 1 Thess 4:4,[26] and that the use of wine in the cult of Dionysus gives a clue for the understanding of 1 Thess 5:7.[27] It is amazing that, as far as I know, nobody has claimed the fifth-century CE Samaritan inscription in order to suggest that Paul must have preached in a Samaritan synagogue!

3. A consequence of such speculations is the breakdown of exegetical sophistication. Once a model of pagan millenarianism has been invented and has been superimposed upon the Letters to the Thessalonians, all eschatological data of these two letters must be made to fit the same situation. Serious differences in the hermeneutical structure of the arguments of the two letters are no longer considered. As long as such data fit into the imaginary bag of pagan apocalyptics, they must all come from Paul's pen. Moreover, not much attention is paid to the possibility that Paul might have had his own eschatological thoughts and expectations that had no relationship at all to the religion of the Kabiros or to the drinking of wine in the cult of Dionysus.

4. This does not imply that Paul's eschatology as it appears in 1 Thessalonians or the eschatology of 2 Thessalonians have no connection with the religion and culture of the Roman imperial period and with matters that can be learned from archaeological data. But the religious horizon of Paul and even of the Christians of Thessalonike was much

---

24. Hendrix in Koester, ed., *Cities of Paul: Thessalonike* #25 and #26.

25. Jewett, *Thessalonian Correspondence,* 130–31. It is noteworthy that these conclusions are based on Witt's ("Kabeiroi," 72) interpretation of the famous 5th-century BCE Kabiros kylix from Thebes. Moreover, the cult of the Kabiroi at Thebes had been subject to a thorough Greek reinterpretation as early as the classical, or even the archaic, period and was by no means representative for the Kabiros cult on Samothrake and in Macedonia; cf. Martin P. Nilsson, *Geschichte der griechischen Religion* (2d ed.; 2 vols.; HAW 5.2; Munich: Beck, 1955) 1.671–72.

26. Donfried, "Cults," 338; and (referring to Donfried) Jewett, *Thessalonian Correspondence,* 127. Indeed, a small herm with a hole for the insertion of a phallus has been found in Thessalonike—indubitable proof for the understanding of σκεῦος (1 Thess 4:4) as *membrum virile* (Donfried, "Cults," 342)! Why not?

27. Jewett, *Thessalonian Correspondence,* 127, with reference to Donfried.

wider than, and perhaps quite different from, the realm to which the very fragmentary finds from one single city belong. The features of religious thought of Paul and of his readers must be determined first of all by an analysis of the traditions used in this correspondence and of their interpretation in the letters themselves.

Apocalyptic Traditions and Interpretation in First Thessalonians

The term *parousia* is a peculiar feature of these two letters. It is used with reference to the coming of the Lord four times in 1 Thessalonians (2:19; 3:13; 4:15; 5:23) and twice in 2 Thessalonians (2:1, 8)—elsewhere in Paul only once (1 Cor 15:23).[28] It has been a general assumption that "parousia" is used as a technical term for the eschatological coming of Jesus or the Son of Man. However, there is no evidence in pre-Christian apocalyptic literature for such technical usage.[29] If there is any "technical" use of "parousia" it appears in the terminology for the arrival of a king or an emperor.[30] In the traditional formula quoted by Paul in 1 Thess 1:9–10 the term does not occur, although this formula ends with an eschatological reference to the coming of Jesus (ἀναμένειν τὸν υἱὸν αὐτοῦ . . . Ἰησοῦν).[31] Also elsewhere in 1 Thessalonians, παρουσία is never part of traditional materials used by Paul.

I would therefore conclude (1) that the term "parousia" has been introduced by Paul in this letter, and (2) that it is a political term that is closely related to the status of the community. The traditional formula quoted in 1:9–10 contains elements typical for Hellenistic Jewish propaganda in which individuals are asked to convert to the true worship of the "Living and True God." But Paul, in his own language, describes the coming of the Lord like the coming of a king or Caesar for whose arrival the community must be prepared. "Parousia" always occurs in contexts in which the preparedness of the entire community is in view: the community in Thessalonike is the "hope, joy, and crown" of Paul in the parousia of the Lord Jesus (2:19). The reference to the parousia in 3:13 is preceded by an admonition to mutual love (3:12). In 4:15 "parousia" appears in a context in which the question of the joint presence of those who are still alive and those who have died is discussed, and 5:23 concludes an admonition to

---

28. The term appears as a variant reading also in 1 Cor 1:8.

29. See the frustrated attempt to establish such a technical usage by Albrecht Oepke, "Παρουσία," *TDNT* 5 (1967) 859–71. The problem is clearly stated by Traugott Holtz, who observes that a per-Christian Jewish use of *parousia* in the technical sense is hardly if at all in evidence (*Der erste Brief an die Thessalonicher* [EKKNT 13; Neukirchen-Vluyn: Neukirchener Verlag, 1986] 119); cf. also ibid., n. 581: "By A. Oepke . . . ist das Problem verwischt."

30. Oepke, *TDNT* 5.857–58; see also LSJ s.v.; especially the references of Rigaux (*Thessaloniciens*, 198) to the use of "parousia" with respect to the arrival of Demetrius Poliorcetes, Ptolemy Philometor and Cleopatra, and Germanicus.

31. Gerhard Friedrich ("Ein Tauflied hellenistischer Judenchristen," *ThZ* 21 [1965] 502–16) has attempted to show that Paul is quoting a Jewish-Christian baptismal hymn. Holtz (*Erster Thessalonicher*, 54–62) rejects this hypothesis, but recognizes that the terminology is not Pauline and has parallels in Hellenistic Jewish conversion language.

the entire community that speaks of their joint and mutual obligations. Paul's personal role is closely related to this event, because his task is fulfilled and his reward certain if the community is indeed found prepared when the Lord arrives.

The discussion of the fate of those who have died in 4:13–18 belongs to this context of community concern. Its topic has often been described as "the delay of the parousia": since Paul was expecting the parousia to occur very soon, he did not say anything about the resurrection of the dead.[32] This is misleading. Neither here nor elsewhere is Paul concerned with this problem. The "recollection of the creed" in 4:14[33] presupposes that the Thessalonians believed that Christ's dying and rising was the basis for the Christians' hope for the resurrection of the dead. But instead of quoting the expectation of the resurrection in the second part of the formula, Paul alters the sentence: "God will lead through Jesus those who have died with him,"[34] that is, Paul replaces the traditional reference to the resurrection by a statement about God leading the dead with him (namely, Jesus). His concerns here are the concerns of the community in Thessalonike: will those who have died be united with us at the parousia? That this question was raised by the Christians in Thessalonike demonstrates that they had very well understood Paul's message and the aim of his missionary work, namely the founding of communities who are united in their expectation of the arrival of the Lord.

The question discussed here is not a religious question ("will there be a resurrection of the dead?"), but a communal question: "will the dead be united with us in order to meet the Lord when he arrives?" The precise definition of the "saying of the Lord" in 4:16–17 can be left aside here.[35] It is important that, in the context of this discussion, another term from the political realm is employed: ἀπάντησις. That this term was introduced by Paul and does not belong to the apocalyptic "saying of the Lord" quoted in 4:15–16 has long been recognized. ἀπάντησις is a technical term describing the festive and formal meeting of a king or other dignitary who arrives for a visit of a city.[36] It is the crucial term for Paul's description of the festive reception of the Lord at his coming. The united community, those who are alive and those who have died and have been raised, will meet the Lord like a delegation of a city that goes out to meet and greet an emperor when he comes to visit.[37]

---

32. More recently again Willi Marxsen, *Der erste Brief an die Thessalonicher* (Zürcher Bibelkommentare, NT 11.1; Zurich: Theologischer Verlag, 1979) 63–65; also Holtz, *Erster Thessalonicher,* 205–6: "Daß die Heilshoffnung auf entgrenztes Leben auch im Durchgang durch den Tod ihre Erfüllung finden konnte, hatten die Glieder der Gemeinde nicht begriffen."

33. Collins, *Studies,* 158. On the complexity of the interpretation of this formula, including its linguistic awkwardness, see Wolfgang Harnisch, *Eschatologische Existenz: Ein exegetischer Beitrag zum Sachanliegen von I. Thessalonicher 4:13—5:11* (FRLANT 110; Göttingen: Vandenhoeck & Ruprecht, 1973) 29–36; however, there is no reason for Harnisch's assumption that such interpretation of the traditional formula was directed against Gnostic opponents (ibid., 37–38).

34. "διὰ τοῦ Ἰησοῦ corresponds to the διὰ τοῦ Χριστοῦ formula" and "must be taken as a modifier of the verb ἄξει rather than as a qualification of the participle κοιμηθέντας" (Collins, *Studies,* 159).

35. It is clear that apocalyptic traditions are used here; see the discussion in Collins, *Studies,* 159–62, who points to the freedom with which Paul uses a number of apocalyptic motifs.

36. The decisive arguments for the political use of this term were presented by Erich Peterson, "Die Einholung des Kyrios," *ZSTh* 7 (1929/30) 682–702; cf. also idem, "ἀπάντησις," *TDNT* 1 (1964) 380–81.

37. It is not possible to understand this passage as a statement about the "rapture" of the believers into heaven.

One might argue that "being caught up into the air on clouds" reflects mythical apocalyptic language and is not taken from the realm of political terminology. To be sure the language is mythological. But at this point of his argument Paul does not quote any particular apocalyptic tradition. Rather, the mythological language serves to transcend the horizon of the earthly realm and to describe the eschatological meeting of the Lord in cosmic dimensions.

The apocalyptic tradition, quoted in the preceding verses as a saying of the Lord, implies a specific sequence of eschatological happenings or has at least been pressed into this service by Paul. However, this sequence of events is not designed to determine the present standing of the community with respect to the apocalyptic timetable. Its only purpose is to argue that, at the parousia of the Lord, the dead will be raised before the ἀπάντησις. As the Lord draws near in his parousia, the archangel, who goes before him like a herald, accompanied by a trumpeter, will effect the resurrection of the dead. If one wants to have a visual image of this event, one may draw on archaeology: everywhere in ancient Greek cities, the cemeteries line the main roads leading into the city, often for miles.

Paul had no interest in an apocalyptic timetable per se. All emphasis is put on "being *with* the Lord" (σὺν αὐτῷ) at all times (cf. also ἄξει σὺν αὐτῷ in 4:14).[38] Paul customarily uses the formula σὺν κυρίῳ to describe the future relationship of the believers to their Lord, although σύν with Χριστῷ or Κυρίῳ is relatively rare—while the present relationship is usually called being ἐν Χριστῷ. Thus the "being *with* the Lord" in 4:18 seems to point to the future. 1 Thess 4:13–18 does not obliterate the line between present and future existence.

In 5:1 we have a new topic (περὶ δέ), the question of the "seasons and times" (χρόνοι καὶ καιροί). The formulation, which says that there is no need to discuss the topic, makes it very unlikely that Paul is answering a question addressed to him by his readers.[39] The following therefore must be read as a deliberate exposition by Paul that does not have any specific reference to concerns of the readers.

The question is whether Paul's own arguments begin in 5:2 or in 5:4. If the former, Paul wants to juxtapose the early Christian view of a sudden coming of the Lord that cannot be calculated to a Jewish apocalyptic understanding that tries to reckon the dates and sequences of the eschatological events. However, Wolfgang Harnisch has shown that this explanation is not possible.[40] Both the discussion of the times and seasons and the emphasis upon the suddenness and inevitability are topics of the prophetic and apocalyptic traditions of Israel, and both occur also in early Christian statements. Also the citation of the metaphor of the thief and the reference to the onset of labor that suddenly comes upon a woman with child remain in the realm of traditional apocalyptic language.[41]

But it is difficult to place the slogan "peace and security" (εἰρήνη καὶ ἀσφάλεια) into the context of apocalyptic language. Because parallels in apocalyptic writings are

---

38. The question where the believers will be after this festive meeting of the Lord is unnecessarily speculative. Paul's only interest lies in the statement that they will be "with the Lord."

39. Cf. Harnisch, *Eschatologische Existenz,* 51–54.

40. Ibid., 54–77.

41. On the traditional apocalyptic character of these verses, see also Collins, *Studies,* 163–66.

lacking, one usually points to Jer 6:14: λέγοντες εἰρήνη· καὶ ποῦ ἐστιν εἰρήνη, and assumes that Paul has replaced the second εἰρήνη with the synonym ἀσφάλεια.[42] But nothing else in this context points to a use of Jer 6:14 or similar prophetic passages. Moreover, the LXX never uses ἀσφάλεια as an equivalent for Hebrew שׁלוֹם. The reference to traditional apocalyptic materials is thus interrupted by Paul with the phrase ὅταν λέγωσιν . . . τότε . . .,[43] in order to introduce the slogan εἰρήνη καὶ ἀσφάλεια. What is the origin of this slogan?

It is unlikely that Paul has coined the slogan. The first of the two terms, εἰρήνη, is never used by Paul for the description of a false illusion of peace. The second term, ἀσφάλεια, never occurs again in the entire Pauline corpus.[44] The term ἀσφάλεια does not occur in the LXX in all of the prophetic characterizations of false security. But it is widely used elsewhere for the security that is guaranteed by treaties or promises or by strong defenses, like "security of the cities" or "safe conduct."[45] With this meaning, it also occurs in the LXX, especially in 1 and 2 Maccabees.[46] It is a political term.[47] As a political slogan, εἰρήνη καὶ ἀσφάλεια = pax et securitas is best ascribed to the realm of imperial Roman propaganda.[48] If this interpretation of the phrase is correct, it would imply that Paul points to the coming of the day of the Lord as an event that will shatter the false peace and security of the Roman establishment. Of course, such a view is entirely in keeping with older Jewish and later Christian apocalyptic protest against imperial establishments.

On this basis, the following discussion of the position of the Christian community becomes much clearer. The Christian community is not one that has to fear the sudden coming of that day.[49] In verse 4, and not earlier, Paul begins with his own arguments

---

42. Rigaux, *Thessaloniciens*, 558; Holtz, *Erste Thessalonicher*, 215–16. Harnisch (*Eschatologische Existenz*, 79–80) feels the difficulty of applying this slogan of Israel's prophets of salvation to the situation in Thessalonike and suggests that this was a Gnostic slogan or that Paul used terms from the prophetic tradition in order to formulate what is, in his opinion, implied in a Gnostic position. But this interpretation stands and falls with the hypothesis of Gnostic opponents in Thessalonike.

43. The construction ὅταν . . . τότε is not unusual in Paul; cf. 1 Cor 15:28, 54; 2 Cor 12:10 (Harnisch, *Eschatologische Existenz*, 76, n. 9); for λέγωσιν see 1 Cor 15:12. I agree with Harnisch, "daß Paulus in 5:3 (ὅταν . . . τότε) selbständig formuliert."

44. In the entire NT, ἀσφάλεια occurs only here, in Luke 1:4, and in Acts 5:24.

45. See LSJ s.v. 2.

46. E.g., κατοικήσετε μετὰ ἀσφαλείας ἐπὶ τῆς γῆς ὑμῶν (Lev 26:5; cf. Deut 12:10); ἀσφάλεια ἔσται ἐν τῇ ἐμῇ πόλει (Isa 18:4); about Simon, 1 Macc 14:37 reports that he forced the Gentiles to vacate the acra in Jerusalem and that he placed Jewish soldiers there: Καὶ ὠχύρωσεν αὐτὴν πρὸς ἀσφάλειαν τῆς χώρας καὶ τῆς πόλεως. In his letter to the Jews, Antiochus writes that he found it necessary to provide for the security of all people (τῆς κοινῆς πάντων ἀσφαλείας, 2 Macc 9:21).

47. That it can also be used as a legal technical term for "pledge" or "bond" can be left aside here.

48. This suggestion was made by Ernst Bammel ("Ein Beitrag zur paulinischen Staatsanschauung," *ThLZ* 85 [1960] 837) but has been largely ignored. Holtz (*Erster Thessalonicher*, 215) takes notice of Bammel's article but states: "Eine kritische Anspielung auf »das Program der frühprinzipalen Zeit«, das in der Formel pax et securitas enthalten ist, . . . liegt jedenfalls kaum vor."

49. There is no indication that it is a polemical discussion directed against an attitude of the community in Thessalonike that Paul criticizes; *pace* Holtz (*Erster Thessalonicher*, 216): "eine allgemeine Stimmung der Sicherheit in diesem Leben, die die Gemeinde bedroht"; and Harnisch (*Eschatologische Existenz*, 80): "die Einstellung gnostisch orientierter Enthusiasten, welche das Telos mit dem Aufstieg des Pneuma-Selbst in die himmlische Heimat bereits erreicht zu haben meinen."

concerning the community. The play on the metaphors "night and day" (thief in the night, children of the day, etc.) is rhetorically fascinating. It serves to introduce a new terminology for the description of the community: they are "children of light."

The terminology of 5:4–9 has been explained as baptismal language.[50] However, most of the arguments for this view are drawn from parallels in the deutero-Pauline letters to the Colossians and the Ephesians, which is a bit anachronistic. Passages from the genuine Pauline letters do not confirm that the terminology of 1 Thess 5:4–9 is baptismal.[51] The mystery-religions language of dying and rising of Romans 6 may be closer to the baptismal language of Paul's churches.

"Children of light" is certainly not typically baptismal, but can hardly be understood without reference to the Qumran literature.[52] The children of light are the elect people of God who are prepared and ready for the eschatological battle, fighting on the side of God against the kingdom of Belial. That this notion of eschatological battle lies much closer to Paul's thought here than some kind of baptismal piety is evident in his subsequent use of the images of the weapons of God.

But before moving to the interpretation of the weapons for the battle of the "children of light," Paul interjects an admonition that is modeled upon traditional apocalyptic calls for watchfulness and sobriety.[53] If the statements about sleeping and drunkenness at night (5:6–8) are not trivialities, they do not speak about the watchfulness required of those who are expecting the "day," but of those who are already now "children of the day." Thus they underline the position of the community in a realm of realized eschatology. To this extent, the distinction between present and future has been obliterated.

The admonition to sobriety is connected closely with the call for putting on the weapons fitting for the children of light (5:8). There are parallels in the Qumran texts for the use of these metaphors.[54] But Paul's terminology is more directly related to the classical text for this language, Isa 59:17. Paul was familiar with that passage and drew directly upon it, that is, there are no intermediary stages like a "tradition" or a baptismal liturgy.[55] Like Isa 59:17, Paul uses only defensive weapons: breastplate and helmet. The latter he connects, like Isaiah 59, with "salvation," and adds the word "hope" (ἐλπὶς

---

50. Ernst Fuchs, "Die Zukunft des Glaubens nach I Thess 5.1–10," in *Glaube und Erfahrung* (Tübingen: Mohr/Siebeck, 1965) 334–63 (for other references to this hypothesis in Fuchs's works, see Collins, *Studies,* 145, n. 54); Harnisch, *Eschatologische Existenz,* 117–25.

51. For a criticism of the hypothesis of Fuchs and Harnisch, see Collins, *Studies,* 149–53.

52. For a discussion of the Qumran parallels to "children of light" and of the relevant older literature on this terminology, see Herbert Braun, *Qumran und das Neue Testament* (2 vols.; Tübingen: Mohr/Siebeck, 1966) 1.219–22 and 234 ("Die 'Lichtkinder' . . . sind eindeutig qumranisch," 221); furthermore Eduard Lohse, "υἱός, κτλ.," *TDNT* 8 (1972) 357–62.

53. Parallels are cited comprehensively in Rigaux, *Thessaloniciens,* 563–66, and in most other commentaries.

54. Braun, *Qumran und das Neue Testament,* 1.222–24; Karl Georg Kuhn, "ὅπλον, κτλ.," *TDNT* 5 (1967) 298–300.

55. Most exegetes prefer to resort to the hypothesis of intermediary stages; cf. Holtz, *Erster Thessalonicher,* 226; see also the extensive discussion and comparison of all relevant materials in Rigaux, *Thessaloniciens,* 567–70. There is, of course, good cause for the assumption that Paul knew both the passage from Isaiah as well as traditional interpretations.

σωτηρίας), but in the former he replaces "righteousness" (δικαιοσύνη) with "faith and love" (πίστις καὶ ἀγάπη). Thus the triad of Christian virtues, already alluded to in 1 Thess 1:3, is established as the community's weaponry for the eschatological battle.

At this point, however, Paul has moved beyond the implications of the traditional apocalyptic language with which he had started the passage. If 5:1–3 seemed to suggest that the "peace and security" of the empire will be shattered by the sudden coming of the "day of the Lord," it is now made clear that, for the believers, "the day" is realized in the presence of faith, hope, and love in the community; these are the weapons in the battle of God. In faith, love, and hope, the "day" becomes a reality in the life of the community. "The children of the day" or "the children of light," in their "work of faith, labor of love, and patience of hope" (1:3), are the architects of the new eschatological community in which the future is becoming a present reality.[56]

This elimination of the distinction between present and future is summarized in the enigmatic statement of 5:10. It is useful to state the problems of the sentence before suggesting a solution: (1) While 5:9 recalls the non-Pauline formula of 1:10 (salvation from the ὀργή), 5:10 connects this very closely with the typical Pauline formula of Christ's death and resurrection that had already been used in 4:14. (2) This latter formula is not quoted in full; only the part that speaks about Christ's death (τοῦ ἀποθανόντος ὑπὲρ ἡμῶν) appears. (3) Before quoting the conclusion referring to the life of believers, Paul inserts the phrase εἴτε γρηγορῶμεν εἴτε καθεύδωμεν. (4) Paul uses καθεύδειν here, as in the preceding verses (5:6–7), where the word refers to physical sleep, albeit metaphorically; but in 4:13–14 he had used the verb κοιμᾶσθαι in order to refer to those who have died. (5) The aorist subjunctive ζήσωμεν is ambiguous, because it does not necessarily refer to the future;[57] if Paul wanted to refer unambiguously to the future, he could have used the future indicative.[58]

Solutions to each of these peculiar features have been suggested by various commentators. A comprehensive interpretation that accounts for all the peculiar features quoted above is difficult.[59] I can do no more here than to make a few suggestions for a solution of the enigma. The intimate connection between the emphasis upon the dying of Jesus Christ for us and the preceding statement (v. 9) makes clear that the result of the possession[60] of salvation has already been accomplished through the death of Christ for us. Salvation from the ὀργή is not, as the traditional formula of 1:10 might suggest, an event to be expected in the future, nor is it an event connected with the believers'

---

56. One should not overlook that the occurrence of the triad of faith, love, and hope in 1:3 and 5:8 forms an *inclusio* within the rhetorical structure of the letter.

57. I assume with most exegetes that the variant readings which have the verb in the future indicative ζήσομεν and present subjunctive ζῶμεν are secondary.

58. For future indicative after ἵνα in Paul, cf. 1 Cor 13:3 (ἵνα καυθήσομαι); see BDF §369.2.

59. Harnisch (*Eschatologische Existenz*, 142–52) has made an eloquent attempt at a comprehensive interpretation that would explain all these features; however, his solution is bedeviled by the assumption that Paul was arguing against Gnostic opponents. Thus Harnisch is tempted to read all statements as emphases upon an anti-Gnostic eschatology that is strictly futuristic, and he excludes the possibilities of realized eschatology.

60. Περιποίησις must be understood as "possession" (not "acquisition"); see Rigaux, *Thessaloniciens*, 571; Holtz, *Erster Thessalonicher*, 228–29.

future resurrection—thus there is no mention of Christ's resurrection in 5:10.[61] Paul speaks about the life of all believers in such a way that salvation is not simply tied to a future eschatological event, that is, the resurrection of the believers.

The recipients of this life are characterized by the εἴτε . . . εἴτε phrase. One can argue that those who watch are the ones who are still alive and those who sleep are the Christians who have died at the time of the parousia, as most exegetes do.[62] But if this is the meaning of the phrase, why does Paul not use terms that clearly describe "to be alive" and "to die"[63] as he does in Rom 14:8? On the other hand, γρηγορεῖν and καδεύδειν cannot simply refer to the physical state of being awake and being asleep.[64] In the preceding verses, both terms had already been used metaphorically; γρηγορεῖν was equated with νήφειν, and καθεύδειν with μεθύειν (vv. 6–8). No reader of verse 10 could have forgotten the metaphorical use of γρηγορεῖν and καθεύδειν in verses 6–8, where Paul emphasized a crucial distinction of attitudes with respect to the future. Deliberately using the very same words, verse 10 makes this distinction irrelevant with respect to "living with him." Without the intervening verse 8, this would be nonsensical. But verse 8 states why the existence of the believers is no longer dependent upon watching for the "day" that comes like a thief in the night: those who belong to the "day" have put on the weapons of the eschatological battle—faith, love, and hope. They are no longer subject to the dangers arising from the lack of watchfulness or, vice versa, the catastrophe of "being asleep" or "dying" when the Lord comes. "To live *with* him" (σὺν αὐτῷ ζήσωμεν) describes the status of a community that is independent of the eschatological timetable. The terms γρηγορεῖν and καθεύδειν are chosen in verse 10 because Paul does not only intend to say that to be alive or to have died at the time of the coming of the Lord is irrelevant—all will go out to meet the Lord; he also wants to emphasize that the believers' existence is not determined by the watchfulness that is focused on the "day of the Lord."

The concept of a community that realizes the presence of the eschatological future in its οἰκοδομή (5:11) and that obliterates the distinctions between being watchful and being asleep, and between life and death, is certainly utopian, especially in its political implications. But that, it seems to me, was exactly what Paul was talking about.

I may be permitted to add a note regarding the notorious question of the "delay of the parousia." I have argued above that 4:13–18 is not concerned with the problem of the resurrection of the dead in general—as if Paul had failed to talk about the resurrection because he expected the coming of the Lord before any deaths would occur. It seems to me that it is altogether wrong to assume that Paul began to talk about the

---

61. In 4:14 mention of the resurrection of Jesus is important, because Paul wants to argue for the future resurrection of those who have died.

62. Cf., e.g., Holtz, *Erster Thessalonicher,* 230–31; Marxsen, *Erster Thessalonicher,* 70.

63. For the latter, at least κοιμᾶσθαι would have been more in keeping with the terminology used in 4:13–18.

64. Jewett (*Thessalonian Correspondence,* 190), taking up a suggestion of T. R. Edgar ("The Meaning of 'Sleep' in I Thessalonians 5:10," *JETS* 22 [1979] 344–49), argues that καθεύδειν here must be understood as physical sleep: "Paul did not really intend to support Christian insomnia, so he sought to allay [the] fear . . . that if Christ returns while you are asleep you are irrevocably lost."

resurrection of the dead only later when he realized that the parousia might be delayed and that people were dying. 1 Thess 5:1–11 makes the existence of the believers independent of the eschatological timetable. They are already now the children of light who have put on the armor of God, faith, love, and hope. That the day of the Lord will come suddenly and unexpectedly is not their concern, but it will be a disastrous surprise for those who proclaim "peace and security." That the existence of the community had thus been freed from such concerns does not imply that Paul no longer expected the day of the Lord, the raising of the dead, and the coming of the Lord. On the contrary, one could argue that the expectation of the nearness of these events was even intensified in the later writings of Paul. Using the same terms employed in 1 Thess 5:1–11 (καιρός, ἐξ ὕπνου ἐγερθῆναι, σωτηρία, νύξ, ἡμέρα, ἐνδύσασθαι τὰ ὅπλα τοῦ φωτός), Rom 13:11–14 even radicalizes the expectation of the nearness: νῦν γὰρ ἐγγύτερον ἡμῶν ἡ σωτηρία ἢ ὅτε ἐπιστεύσαμεν (Rom 13:11). Neither 1 Thessalonians nor Romans was written by someone who was worried about the "delay of the parousia." But both letters base the existence of the community of believers on the statement that they already belong to the "day" in their present existence.

Consolation and the Mystery of the Apocalyptic Timetable

The way in which apocalyptic materials are used and interpreted in 2 Thessalonians obviously affects the decision with respect to the letter's authenticity. Thus one could argue that the interpreter should not decide against authenticity before the actual inquiry into the text has been accomplished. However, the assumption of authenticity as a working hypothesis has resulted in some grotesque interpretations of the Thessalonian correspondence, for which Robert Jewett's work is the most extreme example.

Since Jewett is quite aware that it is extremely difficult to reconstruct *one* historical situation for *both* letters on the basis of the information that these letters provide, he resorts to a reconstruction of the historical situation on the basis of (1) conclusions drawn from observations about pagan cults of Thessalonike, and (2) general assumptions about millenarianism drawn from the phenomenology of religion.[65] Since the statements of both letters have to fit this model, Paul once more becomes the misinformed apostle who did not understand what was going on in Thessalonike at the time he wrote his first letter[66]—a few months after he left the city and a few days after Timothy gave a personal report to him about the situation! The second letter is then interpreted as a desperate attempt at reestablishing order and his own authority in which Paul repudiates most of the things he has said in his first letter.

Fortunately, we have now the excellent work of Wolfgang Trilling on 2 Thessalonians, and most of the last part of my paper is informed by Trilling's studies.[67] Let me high-

---

65. See the discussion of Jewett's hypothesis at the beginning of this paper.

66. Jewett, *Thessalonian Correspondence,* 186–92. "Since the millenarian radicals in Thessalonike were quoting Paul's teaching and writing to support their contention that the Day of the Lord had already come, Paul was forced to write again. . . . The exasperation is visible throughout the letter" (191).

67. *Untersuchungen zum zweiten Thessalonicherbrief* (Erfurter theologische Studien 27; Leipzig: St. Benno-

light two aspects: (1) the situation to which this letter is addressed that is fundamentally different from the situation of the first letter; (2) the method of interpreting apocalyptic traditions, which stands in stark contrast to the method employed in 1 Thessalonians.

The Different Situation

The key passage for understanding the situation is, of course, 2 Thess 2:1–2, where the author quotes the slogan of those who are causing the disturbance: "the day of the Lord is at hand." Most likely, the prophets who proclaimed this used 1 Thessalonians as a justification of their message.[68] However, the real cause for this slogan lies elsewhere, namely in the apocalyptic fervor of the second half of the first century.[69] Parallels are well known. It is not a message that Paul ever expressed in any of his letters. Paul expected the parousia, probably for the near future, but his message proclaims the death and resurrection of Jesus as the turning point of the ages and the presence of the new age in the building of the new community in which the eschatological future is realized in faith, love, and hope, regardless of the nearness of the parousia.

In contrast, the message of the opponents referred to in 2 Thessalonians does not imply the realization of the eschatological future in the work of the community. Rather, it proclaims the nearness of the "day of the Lord" in order to effect a change in the behavior of the established church. That new behavior, however, is *not* understood as the building of the community of the future here and now. On the contrary, it is characterized by the turning away from the pursuits of the world to the enthusiastic expectation of a change that is to come soon; only *after* that change will there be a new eschatological community. The believer is located within a radicalized apocalyptic timetable just *before* the decisive turning point.

The answer given by the author of 2 Thessalonians accepts this timetable. As Trilling has shown, 2 Thess 1:3–12 lays the foundation for the argument.[70] Tribulation (θλῖψις) is the issue. The pronounced emphasis on θλῖψις implies that the church is presently experiencing tribulations. But the author goes to great pains to demonstrate that these tribulations will be answered by God's just retribution at the coming judgment.[71] Nowhere is there any indication that tribulations could be understood as the eschatological tribulations that must be expected to occur just before the very end.[72] The reason

---

Verlag, 1972); idem, *Der zweite Brief an die Thessalonicher* (EKKNT 14; Neukirchen-Vluyn: Neukirchener Verlag, 1980). I am also relying on the excellent discussion by Edgar Krentz, "A Stone That Will Not Fit: The Non-Pauline Authorship of II Thessalonians," unpublished SBL seminar paper, 1983. I will not, in this paper, rehearse the detailed arguments against the authenticity presented in these works.

68. Trilling (*Zweiter Thessalonicher,* 75–78) stresses that one cannot be certain whether a prophecy, a saying, or a letter of Paul is meant, but argues that it is most likely that the opponents referred to a statement of Paul, probably 1 Thessalonians; cf. the discussion in Rigaux, *Thessaloniciens,* 649–52.

69. I fully agree with the reconstruction of the historical situation by Andreas Lindemann, "Zum Abfassungszweck des Zweiten Thessalonicherbriefes," *ZNW* 68 (1977) 35–47.

70. *Zweiter Thessalonicher,* 39–68; cf. also idem, *Untersuchungen,* 69–75.

71. To be sure, also 1 Thessalonians speaks about "tribulations," but characteristically connects these with joy (χαρά): 1 Thess 1:6 (ἐν θλίψει πολλῇ μετὰ χαρᾶς) and 3:1–10; cf. Trilling, *Zweiter Thessalonicher,* 48–49.

72. This is a fundamental belief of Jewish and Christian apocalyptic prophecy; cf. Dan 12:1; Mark 13:19, 24; Matt 24:9–14. A brief survey of Jewish materials is in Heinrich Schlier, "θλίβω, θλῖψις," *TDNT* 3 (1965) 140–43.

for this reticence becomes evident in the course of the letter: the opponents apparently connected the experience of tribulations with their message of the nearness of the day of the Lord. They are thus following a very well established apocalyptic pattern. It is apocalyptic prophecy that the author faces, not Gnostic propaganda.

The author of the letter, in contrast to his opponents, connects the experience of tribulation not to the day of the Lord but to the coming judgment, which will bring equitable retribution. Therefore those who are in tribulation can wait with patience for the revelation of the Lord Jesus from heaven (2 Thess 1:7). The explicitly stated purpose of the parousia of the Lord Jesus is to bring this judgment over all those who are tormenting the Christians. Once the parousia has thus been put into its proper perspective and function, the author can quote the slogan of the opponents and move to the second part of his argument, which establishes a clear distance between the present time and the parousia, 2:3–12.

Traditional topics of the apocalyptic schemata are used now in order to fix stages of events that will lead from the present to the future. The two events that must occur first are (1) the apostasy, and (2) the appearance of the man of lawlessness (2:3). Since they have not occurred, the announcement that the coming of the day of the Lord is at hand is a deception. The conviction that these two events have to take place before the end is drawn from widespread apocalyptic periodization in Jewish and Christian literature.[73] The discussion of the meaning and role of ὁ κατέχων / τὸ κατέχον (2:6–7) cannot be carried on in the context of this paper.[74] The question of the identity of the retarding element and/or person will probably never be solved. The most prominent traditional interpretation that explains it as the Roman Empire is almost certainly wrong. There remains only the choice between an unconsciously vague and a deliberately mysterious reference to a positive factor that prevents, for the time being, the antichrist from becoming revealed. The mysteriousness of this reference enhances the distance between the present time and the future. It does not want to identify the retarding element with any tangible political reality, nor is the antichrist identified with the Roman emperor. References to the political world are consciously avoided.

In 2 Thessalonians the elements from the traditional apocalyptic timetable have been set into a fixed schema that secures a space of life for the community that is not threatened by apocalyptic enthusiasm. Thus the "Pauline" emphasis upon building up the community, which had been interrupted by the disturbance through the prophetic proclamation of the nearness of the day of the Lord, can be resumed. The remainder of the letter is devoted to this topic, often alluding to analogous statements of the first letter, though with striking differences. However, this is beyond the scope of this chapter.

Hermeneutics of Apocalyptic Traditions in the Letters to the Thessalonians

Both letters to the Thessalonians exclusively use traditional apocalyptic materials. There is no evidence whatsoever that the beliefs of the community in Thessalonike are in any

---

73. See the detailed discussion of relevant materials in Trilling, *Zweiter Thessalonicher,* 81–88.

74. See the discussion, materials, and literature in Rigaux, *Thessaloniciens,* 262–71; Trilling, *Zweiter Thessalonicher,* 88–105.

way influenced by the pagan background of the converts or by millenarian propaganda and sentiments related to the specific cultural and social situation of the members of the community.

Traditional apocalyptic sequences of events are, of course, known to Paul and are presupposed in 1 Thessalonians. Some of these elements are used in order to answer specific questions of the community in Thessalonike. This, however, is done in such a way that the distance between present and future is made almost irrelevant. Paul envisions a role for the eschatological community that presents a utopian alternative to the prevailing eschatological ideology of Rome. In doing so, he radicalizes traditional apocalyptic topics, ascribing a dignity to the building up of the community that is equal to the presence of the future in faith, love, and hope. He thus makes traditional apocalyptic postures irrelevant and interprets the situation of the community in a way that even transcends the distinction between life and death.

Also 2 Thessalonians as well as its opponents stay within the framework of the Jewish and Christian apocalyptic traditions. But, in contrast to 1 Thessalonians, the second letter not only accepts the traditional apocalyptic timetable, but reinforces it in such a way that the distance between present and future is increased through the establishment of intermediate stages. While in the first letter the building of the community is authorized by the eschatological role ascribed to this community, in the second letter it is authorized by the distance to the future events that will ultimately lead to the parousia.

7

PAUL AND PHILIPPI

The Evidence from Early Christian Literature

Philippi in 1 Thessalonians and
in the Acts of the Apostles

Philippi is mentioned in the oldest writing of the New Testament, Paul's Letter to the Thessalonians (1 Thess 2:2), written from Corinth probably in the fall of 50 CE. The following events of the same year determine the context for the writing of this letter:[1] (1) In the spring, Paul had come from Troas to Philippi, where he had the opportunity to preach the gospel and to found a community. (2) After being forced to leave Philippi, Paul moved to Thessalonike, where he must have stayed several months. (3) From Thessalonike he traveled to Athens; from there he sent Timothy to Thessalonike (3:1–2). (4) Timothy returned to Paul with good news about the faith of the Thessalonians (3:6). (5) Paul writes to the Thessalonians.[2]

While Paul is writing to the Thessalonians in detail about his mission in their city and about his close relationship with that community, he says nothing about the founding of a community in Philippi. Rather, Paul and his associates state simply that they were able to preach the gospel freely in Thessalonike, "after they had previously suffered and been shamefully treated in Philippi" (προπαθόντες καὶ ὑβρισθέντες ἐν Φιλίπποις, 2:2).[3] We can obtain no other details from the letters of Paul about this first visit. However, the letters to the Philippians, which Paul later wrote from Ephesos (see below), leave no doubt that Paul did indeed establish a community in Philippi during his first visit of the city; as far as we know, he did not visit Philippi again before he wrote those letters.[4] More-

Published in Charalambos Bakirtzis and Helmut Koester, eds., *Philippi at the Time of Paul and After His Death* (Harrisburg: Trinity Press International, 1998) 49–66.

1. On the chronology of the events, see Lukas Bormann, *Philippi: Stadt und Christengemeinde zur Zeit des Paulus* (NovTSup 79; Leiden: Brill, 1995) 118–26.

2. It is not clear whether the letter was written while Paul was still in Athens or after his arrival in Corinth. The subscriptions of the ancient manuscripts of 1 Thessalonians vary; A B 1 0278. 1739. 1881 and the majority of the manuscripts read πρὸς Θεσσαλονικεῖς αʹ ἐγράφη ἀπὸ Ἀθηνῶν (1739 *pc* add διὰ Τιμοθέου). 81 *pc* read πρὸς Θεσσαλονικεῖς αʹ ἐγράφη ἀπὸ Κορίνθου ὑπὸ Παύλου καὶ Σιλουανοῦ καὶ Τιμοθέου.

3. On the hapax legomenon προπάσχειν, see Béda Rigau, *Saint Paul: Les Épitres aux Thessaloniciens* (EB; Paris: Gabalda, 1956) 401–2. The προ- points to an event that happened at a preceding time.

4. According to Acts 18:18–20 he traveled to Ephesos directly from Corinth and then returned to Ephesos after a visit in Caesarea and Antioch (Acts 18:21–23).

over, according to Phil 4:15, the Philippians had supported Paul from the beginning of his missionary work in Macedonia and Greece, and Phil 4:16 even states that the Philippians sent some support to Paul during his ministry in Thessalonike.[5]

Acts 16:11–40 presents a rather lengthy and detailed report about Paul's first visit to Philippi. Coming from Troas, with a stop in Samothrake, Paul, Silas, and Timothy arrived in Neapolis and went from there to Philippi. The city is correctly designated as a Roman colony (Acts 16:12). However, the following statement about the relationship of Philippi to Macedonia is unclear. The best-attested reading, "which is the leading city of the district of Macedonia" (ἥτις ἐστὶν πρώτη μερίδος τῆς Μακεδονίας πόλις),[6] is certainly wrong and cannot be ascribed to Luke, who had a good knowledge of locality and geography; neither was Philippi a capital nor Macedonia a "district." The best reading is the conjecture: "which belongs to the first district of Macedonia" (ἥτις ἐστὶν πρώτης μερίδος τῆς Μακεδονίας πόλις).[7]

The report about the stay of Paul and his two fellow apostles in Philippi need not be discussed in full here. Acts 16:13–14 reports a meeting on the Sabbath day with women, among them Lydia from Thyatira, who was soon baptized at the river outside the city gate at a "place of prayer" (προσευχή).[8] Then follows an episode of a slave girl who had a spirit of divination (πύθων) and the accusation of the apostles by the girl's owners because they had lost their source of income after Paul had exorcised her prophetic spirit. The result is an attack by the mob and the public beating of the three apostles, an imprisonment, an earthquake that opens the door of the jail, and the conversion and baptism of the jailer with his family. Finally, the release of the apostles and their departure after another visit with Lydia and other brothers and sisters are typical for Luke's composition of the travel narrative.

There are a number of problems in this account from the book of Acts. Here, as elsewhere, Paul's stay is depicted as rather short—quite unlikely if one considers that he founded a new Christian community that remained unusually faithful to him during the following years of his mission. The designation of the governors of the city as στρατηγοί, which is the normal translation of *duumviri* (or *duoviri*), is correct and reveals Luke's good knowledge of the local situation. The story of the exorcism belongs to the

---

5. It is also likely that the mention of "the brothers from Macedonia" (2 Cor 11:9), who came to Corinth with support for Paul, refers to delegates from Philippi; see Bormann, *Philippi*, 122.

6. 𝔓[74] ℵ A C Y 33. 36. 81. 323. 945. 1175. 1891 *pc*.

7. See Hans Conzelmann, *The Acts of the Apostles,* trans. James Limburg, et al. (Hermeneia; Philadelphia: Fortress Press, 1987) 129–31.

8. The Greek text is problematic here. It seems that the grammatically incorrect text of A and B (οὗ ἐνομίζομεν [𝔓[45] ἐνόμιζεν] προσευχὴ [*sic*] εἶναι) was the most original reading. "The variants can be explained in the simplest way if the original had an incorrect nominative (προσευχή) instead of the accusative (προσευχήν)" (Conzelmann, *Acts*, 130).

It is strange that Acts 16:13 says, "where we *supposed* that there was a place of prayer." One wonders, moreover, why only women were there. "Place of prayer" (προσευχή) can be used as a designation for a synagogue; see Shaye J. D. Cohen, *From the Maccabees to the Mishnah* (Library of Early Christianity; Philadelphia: Westminster, 1989) 111–12. On the inscription from Philippi that mentions a synagogue (συναγωγή), see its publication by Chaido Koukouli-Chrysantaki, "Colonia Julia Augusta Philippensis," in Charalambos Bakirtzis and Helmut Koester, eds., *Philippi at the Time of Paul and After His Death* (Harrisburg: Trinity Press International, 1998) 28–35.

common stock of stories about powerful deeds enacted by Christian miracle workers; compare *Ps.-Clem. Hom.* 9.16.3:"For pythons prophesy (πύθωνες μαντεύονται), but they are cast out by us as demons and put to flight."The miracle of the earthquake is a response to the singing of hymns in prison—again a motif that has its parallels elsewhere (cf. *T. Jos.* 8.5). Legends formed early around the memory of the visits of famous apostles. They may have been part of the local tradition at the time of the writing of Acts by Luke.

Paul and Philippi according to the Letter to the Philippians

Philippi is next mentioned in Paul's Letter to the Philippians. It is my opinion that this letter of Paul, which is written from prison, was not written from Rome but from Ephesos. The question of the Ephesian imprisonment of Paul is complex and cannot be discussed here.[9] To be sure, the ancient *subscriptio* to this letter, which appears in the majority of Byzantine manuscripts and in the Syriac translation, is probably quite old. It reads ἐγράφη ἀπὸ Ῥώμης δι' Ἐπαφροδίτου. Since, however, Paul writes in this letter of his hope that he might live and return to the church (Phil 2:24), the subscription might rest on a tradition that Paul did indeed die in Rome. Still, no certain conclusion can be drawn from this secondary addition to the letter.

Accepting the hypothesis of an Ephesian origin of the Letter to the Philippians renders a further consideration more plausible, namely, that this letter is a compilation of three letters by Paul to Philippi that were written from Ephesos.[10] The hypothesis of Ephesos as the place of the writing of Philippians and the hypothesis of the division of Philippians into three smaller letters support each other. A quick exchange of letters and messengers, which is clearly indicated in Philippians, is much more likely if Paul was imprisoned in Ephesos, not as far away as Rome; the long and arduous travel between Rome and Philippi would have prevented a speedy correspondence. If the Philippian letters were written from Ephesos, they must be dated in the winter of 54–55 CE—the most likely date for the Ephesian imprisonment of Paul,[11] that is, before 2 Cor 1:8ff., where Paul speaks of the suffering and the threat of death that had been hanging over him during his stay in Ephesos.

While Paul was in prison, he received a gift from the church in Philippi, and he acknowledged this gift in Phil 4:10–20,[12] the first of the three letters that are now com-

---

9. Since the fundamental work of Wilhelm Michaelis (*Die Gefangenschaft des Paulus in Ephesus und das Itinerar des Timotheus* [Gütersloh: Bertelsmann, 1925]), it has been widely agreed that the so-called Imprisonment Letters, at least Philippians and Philemon, must be dated at the time of an Ephesian imprisonment of the apostle. See especially G. S. Duncan, *Paul's Ephesian Ministry: A Reconstruction with Special Reference to the Ephesian Origin of the Imprisonment Epistles* (New York: Scribner's, 1929); T. W. Manson, "St. Paul in Ephesus: The Date of the Epistle to the Philippians," *Bulletin of the John Rylands Library* 23 (1958/59) 43–45.

10. A detailed discussion of the various division hypotheses of the Epistle to the Philippians has been presented by Bormann, *Philippi*, 108–18.

11. See Helmut Koester, *Introduction to the New Testament*, vol. 2: *History and Literature of Early Christianity* (Berlin and New York: de Gruyter, 2000) 111, 135–40.

12. Probably also 4:21–23 belongs to this letter, unless these verses are the conclusion of the second letter, 1:1–3:1.

bined into the extant writing to the Philippians.[13] Epaphroditos came to Paul from Philippi as the bearer of the gift (4:18). This short letter—its genre is a formal receipt[14]—contains significant information about Paul's relationship to the Philippian church: the Philippians had already supported Paul at the beginning of his ministry in Macedonia by sending support to Thessalonike (4:15–16), and while then they did not have an opportunity (ἠκαιρεῖσθε) to show their concern for Paul for some time, they have now once more come to his aid (4:10).

The second letter,[15] comprising Philippians 1:1–3:1,[16] must have been written somewhat later. Some time must have passed; the Philippians had heard meanwhile that Epaphroditos had fallen sick (2:26b). While 4:18 simply mentioned Epaphroditos as the bringer of the gift, Paul now reports that Epaphroditos had stayed with him and had not only served him on behalf of the Philippians (2:30)[17] but had also become sick: "Indeed he was so ill that he nearly died" (2:27a). However, he was now well again, and Paul wants to send him to Philippi soon (2:27b–28).

It is possible that the mission of Epaphroditos on behalf of the Philippians involved more than just the transfer of a sum of money. This possibility has been explored recently by Lukas Bormann,[18] especially in the context of the mention of "those from the household of Caesar" (οἱ ἐκ τῆς Καίσαρος οἰκίας) in Phil 4:22 and of the reference to the "imperial guard" (πραιτώριον)—the official residence of the proconsul, where the trial of Paul was taking place and where also the gospel of Christ had become known (1:13). Philippi was a Roman colony. It is possible that Epaphroditos, a citizen of this colony, was sent to Ephesos because he may have had special connections to freedmen of the praetorium—a very influential group especially at the time of Claudius and Nero—and could therefore influence the outcome of Paul's trial.

It is evident that Paul, when he wrote this second letter to the Philippians, was more optimistic about a positive outcome to his trial. He wants to send Timothy to Philippi as soon as possible (2:19), and should he receive a favorable sentence, he himself would go to Philippi in the near future (1:26; 2:24). This intention fits with Paul's travel plans as they are known from the Corinthian correspondence, where Paul mentions his plan to visit Corinth by way of Macedonia (1 Cor 16:5)—and this is precisely what Paul did after he left Ephesos following his release from prison.[19]

---

13. A detailed explanation of this letter and of the problems of its interpretation is given by Bormann, *Philippi*, 136–60.

14. Phil 4:18 uses the traditional formula for the acknowledgment of such a gift: "I have been paid in full and I have more than enough; I am fully satisfied, now that I received from Epaphroditus the gifts you sent" (NRSV).

15. That the transition from 3:1 to 3:2 is very harsh has been observed often. While 3:1 emphasizes the joy that Paul has in the Lord, 3:2 begins abruptly with a stern warning. It is difficult to reconcile these two statements as part of one and the same letter.

16. It is debated whether also 4:2–7, 8–9, and 21–23 should be assigned to this second letter. The latest investigation of this problem by Bormann (*Philippi*, 115–18) assigns 4:2–7 to the second letter, while 4:8–9 are seen as part of the third letter (3:2–4:1).

17. ". . . risking his life to make up for those services that you could not provide for me."

18. See the discussion in Bormann, *Philippi*, 213–17 and passim.

19. The letter preserved in 2 Cor 1:1–2:13 and 7:5–15 must have been written from Macedonia, perhaps from Philippi. On the division hypothesis of 2 Corinthians, see Dieter Georgi, *The Opponents of Paul in*

A fragment of a third letter of uncertain date is preserved in Phil 3:2–4:1.[20] This letter does not reflect anything about Paul's imprisonment. Since it is only a fragment, however, it is impossible to tell what was said in the letter's proem and greetings. This third letter is a stern warning against a group of Judaizing apostles who had come to Philippi for their own perfectionist propaganda—perhaps the same group that already had caused trouble for Paul in Galatia. However, the problem of these opponents can be left aside here.[21]

If the hypothesis is correct that the extant letter of Paul to the Philippians is a composition of three letters from Paul, it is necessary to ask why the preserved document was edited in this fashion, presumably by the church of the Philippians before or during the process of the first collection of the letters of Paul,[22] sometime during the final decades of the first century CE.[23] Of the three original letters, the second letter, which emphasizes the imprisonment and impending death of Paul most strongly, has been used as the beginning for the edition by the Philippian church. From this letter, the editor drew the prescript and proem (1:1–2 and 1:3–11) as well as most of the corpus of the letter (1:12–3:1). The greeting of this letter has disappeared, while the greetings of the first letter serve as the conclusion for the new edition. The proem of this second letter is dominated by the concept of martyrdom. It is in these verses that Paul emphasizes that the Philippians are fellows (κοινωνία, συγκοινωνοί) in his suffering as well as of the proclamation on the gospel. In the following body of this second letter, it is again the possibility of Paul's death that dominates. It would be a gain if Paul were dying and were with Christ (1:19ff.), and after the quotation of the famous "Christ hymn" in 2:5–11, Paul once more emphasizes that he is already spent as an offering for Christ in the service of the church (2:17). At the same time, the first letter (4:10–23), which describes the financial relations between Paul and the Philippians, is relegated to an insignificant position at the end. This is surprising because the Philippians could have chosen to set a memorial for themselves[24] as a church that had supported Paul financially in his ministry.

The church of Philippi, sometime at the end of the first century, edited these fragments of Paul's letters to their church in such a way that the concept of Paul's martyrdom was most prominently tied to this particular correspondence. Is it possible to assume that already at this time the Philippian church claimed a special relationship to

---

Second Corinthians (Philadelphia: Fortress Press, 1986) 9–18. Also the two letters concerning the collection for Jerusalem, 2 Cor 8 and 9, must have been written from here; see especially 2 Cor 9:4.

20. Perhaps also Phil 4:8–9 must be assigned to this letter; see Bormann, *Philippi*, 18, and the discussion on the preceding pages of his book.

21. See Helmut Koester, "The Purpose of the Polemic of a Pauline Fragment (Philippians III)," *NTS* 8 (1961/62) 317–32.

22. It is quite possible that a knowledge of several letters from Paul to the Philippians is presupposed in Polycarp of Smyrna, who reminds the Philippians in his letter to that church (3.2) that Paul had written letters to them (ὑμῖν ἔγραψεν ἐπιστολάς).

23. Bormann, *Philippi*, 128–36, discusses several hypotheses about the composition of the three letters into one and concludes that the Philippians themselves were responsible for the one-letter edition.

24. Günther Bornkamm ("Der Philipperbrief als paulinische Briefsammlung," in *Geschichte und Glaube II = Gesammelte Aufsätze* 4 [BevTh 53; Munich: Kaiser, 1971] 203), commenting on the position of the first letter at the end, speaks about the intention of the Philippians to establish "a nice memorial" ("ein schönes Denkmal") for themselves.

the martyrdom and death of the apostle? Is the edition of the extant letter a testimony to the death of Paul in Philippi? If one cannot answer these questions definitively in the affirmative, still the possibility that the composition of the letter in its extant form was prompted by Philippi's claim to the martyrdom of Paul cannot be excluded.

The city of Philippi is mentioned once more in the book of Acts, in 20:6, where Paul sailed "out of Philippi" for Troas after the Feast of Unleavened Bread, when he was heading for Jerusalem by way of Corinth. But it is certain that Paul had already come through Philippi once before. In 2 Cor 1:15–16; 2:12–13; and 7:5, Paul reports that after his release from imprisonment in Ephesos, he went from Troas through Macedonia to Corinth, expecting to meet Titus, whom he had sent ahead to Corinth. Thus he must have come through Macedonia twice: first in the fall of the year 55 on his way to Corinth, where he stayed through the winter, and then in the spring of the year 56 on his journey to Jerusalem as reported by Acts 20:6.

The Conclusion of the Book of Acts

There are no further references to Philippi in the New Testament either in the book of Acts or in any of the deutero-Pauline writings. But neither is there any mention of this martyrdom of Paul in Rome or in any other place. This seems strange. To be sure, it would have been counterproductive for the author of Acts to say anything about Paul after his arrival in Rome because the purpose of Acts is to show the triumphal progress of the gospel of Christ from Jerusalem, the ancient capital of Israel, to Rome, the capital of the Roman Empire. Thus its ending with the description of Paul's successful and "unhindered" preaching in Rome for a period of two years would seem an adequate conclusion to the book.

A number of hypotheses have been proposed in order to explain why Luke does not report the martyrdom of Paul in Rome at the end of his work:

1. Luke intended to write a third volume. As it stands now, however, the work is a complete entity that fulfills the explicit purpose of the author's plan, namely, to present the two epochs of salvation history, the time of the revelation in Jesus' ministry and the time of the church.

2. Luke wrote and completed this work before the trial of Paul had begun. This hypothesis assumes a very early date for the composition of Luke's work, which cannot be confirmed by other observations—a date at the end of the century is much more likely.

3. Paul's martyrdom was originally part of the book but has been removed or otherwise lost; yet there is no sign that the conclusion of the book is fragmentary.

4. Paul was not martyred then at all; rather the case was dismissed after a two-year period had expired. His martyrdom took place a few years later, perhaps at the occasion of the well-attested persecution of the Christians in Rome after Nero himself had been accused of setting the fire that destroyed a large part of the city.[25]

---

25. See the summary of these hypotheses and relevant literature in Conzelmann, *Acts;* and Ernst

Paul's Place of Martyrdom in the Pastoral Epistles

Perhaps it is possible to suggest another version of this fourth hypothesis: Luke knew that Paul was not martyred in Rome at all but later returned to the East, where he eventually found his death as a martyr. The New Testament itself does not report such a martyrdom in the East, nor at any other place, and there is no positive indication for such a return to the East. Nonetheless, a few related puzzles are left in the deutero-Pauline Pastoral Epistles, 1 and 2 Timothy and Titus. To be sure, these letters were not written by Paul. Most critical scholars assume a date for their composition between the end of the first century and the middle of the second.[26] What is the situation that these letters presuppose?[27]

The situation described in 1 Tim 1:3, "I commanded you to remain in Ephesos, when I traveled to Macedonia," is difficult to fit into Paul's travels as they are known from the book of Acts and from Paul's genuine epistles. On his first trip to Macedonia, Paul was not alone. According to Acts 16:1ff., Timothy was with Paul, and Paul had not even been to Ephesos yet. In Acts 20:1 the apostle had sent Timothy from Ephesos ahead of him with the intention to meet him again in Macedonia (Acts 19:22; this agrees with Phil 2:19). It is therefore not possible to fit the situation of 1 Tim 1:2–3 into the Pauline itinerary as it is known from Acts as well as from Paul's genuine letters. Thus the situation of 1 Tim 1:3 assumes a stay by Paul in the East after his Roman imprisonment. If Paul was martyred in Rome, one would have to assume that this martyrdom did not take place at the Roman imprisonment reported by Acts 28 but during a second Roman imprisonment that took place after another visit by Paul to Asia Minor, Macedonia, and Greece.

In the last of the Pastoral Epistles, the Letter to Titus, Paul is somewhere in Greece, planning to spend the winter in Nikopolis (most likely Nikopolis in Epirus, then the most important city of western Greece; Titus 3:12). Such a winter stay again does not fit into the locations known from either Acts or the genuine Pauline letters. It must therefore be dated to a later journey of Paul's after his Roman imprisonment.

The situation of 2 Timothy is more difficult to understand. Here Paul is certainly imprisoned and expects possible martyrdom (2 Tim 1:17; 4:16–17; also 4:6–8). But it is unlikely that this refers to a second imprisonment in Rome. Some scholars have spec-

---

Haenchen, *The Acts of the Apostles: A Commentary,* trans. ed. R. McL. Wilson (Philadelphia: Westminster, 1971), on Acts 28:30–31.

26. For the question of the date and authenticity of the Pastoral Epistles, see Martin Dibelius and Hans Conzelmann, *The Pastoral Epistles: A Commentary on the Pastoral Epistles,* trans. Philip Buttolph and Adela Yarbro (Hermeneia; Philadelphia: Fortress Press, 1972) 1–5.

27. The situations of the Pastoral Epistles and the question of whether these situations rely on any historical information have been discussed repeatedly; see ibid., 15–16, 126–28, 152–54. It is doubtful whether the subscriptions of ancient manuscripts are of any help in informing us about Paul's assumed place of authorship. For 1 Timothy, they suggest Nikopolis or Laodikeia in Phrygia; for 2 Timothy, almost all manuscripts designate Rome as the place of composition (except for Codex A, which gives Laodikeia); for the composition of the Letter to Titus, ancient manuscripts list Nikopolis, Macedonia, or Neapolis in Macedonia. However, it is interesting that the manuscript tradition is not unanimous for Rome as the place at which the Pastoral Epistles were composed.

ulated that the letter refers to the Caesarean imprisonment,[28] but this is very unlikely. The various instructions to Timothy, who is in Ephesos, imply rather that Paul is somewhere in the area of Greece or Macedonia: "Make every effort to come to me quickly" (2 Tim 4:9); "Demas . . . has gone to Thessalonike, Crescens to Galatia, Titus to Dalmatia" (4:10); "Tychikus I have sent to Ephesos" (4:12); "Erastus remained in Corinth. I had to leave Trophimus behind in Miletus" (4:20); "When you come, bring the coat I left in Troas with Carpus" (4:13). Philippi is not an impossible place for such a final imprisonment of Paul. If Timothy is coming from Ephesos to Paul in Philippi, Troas, where Paul left his coat, is on the way.

I would reconstruct the assumed situations of Paul in the Pastoral Epistles as follows. After the Roman imprisonment (and missionary activity in Spain?), Paul returned to the East and went to Crete together with Titus. Returning from there to Greece, he intended to spend the winter in Nikopolis and wrote to Titus to join him there. Thus the Epistle to Titus is the first of these three letters. Writing 1 Timothy, Paul is in Macedonia and writes to Timothy in Ephesos. Neither Titus nor 1 Timothy indicates that Paul is in prison. At the writing of 2 Timothy, however, Paul is indeed imprisoned and has just passed through the first part of his trial. Since Paul is writing to Timothy with the request that Timothy come to him and bring a number of things that Paul left in Troas, the place assumed for this writing is most likely a city of Macedonia, perhaps Philippi.

These pieces of personal information about Paul and of the various instructions are either fragments from genuine Pauline letters, which have been used for the composition of the Pastoral Epistles,[29] or they are fictitious. In the first case, they would represent evidence that Paul indeed returned from Rome after the imprisonment mentioned at the end of Acts; they would indicate that Paul's martyrdom must have taken place in a city of Macedonia. In the second case, that is, if the information is fictitious, these pieces of personal information reveal that the author of the Pastoral Epistles knew of a tradition that claimed a period of Paul's return to the East and martyrdom there, in Philippi.[30] In either case, neither the Pastoral Epistles nor any other New Testament writing say anything about a Roman martyrdom of Paul. All information gathered from the books of the New Testament canon would not conflict with the assumption that Paul was martyred in Philippi.

The *Acts of Paul* and the Martyrdom of Paul in Rome

What then is the origin of the information about Paul's martyrdom in Rome? The entire early Christian literature to the middle or even late second century CE knows

---

28. P. N. Harrison, *The Problem of the Pastoral Epistles* (London: Oxford University Press, 1921) 121ff.

29. That there were genuine letters written by Paul that have not been included in the later collection of the letters of the Pauline corpus is evident from 1 Cor 5:9, where Paul mentions an earlier letter that he had written to Corinth before the writing of 1 Corinthians.

30. It must also be mentioned here that the pseudepigraphical correspondence known as *3 Corinthians*, preserved in the apocryphal *Acts of Paul*, locates the imprisoned apostle in Philippi.

nothing about a Roman martyrdom of Paul. The Apostolic Fathers presuppose the martyrdom of Paul. But neither *1 Clem.* 5.5 nor Ignatius *Rom.* 4.3 says anything about the place of this martyrdom. The earliest information about the Roman martyrdom of Paul comes from the *Acts of Paul*, which was written in the last decades of the second century CE.[31] In this book Paul comes from Corinth to Italy. When he is still on the ship, Christ appears to Paul and reveals that he has to be crucified again.[32] The recounting of this episode especially raises the question of whether the author of the *Acts of Paul* possessed any genuine information or sources for his story, because there can be no question that this episode was borrowed from the *Acts of Peter.*[33] Moreover, for the brief description of Paul's activity in Rome, the author reports the episode of the cupbearer of Caesar Patroklos who fell from a window and died in his attempt to hear Paul,[34] a story the author has simply borrowed from Acts 20:9–12. This demonstrates that the author had no materials that could help him to find a cause for Paul's imprisonment, trial, and execution. Everything is invented here, and it is clear that the author of the *Acts of Paul* could not rely on any older report of Paul's martyrdom. He probably did not know anything else but the claim of the Roman church that she occupied the place at which the apostle was martyred.

That Rome indeed claimed at the end of the second century to be the place of the martyrdom of both Peter and Paul is evident from several authors quoted by Eusebius. However, one of these quotations, a sentence from the Epistle to the Romans by Bishop Dionysios of Corinth (ca. 170), does not explicitly mention Rome as the place of Paul's martyrdom: "By so great an admonition you bound together the foundations of the Romans and Corinthians by Peter and Paul, for both of them taught together in our Corinth and were our founders, and together also taught in Italy in the same place and were martyred at the same time" (*Hist. eccl.* 2.25.8).[35] It must be noted that the reference to the martyrdom of both apostles has as little historical value as the information that Peter and Paul taught together in Corinth, which is evidently false. Moreover, Dionysios does not say that both apostles were martyred "at the same place" but "at the same time" (κατὰ τὸν αὐτὸν καιρόν).

Just before the quotation from Dionysios's letter, Eusebius quotes the anti-Montanist writer Caius, who wrote against Montanus's successor Proclus at the time of the Roman bishop Zephyrinus (198–217): "But I can point out the trophies of the apostles (τὰ τροπαῖα τῶν ἀποστόλων), for if you will go to the Vatican or to the Ostian Way, you will find the trophies of those who founded this church" (*Hist. eccl.* 2.25.7).[36] Caius

---

31. See Wilhelm Schneemelcher, "Acts of Paul," in Edgar Hennecke and Wilhelm Schneemelcher, eds., *New Testament Apocrypha,* trans. ed. R. McL. Wilson (rev. ed.; 2 vols.; Louisville: Westminster John Knox, 1991–92) 2.213–37.

32. Ibid., 258.

33. Ibid., 314. The episode is original in the *Acts of Peter* because it serves as a prediction of Peter's crucifixion. In the *Acts of Paul* it makes little sense because the author continues to tell that Paul was not crucified but beheaded.

34. Ibid., 261.

35. Translation by Kirsopp Lake in LCL, 2.182–83.

36. Ibid.

does not mention any of these founding apostles by name, but Eusebius may be right in inferring that he was speaking about Peter and Paul.

Eusebius adduces still another witness, namely, a remark in Origen's commentary on Genesis, although he does not provide an explicit quotation: "What need be said of Paul, who fulfilled the gospel of Christ from Jerusalem to Illyria and afterward was martyred in Rome under Nero? This is stated exactly by Origen in the third volume of his commentary on Genesis" (*Hist. eccl.* 3.1.3).[37] This reference shows that the Roman claim to be the place of the martyrdom of Paul was also known in the East in the beginning of the third century. This does not exclude, however, the possibility that another church, namely Philippi, may have made a similar claim. That this was indeed the case could be concluded from the recent excavations of the Octagonal Church complex in Philippi.

---

37. Ibid., 2.190–91.

8

WISDOM AND FOLLY
IN CORINTH

Ulrich Wilckens's *Weisheit und Torheit* is an important contribution to the debated question of the opponents of Paul in Corinth. Characteristic for the present status of the debate is the controversy between Johannes Munck,[1] who assumes that there was only bickering going on in Corinth but that there were no "parties" with clearly formulated positions, and on the other hand Walter Schmithals,[2] who tried to prove that the Gnostic movement was the cause of the controversy. Wilckens deals specifically with the section 1 Cor 1:18–2:16 and thus with the problem of "wisdom" in Corinth. That the term "wisdom" should not be understood in the sense of a philosophical effort of thought is certainly correctly stated. Only in a secondary sense could one talk about the way in which Paul's arguments would not be "irrelevant and meaningless" even for the Stoic (p. 269).[3] It would therefore be too far-reaching and also beyond my expertise to discuss the instructive last section of the book about "Structure and Purpose of the System of the Stoic School" (pp. 225–68).

The first part of Wilckens's investigation is dedicated to a careful and detailed exegesis of 1 Corinthians 1–2 (pp. 4–96). A good initial step is the elaboration of the close connection of the topics "wisdom" and "divisions," "in which the topic 'wisdom' proves to be primary and fundamental for the solution of the problems of the divisions" (p. 7). Some skepticism, however, is demanded over against the presuppositions for Wilckens's understanding of the connection between these two topics, namely (1) "that each of the Corinthian parties ascribed a lasting authority of salvation to those by whom they had been baptized" (p. 17); and (2) that the opponents identified what they possessed as their salvation, namely Wisdom, with the exalted Christ. This assumes that the divisions resulted from the fact that the opponents derived their right to look down upon Paul's foolish proclamation of the cross on the basis of their sacramental connection to the Wisdom-Christ.

What argues against this assumption is the text of 1 Cor 1:12, which presents Christ on the same level as the names of other apostles. That Christ was also a baptizer is not very likely. Wilckens therefore has to delete "I belong to Christ" from the slogans of the parties. But it is also unlikely that Peter had baptized any of the Corinthians, and even Paul has to confess that he had baptized very few of the Corinthians. Apollos alone remains, but he arrived only much later in Corinth and certainly did not play any role

---

1. *Paulus und die Heilsgeschichte* (Aarhus: Universitetsforlaget, 1954).
2. *Die Gnosis in Korinth* (Göttingen: Vandenhoeck & Ruprecht, 1956).
3. Page references in the text are to Wilckens, *Weisheit und Torheit*.

in the baptism of the first-converted members of the community. It is also not clear why Christ is (as Paul says) divided if all the Corinthian opponents understood themselves as connected to Christ as the primary possession of their salvation. Moreover, why does Paul emphasize that nobody has been baptized in the name of Paul (1 Cor 1:13) and why does he later (1 Cor 3:22–23) explicitly subordinate the community to Christ and then subordinate himself to the community? With all this the Corinthians would heartily have agreed.

Wilckens has well argued that the Corinthians consider "wisdom" as the absolute treasure of salvation. If, however, Christ appears in the text side-by-side with other apostles, the Corinthians seemed to see Christ not as identified with "wisdom," but only as one guide into wisdom among others. This seems to me as a quite reasonable assessment, especially in view of the other apostle who was active in Corinth after Paul's departure, the Alexandrian Jewish Christian Apollos (see below on Philo of Alexandria!). Wilckens does not mention this as a point of departure for an explanation of the Corinthian problem.

One has to agree on the whole with Wilckens concerning his interpretation of 1 Cor 1:18–2:5, although one may not share his presuppositions. Paul's preaching about the cross is critically evaluated and rejected by Corinthian wisdom teaching (pp. 36–37). Opposing this judgment, Paul claims that the wisdom of God is exclusively present "in the cross, that is, as the foolishness of God (μωρὸν τοῦ θεοῦ)" (p. 40). Corresponding to this stands the Christian existence, in which those who are called are saved precisely as those who are weak (pp. 41–44). For Paul, wisdom "is a concept that belongs exclusively to God and does not permit any anthropological analogy" (p. 39), which excludes also any claim of those who believe that they now have found new wisdom (p. 40). Even the proclamation itself lacks wisdom, so that the one who proclaims possesses no more "than the one who is finally condemned" (pp. 45–53).

In the difficult verse 1:21, Wilckens interprets the phrase ἐν τῇ σοφίᾳ θεοῦ ("in the wisdom of God") as Paul's acknowledgment that wisdom was in its original intention "a realm of existence in the world" (p. 33), but the world did not understand wisdom as "an instrument through which one can recognize God" (p. 34). If that is correct, wisdom is seen here as parallel to the view of creation in Romans 1. It seems to me more consistent with Paul's view to understand wisdom here as parallel to his view of the law: it has been decided on the basis of God's wisdom—exactly the wisdom that the opponents claim for themselves—that wisdom should not be the way to lead to the knowledge of God.

In the second part of the exegesis (1 Cor 2:6–16), Wilckens—on the basis of his own presuppositions about the theology of the Corinthians—creates the impression that "everything that Paul says here can be understood without any qualifications as Gnostic teaching of wisdom in the same way as the Corinthians conceived of it" (p. 60). This includes, according to Wilckens, that the terms τέλειος ("perfect") and πνευματικός ("spiritual") are used as synonyms, as is the case also in Gnosticism, and that they designate a specific circle of Christians who have indeed access to a teaching of wisdom. To be sure, Paul originally understood wisdom according to Jewish apocalyptic thinking as the gift of salvation that was predestined to be received at the final revelation (pp. 64–70), but that he thought of it "at the same time in a Gnostic sense" as a hidden possession of salvation (p. 67). Through such a transformation of the apocalyptic concept, "the process of revelation becomes . . . the descent of the redeemer, and the possession of salvation becomes the 'person' of the redeemer" (p. 83). Also in his talk about the Spirit (πνεῦμα), Wilckens suggests that Paul had assimilated his statements "not only terminologically but also in terms of the theological subject matter to the central intentions of Gnosticism to such a degree that the opponents' primary thesis of the identification of the redeemed spiritual person with the Spirit-redeemer foists itself upon the reader" (p. 85). "The theological intention of the apostle everywhere stands under the shadow of this foreign Gnostic concept, and the result is an evident confusion" (p. 87). Therefore "an exegetical criticism of the subject matter" is demanded (p. 93). The author sees a starting point for such criticism in Paul's emphasis upon the cross as the place of God's actions (cf. especially pp. 217ff.) and in the fact that Paul avoids the radical Gnostic consequence ἵνα γένωμεν [*sic*] πνευματικοί ("so that we become spiritual persons"), which "takes the edge of the Gnostic train of thought that Paul had begun" (p. 86).

How was it possible that the author could arrive at such a conclusion? In my opinion, it is because two different things are not clearly distinguished. (1) The understanding of Sophia as "a person-like *mythical* figure" (p. 73; my italics). In this case, I think, one has to talk about Gnosticism as soon as the believers know themselves to be connected spiritually to this nonworldly Sophia; that may have been the case among the Corinthians. (2) Opposed to this is the possibility of speaking of the identity of the apocalyptic possession of salvation with the historical person Christ; this is what Paul is speaking about—even if it may still be debated whether in 1 Cor 2:6ff. σοφία τοῦ θεοῦ ("wisdom of God") and κύριος τῆς δόξης ("Lord of glory") are actually identical (but see 1 Cor 1:24). But the mythological terminology here has a very different meaning from the one used by the Corinthians. It states that the heavenly salvation is hidden insofar as it is historically present. In Gnosticism, however, that it is hidden emphasizes that it is not historically tangible. Yet Wilckens sees the difference simply in Paul's emphasis upon the cross (pp. 217ff.), thus making the cross ultimately into an unexplained mysterious cipher. He disregards that for Paul the cross is a metaphorical reference to the historicity of the revelation, that is, it designates the entire Christ event. In the same way, for Paul, identity with the crucified constitutes a fully historical existence and is not, as in Ignatius of Antioch, reduced to the suffering of martyrdom.

In correspondence to this it would also be necessary to distinguish between the Corinthian and the Pauline concept of the Spirit, and the text says enough about that. It is not sufficient to say that Paul speaks of the Spirit of *Christ* because "Christ is for Paul deliberately and explicitly the crucified one" (p. 95). It is apparent that the Corinthians, for whom Christ was not a central feature of their salvation, talked like true Gnostics only about the Spirit of *God,* and moreover, claimed that exclusively "the perfect person" was in possession of this Spirit. For Paul, on the other hand, it is the Spirit of Christ, which all believers had received, that reveals to them that Christ is the Wisdom of God (1 Cor 2:6–8). For him all those are pneumatics who recognize what God has given to them in Christ (2:12). What is at stake here is no more and no less than the difference between mythical and historical revelation and between spiritualistic recognition of God and the knowledge of God that is bound together with Christ—and it seems that Paul was fully aware of that.

Wilckens's presupposition that mythical Wisdom and Christ were identified by the Corinthians creates difficulties already in the understanding of the text. But can such identification be upheld in terms of the history of religions? This is the topic of the second major part of Wilckens's book (pp. 97–169). Because of the close affinity of the Corinthian teaching as reconstructed by Wilckens, he first turns to the Valentinian Wisdom speculations (pp. 100ff.). Perhaps he should have started with Manichaeism, where Wisdom is clearly identified with Jesus (p. 133). This is not the case in the Valentinian system. His presentation of the role of Sophia among the Valentinians (pp. 100–111), in the Gnostic system described by Irenaeus *Adv. haer.* 1.30 (pp. 118–23), in Barbelo Gnosticism (pp. 123–25), and in the *Sophia Jesu Christi* (pp. 126–31), is highly instructive. It is fundamental in each case that "Sophia is the mythical image of the Gnostic himself" (p. 106). That is also the case in the Valentinian system; the Gnostics identify themselves first with the fallen "lower" Sophia, but subsequently, and substantially analogous, also with the "upper" Sophia, "according to the position of the redeemer, . . . who has already overcome the position of the lower Sophia outside the Pleroma" (pp. 109–10; cf. pp. 106ff.). Sophia is often also designated as the guide (pp. 109–10). But she is always distinguished from Jesus or Christ respectively, who plays the role of the redeemer as her heavenly partner (σύζυγος). A seeming identification appears only in the system of Irenaeus *Adv. haer.* 1.30; here Christ, already as he is descending from heaven, unites "with his sister Sophia" and thus "both are coming down together upon Jesus" (p. 121), but she leaves him again before the crucifixion. But this artificial docetism should not be presupposed for the Corinthians, and "the very close connections between the understanding of Jesus [!] here and among the Corinthians" (p. 121), already claimed by Schmithals, seem to me highly questionable. The substantial identity of Christ and Sophia, that is, of the redeemer and the redeemed cannot be questioned. More important, however, is the joined (συζυγή) structure of the process of salvation, in which redeemer and redeemed are united but not "one" (p. 123). But also here one cannot speak of a "redeemed redeemer." The unity of the συζυγή with the earthly Jesus is actually not interesting in terms of theology. Such an intelligent docetism seems to me to be only the result of the Christian-Gnostic controversy, but not the presupposition for its beginnings, which are evident in 1 Corinthians.

The *Acts of Thomas* presents very complex problems. The Wedding Song of chapters 6–7 is certainly a brilliant example for the Gnostic form of the myth about Sophia and the primordial man, which does not contain any specific Christian elements (pp. 115–17). The redemption consists of the restoration of the συζυγή of God and Wisdom. Characteristically, Christ as a redeemer figure does not appear. Similarly, in the epiclesis, inserted in chapter 50, of the σοφία/μήτηρ ("Wisdom/Mother"), who clearly has the function of the Valentinian Sophia (as Wilckens has shown on pp. 112–13), a Christ figure is originally quite superfluous. Furthermore, the few passages of the *Acts of Thomas* in which Jesus is identified with the Sophia/Primordial Mother or has assumed her functions, seem to be dependent upon 1 Corinthians; here belong the following: 133[4]: . . . ἀπορρήτου μυστηρίου ἀρχῶν τε καὶ ἐξουσίων κεκρυμμένων (= 1 Cor 2:7–8); 47[5]: . . .

---

4. Rianardus Albertus Lipsius et Maximilianus Bonnet, eds., *Acta Apostolorum Apocrypha* (Darmstadt: Wissenschaftliche Buchgesellschaft, 1959) 2, 2.240, 11–12.

5. Ibid., pp. 163, 221–164, 1.

Ἰησοῦ τὸ μυστήριον τὸ ἀπόκρυφον ὃ ἡμῖν ἀπεκαλύφθη (= 1 Cor 2:7, 10); 77[6]: ὅτι αὐ-
τός (sc. ὁ Ἰησοῦς) ἐστι δύναμις θεοῦ καὶ θεοῦ σοφία (= 1 Cor 1:24), ὃς συμπαρῆν τῷ
θεῷ ὅτε καὶ τὸν κόσμον ἐποίησε (= Wis 9:9); cf also *Acts Thom. Syr.* 10. Where such an
evident dependence upon 1 Corinthians does not exist, Jesus is addressed as τῶν σοφῶν
ὁ σοφίστης (chap. 79), μόνε σοφέ and λόγε σοφέ (chap. 80); cf. ὁ σοφίσας ἡμᾶς ἐν τῇ
σοφία σου (*Acts of Philip* 144[7]). Thus he is the bringer of wisdom or the wise, but not Wisdom herself. Wilckens himself admits that an explicit identity of Jesus and Wisdom leads
"into the neighborhood of Manichaean texts" (p. 115; cf. p. 133). One should add that,
before the time of these Gnostic texts, Paul was the only one who claimed an identity of
Jesus and Wisdom, that is, with a polemical intention. That implies, however, that Paul's
opponents denied such an identity because they saw Jesus as the bringer of Wisdom.

Observations of Wilckens in his consideration of other Gnostic texts have to be
corrected in a similar way. The *Epistula Apostolorum*,[8] which lacks a Sophia myth, is
wrongly cited as "direct evidence for the predication of the Gnostic redeemer as σοφία
θεοῦ" (p. 132). Similarly, the interchange of "he" and "she" in *Odes of Solomon* 33 is no
proof for a claimed identity of the partners (συζυγαί), but evidence that here, as in
other texts of the *Odes of Solomon*, disparate elements of mystic language have been
woven together eclectically.

This leads into the interpretation of Jewish wisdom speculations, first Philo. Wilckens follows J. Pascher,[9] thus presupposing that Philo is here influenced by an Alexandrian (Wisdom) mystery cult (pp. 145–57). He concludes from a comparison of this
Philonic mystery cult with the Gnostic Sophia myth "that we are dealing here with an
early form of this Gnostic myth, in which this myth has been embedded into the schema
of a mystery cult" (p. 155). He assumes that at the base was an Isis mystery cult that was
strongly influenced by Gnosticism (p. 156), and he claims that we cannot exclude that
we find here an important root of the Valentinian Gnostic myth of Sophia (p. 157). If
it is the case that in Philo the typical Gnostic element is the figure of Sophia, the question of her origin should have been pursued more rigorously! Neither Apuleius nor
Plutarch presupposes that Isis was the goddess of Wisdom. The androgynous nature of
a deity has possibly some pagan background (pp. 152–54); it is, however, a far cry from
the Valentinian speculations regarding a heavenly union of partners (a syzygy), and allegorical plays with the androgynous character of Sophia on the basis of texts from the
Old Testament are no evidence for the existence of a corresponding Sophia tradition.

On the other hand, Wilckens did not see the possibilities of insights in the Corinthian
teachings on the basis of Philo nor the consequences of his own observations about the
pneumatic in Philo (pp. 157–59). In order for pneumatics to enter into the heavenly
Sophia, no "redeemer" is needed but only a mystagogue as a guide into the mysteries.
Philo speaks about Moses in this way: γίνεται δὲ οὐ μόνον μύστης, ἀλλὰ καὶ ἱερο-
φάντης ὀργίων καὶ διδάσκαλος θείων ("he not only becomes an initiate but also a
guide to the mysteries and a teacher of the divine things," *Gig.* 54; see p. 158 in Wilck-

---

6. Ibid., p. 30, 17–18.

7. Ibid., 2.2, pp. 9–10.

8. Hugo Duensing, "Epistula Apostolorum," chap. 13, in Wilhelm Schneemelcher, ed., *New Testament
Apocrypha*, vol. 1 (Louisville: Westminster John Knox, 1991).

9. *ΒΑΣΙΛΙΚΗ ΟΔΟΣ* (Studien zur Geschichte und Kultur des Altertums 17; Paderborn: F. Schöningh, 1931).

ens). Did the opponents of Paul speak in this way about Christ? If this was the case, Paul's claim that Christ is the Sophia and his statement about the Spirit of Christ would have appeared to them as absurd, as it would have been absurd for Philo to speak about the Spirit of Moses instead of the Spirit of God.

Decisive for the recognition of the origin of Gnosticism is the interpretation of the figure of Sophia in Jewish literature (pp. 160–90). Wilckens has clearly demonstrated that the Jewish figure of Sophia already reveals many features of the later Christian-Gnostic figure of Wisdom, for example, her being sent down from heaven, her role as a revealer figure, and the "radically negative view of the world." What is the origin of such Gnostic features? Wilckens assumes an origin outside of Judaism in a "Gnostic current" that flows from the same source as the Jewish Wisdom myth and that continuously influenced the Jewish developments, especially in the Diaspora (pp. 190–97). One should, however, treat with great mistrust the various references to the cult of oriental mother deities like the Syrian Astarte[10] (pp. 174ff. and elsewhere) as sources for Gnostic and Jewish Wisdom myth. Single features, like perhaps the concept of *synousia,* may have come to Jewish Wisdom myth in this way. But Wilckens does not mention the only existing evidence for a non-Jewish figure of Wisdom. It appears in the oldest version of the Ahiqar legend, extant in the Elephantine Papyri, from which one can learn with certainty that Wisdom is here personified, bearer of the power of the dominion of the heavenly Shamash.[11] In analogy to this pagan concept of the figure of Wisdom, it should have been emphasized that also the Jewish figure of Wisdom bears the features of Yahweh and is characterized by his attributes especially in her role as revealer. From this point of departure, the inner-Jewish possibilities for the development of the Gnostic myth of Sophia must be considered, namely the skepsis, for which this world has become meaningless and the will of God hidden, and apocalypticism, which, bypassing the history of salvation, expects a mythical eschatological action of God that corresponds to the primordial time and can already be anticipated by the individual.[12]

It seems to me therefore that Wilckens's fundamental investigation contributes much to the elucidation of the backgrounds of 1 Corinthians 1–2. But its primary thesis is not tenable on the basis of the materials presented here. Everything speaks against the assumption that the Corinthians had identified Christ in some way or other with Wisdom. That they were Gnostics, namely Jewish Gnostics, seems even more certain to me. However, one should not too rashly presuppose the existence of a myth of a redeemer figure in the sense of a developed christology when one is dealing with pre-Christian Gnosticism and early Christian heretics. We have to learn here to make much clearer distinctions. This is even more necessary as the contours of a Jewish Gnostic Sophia myth begin to stand out, contours that share with the later Gnostic system exactly the fact that a personalized appearance of the redeemer or of the central means of salvation are not significant or do not even appear on the horizon. This, of course, implies that more work is needed in order to arrive at a definition of Gnosticism that is *not* tied to the concept of a redeemer figure.

---

10. Wilckens is here dependent upon Gustav Boström, *Proverbia Studien* (Lund: Gleerup, 1935).

11. Col. 53, 16–24; A. E. Cowley, *Aramaic Papyri of the Fifth Century B. C.* (Oxford: Clarendon, 1923); I owe this reference to my colleague Frank M. Cross.

12. All this has been said *in nuce* already by Gerhard von Rad (*Old Testament Theology,* trans. D. M. G. Stalker [2 vols.; New York: Harper & Row, 1962–65] 1.442ff.).

9

HERO WORSHIP

Philostratos's Heroikos *and Paul's Tomb in Philippi*

About a decade ago, when I was directing our Greek reading club at Harvard Divinity School, called "Graeca," we began reading Philostratos's *Heroikos,* of which no English translation had ever been published. Ellen Aitken and Jennifer Berenson Maclean were members of this class and have now edited and translated this work. We struggled with the often rather difficult syntax of Philostratos and began the composition of a "glossary" (which they have now published with their edition), just for our own learning experience and not yet thinking that this might eventually lead to the publication of an English translation of this important ancient text. It is a pleasure to see that these two former graduate students, with the encouragement and criticism of my colleague and friend Professor Gregory Nagy, have now been able to prepare a readable English translation with introduction, notes, and glossary that will make this text more easily accessible to the student of Roman religion, Homeric tradition, and indeed to the study of early Christianity.

Not too far from the Thracian Chersonnes, where the tomb of Protesilaos recalled the memory of the Trojan War, was the eastern Macedonian city of Philippi, situated just at the border of Macedonia and Thrace. About a century after Philostratos wrote his *Heroikos,* the Christians of Philippi invited the pilgrims who were on their way from central and western Europe to the Holy Land to stop and worship at the tomb of Saint Paul, apostle and martyr. Here, not in Rome, so they claimed, was his tomb: Paul had returned to the East after his sojourn to the West and had died in Philippi as a martyr.[1] A vaulted tomb of a hero from the Hellenistic period still existed in Philippi near the center of the city. The name of the hero who had once been worshiped here, Epiphanes Exekestou, had probably been long since forgotten.[2] After the peace of Constantine, the Philippian Christians chose the location immediately adjacent to the tomb's temple-like superstructure when they built their assembly hall and dedicated it to "Saint Paul in Christ," as a mosaic inscription in the floor of the church reveals.[3] Soon this first

---

1. On the excavation of the tomb and of the church of St. Paul in Philippi and the interpretation of the finds, see Charalambos Bakirtzis and Helmut Koester, *Philippi at the Time of Paul and After His Death* (Harrisburg: Trinity Press International, 1998).

2. The name of this hero was found inscribed on the lid of the sarcophagus that excavators found under the dirt floor of the tomb.

3. The inscription tells that the mosaic floor of the church was given by Bishop Porphyrius, who is known to have been bishop of Philippi in the first half of the 4th century CE.

structure was replaced by a magnificent octagonal cathedral, the typical structure for a martyrion. With its fountain and baptistery the building complex surrounded the ancient tomb. Hundreds of coins from the fifth and sixth centuries that were found in the ancient tomb's superstructure give evidence for the pilgrims' devotion to the memory of the great apostle. A large hostel was constructed next to the martyrion to accommodate the visitors during their stay.

This was characteristic for the developments of the fourth century. To understand the rise of this hero worship it is important to understand and study the hero cult of the Greek and Roman world and especially its popularity in the third century CE, for which the *Heroikos* of Philostratos is an important document. The worship of the great apostles of the past and of the Christian martyrs took over the role of the pagan hero cults and spread very quickly at the time of the new Christian emperor Constantine. While occasionally prayers had been offered to martyrs at their graves as early as the third century, the cult of the martyrs as the heroes of the new religion now became widespread. Eucharistic meals were celebrated at their graves annually on the day of their martyrdom or other designated days. Healing miracles happened at the graves and prayers were offered there for the benefit of the supplicant. Local martyrs took over the role of the old city-protecting heroes, as, for example, Saint Demetrius in Thessalonike stepped into the shoes of the venerated Kabiros, or the Virgin Mary now assumed the role of the city goddess Tyche in Constantinople and elsewhere. The emperor Constantine himself ordered and financed the building of new churches over the graves of the apostles Peter and Paul in Rome. Christianity fully became the heir of the ancient Greco-Roman cult of heroes within a few decades.

But it was a long way in the development of Christian beliefs to make it possible to worship at the tomb of a martyr or apostle or at the tomb of Jesus. Christianity did not begin with worship at the tomb of its founder. In the beginning, such worship was rejected as a typically Jewish and pagan custom. Early Christian belief began with a clear disclaimer of such worship. Jesus was not a hero, and his grave did not play any role as a place of worship after his death. In his quotation of an early formula of faith, the apostle Paul speaks of Jesus' death, burial, resurrection, and epiphanies to many, but never mentions any worship at the tomb of Jesus (1 Cor 15:3–7). After all, "flesh and blood cannot inherit the kingdom of God" (15:50).

The story of the empty tomb that is told variously in the ancient Christian Gospels confirms this belief. Its oldest version is preserved at the end of the Gospel of Mark (Mark 16:1–8 and pars.). It tells about the women who came to the tomb[4] of Jesus in order to do the expected embalming of the body of Jesus. But they found that the tomb was empty and they were told, "You seek Jesus the Nazarene? He is risen. He is not here!" (Mark 16:6). In the traditional interpretation that is shared by most exegetes and indeed in the general Christian understanding, the record of the empty tomb of Jesus is usually taken as a story told in order to give evidence for the bodily resurrection of Jesus. However, it is unlikely that this was its original intention. We should also remember that it was not difficult for the ancient mind to imagine the physical reality of the

---

4. The canonical Gospels use the term μνημεῖον in all reports about the tomb of Jesus; cf. Mark 16:2–8 and pars.; John 20:1–11, although there are a few textual variants in which the term μνῆμα appears.

appearance of someone who had died. In order to say that a dead person had appeared in bodily form, it was by no means necessary to say that the tomb was empty.

The story of the empty tomb belongs to the oldest layer of the formation of the passion narrative. It predates the various stories of the epiphanies of the risen Jesus, which appear in different forms in the several traditions of the ancient Christian Gospels. While these epiphany stories serve as proofs for the reality of Jesus' resurrection, the story of the empty tomb must have a very different purpose, namely, to explain that there would be no hero worship at the tomb of Jesus.[5] Tombs of the great figures of the history of the Bible were everywhere in ancient Israel, especially around Jerusalem. The author of the Gospel of Matthew knew this well when he presented Jesus accusing the Pharisees that they built the tombs of the prophets and decorated the tombs of the righteous (Matt 23:29). It is also reflected in the report that, after the death of Jesus, the tombs opened and many saints came out of their tombs and appeared to many in the city (Matt 27:52–53).

The story of the empty tomb in Mark 16 corresponds to the confession of the centurion standing at the cross when Jesus died, "Truly, this man was the Son of God!" (Mark 15:39). Jesus is here not presented as a hero or a divine man, whom one should worship at his tomb; he was the Son of God—altogether belonging to a very different category of divine beings appearing on earth.[6] In the first part of the Gospel of Mark, Jesus had indeed been presented as a hero as he accomplished marvelous deeds of healing and even demonstrated his power over the forces of nature in the stilling of the tempest (4:35–41). The author of the Gospel of Mark, however, argued that the true dignity of Jesus is not recognized by Peter's confession, "You are the Christ" (8:29), that is, the miracle-working heroic Messiah. Rather, he is the Son of Man who has to suffer and to die. In his death, Jesus truly becomes the Son of God, not a human being endowed with heroic powers but God's beloved Son who gives his own life as a ransom for many (10:45). According to the Gospel of Mark, Jesus is not a hero, legitimized by his miraculous accomplishments, but the Son of God because of his suffering and death.

That the early followers of Jesus explicitly rejected the worship of their dead master as a hero must be seen within the rich tradition in ancient Israel of the tombs of heroized ancestors. The tomb of Sarah and Abraham was situated east of Mamre in the field of Ephron that Abraham had purchased from the son of Zohar the Hittite (Gen 23:5–20). The Jewish historian Josephus (*Bell.* 4.532) tells that this tomb near Hebron, beautifully decorated with marble, was still shown in his days. According to Gen 25:9–10, both of Abraham's sons, Isaac and Ishmael, together buried him there.[7] This tomb

---

5. This interpretation was orally presented some years ago by Dieter Georgi. I have no doubt that it is correct.

6. I agree with Hans Dieter Betz ("Heroenverehrung und Christusglaube: Religionsgeschichtliche Betrachtungen zu Philostrats *Heroikos*," in Hubert Cancik, et al., *Geschichte, Tradition, Reflektion: Festschrift für Martin Hengel zum 70. Geburtstag* [Tübingen: Mohr/Siebeck, 1996] 138–39) that the Christian christology required a model that was different from the worship of the hero. I would add, however, that this difference in christology is indebted to the tradition of Moses and to the Servant of God in Deutero-Isaiah.

7. That this memory was still alive in the early Christian period is indicated by the reference in Acts 7:16.

of Abraham remains a sacred site for both Jews and Muslims to this very day—even the place of the terrible killing of Muslims by a deranged fanatic Jew only a few years ago.

As Josephus tells (*Ant.* 16.179–83), there was also the tomb of David and Solomon near Jerusalem, from which Herod the Great tried to rob some treasures and then built a memorial (μνῆμα) of white marble at the entrance. Josephus also notes that Herod's court historian, Nicolaus of Damascus, mentions this tomb, though—according to Josephus—he suppressed the information about Herod's robbery. It is not clear what is meant by the "tomb of Herod" to which the Roman army moved when it came down from Mount Skopus (Josephus *Bell.* 5.108). Since Herod the Great was buried at the Herodium (*Bell.* 1.673, although the excavations have found no evidence for this whatsoever), it could have been the tomb of members of Herod's family or the tomb of Herod's grandson Agrippa I.

There is also the tomb of Rachel "on the way to Ephrath, which is Bethlehem," where "Jacob set up a pillar to her grave; it is the pillar of Rachel's tomb which is remembered to this day" (Gen 35:19–20). Worship at the tombs is also evident from the remark in Matt 23:29/Luke 11:47 that the Pharisees "build the tombs (τάφοι) of the prophets and decorate the graves (μνημεῖα) of the righteous." Acts 2:29 refers to the fact that the tomb (μνῆμα) of David is still known to this very day. Further references to the known tombs of Israel's kings, prophets, and heroes of old are abundant in the Hebrew Bible.

There is, however, one exception: "Moses was buried in the land of Moab in the valley opposite Beth-peor, but no one knows his burial place to this day" (Deut 34:6). The epilogue of Deuteronomy states that "never has there arisen a prophet in Israel like Moses, whom the Lord knew face to face. He was unequaled for all the signs and wonders that the Lord sent him to perform in the land of Egypt, against Pharaoh and all his servants and his entire land, and for all the mighty deeds and all the terrifying displays of power that Moses performed in the sight of all Israel" (34:10–12). His tomb, however, remains unknown. Moses was not a hero to be worshiped at his tomb. Yet there is a reference to this Moses in a later book of the Hebrew Bible, where also the obscurity of his tomb is especially emphasized: the Servant of God in Second Isaiah. Here the prophet tells about the Servant "who has borne our infirmities and carried away our diseases," and who "was oppressed and afflicted" and "by a perversion of justice was taken away," "for he was cut off from the land of the living" (Isa 53:4, 7–8). "They made his grave with the wicked and his tomb with the rich" (53:9).[8] Like the tomb of Moses, the tomb of this new Moses, the Servant of God, remains unknown. No worship took place at his tomb. The Christians who fashioned their narrative of the suffering and death of Jesus in analogy to the story of the Suffering Servant of Deutero-Isaiah knew that there should be no worship at the tomb of Jesus.

The early Christian church, however, was not able in the long run to reject the worship of the hero Jesus. The Jewish philosopher Philo of Alexandria had already given

---

8. See Klaus Baltzer, *Deutero-Isaiah: A Commentary on Isaiah 40–55* (Hermeneia; Minneapolis: Fortress Press, 2001), especially 417–18.

space to the concept of Moses as a hero in his *De vita Mosis.*[9] The early Christian tradition, however, had apparently resisted for a long time the temptation to pay honor to the tomb of Jesus. The memory of Jesus was kept alive in the Christian Eucharist that was celebrated in his memory in every place where a community gathered for the common meal. At these meals it was believed that Jesus was mysteriously present, as is told eloquently in the story of the Emmaus disciples (Luke 24:13–32). To be sure, Palestine had become the Holy Land as early as the writing of the Gospel of Luke, but it did not yet include the tomb of Jesus as a holy place. If there were heroes, they were the Christian martyrs, whose relics may have been collected as early as the *Martyrdom of Polycarp.*[10] Memorial meals were celebrated in honor of these martyrs in the cemeteries. Dates for these festivals began to be fixed during the fourth century.[11]

Full-fledged hero worship of Jesus, however, did not enter the early Christian world until the time of the emperor Constantine early in the fourth century. The tomb of Jesus had to be found again; nobody remembered where it was. Constantine's mother had to travel to Jerusalem and she was lucky to find it. Constantine ordered the building of a magnificent basilica; its eastern extension was a large rotunda as a house for the tomb of Jesus, which survives to this day as the Church of the Holy Sepulcher. Hero worship had finally gained entry into Christianity. As worship at the tomb of the founding hero Jesus became the primary object of pilgrimages to Jerusalem, also the tombs of the apostles and martyrs were now discovered and monuments built to honor their memory and to invite pilgrims to stop on their way to the Holy Land, as many did at the tomb and the octagonal martyrion of Saint Paul in Philippi. Indeed, the claim of the discovery of the tomb of Saint Peter under the dome of his church in Rome makes this the largest and most magnificent place of Christian hero worship in the whole world.

---

9. But see the conclusion of *De vita Mosis:* "How also he was not laid to rest in the tomb (τάφος) of his forefathers, but was given a monument (μνῆμα) of special dignity which no man has ever seen" (2.291).

10. See *Mart. Pol.* 18.2. It is not certain, however, whether this reference belongs to the original report. It may have been added at a later time.

11. The exact date for Polycarp's martyrdom, which appears at the end of the report (*Mart. Pol.* 21), is certainly a later addition that is characteristic for the attempt of the 4th-century church to regulate the hero worship of Christian martyrs; see Hans von Campenhausen, "Bearbeitungen und Interpolationen des Polykarpmartyriums," in *Aus der Frühzeit des Christentums* (Tübingen: Mohr/Siebeck, 1963) 253–301.

II

READING PAUL'S WORLD

The Cultural and Religious Environment

10

SUFFERING SERVANT AND ROYAL MESSIAH

From Second Isaiah to Paul, Mark, and Matthew

The Expectation of the Royal Messiah, the Son of David

When the prophet Nathan went to King David, he said to him:

> Thus says the Lord of hosts: I took you from the pasture, from following the sheep to be prince over my people Israel, and I have been with you wherever you went. . . . When your days are fulfilled and you lie down with your ancestors, I will raise up your offspring after you, who shall come forth from your body, and I shall establish his kingdom. He shall build a house for my name, and I will establish the throne of his kingdom forever. I will be a father to him, and he shall be a son to me. . . . Your house and your kingdom shall be made sure forever before me. Your throne shall be established forever. (2 Sam 7:8–16)

The Babylonians had conquered Jerusalem in 587 BCE, captured the last Davidic king Zedekiah, burnt the temple, and exiled the upper class of the population to Babylon. But the belief in the reestablishment of the throne of David persisted among the exiled people. The books of the Deuteronomistic History, of which the Second Book of Samuel was a part, composed during the exile, included this prophecy of Nathan to David about the everlasting throne of his house. Moreover, the hope for the reestablishment of the kingdom through a scion of the house of David was revived and kept alive. Yes, one day God will send a son of David, the Messiah, to liberate Israel and to make the kingdom of the Davidic royal Messiah secure forever.

After the return from the exile in 536 BCE, the Persians had appointed Zerubbabel as the governor of Judea. Zerubbabel was a grandson of King Jehoiakin and thus again an offspring of David. One of the prophets at that time, Haggai, proclaimed Zerubbabel as king of Judea, calling him Yahweh's "servant," "chosen one," and "signet ring" (Hag 2:21–22). The Persian reaction was swift; they did not suffer to see a king on the throne in Jerusalem: Zerubbabel disappeared from the scene and was never heard of again, and the Persians did not appoint another offspring of David as governor.

But the hope of the return of a son of David as king and Messiah would not die. It remained alive during the entire postexilic period. It became an important part of the eschatological expectation of Israel that can be best summarized as the expectation of the coming of the Messiah. It was forcefully renewed among the Essenes, as is evident in the texts from the Dead Sea. There two messianic figures are expected to return, the Messiah of Judah as a scion of David and the priestly Messiah. This expectation was also powerfully present in the propaganda at the time of Jesus and it finally resulted in the Jewish War of 66–70 CE, to be renewed once more in the disastrous insurrection of Bar Kochba (132–135 CE).

The Servant of God

On the other hand, the prophetic criticism of the royal establishment and its claims to legitimacy was also still alive. Prophets in that tradition had often rejected the claims of the Davidic kingship. For them Yahweh remained the true and only king of Israel. After the disastrous end of the Zerubbabel affair, the prophetic tradition of Israel that rejected the messianic claims of the royal expectations was renewed by a prophet, who is known to us as "Second Isaiah," who is speaking in Isaiah 40–55. I am following here the lead of the commentary on Deutero-Isaiah by Klaus Baltzer,[1] which has opened up exciting new perspectives regarding the controversy between the royal eschatological expectation of the Davidic Messiah and the eschatological expectation of a prophet like Moses.

Departing from the traditional dating of Second Isaiah to the time of the Babylonian exile in the fifth century BCE, some now think it more likely that this book must be dated sometime in the fourth century, certainly well after the attempt to elevate the governor Zerubbabel to the throne of Israel. The book belongs to a time when the Achemenid Persian kings were in full control of the vast area extending from India to the shores of the Aegean Sea, including Egypt, Palestine with Jerusalem, and all of Asia Minor with the Greek cities Smyrna, Ephesus, and Miletus on the Aegean coast. While the rule of the first Persian king Cyrus was then remembered as enlightened and supportive of the various nations under his rule—it was Cyrus who sent the exiles of Judea home from Babylon and instructed them to rebuild Jerusalem—unrest began to appear under his successors, especially in the fifth century BCE. By the turn of the fifth century, Egypt was even able to throw off the Persian yoke, while the Greek cities on the Aegean coast rose up in an unsuccessful war of liberation from Persian rule.

In the Greek tradition, the cruelty and injustice of the Persian domination became the battle cry in the resistance against the Persians; and indeed the cities of mainland Greece were able to fend off the Persian attempts of conquering them in the famous battles of Marathon, Salamis, and Cheironeia. While the polemics against the Persian kings continued in Greece, Greek tragedians and historians of the fifth century BCE held up the memory of the first Persian ruler Cyrus as an example of a wise and just benefactor to the conquered nations. Israel and Jerusalem were in the same situation as

---

1. Klaus Baltzer, *Deutero-Isaiah: A Commentary on Isaiah 40–55* (Hermeneia; Minneapolis: Fortress Press, 2001).

the Greek cities of Ionia, suffering under Persian rule, governed by people from the Persian court, but also remembering the benefactions of Cyrus, the great king of the past. This is the period in which the prophet appeared in Israel who is known as Second Isaiah.

Who is this "prophet" of the Second Book of Isaiah? He is never named; the central figure in this book is called the "Servant of Yahweh," "the Servant of God." It must be remembered that "Servant" here does not designate a lowly slave, but a high official. As in the ancient Near East generally, so also in Israel "Servant" is often the title of a high official in the king's court, like the grand vizier or prime minister. In Second Isaiah the "Servant of God" is the highest-ranking representative of God on earth. The book speaks about his conduct of office in behalf of God, his successes and failures. An important element in this description of his conduct in office is his suffering and death and final vindication.

The question of the identity of this Servant of God, however, has remained a conundrum. Many solutions have been suggested, including: the prophet himself; some savior figure to come in the future, which the Christians later took as a prediction of the coming of Jesus; a corporate figure designating all the people of Israel; and finally the Messiah. But each of these suggestions has difficulties. The prophet of this book never speaks in the first person about the Servant; moreover, Isaiah 53 implies that the Servant has died; thus the prophet, who is the author of this book, is not identical with the Servant. A corporate figure designating Israel is also unlikely because the Servant is clearly distinguished from Israel as a whole.

Is he the Messiah? Although this identification appears especially in Christian circles, it must be rejected: the titles "Messiah," "Son of David," and "king" are never used for the Servant. On the contrary, the only person appearing in the book who is called "Messiah" is the Persian king Cyrus:

> God says to Cyrus: He is my shepherd, and he shall carry out all my purpose....
> Thus says the Lord to his Messiah Cyrus, whose right hand I have grasped to
> subdue nations before him and strip kings of their robes.... I will go before you
> and level the mountains ... I the Lord, the God of Israel, call you by your name.
> (44:28–45:3)

It is clear that the title "Messiah" is therefore entirely inappropriate for the Servant of God. Nobody in Israel can claim this title. The political rule, according to God's will, has passed to the Persian king, who is now designated as the "Messiah." The entire Second Book of Isaiah does not contain any reference to a scion of David or coming king of Israel. Israel already has a king, but this king is not a human figure but God himself, who is called "King of Israel" throughout Second Isaiah. It even seems that the avoidance of the titles "Messiah," "son of David," and "king of Israel" is deliberate and serves a purpose: Second Isaiah wants to tell the reader that salvation for Israel is not coming through a powerful royal messianic figure, but only through God, the true king of Israel. Israel will be saved when its people listen to the message of God's Servant.

Only more recently, especially in the new commentary of Klaus Baltzer, has an older thesis about the identity of the Servant of God been renewed. Who in the Hebrew Bible is *the* Servant of God? The answer should always have been obvious: it is Moses!

Throughout the Pentateuch, Moses is the "servant of God." He is never called king or designated with any royal attributes. But he is acting as the appointed agent of God on earth, as a lawgiver and, even more so, *as a prophet*, especially in the book of Deuteronomy. Thus says Moses:

> The Lord your God will raise up for you a prophet like me from your own people; you shall heed such a prophet. . . . The Lord replied to me: " . . . I will raise up for them a prophet like you from among their own people. I will put my words in the mouth of the prophet, who shall speak to them everything that I command." (Deut 18:15, 17, 18)

Again after the death of Moses, Deuteronomy says: "Never since has there arisen in Israel a prophet like Moses, whom the Lord knew face to face" (34:10).

This tradition remained alive among the prophets of Israel. The image of the prophet Elijah is clearly modeled on that of Moses, as the many parallels demonstrate. The prophets of Israel also held up the tradition that the real king of Israel is not David or any offspring of David, but God himself. At the end of the prophetic books of the Hebrew Bible, in Mal 4:4–5, the figures of Moses, the servant of God, and of Elijah, the prophet, are set side-by-side: "Remember the teaching of my servant Moses, the statues and ordinances that I commanded him for all of Israel. Lo, I will send you the prophet Elijah before the great and terrible day of the Lord comes."

In the tradition of the prophet Moses, the Servant of God also has to suffer in the conduct of his office. The story of Elijah and especially the book of Jeremiah give ample evidence for that consequence of obeying God in carrying out God's command. The suffering of the Servant of God in Second Isaiah is the centerpiece of the entire story. The "biography of office" of the Servant of God, expressed in the Servant Songs, indicates that the Servant is rejected and that his message does not meet full acceptance. The last Servant Song in Isaiah 53 increases this element in a fascinating judgment scene.[2]

52:13–15: The scene is described as taking place in the divine court, to which the Servant of God is elevated; the Divine Judge speaks:

> See, my Servant shall be "beatified."
> He will rise and be carried up and be very high.

Addressing the Servant:

> Just as many were dismayed over you—

Quoting what the "many" had said:

> so maltreated, no longer human was his appearance,
> and his form not like the form of a human being—

Addressing the "many," among them also the kings

---

2. The following translation and the stage directions are taken from Baltzer, *Deutero-Isaiah,* 394–400.

Above/over him kings will shut their mouth [a gesture of reverence].
Truly, what they had not been told they will have seen,
and what they have never heard they will have understood.

53:1: A member of the Divine Court speaks:

Who has believed our revelation?
And over whom has the arm of Yahweh been revealed?

53:2–3: Answer by the first chorus, looking at the servant from the outside. (This could also be represented as a single voice.)

But he grew up like a young shoot before him,
and like a root out of dry land.
He had no form and no beauty that we should have looked at him,
and no appearance that we should have desired him.
He was despised, and forsook by human beings,
a man of suffering and familiar with sickness,
and like one before whom one covers one's face,
despised—so we held him to be of no account.

53:4–6: The response of the second chorus considering the true meaning of this suffering:

Truly he bore *our* sickness,
and *our* sufferings—he took them upon himself.
But we held him to be one who (had been) touched
by the stroke of a god and humiliated.
But he was <desecrated> for *our* "sin,"
smitten because of *our* "transgressions."
The rebuke leading to *our* healing lay on him,
and through his fellowship/invocation *we* have received healing.

53:7–9: Answer by the first chorus, looking at the Servant from the outside:

He was oppressed and he was bowed down
and does not open his mouth—
like a lamb that is led to the slaughter,
and like a sheep that is dumb before his shearer,
he does not open his mouth.
He has been taken away out of exclusion and condemnation.
But who thinks about his generation?
Truly, he is cut off from the land of the living;
because of the "sins" of <his> people a blow has struck him.
And he gave him his grave among criminals,
and his "place" beside a rich man,
although he had not committed any act of violence,
and there was no deceit in his mouth.

53:10: Response of the second chorus, interpreting the meaning of his suffering:

> But it had pleased God <to let him become dust>.
> He had <desecrated> him.
> If he gives his life to wipe out debt (guilt)/as an offering for sin (guilt),
> he will see descendants and have a long life
> and Yahweh's good pleasure/cause will have success through his hand.

53:11–12: Having heard the opposing witnesses, the Divine Judge now pronounces his judgment:

> After [or "because of"?] the trouble/anguish of his life/soul he shall see <light>
>   <and> be satisfied.
> Through his knowledge he, the one who is just,
> my Servant will make the many just,
> and their "debts" he will take them upon himself.
> Therefore I will give him a share with the many,
> and with the powerful he will share "spoil,"
> because he surrendered his life to death,
> and let himself be numbered among sinners.
> He was the one who bore the crimes/transgressions of many,
> and he will intercede for their sins.

In his commentary Baltzer demonstrates that many details of the description of the Servant in this text have their roots in characterizations of Moses in Exodus and especially in Deuteronomy. While the latter book ends, however, with the death and burial of Moses, the Servant Song of Isaiah 53 goes beyond that in the description of the exaltation and vindication of the Servant of God. Thus we can conclude that this Servant of God, who is like Moses never king or Messiah, is a prophet like Moses. But his task clearly goes beyond that of Moses: he is not just sent to Israel but also to the nations. In Isa 49:6 God says to the Servant: "It is too light a thing for you that you should be my servant to raise up the tribes of Jacob and to restore the survivors of Israel; I will give you as a light to the nations, that my salvation may reach the end of the earth." This clearly falls completely outside of the expectations of the coming of the Davidic Messiah, who is the king of Israel only. For Deutero-Isaiah, Yahweh is the king and God of Israel, but he is also the God of all nations. This universalism of divine rule is now extended also to the task of the prophet, the Servant of God. Yet in one other important respect, Second Isaiah departs from the traditional promises to Israel and its Messiah: there is no mention anymore of the restoration of Israel to the Holy Land promised by God. One may ask why the name of Moses never appears in the entire book. The answer is probably that Moses is an Egyptian name: a person with an Egyptian name would be a red flag under the rule of the Persian kings. But it may also be that a special Jewish-Egyptian name would not be fitting for the universal task of God's Servant.

Jesus as the Messiah

Among the most difficult and as yet unsolved problems of the history of early Christian christology are why and when Jesus was given the title "Messiah." There can be little doubt that this title was applied to Jesus at a very early time. It appears early in the Greek translation *Christos*, "Christ," in the letters of Paul, and it must have existed before Paul's call, although in Paul's letters it has become nothing more than a part of Jesus' proper name. Paul's own christology does not rest on this title, or on any other notion connected with the ideology of the royal offspring from the house of David. On the other hand, the Synoptic Sayings Gospel Q does not use the title "Messiah/Christ."[3] In the final stage of the Sayings Gospel Q, the title "Son of Man" prevails, while in the earlier stages of the sayings tradition titles for Jesus seem to be completely missing. This is borne out by the *Gospel of Thomas,* where Jesus is called the "Living One" but all traditional titles of dignity for Jesus are absent.

The claim that Jesus was indeed an offspring of David is evident in the construction of the genealogy of Jesus that originally must have run from David to Joseph, the father of Jesus.[4] It does not matter whether this genealogy of Jesus is grounded in any older tradition or has been invented ad hoc, although I tend to think that it is not a complete fiction because after the death of Jesus the leadership of the Jerusalem community went to his brother James—another offspring of David. The application of the title "Messiah" to Jesus is surprising also in view of the fact that any connotations of the powerful king, warrior, and ruler over Israel are missing. The only connection with power appears in the characterization of Jesus as a miracle worker; this is evident in the tradition used in the Gospel of Mark and with respect to the opponents of Paul in 2 Corinthians.

Two other traditional images of the divine agent become effective in the early formation of the fundamental christologies of the New Testament. The first is Jesus as wisdom teacher and as the voice or presence of heavenly Wisdom. This is present in the Synoptic Sayings Gospel, the *Gospel of Thomas,* the Gospel of John, and also in several hymns of the Pauline corpus, especially in the Christ hymn of Philippians 2 and in the hymn of Colossians 1. The second image that formed early Christian christology is that of the Suffering Servant. I shall here discuss only the latter.

The Suffering Servant and the Story of Jesus' Suffering and Death

The attempt to reconstruct the development of the passion narrative leads to some very interesting observations and conclusions. The extant Gospels have preserved five different versions of the passion narrative, Matthew, Mark, Luke, John, and the *Gospel of Peter.* Matthew and Luke cannot count as preserving more original versions because

---

3. Paul's use of the title "χριστός" will be discussed further below.
4. I shall comment later on the changes introduced by Matthew.

they are dependent upon the Markan passion narrative, although they may have preserved additional independent materials. This leaves three older versions that are independent of one another: Mark, John, and the *Gospel of Peter*, which are parallel in many ways and yet differ from one another. If one compares Mark's and John's versions, however, it emerges that they show, in spite of all their differences, almost exactly the same sequence of episodes beginning with Jesus' entry into Jerusalem and ending with the burial of Jesus and the story of the finding of the empty tomb. The older consensus was that an earlier account, which can be called a "historical report" of the actual events, lay at the base of all the surviving versions of the passion narratives. This has been challenged more recently by John Dominic Crossan in two ways: (1) There was an older written version of the passion narrative, which he calls the "Cross Gospel," that is most faithfully preserved in the *Gospel of Peter* and upon which all extant versions depend. (2) This older "Cross Gospel" had no relationship to the actual events and their sequence in Jesus' suffering and death, but it was entirely developed on the basis of passages from the prophets and some psalms. Crossan therefore emphasizes that the passion narrative is not history with annotated references to prophetic passages but rather prophecy historicized.[5]

I am somewhat critical of Crossan's reconstruction of the "Cross Gospel," but I find Crossan's arguments convincing that the passion narrative is "prophecy historicized" or, as I would rather formulate, "history told in the words and images of prophecy." There are indications that the passion narrative must have existed in oral form for a longer period and that differences of the extant written versions ultimately have their roots in the continuing oral performance of the passion narrative in a liturgical context that included the repeated reading of Scripture, especially about the Servant of God in Deutero-Isaiah and a number of Psalms that were speaking of the suffering righteous. Long before it was eventually written down, the story was told in the context of the liturgy of the celebration of the Eucharist.

Here is what I imagine happened after the death of Jesus. The disciples and friends of Jesus would have gathered again after Jesus had died and had been buried. What did they do then? They certainly did not form a committee that was charged to collect and write down everything that they could remember and gather, with pencil in hand like good journalists, including further information from eyewitnesses. Note that all extant versions of the story tell that the disciples had fled and did not witness what happened! Rather, the friends and disciples of Jesus did what they had always done in the company of Jesus: they gathered together, read the Scriptures, sang psalms, and prayed as they broke the bread and blessed the cup. When they did this, they realized that Jesus was mysteriously present among them.

This is told in a moving way in the story of the Emmaus disciples in Luke 24:13–31. Two disciples of Jesus are on the way to Emmaus after Jesus' death. A stranger joins them and asks them about their grief. When they tell him what has just happened in Jerusalem, the stranger—it is Jesus but they do not recognize him—explains to them

---

5. My formulation of the thesis of *The Cross That Spoke: The Origins of the Passion Narrative* (San Francisco: Harper & Row, 1988).

beginning with Moses and all the prophets that this had to happen to the one they thought was the Messiah in order to save Israel. When they invite the stranger to share supper with them, he blesses and breaks the bread, and they realize that it is Jesus—and he disappears before their eyes. To be sure, that wonderful story is a relatively late novelistic account. But it seems to me that it captures the essence of the actual events after the death of Jesus.

Not historical memory but the reading of Scripture in the context of the liturgy of the Eucharist gave the language to the development of the passion narrative. Constant retelling in the context of the rereading of Scripture provided new insights. Thus the narrative was continuously enlarged in the process. Only decades later, once the passion narrative had been written down in several related versions, did Matthew's learned knowledge of the Bible bring additional clarification into the final account by adding explicit references to the relevant scriptural texts. But the beginnings, more than half a century before the writing of the Gospel of Matthew, are evident very early, namely in the writings of Paul.

Paul was called no later than 35 CE, that is, within five years or less of Jesus' death. In 1 Corinthians 11 he quotes a tradition regarding the institution of the Eucharist saying that he had received this tradition; it must therefore have existed before Paul joined the circles of the followers of Jesus as a new missionary. In the introduction to the words of institution, he states that "Jesus in the night in which he was handed over broke the bread" (11:23). This reveals that Paul and the readers of his letter must have already known the context of the passion narrative; otherwise the reference to a particular moment in that narrative would make no sense to the readers. The formulation "in the night in which he was handed over (παρέδωκεν)" (not our usual "in the night in which he was betrayed"—there is no reference in the story to Judas, who betrayed Jesus) is a clear reference to the Greek text of Isa 53:6: "The Lord handed him over for our sins" (καὶ ὁ κύριος παρέδωκεν αὐτὸν ταῖς ἁμαρτίαις ἡμῶν). A reference to Isa 53:6 reappears in 1 Cor 15:3 in the famous summary of the "gospel" that Paul had received and passed on to the Corinthians. Here Paul says that "Christ died for our sins according to the Scriptures" (Χριστὸς ἀπέθανεν ὑπὲρ τῶν ἁμαρτιῶν ἡμῶν κατὰ τὰς γραφάς). This is again a reference to the same passage of Second Isaiah. "According to the Scriptures" here, of course, does not mean that one can prove it by a reference to the scriptural prophecy; rather, it must be understood in the sense of "Scriptures of old have already told this story." Which Scriptures? No doubt, the story of the Suffering Servant of God told in Isaiah 53.

Thus at a very early date in the history of the followers of Jesus the story of the Suffering Servant of God from Second Isaiah has become the foundation story for a new people. But it is also connected to a particular ritual, namely, the celebration of the Eucharist, a ritual that is again closely tied to the death of Jesus. What is happening here is of fundamental significance because it stands in close relationship to the general function of story and ritual in antiquity.

In antiquity the primary constitutional elements of community are widely accepted cults and rituals connected with the telling of a story that orally restates the tradition in ever new versions until it finally reaches the stage of canonization. Professor Gregory

Nagy of Harvard University has analyzed this pattern masterfully and instructively in a chapter on "Panhellenism" in his book *Pindar's Homer*.[6] The cult, rituals, and athletic competitions of the Panhellenic sanctuaries, especially Olympia and Delphi, were closely connected with performances of the Homeric epic by the lyric poets like Pindar. As these poets reached back to the mythical past of the Homeric story, their recastings of this story, in contrast to local versions, are aimed at creating a statement of truth (*alētheia*) "in the overarching process of achieving a convergent version acceptable to all Hellenes." This process remains fluid "to the point where the latest version becomes the last version, a canonization that brings to a final state of crystallization what had been becoming an ever less-fluid state of variation in performance."[7]

An analogous process can be observed in the creation of a new ritual and narrative in Rome at the time of Augustus through which the beginning of a new age was proclaimed and celebrated. When Julius Caesar had been assassinated, a cult for the Divus Julius, the deified Caesar, was immediately established. After the consolidation of his power, Caesar's heir, Augustus, took advantage of the existence of this cult, which honored a person who had died and had become a god, and refashioned it into a comprehensive cult that could be renewed with the deification of every succeeding emperor. At the same time, Virgil created in his *Aeneid* the story that would become the national epic of Rome. It is a new story, but at the same a story that reaches back to the oldest Greek myth and epic tradition by connecting the founder of Rome to the story of Troy from Homer's *Iliad*. The celebration of the beginning of a new era in the Secular Festival of 17 BCE was again accompanied by the words of a poet in Horace's *Carmen saeculare*. A decade later, Augustus consecrated with a festive procession and sacrifices the new Altar of Peace, the *Ara Pacis*. Among the preserved reliefs of this monument appear not only a symbolization of a peaceful and fruitful mother earth but also a depiction of the Trojan hero Aeneas's sacrifice at the founding of Rome.[8] It would be interesting to investigate the subsequent establishments of the cult of Caesar and Dea Roma or of Augustus and Rome in the cities of the empire. As in Virgil's epic, there is clear evidence for attempts to relate the new imperial cult to time-honored religious rituals and stories of traditional deities. For example, in Athens the new cult of Roma, the city goddess of the Roman Empire, and of Augustus, the founding hero of a new state, was set up as an analogy to the cult of the ancient city goddess Athena and to Athens' founding hero, Erechtheus. There is also evidence that Virgil's epic was by no means an unalterable canonical text. Under Domitian, who attempted to renew the eschatological spirit of the time of Augustus, several new versions of epic narrative appeared.

The same pattern is evident in the history of Israel. If the exact relationship of the narrative of the exodus to the festival and ritual of the renewal of the covenant is still debated, there can be no question that the retelling of the exodus story and the reformulation of the giving of the law was intimately related to the creation of pan-Israel, the new nation consisting of the twelve tribes, until canonization finally took place in

---

6. Gregory Nagy, *Pindar's Homer: The Lyric Possession of an Epic Past* (Baltimore: Johns Hopkins University Press, 1990) 52–81.

7. Ibid., 60.

8. See plates 15 and 16.

PLATE 15. Ara Pacis: The fertile earth. Museum of the Ara Pacis, Rome, Italy. Scala/Art Resource, NY.

PLATE 16. Detail of the Sacrifice of Aeneas. Museum of the Ara Pacis, Rome, Italy. Scala/Art Resource, NY.

the establishment of the five books of Moses as Scripture. With respect to the Passover, the close connection between the ritual and the remembering of the exodus is evident. Here, as in Greece with its several national festivals (in addition to Olympia and Delphi also Nemea and Isthmia), the narrative does not have to be limited to one particular ritual. It can be observed that the story of Jesus' suffering, death, and resurrection not only accompanies the celebration of the Eucharist but also can be connected with the ritual of baptism.[9]

Our evidence for this fundamental pattern was not drawn from the world of religious history. Rather, the parallels belong to the realm of political history. In Greece as in Israel and in imperial Rome, we have been discussing the political process of the creation of a nation, in the case of Rome, a creation of a new area of peace for all nations under an eschatological perspective. The founding of early Christian communities, from Jerusalem to Antioch and to the Pauline churches in Asia Minor and Greece, should not be seen as a feeble attempt of the establishment of a new religious sect—however modest the beginnings may have been. The designations that these new communities used for themselves demonstrate the political dimension of this venture. Typical terms for the designation of religious communities, such as *synagōgē* or *thiasos* and *koinon* (the Greek terms for religious associations) are missing. Instead, the term *ekklēsia* predominates—the Greek term designating the democratic assembly of all free citizens. Also the term "new Israel" appears. Moreover, the term "gospel" for the Christian proclamation was also drawn from the political realm: it was used for the messages issuing from the Roman emperor Augustus in his announcement of the new age of peace.

Like the stories of Greece and Rome, also the new Christian story is rooted in a venerable ancient tradition from which it draws its images and language. But as Virgil's epic develops its story from ancient Troy and relegates the older story of the founding of Rome by Romulus and Remus to a secondary position, so the Christian cult narrative is developed in a recourse to Israel's story of the suffering righteous, thus replacing Israel's story of the exodus and with it also ending the validity of the law of Moses. At the same time, the death of Jesus and his vindication is remembered in the ritual of the Eucharist as the founding sacrifice of a new political order. The cult of the Kyrios Christ and the story that legitimizes the new Israel as an eschatological event are anchored in the traditional language of Israel and, at the same time, in the actual suffering and death of the historical Jesus of Nazareth.

Suffering Servant and Messiah in Paul

Jesus is for Paul and his churches the Servant of God, not the Messiah. This is most evident in the fact that "Messiah" in Paul's letters no longer functions as a title but as part of a proper name: Jesus Christ or Christ Jesus. This should not be translated as "Jesus *the* Christ." Also in those instances in which Paul uses only the name "Christ," it is just a reference to a part of the proper name of Jesus and does not mean "Messiah"; for

---

9. See especially Rom 6.

instance: "Christ died for us, when we were still sinners" (Rom 5:8), or "If we have died with Christ" (Rom 6:8). In these passages, Paul does not say that "the Messiah" died for us. The concept of a suffering and dying Messiah is never found in the tradition of Israel and would be a very strange thing in this tradition. That "the Messiah suffered" is purely based upon a later Christian misunderstanding, and it is entirely wrong, if one wants to base such assumption on the text of Isaiah 53; the one who dies here is not the Messiah but the "Suffering Servant," who is Moses or a prophet like Moses.

Also in 1 Cor 15:3, in the gospel formula that begins with "Christ died for our sins" Christ is a proper name and not a title. There are perhaps two instances in which Paul deliberately uses the title "Christ." The first occurs in the discussion of the fate of Israel in Romans 9–11, where "Christ" appears seven times, but "Jesus Christ" is absent. But even here, Paul speaks once of "Christ according to the flesh" (9:5), which plays down the possible titular implications. The other instance is 2 Cor 5:16: "Even if we had known Christ according to the flesh, we no longer know him." Paul is here fighting miracle-working super-apostles, who claimed to be imitators of the powerful miracle-working Christ/Messiah. This points to an understanding of the title Christ = Messiah in the tradition of the divine man, whose powerful deeds reveal the presence of divine authority. Paul rejects this authority because for him the real presence of God is not the powerful miracle worker but Jesus suffering and dying on the cross. We will again encounter this problematic understanding of Christ = Messiah in the discussion of the Gospel of Mark.

There is also evidence that Paul is suspicious of the claim that Jesus comes from the house of David, the primary prototype of the Messiah. Paul knows the title "Son of David" because in Rom 1:3 he quotes an older formula that speaks of "the gospel concerning his Son, who was descendant from David"; but Paul emphatically adds "according to the flesh." Although the term "Servant" or "Servant of God" plays almost no role in the letters of Paul, it is clear that Paul's christology is in no way related to the messianic expectations of Israel, but it is deeply rooted in the story and the expectation of the Suffering Servant of God. Jesus is not the Messiah because of his descent from David; rather, he is the Son of God because of the power of his resurrection.

Messiah and Servant of God in the Gospel of Mark: Sources, Composition, and Christology

I have no doubt that Mark must have been written before Matthew and Luke, who both use Mark in the composition of their writings. Thus I am accepting the two-source hypothesis as the basis for my arguments. Mark's composition falls into a time about two decades later than the writing of Paul's letters. Most scholars would assign a date right after the Jewish War (70 CE) to the composition of Mark. It must therefore be considered the very oldest Gospel writing that we now possess. Mark's Gospel cannot be dated before 70 CE because it presupposes the destruction of the Jerusalem Temple. Among the different choices of the interpretation of Jesus, Mark, like Paul, belongs into the tradition of understanding Jesus as the Suffering Servant. This is clear in Mark's adoption of the passion narrative as the fundamental and principal genre for the composition of his writing, but also in the fact that the model for the genre of Mark is the biography of the prophet.[10]

In addition to a written passion narrative, however, Mark (in addition to some oral materials) uses several other written sources. The first recognizable written source in the Gospel of Mark is a written collection of parables, used in Mark 4.[11] The christological orientation of this parable collection is evident from the element of esoteric teaching: the parables are stories told to conceal to the outside world their real message, the mystery of the kingdom of God, which is given to the disciples only in private instruction (Mark 4:10–12). Two other written sources were used by Mark in 4:35–8:26; they are two catenae of miracle stories. This is evident because (1) several stories appear in two different versions, and (2) several of the miracle stories are also found among the sources of the Gospel of John, the so-called signs source (*semeia* source).[12]

The author of the Gospel of Mark has inserted other materials into the framework that these two written sources provided. Such additional materials are of a different character. This compositional technique does not have to concern us here. Suffice it to say that some of these additional materials inserted into the older written collections are also miracle stories: the Gerasene demoniac (5:1–20) and two healing summaries (6:53–56 and 7:31–37), the latter including also the brief account of the healing of a deaf-mute. There is also a good possibility that other materials were available to Mark in written form, such as the Synoptic Apocalypse in Mark 13 and the controversy stories of Mark 12.

Most important is Mark's use of a written passion narrative. The sequence of the events in the passion narratives of Mark and John is almost exactly the same. Because I do not think that the Gospel of John is dependent upon Mark, both authors must have used a very similar written document that began with the entry into Jerusalem (Mark 11:1–11) and the anointing in Bethany (Mark 14:3–9; the two stories appear in John 12:1–19 in reverse order) and ended with the story of the finding of the empty tomb (Mark 16:1–8; John 20:1–10). Both Mark and John use the general framework of the passion narrative to insert additional materials: Mark inserts the discourses and debates in Jerusalem in chapter 12 and the apocalyptic discourse in chapter 13. John inserts the farewell discourses in chapters 14–17. Minor discrepancies can here be left out of consideration.

Using these various materials, Mark presents a *christological* (not historical) outline of the ministry of Jesus in three parts:

1. Mark 1:1–8:26: Jesus' public ministry. Here Jesus moves from place to place, teaches publicly, and performs many miracles. But he often forbids the demons to proclaim him openly and repeatedly tells people who have been healed not to tell anybody. Sometimes Jesus' teaching is also shrouded in a veil of secrecy: the purpose of the para-

---

10. Helmut Koester, "Evangelium II: Gattung," *RGG* (4th ed.; Tübingen: Mohr/Siebeck, 2000) 2.1736–41.

11. Heinz-Wolfgang Kuhn, *Ältere Sammlungen im Markusevangelium* (StUNT 8: Göttingen: Vandenhoeck & Ruprecht, 1971).

12. Paul J. Achtemeier, "Towards the Isolation of Pre-Markan Miracle Catenae," *JBL* 89 (1970) 265–91; idem, "The Origin and Function of Pre-Markan Miracle Catenae," *JBL* 91 (1972) 198–221.

bles is to hide the true meaning of Jesus' message from those outside, while only the disciples receive privately an explanation. Notwithstanding Jesus' repeated private instruction to the disciples, they remain without understanding.

2. Mark 9:14–16:8: Jesus leads the disciples to his suffering and death. Though there are still two more miracles reported (the boy with a spirit, 9:14–29, and the blind man Bartimaeus, 10:46–52), they are followed neither by a public acclaim of Jesus' deed nor any command of Jesus to keep the deed secret. This entire section stands under the shadow of Jesus' expected suffering and death. Jesus predicts the suffering, death, and resurrection of the Son of Man three times before arriving in Jerusalem.[13] All along the way to Jerusalem, Jesus instructs his disciples about the sacrifice and self-denial that is required if they want to follow after him. At his arrest, the disciples flee; only Peter stays, but he denies Jesus. The disciples never appear again. Only the women stay to witness Jesus' death, and the women are the ones who discover that the tomb is empty.

3. Mark 8:27–9:13: In the center of the Gospel of Mark stands a special section that includes the confession of Peter at Caesarea Philippi, the first prediction of the passion, and the story of the transfiguration. Here Jesus' assumed dignity is revealed by Peter in his confession: "You are the Messiah" (Mark 8:29), but this is immediately countered with Jesus' prediction of the suffering, death, and resurrection of the Son of Man (Mark 8:31). In the transfiguration, the disciples get a glimpse of Jesus' true heavenly dignity as Jesus appears to them in the company of Moses and Elijah—the two most important figures of the prophetic tradition of Israel. Then the disciples are told not to tell anyone what they had seen "until the Son of Man is raised from the dead." This is the last time that the command not to tell appears in the Gospel of Mark.

This general outline of the Gospel of Mark is not based on historical memory of the actual sequence of events in the course of Jesus' ministry, but on a christological concept, by which the author tries to reconcile different images and dignities of Jesus that are presented to him in his sources. The outline of the Gospel of Mark is thus the result of a theological design.

On the one hand, Mark is confronted with a fully developed memory of Jesus as a famous miracle worker, a "divine man." This tradition existed prior to Mark and was widely propagated by the telling of stories about Jesus' great and powerful miracles. These miracles were told in order to emphasize that Jesus was indeed the *Messiah*. The use of the title "Messiah" for the miracle-working Jesus was already present in the controversy of Paul with the super-apostles in 2 Corinthians. But Mark was also aware of another important concept of Jesus that consisted of two elements: (1) A passion narrative that proclaimed Jesus as the *Suffering Servant*, and (2) a prophetic proclamation that called Jesus the *Son of Man*, who would return for judgment in the near future. Mark's Gospel confronted the challenge to reconcile the christology of Jesus as the miracle-working Messiah with the christology of the Suffering Servant/Son of Man.

Mark accomplished this task by making the narrative of the suffering and death of Jesus the fundamental paradigm of his writing. He did not call this story a "gospel." In the beginning of the book, "the beginning of the gospel of Jesus Christ the Son of

---

13. Mark 8:31; 9:31; 10:32–34.

God"[14] (Mark 1:1) does not mean that this is the beginning of a writing that can be called "gospel." It simply means that the proclamation of Jesus' message ("gospel") is beginning with the appearance of John the Baptist and Jesus' appointment by the heavenly voice. The reader knows: *Son of God* is the bracket that spans the entire writing from the proclamation by the heavenly voice at the baptism of Jesus to the confession of the centurion at the end of the Gospel of Mark (15:39). In the first part of the Gospel, the messianic activity is shrouded in secrecy by the repeated commands of Jesus not to tell what they had witnessed, by the lack of understanding among the disciples, and the theory that the parables are esoteric instructions; we must remember that this is a secret only for the actors appearing in the story. The reader, however, is fully informed by the first verse of the Gospel: "Jesus Christ is the Son of God." The reader also knows what the heavenly voice says to Jesus, "You are my Son," while the heavenly voice is not heard by the bystanders in the story (Mark 1:9–11). Thus the readers' knowledge of Jesus' true dignity is not shared by those who were present at Jesus' baptism.

Is the Son of God the Messiah or the Suffering Servant? Mark 8:27–9:13 is the turning point in the story. Peter reveals in his confession that the one who performs all these miracles must be the Messiah (Peter's confession is thus correctly translated with "You are the Christ," i.e., the Messiah). When Jesus responds to that confession with the announcement that the Son of Man has to suffer, Peter correctly rejects that statement, not because he has some warm feelings and does not want his friend Jesus to die; rather, Peter is presented as the one who knows that there is no such thing as a suffering Messiah. But Jesus rejects Peter, calling him "Satan" (Mark 8:27–33). The disciples must learn to follow Jesus, the Suffering Servant (Mark 8:34–38). The transfiguration confirms for the reader once more that Jesus' ultimate dignity is as Son of God: "This is my Son the Beloved; listen to him!" (Mark 9:7). Jesus does not belong with David as the Messiah but with the prophets Moses and Elijah. As the discourse during the descent from the mountain shows, also John the Baptist belongs to this line: he was Elijah, a prophet like Moses (Mark 9:9–13).

At this point, the change of the titles for Jesus is striking. Not the Messiah, whom Peter just confessed, but the "Son of Man" is going to suffer and to die. This title appears here in the Gospel of Mark for the first time; I believe that "son of man" in Mark 2:10 and 2:28 is not used in a titular fashion but simply means "human being": human beings can forgive sins and human beings are master over the Sabbath. Thus the title Son of Man appears without preparation in Mark 8 for the first time and is then repeated in every following prediction of the suffering and death of Jesus. The close relationship of the understanding of Jesus as the Son of Man and Suffering Servant is explicitly stated in Mark 10:46 with a clear allusion to Isaiah 53.

Closely connected with the Son of Man as the Suffering Servant is the tradition that proclaims Jesus as the Son of Man coming for judgment at the end of days. The origin of this title cannot be further discussed here. Possibly this designation was already used in the prophetic tradition for the Servant of God, a human who would suffer in

---

14. This should not be translated "Jesus *the Messiah*, the Son of God"; "Christ" is here part of the proper name "Jesus Christ," as it is used already in the letters of Paul.

his service but ultimately be vindicated by God. The title was not known to Paul and did not play any role in the corpus of the New Testament epistles. In the Christian tradition, it appears for the first time in the final redaction of the Synoptic Sayings Gospel and in the Synoptic Apocalypse that Mark uses in chapter 13. In both documents it belongs to pronouncements of Christian prophets, dating to the time of the increasing messianic propaganda that preceded the Jewish War of 66–70 CE.[15] The Christian communities were told by these pronouncements that they should stay away from the messianic war propaganda and should not be misled by false prophets saying, "Look, here is the Messiah!" (13:21; see 13:22), because their salvation was bound to the sudden and unpredictable appearance of Jesus as the Son of Man (13:26). In Mark's Gospel Jesus confirms this explicitly in his statement before the high priest: if he is the Messiah he deserves this title only as he is the Son of Man to come on the clouds of heaven (14:62). The passion narrative thus radically reconceived also the concept of Jesus as the coming Son of Man. The Son of Man coming on the clouds of heaven is indeed no other than the Suffering Servant.

This dramatically changes the position of the disciples, although they have seen the glory of Jesus in his transfiguration. When they try to imitate Jesus the Messiah's great miracles, they fail and Jesus has to come to their rescue (9:14–29). Immediately after this story, Jesus repeats his prediction that the Son of Man has to die (9:30–32). The disciples are now the people who have to follow Jesus on his way to the cross, albeit with fear and trembling. All the materials that follow until the end of chapter 10 are related to the order of the church. Prominent in these materials are the rejection of all aspirations to rank and dignity (9:33–37) and the admonition that the "little ones" not be despised (9:42; 10:13–16). The section ends with the request of John and James to sit on Jesus' right and left hand in the kingdom of God. In his response, Jesus says that those who want to be great in the community of the disciples must be the servant and slave of all, "for the Son of Man came not to be served but to serve and to give his life as a ransom for many" (10:35–46). With this clear allusion to Isaiah 53 ends the church order section of the Gospel of Mark.

Is Jesus then not the Messiah? The Son of David pericope (12:35–37a) says: Yes, he is the Messiah, but not that kind of Messiah, not the Son of David. The final juxtaposition of the titles "Christ" and "Son of Man" marks the high climax of Jesus' trial before the synedrion: the high priest's question, whether he is the Christ the Son of the Blessed One, is answered positively, but from then on the title "King of the Jews" is used only in mockery by the soldiers (15:16–19), by Pilate in the inscription on the cross (15:26), and by those mocking the crucified Jesus ("the Messiah the King of Israel," 15:32). Only the centurion at the cross knows: "Truly this man was God's Son" (15:39). Thus the confession of the centurion reaches back to the acclamations of Jesus' true dignity at his baptism and at the transfiguration.

But Mark does not set the aretalogical materials, which tell of the powerful deeds of Jesus, completely aside. Rather, he combines them with the passion narrative; they are part of the conduct of Jesus' prophetic office. Telling the story of the office conduct

---

15. Egon Brandenburger, *Markus 13 und die Apokalyptik* (FRLANT 134; Göttingen: Vandenhoeck & Ruprecht, 1984).

and of the suffering of the Servant of God, Mark produced for the first time what can be called a "biography of Jesus." This, however, is not an accidental creation. There was a model for this genre of writings in the tradition of Israel, namely the biography of the prophet.[16] This genre of the biography belongs to the category of office biography, as it justifies the conduct of an appointed official in the face of adversity and suffering. This office biography has its roots in ancient Egypt and can be found in the Bible in the biographical elements of the story of Moses (especially in the book of Deuteronomy), in Jeremiah, Deutero-Isaiah, and Nehemiah. Such biographies are fundamentally different from the genre of biography that had been developed in the Greek world. In the latter, the primary interest is in the development of an individual's character, personal conduct, and ethos.[17] These elements are completely absent from the prophetic biography, which is exclusively concerned with the conduct and experiences that arise out of the official's faithfulness to the charge of his divine sovereign.

The appearance of John the Baptist in Mark is introduced by a quotation from Isa 40:2–3. The location of John the Baptist in the wilderness and the baptism in the Jordan recalls the motif of the exodus. Jesus' baptism is then told as the story of the call of a prophet. The prophetic call for repentance opens also the preaching of Jesus (Mark 1:15). The hostility that Jesus experiences is the result of his conduct of office. Jesus' interpretation of Israel's law and ritual is "prophetic Torah." He suffers the fate of the prophet in his death and is vindicated. But his tomb is empty, and the memory of its location is not preserved. There is no hero worship at the tomb of Moses, at the tomb of the Servant of God, or at the tomb of Jesus, while such worship was well established at the tombs of Abraham and of the kings of Israel (David, Solomon, and others).[18] The literature that was much later called "gospel" by the Christians is thus continuing the venerable genre of the office biography of the tradition of Israel that begins with the biography of Moses in Deuteronomy and culminates in the story of the Suffering Servant of Second Isaiah, the prophet like Moses.

The Gospel of Matthew: Sources, Composition, and Christology

One might be tempted to include in the further discussion also the Gospel of Luke and perhaps the Gospel of John. These two Gospels, however, are concerned with a different set of christological problems. Mark's dilemma, whether Jesus is the Messiah and the Son of David, or the Son of Man and the Suffering Servant, continues to concern only the author of the Gospel of Matthew.

The first major source for Matthew is the Gospel of Mark. Mark's basic outline dictates the framework of the Gospel of Matthew. Although Matthew has rearranged some

---

16. Klaus Baltzer, *Die Biographie der Propheten* (Neukirchen-Vluyn: Neukirchener Verlag, 1975).

17. Albrecht Dihle, "Die Evangelien und die griechische Biographie," in Peter Stuhlmacher, ed., *Das Evangelium und die Evangelien* (Tübingen: Mohr, 1983) 383–411.

18. See my essay "Hero Worship: Philostratos's *Heroikos* and Paul's Tomb in Philippi," chapter 9 in this volume.

of the materials, especially the miracle stories, whenever he agrees with Mark's sequence, he also agrees with Mark's sequence reflected in the Gospel of Luke. The second major source of Matthew is the Synoptic Sayings Gospel Q, from which he drew most of its sayings. In addition, Matthew is using some special materials, which do not occur elsewhere in the gospel tradition, but are sometimes paralleled by the *Gospel of Thomas*.

Although Matthew relies on Mark's outline of Jesus' ministry, his general composition is dominated by a different concept that appears in the composition of five major speeches:

1. The Sermon on the Mount (Matt 5–7)
2. The Mission Instructions for the Sending of the Twelve (9:35–11:1)
3. The Parable Speech (13:1–53)
4. The Church Order Speech (18:1–19:1)
5. The Eschatological Speech (24:1–26:1)

The scene is carefully set at the beginning of each speech (Jesus on the mountain, or gathering the disciples), and each of the speeches ends with the sentence: "And it happened when Jesus had finished these words." Only at the end of the last speech, the eschatological speech, the conclusion reads: "And it happened when Jesus had finished *all* these words." This systematic introduction and conclusion of the speeches indicates that Matthew's primary purpose in the composition of his Gospel was to present Jesus as a teacher, who left for his churches a comprehensive manual for their understanding, conduct, and organization. That there are five speeches demonstrates that Jesus, like the prophet Moses, is the giver of the new law of Israel. Although Jesus is never explicitly designated as the new Moses, the parallelism with the five books of Moses could not be lost on the reader. Matthew's purpose was to establish the church as the new Israel, not as a departure from the Israel of old but as a renewal of Israel's law through Jesus. Note, however, that Jesus will return not just in order to judge Israel; rather he will judge all the nations, and they will be judged not according to their fulfillment of the law but according to the deeds they have done to the least of Jesus' brothers and sisters (Matt 25:31–46).

Infancy Narrative—Passion Narrative—Inclusions and Key Words

In Mark the story of Jesus was developed in two acts. The first depicts Jesus' powerful ministry up to the confession of Peter. The second act leads the disciples into the story of Jesus' suffering and death. Matthew changes this concept radically. The primary structuring elements, as we have seen, are the five great speeches of Jesus, while the course of the narrative reveals a development that is different from the two-stage drama in Mark's story of Jesus' ministry. In Matthew the reader is asked to discover the symbols and signs that connect and move various parts of the narrative.

Most important is the inclusion through which Matthew binds the entire story into a meaningful whole: the birth narrative forms the prologue of the Gospel, while the passion narrative, no longer dominating the entire story as in Mark, becomes the conclusion of the Gospel. Prologue and conclusion are connected through inclusions in the use of titles. "King of the Jews" appears in the story of the wise men (Matt 2:1–12) and again in the inscription on the cross (27:37). Similarly, that Jesus is the Son of God is proclaimed in the heavenly voice at Jesus' baptism (3:17), and it appears again in the confession of the centurion and the soldiers at the cross (27:54). Thus the pointers in the beginning find their solutions at the end, while they are only hinted at in the course of the development of the narrative.

The Formula Quotations

Fourteen times in his Gospel, Matthew adds a reference to Scripture with the words, "This has happened in order to fulfill what had been said through the prophet" (or similar formulations). These references, however, are unevenly distributed: five occur in the birth narrative (1:23; 2:5, 15, 17, 23), three in the passion narrative (21:4; 26:56; 27:9). The remaining six are distributed over the rest of the Gospel at significant points: the first two at the beginning of the Baptist's appearance (Matt 3:3 = Isa 40:2) and of Jesus' preaching (Matt 4:14 = Isa 9:1–2; including the phrase "Galilee of the Gentiles"); the third as a characterization of his healing activity (Jesus brings healing, Matt 8:17 = Isa 53:4); the fourth at his healing of the multitudes, ending with the sentence, "And in his name the Gentiles will hope" (authorizing Jesus' ministry to the Gentiles, Matt 12:18–21 = Isa 42:1–45); and the next emphasizing the rejection of Israel (Matt 13:14 = Isa 6:9–10); and finally introducing a quotation of Ps 78:2 in explaining the meaning of Jesus' parable teaching (Matt 13:35). Together, these scriptural references mark for the reader the direction in which the story of Jesus is developed. As it begins, it is wholly enveloped in the tradition of Israel and its prophecy of a royal figure, the Son of David and king of the Jews, who will rule Israel. There could be no question about the legitimacy of this newborn child as the heir of David's promised kingship. Strangely enough, however, the wise men who came to worship the child are not from Israel but foreigners from the world of the Gentiles. In the course of the Gospel's story, the formula quotations point to the mission to the Gentiles, the rejection of Israel, and the Suffering Servant.

The Church of Saint Matthew

Though we cannot know who the author of this Gospel was, he was not an apostle or eyewitness but certainly an Israelite. More specifically, he came from the Greek-speaking Diaspora of Israel. His native language was Greek, although he did know some Hebrew and was familiar with Hebrew-language interpretations of the Bible as they appear in the Dead Sea Scrolls and later in rabbinic writings.[19]

What was Matthew's and his community's relationship to Israel? It is evident that Matthew was fully convinced that his community was the heir of Israel and of the promises of Scripture as well as of the law of Moses. Moreover, whatever happens in the

---

19. The most important work on the question of the biblical quotations in the Gospel of Matthew is Krister Stendahl, *The School of St. Matthew* (rev. ed.; Philadelphia: Fortress Press, 1968).

story of Jesus is seen as a fulfillment of Israel's prophecy, as the typically Matthean formula quotations demonstrate.

At the same time, the Pharisees are rejected, and the authorities in Jerusalem (high priest and synedrion, called "Jews" by Matthew[20]) are assigned the full responsibility for the death of Jesus. All this, however, does not describe the situation of Jesus' time but reflects the situation at the end of the first century, when the Gospel of Matthew was composed. What was that situation? It seems that Matthew's community had originally been part of the Greek-speaking Jewish synagogue community in the Diaspora, not in Palestine but somewhere in Syria. These followers of Jesus knew and used a written Greek document, namely the Synoptic Sayings Gospel.

In this synagogue, followers of Jesus were not rejected as long as they accepted the law like everyone else. To be sure, there were different interpretations of the law. Matthew's community codified its interpretation in the Sermon on the Mount (Matt 5–7). Jesus did not present a new law but the very same law of Moses that was accepted by other members of this Jewish Diaspora synagogue. Thus Matthew's Jesus says:

> Do not think that I have come to abolish the law and the prophets. I have not come to abolish but to fulfill. Truly I say to you, until heaven and earth pass away, not one letter, not one stroke of a letter will pass from the law until all is accomplished. Therefore whoever breaks one of the least of these commandments, and teaches others to do the same, will be called least in the kingdom of heaven; but whoever does them and teaches them will be called great in the kingdom of heaven. (5:17–19)

It is difficult not to recognize here a clear polemic against the Pauline Gentile mission and its thesis that Christ is the end of the law. This polemic reappears at the end of the Sermon on the Mount:[21]

> Not everyone who says to me, "Lord, Lord," will enter the kingdom of heaven but only one who does the will of my Father in heaven. On that day many will say to me, "Lord, Lord, did we not prophesy in your name and cast out demons in your name, and do many deeds of power in your name?" Then I will declare to them, "I never knew you; go away from me you who have done works of lawlessness."[22] (7:21–23)

The antitheses of the law in 5:21–48—"You have heard that it was said to those of ancient times, but I say to you"—should not be understood as a new legislation that replaces the law of Moses. Rather, these antitheses are intensifications of the law that try to make the law even more relevant.

---

20. It must be noted that the term "Jews" here does not designate the whole people of Israel.

21. See Hans Dieter Betz, *Essays on the Sermon on the Mount* (Philadelphia: Fortress Press, 1985) 19–21; idem, *The Sermon on the Mount: A Commentary on the Sermon on the Mount* (Hermeneia; Minneapolis: Fortress Press, 1995), on 7:21–23.

22. Note that the NRSV translation here is "go away from me you *evildoers*." This, however, translates the text of the Lukan parallel (ἀδικία), whereas Matthew's text has the term ἀνομία = "lawlessness."

The situation of Matthew's community, however, must have changed radically after the end of the Jewish War of 66–70. During the Jewish War, a group of Pharisees who had opposed the war received permission from the emperor Vespasian to relocate to Yavneh (Jamnia) in the coastal plain of Palestine in order to found a school for the reorganization of whatever was left of Judaism; later this group moved to Galilee. These new leaders of Judaism were convinced that the cause of the disaster that had befallen Israel was its disobedience to the law. Therefore a unified interpretation of the law had to be established for all Jews in order to secure a perfect fulfillment. There was no longer room for the freedom of interpretation that had prevailed up to then. This seems to have resulted in a separation of the followers of Jesus from the Jewish synagogue, often through excommunication, and in the establishment of distinct communities of law-abiding followers of Jesus. At the same time, the Pharisees as the representatives of the reestablishment of the Jewish rabbinic synagogue became the enemies of Matthew's community, which observed the law but followed a more liberal understanding of the law that allowed Gentiles to participate (circumcision and ritual law are never mentioned in Matthew!). Matthew's "anti-Semitism" is an inner-Israel conflict between two law-abiding factions of Israel, one group (the "Jews" and Pharisees) insisting on the ritual law and the exclusion of Gentiles, the other group (Matthew's church) radicalizing the moral law and accepting Gentiles.

The apostolic authority for this new departure—acceptance of the Gentile mission, but continued observance of the law without its ritual prescriptions—becomes Peter. He is praised as the rock on which Jesus will build his church and who thus receives the power of the keys (Matt 16:17–19). This statement is to be understood as a confirmation that the tradition under the name of this apostle Peter is legitimate.[23]

The move in the history of Matthew's community from the belief in Jesus as the Davidic Messiah for Israel to an understanding of Jesus as the Servant and Son of God and Savior for the Gentiles is described in this Gospel as a "story." Matthew does not write a theological essay about Jesus and his dignity, nor does he simply translate traditions and historical information into dogmatic statements about Jesus. Rather, he writes a *story*. Whenever Jesus is presented in his special role as revealer, teacher, Son of God, or Lord, it is still in the form of a story that is told. In this story, real people encounter Jesus—his family, followers, sick people, opponents. They ask questions, understand or do not understand, get healed, worship Jesus, and are addressed by Jesus' words. But, as Ulrich Luz has argued, though it is written as the story of Jesus, it is really the story of Matthew's church projected back into a story of Jesus.[24] Jesus' story in this Gospel tells the story of the church of Matthew.

---

23. Only late in the 2d century was this statement adopted by the Roman church as an endorsement of Peter as the first legitimate bishop of Rome and thus as an endorsement of the universal leadership of all of Peter's successors as bishops of the Roman church.

24. See his commentary on the Gospel of Matthew, published in three volumes in the Hermeneia commentary series: Ulrich Luz, *Matthew 1–7*, trans. James Crouch (Minneapolis: Fortress Press, 2006); *Matthew 8–20*, trans. James Crouch (Minneapolis: Fortress Press, 2001); *Matthew 21–28*, trans. James Crouch (Minneapolis: Fortress Press, 2004); see also idem, *Matthew in History: Interpretation, Influence, Effects* (Minneapolis: Fortress Press, 1994).

As the story begins, it is a story of a man from Israel, or as we would say today, as a story of a "Jew." The older genealogy of Jesus used by Matthew at the beginning of his Gospel (1:2–16) must have originally begun with David because its interest was to prove Jesus' legitimacy as the Messiah, the son of Joseph, the son of David (there was then no knowledge of Jesus' birth by a virgin). Matthew, however, wants to show that Jesus fully belongs to Israel; thus he extends the genealogy back to Abraham; this origin does not prove Jesus' messianic dignity but his "Jewishness"—all Jews are children of Abraham.

At the beginning of the Gospel, Jesus' dignity is not expressed in general Hellenistic terms, but in very specific Jewish terms: he is the newborn king of Israel and thus David's son and heir. However, a signal is set here that the reader should note: why are there no Jews coming to worship the newborn child but only three wise men from the Gentiles? And King Herod, the highest Jewish authority in Jerusalem, tries to kill him, so that his parents have to flee to Egypt with the child. How Jesus is bound to Israel and its tradition is developed in the Gospel of Matthew in the use of the titles "Son of David" and "King."

The use of the titles "Son of David" and "King" is strangely mysterious in this Gospel. Matthew intentionally makes the reader wonder what these titles mean. At the beginning of the Gospel, the reader would certainly agree that this newborn child is the designated king of Israel, the Messiah.[25] The titles used at the beginning of Matthew's Gospel are the traditional royal titles of Israel, with no suspicion attached to them that they may be inappropriate. That question arises only in the final chapters of Matthew's story. In the conclusion of the Gospel of Matthew the use of the titles "Son of David" and "King of the Jews" appears in a problematic light. Who Jesus really is, the reader should understand, has gone far beyond the boundaries of Israel's messianic expectations.

During the narrative of the Gospel, from chapter 3 to chapter 19, the title "King of the Jews" never appears, but "Son of David" is used four times. It occurs several times in addresses of people who seek healing from Jesus,[26] twice by blind men who seek healing and once by the Canaanite woman, a Gentile, whom Jesus first refuses to receive but then accepts because of her faith. Once it is used after Jesus has driven out demons, and the people wonder whether he is the Son of David. Yes, Jesus is the Son of David, not however as a king but as a healer. But this does not yet reveal Jesus' ultimate dignity. The use of the titles "King" and "Son of David" in the story of the entry into Jerusalem (21:5, 9) only seems to suggest this. Indeed, Matthew has inserted the messianic titles here; they do not appear in the Markan version that Matthew uses. Why? Probably because Matthew wants to show that the crowds, who hailed Jesus as the Son of David, would be calling for his crucifixion only a few days later. These crowds do not know who Jesus really is. There follows the strange apophthegma (22:41–45) in which Jesus argues that the Messiah cannot be David's son because David calls him Lord in the Psalms (Ps 110:1). After that, "Son of David" is never used again, and the crowds that hailed him as Son of David, asked by Pilate what should be done with the "Messiah,"

---

25. Matt 1:1, 18; 2:2, 6.
26. Matt 9:27; 12:23; 15:22; 20:30–31.

now cry, "Crucify him!" (Matt 27:22). Yet the emphasis upon "Jesus the King" also returns, though only in the mouth of Jesus' enemies. Pilate asks "Are you the King of the Jews?" (27:11); the soldiers mock him as the "King of the Jews" (27:2). Then Pilate sets the inscription on the cross, "This is Jesus the King of the Jews" (27:37)—the only words that were ever written about Jesus during the time of his life—and Jesus is mocked once more as "King of Israel" (27:42). It is evident that the title "King" is now totally inappropriate for the description of Jesus' true dignity. The Roman soldiers at the cross tell the reader of the Gospel that this is not Jesus' true title; rather, he is the "Son of God" (27:54).

Son of God: The one who announces Jesus' coming, John the Baptist, is clearly a prophet from Israel; he resembles the prototype of all of Israel's prophets, Elijah. However, hostility against the leaders of Jerusalem immediately emerges: the Pharisees and Sadducees are addressed as "brood of vipers!" (3:7–9). It is clearly Matthew who has introduced the Pharisees here. Is this Jesus, who comes to be baptized, just another Israelite or another prophet? John the Baptist knows better and refuses to baptize him, though Jesus insists "in order to fulfill all righteousness" (3:13–15). Jesus is therefore again one who fully belongs to law-abiding Israel. This heightens the contrast to the proclamation of the divine voice to the crowd: he is the Son of God (3:17).

The heavenly voice at Jesus' baptism, addressing the crowds (not to Jesus alone as in Mark), declares for the first time openly that this man from Israel is the Son of God. As in the Markan parallel, the words of the heavenly voice are drawn from Deutero-Isaiah (Isa 42:1). As the story develops, however, only a very few people seem to be aware of this dignity. As in Mark, Satan knows it (Matt 4:3, 6), and the demons know it (8:29). Finally the disciples acknowledge that Jesus is the Son of God after he walks on the water (14:33). In the confession of Peter (16:16), Matthew changes Mark's text so that Peter does not designate Jesus as the Messiah but as the Son of God. This is soon confirmed by the second heavenly voice in the story of the transfiguration (17:5). Yet again there is silence with respect to this title until the high priest asks at the trial of Jesus: "Are you the Messiah, the Son of God?" (26:63), and it is repeated in the mocking of Jesus on the cross, "If you are the Son of God, climb down from the cross" (27:40)—a clear reference to the words of Satan at the temptation, "If you are the Son of God, throw yourself down" (4:6). The conclusion is reached finally in the confession of the Gentile soldiers, "Truly this man was the Son of God."

I shall not discuss the title "Son of Man" here. With respect to this title, Matthew follows the concept of Mark that the "Son of Man," who has to suffer and to die, is identical with the Son of Man who will appear on the clouds of heaven in his parousia. This is even heightened in Matthew by the statement that the "sign of the Son of Man" (perhaps the cross?) will appear in the sky first as he returns. As the man who suffered on the cross, Jesus is no longer the Messiah, the King of the Jews and the Son of David. Rather, he is the Son of Man/Suffering Servant, who deserves the title "Son of God."

In this paradoxical presentation of Jesus of Nazareth and the story of his ministry, Matthew transfers his own tradition, namely that of a community from Israel, back into the story of Jesus. The story of Jesus in Matthew's Gospel mirrors the story of his own community, a community that has moved out of the boundaries of Israel and out of the belief in Jesus as the Davidic Messiah into the Gentile mission and the belief in Jesus as the Servant and Son of God. In Mark there is no doubt that Jesus' ministry takes place in Israel; but there is no emphasis upon the Jewishness of Jesus. Matthew emphasizes exactly this point. Like all members of Matthew's earliest community, Jesus is a descendant of Abraham and he begins his ministry as a mission to Israel alone. In the missionary instruction he asks his disciples not to go into the houses of the Gentiles (10:5–6). He first refuses to heal the Canaanite woman's daughter, saying that he has been sent only to the lost sheep of the house of Israel (15:21–28), just as originally Matthew's community rejected the Gentile mission. In this story Jesus' move from a focus on Israel alone to a mission to the Gentiles is highlighted several times by quotations from Second Isaiah; it appears that Matthew's church was guided by this prophetic book in its move out of Israel into a church for the Gentiles. This has nothing to do with the memory of the historical Jesus. Rather, it is part of the self-reflection of Matthew's church and its Jewish-Christian heritage. Can these Christians bring their "Jewish" Jesus with them as they moved into the church of Jews and Gentiles, or even mostly Gentiles? Matthew's answer is yes. He argues in his story that this is exactly what Jesus did, born as a Jew and greeted at his birth as the messianic Son of David, King of the Jews, and ending with the command of Jesus, the Son of God, to preach to all the Gentiles, just as Matthew's church has emerged from a law-abiding Judaism and has developed into a church that is now Israel of the Gentiles.

By placing Jesus' story more intimately into the tradition of Israel, Matthew places the tradition about Jesus more clearly into a Jewish context, from which also his own community emerged. He stresses that Jesus was indeed a Jew, the Son of David and the offspring of Abraham and the one who renewed the law of Moses in a legitimate Jewish interpretation. Jesus is a man who is depicted as having great personal difficulties when he is faced with the challenge of a Gentile woman who sought healing for her daughter, just as Matthew's church once must have found it difficult to accept Gentile converts. But Matthew remembered that those people who had now excommunicated his community were the same people who shared responsibility in the death of Jesus. Therefore the kingdom of God is taken away from them and is now given to the Gentiles. Thus the Gospel of Matthew ends with Jesus' command "to go to all Gentiles [not: nations!] and teach them whatever I have taught you" (Matt 28:19–20), namely to keep the law of Moses in the way the Sermon on the Mount understands it. With this teaching, Matthew has also preserved the validity of the law of Moses for the Gentile churches. But the Jesus who renewed this law of Israel for the Gentiles is no longer for them the Messiah, Son of David, and King of the Jews but is the Suffering Servant and the Son of God.

Acceptance of the community of Matthew and its Gospel in the church of the Gentiles and the eventual canonization of this Gospel had far-reaching consequences. Not only might it otherwise almost have been forgotten that Jesus came from Israel. It also assured the remaining significance of the Scriptures of Israel and it reintroduced the law of Moses in the form of a prophetic Torah, without the demand for circumcision and purity regulations, as the law of Christianity—however interpreted.

11

THE FIGURE OF THE DIVINE HUMAN BEING

The belief in the greatness of individual human beings, who are acknowledged as bene-factors of the city, the nation, and humankind, is as old as the beginnings of Western cul-ture.[1] When the first Christian apostles encountered this belief, it was already well established in the Greco-Roman world. And, with all its intriguing allure, it is still an important and pervasive current in our present situation. Indeed, this belief is very much alive as all of us face the demand for excellence in our teaching and our studies, as well as the expectation that graduates will emerge as recognized leaders in religious com-munities and in our society at large.

The beginnings of the concept can be found in the momentous discovery by the Greeks and the Hebrews that gods resembled human beings—albeit more powerful, more beautiful, wiser, and immortal. According to the book of Genesis, human beings, male and female, were created in the image of God. Therefore the temptation becomes possible, *eritis sicut deus*: "You will be like God." In the world of classical Greece the art of the representation of divinities in the form of human beings found its perfection. As a result, the dividing line between humanity and deity was partially obliterated.

The ascription of such divinity to human beings, however, was not generally avail-able. It was reserved for those special individuals who, by their powerful and inspired deeds, had demonstrated that they were more than just human—they were "gods," or "sons of a god," or "heroes," or "divine men."

What kinds of human achievement especially qualified as the demonstration of divine power? It is interesting that in the early classical period one finds few, if any, politicians or military leaders singled out for such honor. The rise of this belief in divine individuals is closely related to the growing sense of freedom and self-determination possessed by citizens of the Greek cities, especially Athens, after liberation from the rule of the tyrants. Poets, orators, philosophers, and athletes found their audience and their admirers from among these free citizens. The symbol for the divinity of human beings was therefore the great poet Homer, and philosophers and athletes had a better chance

---

An address given at the Convocation of Harvard Divinity School on Monday, 23 September 1985, and subsequently published in *HTR*. I am dedicating this address to George MacRae, who died on Friday, 6 Sep-tember 1985. His greatness as a human being is remembered in his selfless service to students, colleagues, and friends, and in his tireless work devoted to scholarship, the university, and the church universal.

1. The basic work on the concept of the divine human being in antiquity is Ludwig Bieler, *ΘΕΙΟΣ ANHP: Das Bild des göttlichen Menschen in Spätanlike und Frühchristentum* (repr. Darmstadt: Wissenschaftliche Buchgesellschaft, 1967); a comprehensive essay with full bibliography was published more recently by Hans Dieter Betz, "Gottmensch II (Griechisch-römische Antike und Urchristentum)," *RAC* 12 (1982) 234–311.

of becoming divine than did kings and generals. Three elements were important: (1) legitimate divine power was not tied to heredity or office, but could be found in the extraordinary life and achievements of any human being; (2) the fruits of such an individual's life and deeds were benefactions given freely to all; and (3) the lives and deeds of such divine men could serve as examples, and their "virtues" could be imitated.

In the subsequent Hellenistic and Roman periods, the belief in the divinity of human beings became a very important factor both in the shaping of philosophical theory and in religious propaganda. But its most powerful effects can be seen in the political realm, where it became the seminal concept for the development of the Hellenistic ruler cult and the Roman cult of the divine emperor. The limitations of this concept are evident also: it is elitist and antidemocratic, since only the few chosen people could claim this status, giving them a position apart from the masses; it is also clearly a male concept, because the structures of the society did not allow women to withdraw from the regular pursuits of life to the same degree as men. The elitist and male-oriented nature of the concept has continued to be basic even in its modern version.

For the philosophers, the divine man was the one who had reached the perfection of virtue and thus had come into possession of complete bliss and happiness. This achievement of divinity could and should be imitated. Thus the harmony of conduct, character, and life was presented as an example for the student of philosophy who was striving to reach such harmony for himself. Although the concept of the divine man remained in this way a symbol for human freedom, it became restricted to a small elite, since it was reserved only for those who endeavored to lead a philosophical life. Such a philosophical life, moreover, was not designed to be beneficial to the society at large, and had no political consequences. Rather, the goal that the philosopher pursued through the imitation of divinity served only his own personal perfection and happiness. Godly perfection had effects merely on the formation of the individual self: ethical achievement was identical with the ultimate realization of one's true self as divine. This is the meaning of *nosce te ipsum*, "know yourself," that is, that you are gods, in the much admired Stoic morality.

In the religious propaganda of Hellenism the presence of divine *aretē*, "virtue," in human beings meant power rather than morality. In the earlier Greek formation of the concept of the divine man, this element had already played an important role. The Greek word *aretē* does not mean virtue in the rational-moral sense, but virtue achieved by inspiration, that is, possession of divine spirit. Extraordinary persons who brought the message of a new religion demonstrated the presence of the virtues and the possession of divine power in their lives, and taught the way to salvation, or the laws for the perfect society were described by divine human beings. In Judaism, Moses—prophet, king, legislator, and guide into the divine mysteries—became the archetypical divine man in the writings of Philo of Alexandria. Similarly, Abraham was depicted as the prototype of the human being who strives after perfection in virtue, and thus achieves divine nature. Both Moses and Abraham served as examples to be imitated by those who would earnestly pursue a life of virtue, and of perfection of the soul, as their ultimate divine destiny.

In the pagan world one of the divine men whose life has been described in detail in a biography of virtue and power was the first-century Neo-Pythagorean philosopher and wonder-worker Apollonius of Tyana. His wonderful birth in a meadow of flowers, certified by a thunderbolt, his teachings full of deep divine wisdom, his miracles (including the raising of a dead person), his ascetic lifestyle, his travels to India, his miraculous disappearance from a courtroom and equally miraculous appearance afterward to his disciples, all attest to the fact that he is a god rather than a human being.

Christian missionary propaganda presented the divine man Jesus in a very similar fashion. Born miraculously of a virgin, demonstrating his wisdom at an early age, performing wonderful healings and raising the dead, teaching with authority and legislating the rules of conduct for the new eschatological community, rising after his death and appearing miraculously to his disciples, Jesus became the most convincing example of the presence of divine power in a human being. The Gospels of the New Testament give a striking testimony to the divine-man ideology that has formed the tradition about the founder of this new religion.

There are a number of problems, however, in this Christian understanding of the divinity of Jesus of Nazareth. To be sure Jesus is even today presented as an example to be imitated, certainly as the prototype of Christian piety and morality—if not in his exercise of miraculous power. The image of Jesus has always played a role in the history of Christianity, but a different concept of the imitation of Christ had been more influential in the formation of the early Christian communities, namely the concept of the imitation of Jesus' humanity rather than of his divinity.

This concept of *imitatio Christi* is rooted in Jesus' own pronouncements about discipleship, and in the Christian proclamation of the cross of Christ as God's giving of his beloved child for the salvation of all humankind. Jesus' words about discipleship clearly emphasize service to others, as he had come to serve others and to give his life for them. This democratizes the concept of imitation: serving the welfare of others is a possibility open to everyone, regardless of social status, gender, or race—it is a fundamentally human possibility. Moreover, such service, as summarized in the Christian command to love one's neighbor as well as one's enemy, does not aim at building up and perfecting one's own personality; rather its focus is on the humanity of the other one. This explains the striking phenomenon that the concept of virtue and moral perfection for one's own sake—the central feature in the Hellenistic idea of the imitation of the divine man—is completely absent from Jesus' teaching. The reference to perfection, "you will be perfect as your Father in heaven is perfect," characteristically follows upon the commandment to love one's enemies. Perfection is giving oneself rather than becoming oneself.

On this basis the Christian message was capable of founding communities of people from all classes, races, and genders. One of the oldest formulae for Christian baptism, the entrance rite into the Christian communities, explicitly states the elimination of all ethnic, social, and gender qualifications: "In Christ there is neither Jew nor Greek, neither slave nor free, neither male and female" (Gal 3:28). The concept of the divine human being has been radically reinterpreted: the truly divine human beings are those who give themselves for others, even to death on the cross; because God has appeared in Jesus—neither the most powerful nor the most virtuous—but as self-giving love. God is not power, rather God is love.

The development of these communities and the formation of Christian churches, however, fell in a period of history in which the concept of the divine man became a dominant political image in the cult of the Roman emperor. Beginning with Augustus the Roman emperor was the most powerful and most visible presence of divinity on earth. The *Res gestae* of Augustus, the account of all his accomplishments published by Augustus himself toward the end of his life, leave no doubt that he is *the* divine man: the son of the divinized Caesar, who has brought peace to the whole world, who had become the benefactor of all humankind, and who had established law and order for all people—an order, indeed, of cosmic dimensions, demonstrated by the introduction of the new solar calendar; inscriptions celebrating the establishment of this calendar also greet the message of the birthday of the emperor as "gospel" initiating a new era in history.

The Roman imperial period thus begins with two diametrically opposed developments of the concept of the divine human being: the democratized version of the crucified Jesus whose self-giving service opens up for everyone the opportunity of becoming divine, and the elitist version of the divine Caesar whose rule promises peace and well-being for all people. It is no accident that for Christians the test of political and religious loyalty became the demand to worship Caesar. At least for the first three centuries of the Common Era, the issue was clear and unambiguous for Christians: against the claim of the institutionalized presence of divine power in the person of the Roman emperor, Christians maintained their belief that true divinity is present in the willingness of the powerless to die for their faith. The honor of becoming divine human beings in martyrdom was not denied to anyone, whether slave or free, whether female or male.

With the victory of Christianity at the time of Constantine, the Christian churches found themselves in a dilemma that has haunted Christian thinkers ever since: to what degree should Christians acknowledge as legitimate the presence of divine power in political authorities who, explicitly or implicitly, claim to be authorized by the same God whom Christians worship? Although this problem has been solved variously during the history of the Western world, the church institutionalized its version of the concept of the divine human being in the canonization of its saints who are not primarily politicians, but martyrs, wonder-workers, and self-giving servants—from Saint Antony in the Egyptian desert to Mother Teresa.

There is, however, a new, albeit secularized, concept of the divine human being that has arisen in modern times.[2] It is not without its direct ties to the ancient concept, and the analogies to the Greco-Roman period are striking. As in the classical Greek period, the concept is first developed in a time of liberation. In the eighteenth century the Enlightenment prompted the emancipation of citizens from the rule of the princes. The symbols for this liberation were, once again, not the political leaders but the poets. The "new Homer" is Shakespeare. English writers, beginning in the late seventeenth century, had already discovered Shakespeare as the true genius, the man taught by nature

---

2. Throughout the second part of this address I am indebted to the work of Jochen Schmidt, *Die Geschichte des Genie-Gedankens in der deutschen Literatur, Philosophie und Politik 1750–1945* (2 vols.; Darmstadt: Wissenschaftliche Buchgesellschaft, 1985). Individual references are given in the following notes only in those instances in which I am quoting specific works of German authors.

rather than by artificial learning, truly inspired and inspiring. German idealism, which fully developed the concept of the genius, was directly influenced by this new English view of Shakespeare, from Dryden's "Essay of Dramatick Poesy" of 1668 (translated one hundred years later by Lessing), to Addison's statement in a *Spectator* article of 1711 that became the Magna Carta of the genius theories of the eighteenth century.

In the Odes of Johann Wolfgang Goethe it is most evident that the genius is, indeed, the divine human being of ancient Greece resurrected. As in antiquity, the divine human being is always male, autonomous, defiant, and endowed with the power to do miracles in the creation of his works. But this divine man now fully assumes the privileges of divinity for himself. In Goethe's ode "Prometheus," Zeus is sent back into the heavens, and Prometheus says:

> You [Zeus] must cede my earth to me
> And my house that you have not built
> And my hearth
> Which is your envy.
> I know nothing more wretched
> Under the sun than you, the gods.
> . . .
> Is it not my own sacred fervent heart
> that has accomplished everything by itself?
> . . .
> Here I am, forming human beings
> according to my own image
> a generation that will be like myself.[3]

The genius is like God, and his works demand that one should worship the glory of the genius who created them. What the genius produces does not only reveal freedom, independence, and autonomy—it is sacred. Accordingly, only the small elite of the initiated can truly behold what such works reveal. But such beholding of inspired art carries with it the claim that here, and only here, can whatever is meant by "divinity" be obtained, and the achievement of ultimate happiness results. Other human endeavors, especially the efforts of the scholar, are explicitly excluded. Goethe's "Faust" begins with the description of the bankruptcy of scholarship, that is, of all human efforts that are not the products of inspiration by nature (for which "the gods" may sometimes appear as a metaphor).

The transfer of the concept into the political realm had far-reaching consequences. Here Napoleon replaced Shakespeare. The enemy of the genius is no longer primarily the methodical scholar but uninspired bourgeois traditionalism and its morality. Napoleon's greatness was manifested in that he stood above and beyond all limitations of moral criteria; his eyes could see all things in the world at once, says Heinrich Heine, as only the gods can see; and St. Helena he sees as the Holy Sepulcher to which all the people of the Orient and the Occident made their sacred pilgrimages.[4]

---

3. "Prometheus," *Goethes Poetische Werke: Vollständige Ausgabe* (Stuttgart: Cotta, n.d.) 1.319–21.

4. Heinrich Heine, *Sämtliche Schriften* (ed. Günter Häntzschel; Munich, 1969) 2.234.

There were voices that tried a critical evaluation of the concept of the genius: Goethe himself had shown the self-destructive tendency of the genius in his later works, especially in the tragedy of Faust; Kant emphasized the high value of gradual moral and rational learning; the Swiss poet Gottfried Keller proclaimed the ideal of a rationally motivated realism in a bourgeois society based on the ideals of liberalism; Karl Marx presented a radical translation of the concept of the genius into the divinely sanctioned eschatological (or utopian) mission of the proletariat. Most influential on the European continent, however, was the voice of Alexis de Tocqueville and his observations made in America; what he had to say about American democracy produced a negative reaction in view of the failure of the liberal bourgeois revolution in Germany in 1848/49. The spokesman of this reaction became Nietzsche; his foil in the field of the arts was Richard Wagner; and in the area of politics the celebrated genius was once more Napoleon.

Nietzsche's cultural criticism in the name of genius is entirely reactionary and anti-democratic. In his view what de Tocqueville had reported about the American democracy and what Marx and Engels propagated was one and the same: a fundamental threat to all divinely authorized human greatness. However, the understanding of "divine authorization" had already been thoroughly secularized. Nietzsche found the criteria for the identification of genius in the theories of English and American Darwinists: nature could authorize "genius" by the preservation and propagation of the pure race of those destined to be rulers and leaders and to produce the geniuses for all humanity. The concept of genius was thus transferred into the realm of natural-science theory. The rediscovery, in Richard Wagner's work, of the Germanic essence of the race destined for leadership for some time inspired Nietzsche's prophetic message—and also encouraged programs of eugenic selection in Germany as well as in the English-speaking world.

Genius and race were finally welded together into the one powerful principle of all human history by the son of a British general, Houston Stewart Chamberlain. Adopting Germany as his home country, he married the daughter of Richard Wagner and moved to Bayreuth, where Adolf Hitler visited him in Wagner's villa in 1927 (he died shortly thereafter). According to his tremendously influential work "The Foundations of the Nineteenth Century" (published in 1898),[5] all human greatness is produced by the heroic genius and must be embedded in the pure race of a chosen people, like Homer and the Greeks, and Goethe and the Germans.

After the catastrophe of World War I, all of the ingredients were ready in Germany for the creation of the messianic genius-religion with its expectation of the political genius, the great *Führer*, who would come from the natural soil of the chosen race to redeem his people: an Aryan, male, all-knowing and all-seeing, above the law and a law to himself, a persuasive speaker, and a powerful commander of those who were ready to die for the mission of their race. In *Mein Kampf*, Hitler writes:

Whatever we possess today in terms of human culture, works of art, scholarship, and science is almost exclusively the creative product of Aryans. Exactly this fact

---

5. Houston Stewart Chamberlain, *Die Grundlagen des 19. Jahrhunderts* (Munich: Bruckmann, 1899).

allows the well-founded conclusion that the Aryan alone is the originator of a higher order of humanity and thus the prototype of everything we designate with the word "human." The Aryan is the Prometheus of humanity from whose luminous head went forth at all times the divine spark of the genius.[6]

This race is, therefore, also destined to stand tall among all the races and nations of the world and to make them subject to its own interests and purposes—indeed, in doing so it fulfills its own divinely sanctioned mission.

It may seem to us that this particular instance of the development of the concept of the genius is but a horrible caricature of much that has been great and inspiring in the modern West. The liberal-democratic tradition of countries like Great Britain and the United States has prevented the unchallenged rise to political power of a genius, supported by the ideological agreement of a large part of the population. But there are signs of danger.

The Christian tradition and the interpretation of its heritage today is full of the belief in the divine man, from the understanding of its heroes, such as Jesus and Luther, to the suggestion that true piety will also carry the reward of human greatness and extraordinary accomplishment for ourselves, both as individuals and as a nation. That we are under the spell of this idea also implies the pervasiveness of male and white imagery—and nothing is lost if we add a few female and black heroes to this gallery of religious geniuses.

As a nation we may not be in danger of contrasting our own superior and divinely authorized genius with the inferior race of the Jews, as did Hitler and his Aryan movement. But we constantly reaffirm our own mission by contrasting ourselves with other nations that are downgraded as less democratic, less wealthy and successful, less peace-loving, or even barbaric or satanic—as we seek our own interests and not those of others. Moreover, in the hour of national need we might be quite willing to overrule the democratic processes and to bow to the will and wisdom of a great leader, praying that God will inspire him to make all the right decisions on our behalf.

For students of religion it is all the more important to make a commitment to another vision of the divine human being, one that recognizes the presence of divinity in all human beings, regardless of race or gender, in friend and enemy alike. This vision requires an acute awareness, and fundamental rejection, of the elements that constitute the concept of the divine man and the genius: imitation of the divine man's inspiration and accomplishments, scorn for scholarship and intellectual pursuits, contempt for moral principles if they stand in the way of ideological or religious achievement, disdain for democratic processes both in the secular realm and particularly in religious communities, and finally the definition of community as a chosen elite.

The new vision implies that in scholarship, in democratic society, and in religious communities there is no place for the divine man, the genius, and the leader; but there is a place for and much work to be done by women and men who are not seeking

---

6. Adolf Hitler, *Mein Kampf* (15th ed.; Munich, 1932) 321. Quoted by Schmidt, *Geschichte des Genie-Gedankens*, 2.228.

themselves and their own religious perfection, but are willing to give themselves, their erudition and insight and moral strength for the service of others. Nor is there a place in the world for a chosen race or a chosen nation, powerful in its lording over others; but there is place for a nation that is willing to serve selflessly, giving of its learning and knowledge and wealth to all others.

12

NATURAL LAW (Νόμος Φύσεως) IN GREEK THOUGHT

I

It is widely assumed that the concept of "natural law" is of Greek origin. In treatments of a more general, albeit scholarly, character, one may find statements such as these:

> The early Greek philosophers of natural law had no difficulty in finding an answer on the basis of their pantheistic philosophy.... Stoic philosophy, because of its belief in a well-ordered Cosmos, attempted to revive the original idea of natural law. Still the Stoics had to admit that human laws ... are but imperfect ... realizations of the law of Nature. The idea of a dual order has formed the basis of most natural law speculation ever since.... The [Greek] dualistic theory of law fitted in with the Christian dogma of the Fall of Man and was, therefore, made part of the Christian system of natural law.[1]

Established and dignified assumptions are not easily challenged. Furthermore, there can be little doubt that early Christian, medieval, and modern concepts of natural law include basic elements that are ultimately of Greek origin. My concern in this paper is specifically with the term "law" as it occurs as a component of the legal and moral concept "law of nature."[2] Insofar as this conception also appears under the term "natural rights,"[3] this inquiry is relevant only inasmuch as such natural rights are said to derive from a universal law of nature, which stands over against codified or positive law.

It is questionable whether the assumption that Greek thought ever conceived of the basic moral and legal principles inherent in nature as a universal natural law can be justified. There is, in fact, very little evidence for the occurrence of the term "law of nature" (νόμος φύσεως) in classical Greek texts. The term never appears in any of the fragments of the pre-Socratic philosophers, nor among the Sophists. It is also absent from the extant fragments and writings of the Greek Stoics (with a few exceptions that will

---

1. Friedrich Kessler, "Theoretic Bases of Law," *The University of Chicago Law Review* 9:1 (1941/42): 98–112; quotation from 100–101; for a substantially similar, although more detailed, presentation of the same view see J. L. Adams, "The Law of Nature in Greco-Roman Thought," *JR* 25 (1945) 97–118.

2. For "law of nature" as a term of natural sciences in antiquity see Robert M. Grant, *Miracle and Natural Law in Graeco-Roman and Early Christian Thought* (Amsterdam: North Holland Publishing, 1952).

3. Cf. the German *Naturrecht,* which, however, is largely equivalent to "natural law" = *lex naturalis* or *naturae.*

be discussed below). There is still the possibility that the Pythagoreans and, with quite different connotations, the Epicureans might have used the term; but the scanty sources that are left to us do not permit any firm conclusions.

For the first time in Greek literature the term "law of nature" is liberally employed in the writings of Philo of Alexandria. The question arises, thus, whether the thought of this Jewish philosopher from the first century CE was the melting pot in which the Greek concept of nature as a universal power and the Jewish belief in the universal validity of the divine law coalesced and were amalgamated into the new concept of a "law of nature." It is necessary, however, to note that the Latin equivalent *lex naturalis* occurs even before Philo, and seems to have arisen independently of the formulation of the Greek term νόμος φύσεως.[4]

Since this paper is concerned primarily with Philo of Alexandria, it seems appropriate to dedicate it to the memory of Erwin Goodenough, whose work has contributed so much to Philo scholarship.[5]

II

In pre-Socratic Greek thought the law of the polis was understood to exist by divine sanction and to derive from the one and only divine law, which sustains the existence of all human beings.[6] What one does not find here, however, is the appeal to nature as the source of law. Although the particularity of the existing laws and constitutions is recognized quite early (at least in the 5th century BCE), the conflicts that arise are not seen as the antagonism of particular laws and a "law of nature," but rather as conflicts between the law of the polis and the law of the gods[7] or between written and unwritten law.[8]

In the famous Pindar fragment 169, "According to a law that belongs to nature" (κατὰ νόμον τὸν τῆς φύσεως), a correlation between law and nature is not yet developed. The term "law of nature" is extremely rare, even in the following centuries. The two earliest occurrences are in Plato[9] and in Theophrastus.

In Plato's *Gorgias* 483e, Callicles says about the right of the stronger one that it exists

---

4. On the occurrence of *lex naturae* in Cicero, see below.

5. The paper was read on December 4, 1965, at the Harvard History of Religions Club, of which Erwin Goodenough was a member during the last years of his life.

6. Cf., e.g., Heraclitus frg. 114; see further Hermann Kleinknecht, "νόμος," *TDNT* 4 (1967) 1025ff., and the literature given on pp. 1023–25. See also my article "φύσις," *TDNT* 9 (1974) 251–77.

7. Cf. Rudolf Bultmann, "Polis und Hades in der Antigone des Sophokles," in *Glauben und Verstehen* (4th ed.; Tübingen: Mohr/Siebeck, 1965) 2.20–31.

8. R. Hirzel, "ΑΓΡΑΦΟΣ ΝΟΜΟΣ," *Abhandlungen der Sächsischen Akademie der Wissenschaft* 20 (Leipzig: Teubner, 1900) 65ff.

9. A second occurrence in Plato would be *Tim.* 83e, where disease is said to be παρὰ τοὺς τῆς φύσεως νόμους. Here, however, the term refers to the normal and natural functioning of the body. But even the use of this term for the physical laws of nature is unique. The only other early example is Aristotle's statement that the Pythagoreans speak of numbers as if they had received them παρὰ τῆς φύσεως ὥσπερ νόμους ἐκείνης (*De caelo* 1.1, 268a13); Aristotle himself prefers to use the simple term "nature." On the physical law of nature see further Grant, *Miracle and Natural Law,* 19–28.

"according to the law of the nature" (κατὰ νόμον τὸν τῆς φύσεως). There is no doubt that the phrase here has to be understood, as Leisegang says, as "a paradox, in which the two antonymous terms have been forced together."[10]

Theophrastus frg. 152 says that he who does not give due respect to the divine but is neglectful of "both the laws of the polis and those of nature" (τῶν τε τῆς φύσεως τῶν τε τῆς πόλεως νόμων) has transgressed the two due requirements of righteousness. Obviously the desire to find an all-encompassing formulation and a parallelism with the traditional "laws of the polis" has caused this unusual expression.

But even for the two last pre-Christian centuries it is possible to list only two more occurrences of the term "law of nature" (νόμος τῆς φύσεως); once in the pseudepigraphical work *On Nature* under the name of Ocellus Lucanus[11] (49.23.8, ed. Harder) that has to be dated about 150 BCE, and the second time in a passage in Dionysius of Halicarnassus 3.11.3.[12]

III

As the words "nature" and "law" are terminologically developed and brought into correlation with each other in Greek thought before Plato, they designate two realms of human experience that are quite different in scope and character. They may supplement each other, but more often they are opposed to each other. "Nature" is the realm of self-sustained "natural" things and events, a realm that is not called into being and not ordered by human activity. "Law," on the other hand, does not designate just any law or rule one might find somewhere; but "law" also is a realm, the world of human beings and their activities, customs, morality, and deliberate efforts of ordering.

It was probably in Greek ethnography that the two terms were brought together for the first time.[13] Herodotus uses the term "nature" frequently for the "character" of a country (φύσις τῆς χώρης, Herodotus 2.5[14]) and, in one instance, also of human beings side by side with the term "law": "The Greeks who say this seem to me to be without

---

10. Hans Leisegang, "Physis," PW 20.1144; cf. Grant, *Miracle and Natural Law*, 20.

11. Ocellus is known as a Pythagorean, but this work is certainly spurious and its orientation is peripatetic. The occurrence of this term in "Ocellus," however, is of some interest, since Philo uses "Ocellus" in *De aeternitate mundi*. Yet although Philo shares the view of "Ocellus" that it is "against (the law of) nature" to marry a barren woman (*Spec. leg.* 3.34, 36), there is no indication that he is deriving either this view or the terminology from "Ocellus."

12. On the question of the use of this term in the Stoa see below. An interesting occurrence of the term "law of nature" in the 1st century CE is Dio Chrysostom *Or.* 80.5; here the law of nature that has been forsaken by men is contrasted with written laws and rules engraved in stone.

13. For a detailed study of the origin of the combination and antithesis of the terms see Felix Heinimann, *Nomos und Physis* (Schweizerische Beiträge zur Altertumswissenschaft 1; Basel: Reinhardt, 1945); cf. further Max Pohlenz, "Nomos und Physis," *Hermes* 81 (1953) 418–38.

14. See further 2.19, 35, 68, 71. Possibly Herodotus had learned this usage of the term from Hecataeus; cf. Heinimann, *Nomos und Physis*, 106–7. It is doubtful, however, whether this would also prove that the antithesis νόμος-φύσις had its origin in Ionic natural philosophy, as Heinimann (pp. 40, 107–8) believes; cf. Pohlenz, "Nomos und Physis," 425.

any knowledge of the nature and the laws of the Egyptians" (τῆς Αἰγυπτίων φύσιος καὶ τῶν νόμων, 2.45). But neither this passage nor Sophocles *Ajax* 548–49, which speaks about the habit of life (νόμος) and the character (φύσις) of Ajax, is sufficient evidence to show that the two terms were used antithetically before the Sophists.

A parallel to such an antithetical usage has been seen in Parmenides' antithesis "appearance" and "truth" (δόξα-ἀλήθεια).[15] But this shows a terminological difference, even if in one instance Parmenides can use "it is an accepted convention" (νενόμισται, frg. B 6.8) in contrast to "truth."[16] Any other evidence for the antithesis from pre-Socratic philosophy is even less conclusive. If genuine, Philolaus's "by nature and not by law" (φύσει καὶ οὐ νόμῳ, frg. B 9) would be an early witness; nothing of the context, however, is preserved. Diogenes Laertius 2.16 reports as doctrine of Archelaus, Socrates' teacher, who is said to have introduced Ionic philosophy to Athens, "that the good and the bad is not by nature, but by law" (οὐ φύσει, ἀλλὰ νόμῳ); yet this sharply antithetical formulation probably does not represent Archelaus's own wording but that of the doxographer.[17]

The terminological juxtaposition of νόμος and φύσις is firmly established in one of the oldest writings of the Hippocratic corpus, *De aere aquis locis* (ca. 430 BCE): the author wants to discuss only those nations that differ widely "both in their nature and in their conventions" (ἢ φύσει ἢ νόμῳ, 14). Quite different from the use of these terms in ethnography, "law" and "nature" here are not understood as descriptive but as causal categories. They are the ultimate reasons for the development of different features in the character of various people. At the same time, νόμος and φύσις are clearly distinguished as factors of quite different properties. They can also be seen in conflict with each other, for example, in the description of the courage of the Asian people (*De aere aquis locis* 16): If someone is by nature (φύσει πέφυκεν) courageous and noble, his character will soon be changed through the laws (ὑπὸ τῶν νόμων).

The further elaboration of this contrast into a real antithesis was achieved by the Sophists, resulting in the creation of the first formulated doctrines of natural rights of human beings (not, however, of natural law!). Not only is there no evidence for the term "law of nature" in the extant fragments of the Greek Sophists, but such a concept could not have found any place whatever in their teachings. Law and nature are mutually exclusive. The best extant example is the Antiphon fragment *Pap. Oxy.* 11.1364 (frg. B 44 A in Diels). The contrast is between "that which pertains to the laws" (τὰ τῶν νόμων) and "that which pertains to nature" (τὰ τῆς φύσεως). Even when the transgression of the laws and its consequences are contrasted to the violation of the things pertaining to nature, Antiphon never conceives of the latter as if they were something like laws in their own right, albeit of a different order. On the contrary, what pertains to nature does not have the character of "law." Nature's ways are "of necessity" (ἀναγκαῖα, not

---

15. Cf. Karl Reinhardt, *Parmenides und die Geschichte der griechischen Philosophie* (2d ed.; Frankfurt: Klostermann, 1959) 81–88.

16. Werner Jaeger, *Theology of the Early Greek Philosophers,* trans. Edward S. Robinson (Oxford: Clarendon, 1947) 251 n. 69, believes that here we have a prefiguration of the later antithesis νόμος-φύσις. For νόμος as "convention" in contrast to "truth" cf. Heinimann, *Nomos und Physis,* 85–89.

17. Cf. Heinimann, *Nomos und Physis,* 110–14; Pohlenz, "Nomos und Physis," 432–33.

"ordered," ἐπίθετα); they have come about "through natural growth" (φύντα, not "by common agreement," ὁμολογηθέντα), are "ingrown in human nature" (σύμφυτα), and their violation implies disaster as a natural consequence, that is, laws regulating punishment would be superfluous for nature's trials. Of course, nature requires that human beings should give to their lives a certain direction. This, however, is not identical with the recognition of any laws, whatever their character may be, but is rather the insight into the true conditions of human nature, namely that "by nature we are all equal" (πάντα πάντες ὁμοίως πεφύκαμεν)—since all human beings are breathing with nose and mouth—and thus we can recognize "the things which are by nature necessary for all human beings" (τὰ τῶν φύσει ὄντων ἀναγκαίων πᾶσιν ἀνθρώποις).[18]

It seems to me that the limited intention and function of these teachings of the Sophists are often overlooked. What they have said, of course, implies nothing less than the discovery of the one and common nature of all humans. Consequently they fight against artificially established political and social distinctions, which are controlled by the laws that give specific rights to certain classes, cities, and nations, and deny the same rights to others. But they do not speak of nature as if it were a divine lawgiver. In their concept of education, the Sophists share with earlier philosophers—and elaborate even further—the threefold schema of φύσις, ἄσκησις, and διδασκαλία (cf. Protagoras, frgs. B 3 and B 10), and men like Plato have no quarrel with the Sophists at this point.[19] Furthermore, Plato's and Aristotle's criticism of the Sophists never implies that their nature doctrines lead to dangerous consequences for legislation, but rather that any concept of nature is completely mute with respect to legislation. The Sophists, Plato, and Aristotle agree that anything like a law of nature would be absurd. Plato and Aristotle differ from the Sophists in their rejection of the concept of "the right life according to nature" (κατὰ φύσιν ὀρθὸς βίος, Plato *Leges* 10.890a) and in their emphasis upon the necessity of law for the education (*paideia*) of human beings. Law, however, has its origin not in nature, but in the "mind and reason" (νοῦς and λόγος): law originates from the "mind according to reason" (νοῦς κατὰ ὀρθὸν λόγον, Plato *Leges* 10.890d).

Aristotle emphasizes that no virtues for moral and political action can be derived from nature (οὐδεμία τῶν ἠλικῶν ἀρετῶν φύσει ἡμῖν ἐγγίνεται, *Eth. Nic.* 2.1, 1103a19). Virtue and vice are independent of nature: "we are empowered by nature, but we are not become good or bad according to nature" (δυνατοὶ μέν ἐσμεν φύσει, ἀγαθοὶ δὲ ἢ κακοὶ οὐ γινόμεθα φύσει, *Eth. Nic.* 2.4, p. 1106 a 9–10). Although one may speak of a "physical right" (δίκαιον φυσικόν), to which, for example, belongs love between husband and wife (cf. *Eth. Nic.* 5.10, p. 1134b), the knowledge of virtue belongs to the Logos that nature has given to human beings for this purpose (*Polit.* 1.2, p. 1253 a 9ff.). To be sure, it was nature who endowed humanity with the Logos, and thus a human being is "by nature a political animal" (φύσει πολιτικὸν ζῷον, *Polit* 1.2, p. 1253 a 2–3). But far from drawing from nature any criteria or laws, Logos and Nous, as the true sources of law and art (τέχνη), are rather the fulfillment of "nature's purpose" (τῆς φύσεως τέλος, *Polit.* 7.15, p. 1334 b 14–15).

---

18. The characterization of the Sophists' teaching about nature in the statement of Hippias in Plato's *Protagoras* 337 c–d is essentially the same.

19. Cf., e.g., Plato *Res Publica* 2.374 e; but also Aristotle *Polit.* 7.13, 1332a39–40.

IV

The goal of Stoic philosophy was to overcome the split between φύσις and λόγος. This certainly had to include reconciliation of φύσις and τέχνη = the human ability to create things through the mind and skill: Nature is the master technician whom humans imitate. Whether such a view also implied the reconciliation of φύσις and νόμος is more than doubtful. Νόμος is a social and political category. Concerns in this realm, for the Stoics, were only preliminary and without ultimate value. The real concern for the truly wise man was with the positive correlation of reason and nature (λόγος and φύσις), whereas the relation of law and nature was still seen as an irreconcilable antithesis.

It is necessary to emphasize here that the oldest form of the Stoic Telos formula in Zeno does not contain the term φύσις but was simply: τέλος τὸ ὁμολογουμένως ζῆν,[20] and is to be translated "to live in agreement with the Logos."[21] Zeno's aim was to express the agreement with a person's essential self, that is, the Logos. The intention of the formula, thus, is to express harmony qua harmony and not agreement with something else outside as, for example, with certain laws of nature. It was Cleanthes who added to Zeno's formula the term φύσις, thereby eliminating the awkwardness of Zeno's impossible etymology of ὁμολογουμένως = "in harmony with the Logos" and creating what was to become the classical form of the Telos formula: "The goal is to live in harmony with nature" (τέλος ἐστὶ τὸ ὁμολογουμένως τῇ φύσει ζῆν).[22] Through this alteration the divine nature of all things, rather than the specific nature of humanity (the Logos), became the ultimate criterion for human moral decision. The divine nature of all things, however, is by no means identical with the external world of natural appearances. As the further development of the Telos formula demonstrates, "according to nature" means "according to human nature which is reason"; see, for example, Panaetius: "to live according to the inclinations that are given to us by nature (ἐκ φύσεως ἀφορμαί),"[23] similarly in Epictetus, where "to live according to nature" is understood as "to live λογικῶς" = "after the manner of the Logos" (*Diss.* 3.1.25). The Logos that humans have received from their nature and that thereby is their true "nature" enables them to the right use of the perceptions (χρῆσις τῶν φαντασιῶν, *Diss.* 1.28.12) and thus to find their moral purpose (προαίρεσις, *Diss.* 1.14.18). Consequently, human beings find their true nature in the agreement with internalized reason.

---

20. Johannes von Arnim, *Stoicorum Veterum Fragmenta* (3 vols.; Leipzig: Teubner, 1903–1905) 1.54.24; for the history and interpretation of the Telos formula cf. Max Pohlenz, *Die Stoa* (Göttingen: Vandenhoeck & Ruprecht, 1948) 1.116; vol. 2 (2d ed. 1955) 67; Günther Bornkamm, "ΟΜΟΛΟΓΙΑ," *Hermes* 71 (1936) 338–93; Hans Jonas, *Augustin und das paulinische Freiheitsproblem* (2d ed.; Göttingen: Vandenhoeck & Ruprecht, 1965) 27–29. A useful compilation of the various forms of the Telos formula is given by Clement of Alexandria *Strom.* 2.129.1ff.

21. It is known that Zeno understood the word ὁμολογουμένως (= "conformably," "admittedly") to express the thought "conforming with the logos," or he may have understood the word to mean simply "to live consistently."

22. Cleanthes frg. 552, von Arnim 1.125, 18ff.

23. Quoted in Clement of Alexandria *Strom.* 2.129; cf. also: "All humans by nature have inclinations toward virtue" (Cleanthes frg. 566; von Arnim 1.129, 18–19).

At the same time, moral decision is primarily characterized in its form, but not in its content, according to an explicit code of moral values. The question as to the content of the life "according to nature" is answered by the statement that it is righteousness that comes from God and out of the "common nature" (κοινὴ φύσις).[24] If the goal is "to do everything in our power, continuously and steadfastly, in order to achieve what is principally according to [our] nature" (τῶν προηγουμένων κατὰ φύσιν),[25] then the goal is found in humans acting according to nature as such and in the development of their own nature, but not in the things that are according to nature in the manner of independent or external laws of moral values.[26] Following this maxim, humans do not transcend their own self through an encounter with a greater challenge, but only become what they already are.

It is not surprising to find that Stoicism would not attempt to produce any independent set of moral values and would not establish the claim to possess the knowledge of the law of nature in any way whatsoever. It is "according to nature" that human beings accept their social and political role, whatever that may happen to be (general, husband, father, etc.), that is, Stoicism accepts any existing order, and only requires that human beings in such a state behave "according to nature" (ἐν τούτῃ τῇ ὕλῃ κατὰ φύσιν ἔχοντα αὐτὸν τηρεῖν, Epictetus *Diss.* 4.5.6). And to say that it is against nature (παρὰ φύσιν) if a man goes to bed with his neighbor's wife and destroys his marriage[27] does not require recourse to any doctrine of natural law—and no Stoic believed that it did.

The term "natural law" is, thus, almost totally absent from Stoic writings. It is quite certain that Zeno never used this term. He, as well as Chrysippus, would rather speak of the "right reason" (λόγος ὀρθός),[28] although Chrysippus could say that the "what is just" (δίκαιον) does not exist on the basis of arbitrary determination (θέσει) but on the basis of nature (φύσει), as do the νόμος and the right reason (ὀρθὸς λόγος).[29] Only one passage approaches the term "law of nature": "The world is the city of gods and human beings, since they share the fellowship of the Logos that is law by nature" (ὅς ἐστι φύσει νόμος). This passage, however, is of a somewhat doubtful origin; it is quoted by Eusebius *Praep. ev.* 15.15 from Arius Didymus, a first-century CE doxographer, although it is commonly ascribed to Chrysippus.[30]

All evidence for the concept "natural law" in Stoicism comes from Cicero or from Philo. Cicero (*De nat. deor.* 1.36) says: "Zeno says that the natural law is divine and that

---

24. Chrysippus frg. 68 (von Arnim 2.17, 4–7); frg. 326 (von Arnim 3.80, 34–36). Cf. also the frequent identification of τὸ κατὰ φύσιν ζῆν with τὸ καλῶς ζῆν, τὸ καλὸν κἀγαθόν, ἀρετὴ καὶ τὸ μέτοχον ἀρετῆς, e.g., von Arnim 2.6, 16ff.; 6, 7ff.

25. Antipater frg. 57 (von Arnim 3.252, 39–53, 1).

26. The moral orientation according to the appearances of external nature are only τὰ πρῶτα κατὰ φύσιν (like health, strength, etc.), and thus only a preliminary stage toward the things that are truly according to nature, i.e., τὰ περὶ τὴν ψυχὴν κατὰ φύσιν ὄντα. Cf. von Arnim 3.34, 14–18; 33, 14–16.

27. Zeno frg. 244 (von Arnim 1.58, 13–15).

28. There is overwhelming evidence for the technical use of these two terms in Stoic writings; cf. von Arnim 1.43ff., 2–3; 81, 23–24; 158, 10–11, 18–20.

29. Frg. 308 (von Arnim 3.76, 4–5).

30. Von Arnim 2.169, 26–29.

it commands to acquire what is right and to prohibit what is the opposite" (Zeno naturalem legem divinam esse censet eamque vim obtinere recta imperantem prohibitenque contraria).[31] It has already been observed that other Latin sources for the same sentence of Zeno (Lactantius *Instit. div.* 1.5 and Minucius Felix *Octavio* 19.10) are dependent upon Cicero and thus have no value as independent witnesses.[32] This quote from Cicero is obviously a translation of the frequently quoted Stoic sentence about the "constitution" (νόμος) of the universe that is said to be the "right reason" (λόγος ὀρθός) or "the reason of nature that champions on the one hand what should be done and on the other hand forbids what should not be done" (λόγος φύσεως προστακτικὸς μὲν ὧν πρακτέον, ἀπαγορευτικὸς δὲ ὧν οὐ ποιητέον),[33] which otherwise, even in Cicero, is translated with "the law is the highest reason" (*lex est ratio summa*), or "the right reason" (*recta ratio*).[34] In particular the Greek phrase λόγος φύσεως ("natural reason") apparently has given rise to the Latin *lex naturalis* ("natural law"), since the precise translation *ratio naturae* ("natural reason") seems to be absent from Latin Stoic sources. Thus what actually corresponds to the Latin *lex* in the term *lex naturalis* is not the Greek term νόμος ("law"), but the Greek term λόγος ("reason").

There are, in fact, two occurrences of νόμος φύσεως ("law of nature") in Epictetus (*Diss.* 1.29.19 and 2.17.6). In both instances Epictetus quotes as a law of nature the same proverbial triviality, namely that the one who has something has more than the one who has nothing (τὸν κρείττονα τοῦ χείρονος πλέον ἔχειν). This confirms that, even in Stoic thought, the concept of a "law of nature" that is the superior guide and criterion for morality and institutional law does not exist.

It is true that on occasion "law" (νόμος) can be used to designate the constitution of the universe and the rule through which Zeus governs all things as, for example, in the famous *Zeus Hymn* of Cleanthes: "Zeus, the beginning of the world of nature is from you; and with law you rule over all things" (Ζεῦ, φύσεως ἀρχηγέ, νόμου μέτα πάντα κυβερνῶν).[35] But with respect to moral values, Stoicism has not overcome the deeprooted Greek antithesis of νόμος and φύσις. Neither does nature ever have the status of a divine legislator, although it does have divine dignity in Stoicism; nor could law lose its connotation of existing by "thesis" (i.e., by enacted agreement and contract), and thus it does not quite agree with all things that exist by φύσις.

V

Compared to the rare and problematic occurrences of the term "law of nature" in Greek literature (not even half a dozen in all extant Greek literature of pre-Christian times)

---

31. Cf. von Arnim 1.42, 35–37.

32. Cf. Grant, *Miracle and Natural Law*, 21.

33. Stobaeus *Ecloge* 2.7 (Curtius Wachsmuth and Otto Hense, eds., *Joannis Stobaei Anthologium* [Berlin: Weidmann, 1884], 96 = von Arnim 3.158, 11–13); Philo *De Josepho* 29 (= von Arnim 3.79, 38–41); cf. Clement of Alexandria *Strom.* 2.166, 5 where Clement refers to those who identify λόγος ὀρθός with the law of the Old Testament.

34. Cicero *De legibus* 1.6, 18; 15,42 (= von Arnim 3.78, 2.4; 79, 9).

35. Von Arnim 1.121, 35.

the evidence from Philo of Alexandria is overwhelming: there are at least thirty occurrences of "law of nature" (νόμος φύσεως) in his works; in addition there are numerous equivalent formulations such as "ordinances of nature" (θεσμοὶ φύσεως), "edict of nature" (διάταγμα φύσεως), and prescriptions of nature" (νόμιμα φύσεως).

As we have seen, it is not possible to posit a Greek background for Philo's frequent use of the term "law of nature,"[36] and it seems more advisable to understand this term as a fruit of Philo's efforts to unite basic elements of Jewish tradition with the inheritance of Greek thought. Does the formulation of the concept "law of nature" have its origin in this process of amalgamation of Greek and Jewish thought? In order to answer this question it is convenient to begin with a few remarks about the term "nature" in Philo's writings.

As is well known, the Greek term φύσις ("nature") has no Hebrew equivalent in the Old Testament. The word occurs more or less occasionally only in such books of the Septuagint that were composed originally in Greek (Wisdom of Solomon, *3* and *4 Maccabees*). It is also used in a few passages of the *Testaments of the Twelve Patriarchs*, notably in *T. Naph.* 3.4–5, which says that the order of nature (τάξις φύσεως) has been perverted by the guardians of Gen 6:1–6 and by the Sodomites. It is quite typical that this refers to sexual perversion, which is perhaps the only violation of a moral value that, ever since Plato, has been characterized consistently as "against nature" (παρὰ φύσιν).[37]

Philo is the first Jewish writer who uses the word "nature" more frequently and more specifically. In fact, "nature" is one of the most regularly employed terms throughout his writings. In this usage it is also apparent that Philo has directly borrowed a number of specific meanings and particular connotations from Greek philosophical conceptions of nature, notably from Aristotle.[38] Nevertheless, the Greek concept of nature in the process of this adaptation has been reevaluated. In Philo the Aristotelian conception of the "creator nature" (*natura creatrix*) was combined with the Jewish belief in the Creator God. Thus the Greek view of the universe as an impersonal yet harmonious and inventive nature was merged with the Old Testament doctrine of creation.

Erwin Goodenough has shown that there are numerous occasions where Philo's discourse about nature, almost unnoticed, passes over into speaking about God, and vice versa.[39] One example must suffice: "Nature gives a thousand gifts to humans, although she has no part in them; she is unborn, yet gives birth, etc. . . . [she gives] a happy old age and a happy death, and yet in neither has nature any share. . . . Even the phrase 'as a man' (Deut 1:31) is not used of God in the literal sense. . . . Separate, therefore, my soul,

---

36. It is very unlikely that Philo should have developed his concept of the law of nature on the basis of any of the very rare occurrences of this term in older Greek literature, even if he knew "Ocellus," who uses the term once in a way very similar to Philo's usage; see above, n. 11.

37. Against homosexual intercourse see Plato *Leges* 8.836c; cf. 2.636b; Josephus *Contra Apion* 2.273; Athenaeus 13, 605d; and more often.

38. On the use of the term φύσις in Philo, see especially Erwin Goodenough, *By Light Light* (New Haven: Yale University Press, 1932) 501–2 and passim; Harry Austrin Wolfson, *Philo* (2 vols.; Cambridge: Harvard University Press, 1947–48) 1.332–47; 2.165–200.

39. *By Light Light,* 51.

all that is created, mortal, mutable, profane, from thy conception of God, the uncreated, the immutable, the immortal" (*Sacr.* 98ff.).[40]

Thus the predicates that are allotted to God can also be given to nature, and the terms "God" and "nature" are often interchangeable. Traditional statements about the divine creation and preservation of the world, regardless of their Greek or Jewish provenience, are sometimes assigned to nature, sometimes to God. The creation of the world by God is interpreted in terms of Aristotle's description of the *natura creatrix*,[41] and about the creation of humans Philo can say that nature created all human beings free (*Vit. cont.* 70)—a clear reflection of a sophistic tenet. On the other hand, statements about God's ordering of the world by means of legislation (before and through Moses) can now be described as activities of "nature."[42]

In this syncretistic process of adaptation of Greek concepts the notions of a divine legislator and of a divinely sanctioned law are apparently a genuinely Jewish contribution. This can be observed in the adjustments that Philo makes in his reproductions of Stoic concepts.

In *Jos.* 29–31 Philo reproduces the well-known Stoic topic about the world, the megalopolis of gods and human beings. He repeats the traditional statement that the "(right) reason of nature" ([ὀρθὸς] λόγος φύσεως) is the constitution and law (πολιτεία and νόμος) of this city. But then he introduces the term "ordinances of nature" (θεσμοὶ φύσεως) when he speaks about the rejection of the laws of the universe by human beings and their replacement by human-made laws. The use of θεσμός in this context is striking, since it is an archaic word that denotes the act of divine or human legislation (e.g., by Solon, or in such terms as θεσμοὶ ἀρχαῖοι, πάτριοι θεσμοί).[43] It was not a word in ordinary usage in Hellenistic Greek,[44] and the older Stoics did not use it.[45] This is not surprising since θεσμός refers to an act of legislation and implies the notion of a lawgiver that would not accord with the Stoic concept of the "right reason of nature" (ὀρθὸς λόγος φύσεως, cf. also Chrysippus's statement: φύσει τε τὸ δίκαιον εἶναι καὶ μὴ θέσει).[46]

In another passage, *Op. mun.* 143, Philo is even more explicit. After the mention of the "right reason of nature" as the constitution of the universe, he adds: "this should be more properly called ordinances (θεσμοί), since it is a divine law (νόμος θεῖος ὤν), in accordance with which there was duly apportioned to all existences that which falls to

---

40. Other instances are *Rer. div. her.* 114–16; *Fuga* 170–72; *Spec. leg.* 2.172–73.

41. Cf. Goodenough, *By Light Light,* 51.

42. There is a conflicting concept in Philo where he sees "nature" as subject to God, limited, and inferior. But this is not our concern here.

43. Cf. LSJ s.v.

44. Friedrich Preisigke (*Wörterbuch der griechischen Papyrusurkunden* [Berlin: Selbstverlag der Erben, 1925] s.v.) lists only an occurrence of the word in a Byzantine papyrus.

45. Von Arnim lists two occurrences; one of them (3.82, 32) is a passage from Philo (*Op. mun.* 143; see below); the second is Dio Chrysostom's reproduction of the above Stoic topic (3.82, 18) where θεσμός is used parallel to νόμος. This writer, who flourished half a century after Philo, is also the first pagan writer to use the term "law of nature" in a pregnant sense (although there is only one occurrence of the term in his writings; see above n. 12).

46. Von Arnim 3.76, 4–5.

them severally." It is unmistakable that Philo prefers the terms νόμος and θεσμός as also his concept in these passages is quite un-Stoic. Goodenough has already observed, commenting on *Op. mun.* 143, that nature here is not the nature of things, but it is the nature of God, who stands in direct opposition to the world of existing things and imposes his law upon them.[47] The law of nature is not an immanent law, but it is the law of the transcendent Creator who rules his creation "through the laws and ordinances of nature" (φύσεως νόμοις καὶ θεσμοῖς, *Op. mun.* 171).[48]

If Philo can speak of "following nature" (φύσει ἕπεσθαι, ἀκολουθία) as the truly right way of life, distinguished from those things that often people suppose to be right (*Spec. leg.* 4.46), he is simply quoting a common Stoic thought. However, instead of juxtaposing the ever-changing laws of the nations with nature,[49] Philo also contrasts these human laws with the laws (νόμιμα)[50] of Moses, "which stand firm, unshaken . . . stamped with the seals of nature herself" (*Vit. Mos.* 2.13–14).

There can be no doubt that for Philo the law of nature is the Torah, and that the new term "law of nature" was designed to express a new concept that did not exist before in the Hellenistic world: "that the Father and Maker of the world was in the truest sense also its Lawgiver (νομοθέτης)" and "that he who would observe the laws [νόμοι = law of Moses] will accept gladly the duty of following nature and live in accordance with the ordering of the universe" (*Vit. Mos.* 2.48).[51] Only if one considers the impact of Jewish belief in the law of Moses can one explain that the earliest formulation of natural law in Greek literature can find its appropriate expression in a sentence that is a monstrosity within the Greek concepts of law and nature: "For law is an invention of nature, not of human beings" (νόμος γάρ ἐστι φύσεως εὕρημα ἀλλ᾽ οὐκ ἀνθρώπων, *Q. Gen.* 4.90).[52]

The fundamental Greek antithesis of law and nature is overcome here by virtue of the Jewish belief in the universality of the law of God. The new antithesis has now become that of the "law of nature" and the numerous human laws; this is exemplified in many instances of Philo's writings. He who looks up to semblance (τὸ δοκεῖν) writes up laws that are in opposition to those of nature (νόμους ἐναντίους τοῖς τῆς φύσεως— about Jethro as distinct from Moses, *Ebr.* 37; cf. about Laban, ὃς τοὺς ἀληθεῖς τῆς φύσεως νόμους οὐ κατιδὼν ψευδογραφεῖ τοὺς παρὰ ἀνθρώπους, *Ebr.* 147). In these

---

47. *By Light Light*, 51–52.

48. Cf. *Praem. poen.* 42; *Spec. leg.* 3.189; also the fragment quoted by Eusebius *Praep. ev.* 8.14.3.

49. Cf. *Jos.* 29–31.

50. The term τὰ νόμιμα is again (see above on θεσμός) an archaizing term that was not part of the Stoic vocabulary. It was used in particular as an equivalent of νόμος in the meaning of "customs," "practices" (cf. the title of Aristotle's treatise *Barbarian Customs*) and is thus a precise parallel to νόμος in contrast to φύσις in the terminology of the Greek physicians (see above). The term, however, is frequent in the LXX, usually in the singular as a translation of חֹק and חֻקָּה (especially in the phrase νόμιμον αἰώνιον, Exod 12:14, 17; 27:21; etc.), a few times in the plural for תּוֹרֹת (Gen 26:5; Jer 33:4; Ezek 43:11; 44:5, 24; etc.).

51. Translation by F. H. Colson in LCL.

52. On the other hand, Philo is fully aware of the traditional Greek distinctions. He employs them, e.g., in the interpretation of the words προστάγματα, ἐντολαί, δικαιώματα, νόμιμα, Gen. 26:5, where he says that "the δικαιώματα exist φύσει but the νόμιμα exist θέσει, thus, since things existing by nature are older than those existing by convention, that which is right (τὸ δίκαιον) is older than the law" (*Q. Gen.* 4.184).

passages, the traditional Greek contrast between written and unwritten law is renewed; that the law of Moses, the representative of the true law of nature, is also written is only for the benefit of later generations. In the true sense, it is written on the "tables of nature" (*Spec. leg.* 1.31; cf. *Abr.* 60).

On the other hand, the contrast to the obedience to the law of nature can also be described in traditional Jewish terms of sin and disobedience (cf. *Somn.* 2.174; παρανομεῖν, *Spec. leg.* 1.155).[53] Fulfillment of the law is at the same time understood as harmony with nature. But although Philo uses the Stoic term "right reason of nature" (ὀρθὸς λόγος τῆς φύσεως) in this context, he does not intend to suggest the Stoic thought of harmony with one's own true self. The logos of nature is that which pours out ablutions into the souls of those who love God (*Spec. leg.* 1.191); thus harmony is agreement with the divinely ordained "laws and ordinances of nature" (νόμοι καὶ θεσμοὶ τῆς φύσεως) in a life truly blameless with respect to the law of God (*Spec. leg.* 1.202).

When Philo speaks about the life that follows nature, the men of old are his primary examples, especially Abraham, whose life and obedience are often described in well-known Greek terms. When "Abraham journeys, even as the Lord spoke to him," he "follows nature," the aim extolled by the best philosophers (τὸ ἀκολούθως τῇ φύσει, *Migr. Abr.* 127–28).[54] But this does not mean that Abraham is subject to a guide other than the Torah, even though he sojourned before Moses gave the law. It is precisely the Torah as the divine law of nature that is his guide: "the unwritten law that nature has ordained" (ἄγραφος νόμος, ὃν ἡ φύσις ἔθηκε, *Abr.* 16). The Greek notion of an unwritten law is strangely altered in this formulation, since it is presented as the result of a divine legislation, which includes all laws and commands (i.e., of the Torah), albeit unwritten. Thus Abraham is characterized by a passage that recalls typical Greek phrases but actually describes an exemplary observer of the law of the Bible. Moses confirms that "this man did the divine law and all the divine commands" (τὸν θεῖον νόμον καὶ τὰ θεῖα προστάγματα πάντα); "he was not taught by written words, but by unwritten nature" (οὐ γράμμασιν ἀναδιδαχθείς, ἀλλ᾽ ἀγράφῳ τῇ φύσει); "he was law-abiding" (νόμιμος), "being himself law and unwritten statute" (νόμος αὐτὸς ὢν καὶ θεσμὸς ἄγραφος, *Abr.* 275–76).

However, this theory about the unwritten Torah being available to the men of old before the legislation of Moses does not serve as merely a convenient stopgap for that period in history between creation and Moses. The theory has much wider ramifications and consequences for the understanding of law and of a truly law-abiding life. It produces the extremely momentous insight that a true law of nature is in fact an ultimately superior criterion for the life of the truly wise man. Thus Philo's aim is to show that such a divine law is recognizable, if only one can synthesize the (Greek) concept

---

53. When Philo says here that παρανομεῖν carries its punishment in itself, he repeats a Sophistic sentence about the violation of the things of nature.

54. The same sentence is quoted with explicit reference to Zeno in *Omn. prob. lib.* 160; cf. *Plant.* 49. Furthermore cf. *Vit. Mos.* 1.48 about Moses, who had set before himself the ὀρθὸς τῆς φύσεως λόγος as the only source and fountain of virtues.

of nature's right reason and the (Jewish) knowledge of the Torah of God—those two seen as one: the "law of nature."

Such a synthesis is present and personified in the men of old who lived "according to the law, the right reason of nature" (κατὰ νόμον, τὸν ὀρθὸν φύσεως λόγον, *Omn. prob. lib.* 62). Especially Philo's introduction to his treatise on Abraham sets forth the principles of this concept (*Abr.* 3–6): The more universal (καθολικώτεροι) laws are those that existed before the written legislation of Moses. They are the originals (ἀρχέτυποι) of the particular laws given through Moses, which Philo calls their copies (εἰκόνες). Since the men of old have followed the archetypal unwritten legislation (ἄγραφος νομοθεσία), holding that nature itself was the most ancient statute (τὴν φύσιν αὐτὴν πρεσβύτατον θεσμὸν εἶναι), these men are "rational laws endowed in their souls" (ἔμψυχοι καὶ λογικοὶ νόμοι). The particular and written legislation of Moses appears as that which is "not inconsistent with nature" (τὰ τεθειμένα διατάγματα τῆς φύσεως οὐκ ἀπᾴδει).

But this particular legislation did not preclude the possibility of direct access to the laws of nature; on the contrary, it is the immediate representative of nature's law and leads the wise man into the following of nature; see, for example, Philo's conclusion about the meaning of the first commandment: God gave this commandment to lead the human race "that following nature (ἕπεσθαι τῇ φύσει) they might win the best of goals (τέλος!), knowledge of him that truly is" (*Decal.* 81; cf. *Poster. C.* 185). A righteous man is one who follows nature and its ordinances (*Spec. leg.* 2.42). The law-abiding true citizen of the world regulates his doings by the will of nature (βούλημα τῆς φύσεως, *Op. mun.* 3).

There is perhaps one particular reason for the designation of the Torah as the law of nature. Since this is the archetypal law it is part of the world of reason as distinct from the sphere of sense perception. In this respect Philo's concept of the law of nature is an integral part of the Platonic (not Stoic) structure of his philosophy. It is, therefore, specifically the mind (νοῦς) that is taught by the law of nature and therefore enabled to guide the soul (*Agric.* 66). Obedience to the laws of nature is identical with pruning away the superfluous passions from the mind (ἡγεμονικόν, *Spec. leg.* 1.305–6; cf. 1.191).

But on the whole, this Philonic identification of Torah, divine order, and nature's law is rooted in his understanding of the unity of all realms of human experience. The Greek concept of the world assigned fundamentally different qualities to the two realms of human experience, to the realm of human activity—the law—on the one hand, and to the world of nature on the other; and even the monistic system of the Stoics was unable to overcome this dichotomy, or rather: the Stoics sacrificed large portions of the realm of law, since they declared that the region of political and social involvement was ultimately irrelevant. Philo, on the contrary, knows only one realm of human experience, which can be variously characterized either through his concept of God, or through the investigation of nature, or through the interpretation of the legislation of Moses. But in every case, the one and only unifying principle remains the Torah, the law par excellence.[55]

---

55. On this Jewish apologetic concept of the Torah in which the "basic identity of the understanding of God, world, and human existence is defined," see Günther Bornkamm, "Die Offenbarung des Zornes Gottes,"

A final problem that has to concern us is the question of the particular content of specific laws of nature, or specific implications of the law of nature, to which Philo refers on many occasions. That there will be any individual sets of commandments that are law or laws of nature in particular seems to be quite unlikely.[56]

That the law of nature is understood as the law of numbers may reveal Pythagorean influence upon Philo.[57] According to the laws of nature, the number 6 is most suitable for productivity, thus the creation of the world in six days (*Op. mun.* 13). Since 6 is 3 times 2 (= male and female), "these two were the source of origin κατὰ φύσεως θεσμοὺς ἀκινήτους" (*Spec. leg.* 2.58).[58] The celebration of the seventh day, accordingly, was ordered by Moses for all who were inscribed on his holy roll of citizenship (of the universe) and who followed the "ordinances of nature" (θεσμοὶ φύσεως, *Vit. Mos.* 2.211).

Specific structures in the functioning of the world or in the life of human beings are often called "laws of nature." Sometimes such structures are part of Philo's philosophical and theological tenets, and not necessarily the result of his observation of nature.[59] Thus sense perception appears as the handmaiden of reason "by the laws of nature" (*Vit. Mos.* 2.81).[60] That the Creator cares for the creation since this is necessary because of nature's laws and ordinances (*Opif. mun.* 171; *Praem. poen.* 42)[61] is primarily a theological sentence, even if it is supported by the reference to parents who normally care for their children.[62]

---

in *Das Ende des Gesetzes* (2d ed.; Munich: Kaiser, 1958) 14–15. Goodenough (*By Light Light,* 49) has emphasized that nature and its laws sometimes seem to be placed above the Torah and the world, and, on occasion, even above God; but it appears to me that these observations only describe inconsistencies of secondary importance and functional distinctions; this is the case, e.g., when the relation of the archetypal law to the legislation of Moses is seen in terms of a Platonic schema.

56. About the relationship of Philo's laws of nature to the so-called Noachite laws, cf. Wolfson, *Philo* 2.183–87. Although a certain similarity cannot be denied, the scope of Philo's term is much wider. One might also ask whether the rabbinic concept of the Noachite laws is related to Philo insofar as both depend upon the tradition of Jewish apologetics.

57. Goodenough (*By Light Light,* 52–53) has pointed out that this challenges the sovereignty of God, since even God, in his work of creation, is subject to the superior rule of certain numerical laws. This consequence is, of course, not intended by Philo.

58. On the male-female principle cf. also *Spec. leg.* 2.29–30; *Ebr.* 33–34.

59. There are also some general rules that Philo calls "law of nature," e.g., that the place of creation is in all respects lower than the Creator, since that which is made is later than its maker (*Plant.* 132); or: "the wise man by the law of nature has all fools in subjection" (*Omn. prob. lib.* 30). These rules are similar to the law about superiority and inferiority, which is called a law of nature in Epictetus. In those instances Philo is perhaps reflecting a proverbial usage of the term; cf. also the quotation of the people's excuse for the suicide of Tiberius Gemellus forced by Gaius: "Sovereignty cannot be shared; that is a θεσμὸς φύσεως ἀκίνητος" (*Leg. Gaj.* 68).

60. Cf. also the reference to the Virgin Charites (representing the four faculties of king, lawgiver, high priest, and prophet, as they are combined in Moses) "which an immovable law of nature forbids to be separated" (*Vit. Mos.* 2.7).

61. Different is *Spec. leg.* 3.189, where Philo speaks of the Creator's care for his creation by means of the law of nature; cf. the fragment in Eusebius *Praep. ev.* 8.14.3.

62. That "his creation is itself necessitated by a Law of Nature which seems to antecede it, at least logically" (Goodenough, *By Light Light,* 53), is, of course, quite right; but this statement only emphasizes the harmony that is part of Philo's unity of the understanding of God, nature, and law.

But usually the commonsense observation of the natural order is the main point of reference, for example, in the statement about the firmly established seasons for fruits and crops, established by nature (φύσεως προθεσμία, *Spec. leg.* 4.208; φύσεως νόμιμα, ibid., 212; or φύσεως θεσμοί, ibid., 215).

Here, as well as in the following instances, the reference to the laws of nature purports to argue that certain laws given by Moses are absolutely necessary and indispensable. In the interpretation of Exod 23:26a ("No one shall miscarry or be barren in your land") Philo relates Moses' and nature's law in a very characteristic way that, again, expresses the harmony of his understanding of law, nature, and humans: For those who keep the divine writing of the law, God "grants as a prize the more ancient law of immortal nature" (παρέχει τὸν ἀρχαιότερον νόμον τῆς ἀθανάτου φύσεως), that is, the begetting of sons and the perpetuity of the race (*Q. Exod.* 2.19). At the same time, the injunction to produce children is called a "law of nature" (*Praem. poen.* 108; cf. *Abr.* 249; *Spec. leg.* 2.233).[63]

Other laws that are based on the law of nature in a similar way are: the law of inheritance, from parents to children and not vice versa, since children do not naturally die before their parents (*Vit. Mos.* 2.245; cf. *Migr. Abr.* 94).[64] The law against killing infants at birth is given, since to do this would tear down what nature builds up, and this violates the laws of nature (*Virt.* 132; *Spec. leg.* 3.112). A similar argument appears with respect to the general law against killing (*Decal.* 132).

In a great number of instances Philo uses the traditional Greek phrases κατὰ φύσιν ("according to nature") and παρὰ φύσιν ("against nature") in his discussion of the laws given by Moses, although it is not possible to discuss these passages in detail in this context. These two terms in Philo became precise equivalents of "lawful" (νόμιμος, etc.) and "unlawful" (ἄνομος, etc.). It is remarkable, however, that in Philo the use of κατὰ/παρὰ φύσιν in the moral sense is not limited to sexual matters, as is normally the case in Greek literature.[65] However, this is one of the three topics in which Philo continues the traditional Greek reference to nature. The other two are arguments against the breeding of animals of different species and against slavery. But in these cases as well, the use of the term "law of nature" is specifically Philonic.[66]

With the designation of the sin of the Sodomites as a violation of the law of nature, Philo repeats a traditional argument of Jewish apologetics (*Abr.* 135).[67] Similarly, the passions of love between man and woman are described as the fulfillment of the laws of nature; the opposite is homosexuality (*Vit. cont.* 59).[68]

---

63. See also the reason for the law against touching a woman when the menstrual issue occurs, since the seed would be wasted; thus this law was given in order to respect the law of nature (*Spec. leg.* 3.32).

64. Cf. also the use of the term νόμος φύσεως opposed to the ἀνομία among men in the allegory about the right of the firstborn who represents virtue, *Sobr.* 25.

65. Cf., e.g., Diodorus Siculus 32.10.4; Athenaeus 13, 605d; also Josephus *Contra Apion* 2.273.

66. See the different terms in a corresponding usage in one instance in Plato with respect to sexual morality: to introduce a law against homosexuality ἀκολουθῶν τῇ φύσει, Plato *Leg.* 8.836c.

67. Cf. *T. Naph.* 3.4–3.

68. In another instance Philo says that men who belie their sex are affected with effeminateness, since

Philo also calls it a law of nature that unequal animals should not be yoked together (*Spec. leg.* 4.204; cf. Deut 22:10). But he goes further than the Mosaic law suggests when he not only repeats the injunction against breeding different kinds of animals (Lev 19:19), since it is against a δόγμα φύσεως to do so (*Spec. leg.* 3.46), but also applies this specifically to the breeding of mules (*Spec. leg.* 3.47). In this specification of the law, Philo perhaps depends upon Greek tradition, since Aristotle had already pointed out that it is against nature for a horse to beget a mule.[69]

Also the interpretation of the law against slavery reveals Greek influence upon Philo. That nature has borne and reared all humans alike as brothers is an old Sophistic statement[70] that Philo echoes when he describes the Essenes who denounce slaveholders for violating the equality of all humans and act against an ordinance of nature (θεσμὸς φύσεως, *Omn. prob. lib.* 79).[71]

VI

It seems that there can be little doubt that Philo has to be considered as the crucial and most important contributor to the development of the theory of natural law. Most probably, Philo was its creator, at least insofar as the evidence from the Greek literature is in question. Only a philosophical and theological setting in which the Greek concept of nature was fused with the belief in a divine legislator and with a doctrine of the most perfect (written!) law could produce such a theory, and only here could the Greek dichotomy of the two realms of law and nature be overcome. All these conditions are fulfilled in Philo, and the evidence for the development of this theory of the law of nature in Philo is impressive.

The still unanswered problem is the Roman concept of *lex naturalis*, which is apparently developed independently by a productive misunderstanding and mistranslation of a Greek Stoic concept. That this Roman *lex naturalis* later has influenced especially the Latin church as well as Roman and Western law cannot be doubted. I believe, however, that for the further development of the concept of the law of nature in the early church, beginning with Clement of Alexandria and Origen, the Philonic doctrine was the most vital element. To show this, of course, would require a fresh analysis of the pertinent texts.[72] A detailed investigation of the history of Philo's doctrine of the law of

---

they debase "the currency of nature" (τὰ νόμισμα φύσεως, *Spec. leg.* 1.325; cf. 3.38). The same term is used parallel to θεσμὸς φύσεως and ἔπεσθαι in an argument against the beholding of the nakedness of the other sex (*Spec. leg.* 3.176). This argument is, of course, as convincing as St. Paul's argument from nature for the short hair of men and the long hair of women (1 Cor 11:14–15).

69. Aristotle *Metaph.* 7.8, 1033b32–33.

70. Cf. the Antiphon fragment, *Pap. Oxy.* 11.1364 (see above); see also Philemon Comicus 95, 2–6 (T. Kock, *Comicorum Atticorum Fragmenta* [3 vols.; Leipzig, 1880–1888] 2.502).

71. In a similar context (*Omn. prob. lib.* 37), Philo speaks of the νόμοι φύσεως in contrast to the "laws of the lower world."

72. See, however, Pohlenz, *Stoa*, 2.218, 222; Grant, *Miracle and Natural Law,* passim.

nature in the early church is urgently called for, and as far as I can see, it would most probably confirm the results of this study.[73]

Furthermore, the study of the reevaluation of Greek concepts of nature in the light of Philo's doctrine of the law of nature by the church fathers (and also in later pagan writers?)[74] should be a most rewarding task.

---

73. Even a superficial review of the material in question (now more easily accessible through Lampe's *Patristic Greek Lexicon* [Oxford: Clarendon, 1961]) shows a surprisingly great number of echoes from Philonic passages; examples are frequently drawn from the figures of the Old Testament before Moses; and a number of terms that have been reintroduced into the technical vocabulary by Philo, such as θεσμός and νόμιμα (the latter from the LXX), are used very often in these contexts, although they continue to be rare in pagan sources.

74. In this connection it would be most important to evaluate the context and origin of the unique and striking reference to the "law of nature that men have forsaken to follow written laws," in Dio Chrysostom *Or.* 80.5 (referred to above, n. 12). Is Dio Chrysostom dependent upon Philo and Jewish apologetics and propaganda? Or is he influenced by Cicero and Latin Stoic terminology? Or does he just reflect the general temperament of his time?

13

THE CULT OF THE EGYPTIAN
DEITIES IN ASIA MINOR

Evidence for the Egyptian Cult in Pergamon

The Sanctuary of the Red Hall in Pergamon raises important questions with respect to the development of the worship of the Egyptian gods in the Roman period, and especially in the early second century CE. There can be no doubt that this sanctuary served the cult of the Egyptian deities.[1] The evidence rests not only on the Egyptianizing caryatids of the stoas north and south of the Red Hall,[2] but also on at least one other find. A small terra-cotta head of Isis with sun disk and horns was found in the area of the *temenos*.[3] Two other finds from the Roman period are uncertain. One is a mutilated marble plaque that mentions θεραπευταί, but the name of the deity is not preserved.[4] The other piece is a small marble altar, mentioning a βωμοφόρος that was found in the cisterns of the upper agora.[5]

The earliest evidence for the Egyptian cult in Pergamon is a fragment of a small marble altar with the inscription Σαράπει Ὅρκανος ἀνέθηκε ("Orkanos dedicated this to Sarapis") that has been dated to the third or second century BCE;[6] but this does not yet indicate the existence of an official cult. Before the building of the vast structure of the Red Hall complex, however, there must have been a sanctuary of the Egyptian gods in Pergamon. An inscription, dated to the first century CE and found near the Armenian Church in the lower city, presupposes the existence of an earlier sanctuary.[7] This

---

1. Otfried Deubner, "Das ägyptische Heiligtum in Pergamon," in *Bericht über den 4. internationalen Kongress für Archäologie* (Berlin: de Gruyter, 1940) 477–78. See also Helmut Koester, "The Red Hall in Pergamon," chapter 15 in this volume.

2. It is difficult to understand why Robert A. Wild ("The Known Isis-Sarapis Sanctuaries of the Roman Period," *ANRW* 2.17.4 [1984] 1806) thinks that this evidence is not conclusive.

3. According to Regina Salditt-Trappman, *Tempel der ägyptischen Götter in Griechenland und an der Westküste Kleinasiens* (EPRO 21; Leiden: Brill, 1972) 13–14, plates 18–20.

4. M. Fränkel, *Die Inschriften von Pergamon* (Berlin: W. Spemann, 1895) 249, no. 338; Ladislav Vidman, *Sylloge inscriptionum religionis Isiacae et Sarapiacae* (RVV 28; Berlin: de Gruyter, 1969) no. 314.

5. It was found by Hugo Hepding in 1911; see Vidman, *Sylloge,* no. 315.

6. Fränkel, *Inschriften von Pergamon,* 249, no. 337; Vidman, *Sylloge,* no. 312.

7. Fränkel, *Inschriften von Pergamon,* 248, no. 336; Vidman, *Sylloge,* no. 313: Π. Εὔφημος [κ]αὶ [Τ]υλλία Σ[π]ένδο[υ]σ[α] οἱ ἱεραφόροι καθιέρωσαν | τοὺς θεούς, ὃν ὁ θεὸς ἐκέλευσε, Σάραπιν. Εἶσιν, Ἄνουβιν, Ἀρφοκράτην, Ὄσειριν, Ἄπιν, Ἥλιον ἐφ᾽ ἵππῳ καὶ ἱκέτην παρὰ τῷ ἵππῳ, Ἄρη, Διοσκούρους, σίνδονα, ἐν ᾗ ἐζωγράφηται ἡ θεὸς καὶ περὶ τὴν θεὸν ‖ πάντα, ἄλλας σινδόνους λαμπρὰς τρεῖς, πέταλα χρυσέα ὀγδοήκοντα. Ἐπεσκεύασεν δὲ καὶ τὰ ἀκρόχειρα τῶν ἀγαλμάτων, συνδάλια, χαλκεῖα καὶ περιραντήριον πρὸ τοῦ πυλῶνος.

inscription tells that Euphemos and Tullia Spendousa, the ἱεροφόροι ("bearers of holy objects"), gave to the gods a number of statues as the goddess had commanded: "Sarapis, Isis, Harpokrates, Osiris, Apis, Helios on a horse, . . . Ares, and the Dioskouroi."[8] Although this group includes a number of deities, Isis is the goddess who gives the command and for whom a special painted linen is part of the dedication. That Isis was indeed the primary deity of the Egyptian worship in Pergamon seems to find a confirmation by a papyrus from Oxyrhynchos, which calls Isis ἡ ἐν Περγάμῳ δεσπότις ("the one who rules over Pergamon").[9] The Red Hall complex, however, includes three temples, the Red Hall itself and two flanking round temples. One must therefore assume that the entire complex was dedicated to three deities, probably Isis, Sarapis, and Anubis.

While there is little evidence in Pergamon for the establishment of the Egyptian gods in the Hellenistic period, the Red Hall complex certainly demonstrates that the worship of the Egyptian gods must have enjoyed wide public acceptance and official support in the early second century CE. This popularity may not have been a unique Pergamene phenomenon. I shall therefore try to survey the evidence for the cult of the Egyptian gods and its development from the Hellenistic to the Roman imperial period in Western Asia Minor and the adjacent Aegean islands (see the map on p. xvi). I must state at the outset that in most instances conclusions from the extant materials are problematic. I think that Robert Wild uses a criterion that is too narrow, if he demands that certainty about the existence of a cult, or an officially recognized cult for the Egyptian deities can be established only if there is a clearly identified building dedicated to these gods.[10] Inscriptional evidence of an instituted priesthood in any given city should also be considered as evidence, and the numismatic materials should not be neglected. On the other hand, votives, dedications, testimonies for the existence of religious associations, and casual finds of sculpture out of context must be weighed more carefully.

Rhodos

Evidence for the worship of Sarapis and/or Isis and Anubis appears as early as the beginning of the third century BCE in the areas of Asia Minor and on Aegean islands that were in the domain or under the political and economic influence of the Ptolemaic kings of Egypt during the third century BCE. The earliest and richest testimonies come from the island of Rhodos and from Karia. However, the patterns in which the Egyptian deities appear are very different from place to place. It is evident that the spread of the Egyptian cult was not directed by any central agency, certainly not by the kings of Egypt.

Rhodos City: For Rhodos, where the evidence for the worship of the Egyptian gods is especially rich in the Hellenistic period, the political independence of the island

---

8. On the evidence of this inscription for the not yet identified older sanctuary, see Françoise Dunand, *Le culte d'Isis dans le bassin oriental de la Méditerranée,* vol. 3: *Le culte d'Isis en Asie-Mineure* (EPRO 26; Leiden: Brill, 1973) 93–97.

9. *Pap. Oxy.* 1380, 108. On this papyrus see Dunand, *Culte d'Isis,* 97, n. 3.

10. Wild, "Isis-Sarapis Sanctuaries," passim.

excludes any official control by the Ptolemaic court anyway.[11] What promoted the Egyptian cults here were certainly Rhodos's lively economic and cultural ties with Egypt during this period. Moreover, the Egyptian cult appears in very different forms in the city of Rhodos on the one hand, and in Lindos and Kameiros on the other hand. In the city of Rhodos, Isis is the predominant deity.[12] Coins issued from Rhodos between 166 and 88 BCE feature particularly Isis with cornucopia, while Sarapis radiate and with kalathos appears only late.[13] Also in inscriptions, while Sarapis is not absent,[14] Isis prevails as Ἶσις Σώτειρα,[15] and coupled with Tyche.[16] Also a guild of Isiasts is mentioned several times.[17]

Kameiros: In inscriptions from Kameiros and Lindos, Sarapis appeared as the principal god, while Isis took second stage.[18] In inscriptions from Kameiros, lists of priests (ἱερεῖς and ἱερατεύσαντες) and cult supervisors (ἱεροποίοι) of the various divinities[19] often include toward the end of the list a priest or priests of Sarapis.[20] Thus the cult of Sarapis was officially recognized. A guild of Sarapiasts is mentioned several times.[21] There is also one dedication to Sarapis for rescue from great dangers.[22] All these inscriptions belong to the Hellenistic period, while no analogous evidence is extant from the Roman period. Isis, on the other hand, appears once in Kameiros in an inscription on a marble altar, dedicated to Hestia, Sarapis, and Isis, from the early Imperial period.[23]

Lindos: Official lists of priests from Lindos also include a priest of Sarapis, named after priests for Athena Lindia, Zeus Polios, Apollo Pytheos, and other deities.[24] The priest of Sarapis, however, does not always appear at the very end of such lists as in Lindos; in later inscriptions he is even named right after Athena Lindia, Zeus Polios, and Apollo Pythios, while Artemis, Dionysus, Poseidon, and other Apollos follow.[25] A

---

11. It should be observed that even on the island of Delos, under the control of the Ptolemies for many decades of the 3d century BCE, the worship of Sarapis, Isis, and Anubis had very humble beginnings. It began as a kind of private house sanctuary (Sarapeion A), while the large officially recognized Sarapeion C was built when Delos was under Athenian influence and dominated by Rome.

12. Dunand, *Culte d'Isis,* 24.

13. Ibid., 21.

14. Vidman, *Sylloge,* no. 174 ("priests of Sarapis," 2d–1st century BCE).

15. Ibid., no. 179 (1st century BCE).

16. Ibid., no. 180 (no date).

17. Ibid., nos. 177, 178. A κοίνον of Sarapiasts is mentioned ibid., no. 176 (2d century BCE); see also ibid., no. 181 (Hellenistic): ἱερατεύσαν]τες Σαράπι.

18. Dunand, *Culte d'Isis,* 24–27.

19. Athena Polias and Zeus Polios usually stand at the head of these lists, followed by Apollo Pythios and Apollo Karneios, Asklepios, Dionysos and the Muses, and Aphrodite.

20. Vidman, *Sylloge,* 182–94. These lists date from the mid-3d to the mid-2d century BCE.

21. Ibid., nos. 195–97 (dated to the 2d and 1st centuries BCE).

22. Ibid., no. 198 (1st century BCE).

23. Ibid., no. 199.

24. Ibid., nos. 200 (ca. 242 BCE), 202 (ca. 215 BCE), 203 (ca. 208 BCE), 204 (ca. 184 BCE), 205 (ca. 182 BCE), 206 (ca. 171 BCE), 210 (ca. 149 BCE). In the first of these inscriptions, he is referred to as ἐπὶ τὴν θεραπείαν τῶν ἱερῶν τοῦ Σαραπίου.

25. Ibid., 211 (148 BCE), 211a (ca. 138 BCE), 211b (ca. 137 BCE), 213 (ca. 118 BCE), 214 (125–100 BCE), 215 (ca. 100 BCE), 216 (ca. 98 BCE), 216 (98 BCE), 217 (91 BCE), 218 (86 BCE), 219 (85 BCE), 221 (74 BCE), 222 (65 BCE), 223 (63 BCE), 224 (49 BCE), 227 (42 BCE), 228 (39 BCE), 229 (38 BCE), 230 (27 BCE), 231 (10 CE).

number of other inscriptions of priests, honors, and votives also mention Sarapis.[26] In several honorary inscriptions from the Roman period, the priest of Sarapis is also mentioned prominently among the priests of Lindos.[27] Lindos boasts a guild of Sarapiasts.[28] The title Σάραπις Σωτήρ ("Sarapis the Savior") appears once in an inscription from the early Roman period.[29] Moreover, also Isis seems to have had her place in Lindos. A priest (ἱερατεύσας) of Sarapis and Isis is named several times, though Isis appears always in second place.[30] Sarapis and Isis, with Isis again in second place, also appear together in Hellenistic inscriptions from the Rhodian islands of Chalke and Syme.[31] The secondary position of Isis is perhaps mirrored in a marble relief from Rhodos, which shows Isis standing in front of an enthroned Zeus-Sarapis, between them a bull's head before a pillar.[32] Two other finds of sculpture of Egyptian deities from Rhodos also present Sarapis.[33]

What is most remarkable of all Rhodian evidence is that the familiar Egyptian triad of Isis, Sarapis, and Anubis does not appear a single time.[34] It may also seem striking that the rich attestation of official inscriptions from the Hellenistic period is not matched by anything analogous from the Roman imperial period, although such lists continue somewhat into the later period in the finds from Lindos. Evidence, however, for a renewed popularity of the Egyptian cult in the Roman imperial period does not exist on Rhodos, in spite of the well-attested establishment especially of the cult of Sarapis in Lindos and Kameiros in the Hellenistic period.

Islands of the Western Aegean

Dodekanesos Islands: The few finds from the island of Kos regarding the Egyptian cult demonstrate a large variety. The earliest inscription, probably from the third century, appears on an altar that was set up by the *neokoros* (temple warden) Glaukis for Isis Soteira.[35] Another Hellenistic inscription, dated to the second century BCE, lists the members of a guild (σύνοδος) of Osiriasts.[36] For the early Roman period, a guild of Isiasts is attested;[37] it was appar-

---

26. Ibid., nos. 209 (2d century BCE), 212 (ca. 121 BCE), 220 (82 BCE), 232 (23 CE), 233 (50 CE), 236 (121 BCE).

27. Ibid., nos. 223 (ca. 50 CE), 234 (ca. 100 CE), 238 (ca. 160 CE).

28. Ibid., nos. 237 (1st century BCE), 238 and 239 (both 10 CE).

29. Ibid., no. 240.

30. Ibid., nos. 207–8 (dated ca. 170 and 200–170 BCE, respectively).

31. Ibid., nos. 241 (2d to 1st century BCE), 243 (2d century BCE).

32. G. J. F. Kater-Sibbes, *Preliminary Catalogue of Sarapis Monuments* (EPRO 36; Leiden: Brill, 1973) no. 361; see also Dunand, *Culte d'Isis,* plate V. A similar relief from Rhodos, showing a goddess standing before an enthroned god (Kater-Sibbes, *Catalogue,* no. 360) may also present Isis in a subordinate position to Sarapis.

33. Kater-Sibbes, *Catalogue,* nos. 362 and 363.

34. Dunand, *Culte d'Isis,* 23.

35. Vidman, *Sylloge,* no. 247. Dunand (*Culte d'Isis,* 30) argues for a close association of this title with Egypt.

36. Vidman, *Sylloge,* no. 248.

37. Ibid., no. 250.

ently a funerary association.[38] An inscription from Kardamina on Kos, perhaps also from the first century CE, mentions a gymnasiarch of an association of the Sarapiasts.[39] A longer inscription on a statue base, coming from the city of Kos, honors a famous physician, C. Stertinios Xenophon, who served under Claudius in Britain. He is priest for life of the Sebastoi, Asklepios, Hygeia, Epione, Merops, Isis, Sarapis, and priest of Rhea, Apollo Karneios, Apollo Pythios, Zeus Polios, Athena Polias (Hera, Apollo, and Hekate follow).[40] The inscription is firmly dated to the time of Claudius, who is explicitly mentioned in the beginning. What is interesting here is the sequence of the listing of priesthoods, with the Θεοὶ Σεβαστοί ("the divine Augusti") at the beginning, followed by Asklepios and Hygeia and the legendary Koan king Merops and his daughter Epione, who is said to have married Asklepios and to have borne him several children. Isis and Sarapis are named next and before Zeus Polios and Athena Polias and a number of other priesthoods. This gives the cult of the Egyptian gods—note that Isis is named first—not only prominence and special official standing; it also connects them closely with the important Koan healing deities.[41]

The familiar triad of Sarapis, Isis, and Anubis appears in a Hellenistic inscription from Karpathos, set up by the gymnasium association of the young men,[42] which attests, like the Kos inscription of the Sarapiasts, a close association with the gymnasium. The triad is also found in an inscription from Vathy on Samos, from the Roman imperial period,[43] and in reliefs on a Hellenisitic round marble altar from Tigani on Samos (near the ancient city at modern Pythagorio), which shows Isis standing, Sarapis enthroned to the right, and Anubis standing on the left.[44] A Roman-period inscription from Chios adds Harpokrates to this triad and designates the four gods as θεοὶ συννᾶοι καὶ σύνβωμοι ("the gods sharing temple and altar")[45]—clearly an indication of the official standing of the cult.[46] The testimonies for the existence of the Egyptian cult on both Samos and Chios begin in the second century BCE. A dedication to Sarapis from Chios from the Hellenistic period, however, does not necessarily indicate that an official cult was established.[47] But on Samos a decree of the second century BCE responds to the request of the priest of Isis to undertake a collection for the goddess.[48] From the same century come two private votives, one addressed to Sarapis and Isis, the other in both Greek and Demotic to Apollo (= Harpokrates) on an ornate stele in the type of the Egyptian canopos.[49]

---

38. Dunand, *Culte d'Isis,* 31–32.

39. Vidman, *Sylloge,* no. 251.

40. Ibid., no. 249.

41. Dunand, *Culte d'Isis,* 31, 143.

42. Vidman, *Sylloge,* no. 246 (2d century BCE). The dedicators are the κοινὸν τῶν ἀλειφομένων; see Dunand, *Culte d'Isis,* 29.

43. Vidman, *Sylloge,* no. 254.

44. Kater-Sibbes, *Catalogue,* no. 365.

45. Vidman, *Sylloge,* no. 257.

46. Dunand, *Culte d'Isis,* 77.

47. Vidman, *Sylloge,* no. 256; see Dunand, *Culte d'Isis,* 77.

48. Vidman, *Sylloge,* no. 252; on the sometimes precarious financial situations, see Dunand, *Culte d'Isis,* 195–96.

49. Vidman, *Sylloge,* nos. 253 and 255; on the latter see Dunand, *Culte d'Isis,* 61.

Lesbos (Mytilene):[50] Also on this island the Egyptian deities may have arrived as early as the third century BCE, if a fragmentary marble base dedicated to Sarapis and Isis can be dated to this time.[51] All other evidence is later. A votive for Isis Pelagia by a woman may come from the first century CE,[52] and the inscription from Methymna on Lesbos of a guild of the Sarapiasts, who celebrate the "Great Serapeia," is given a late Hellenistic date.[53] A priestess for Isis is first attested in the first century CE,[54] and a second-century CE votive inscription, [Δ]ιὶ ῾Ηλίῳ μεγάλῳ Σαραπίδι [κ]αὶ κυρᾷ ῎Ισιδι ("to the great Sun-God Sarapis and the Lady Isis"), for salvation from a disease by a man from Alexandria,[55] says little about the Egyptian cult on Lesbos but reflects the titles of the gods as they are used in his Egyptian home city.[56]

Attestation for the cult of the Egyptian gods on these islands proves an arrival of the cult at the beginning of the Hellenistic period, but perhaps first as a private cult. Official recognition does usually not come until the late Hellenistic period. Sanctuaries have not been identified archaeologically on any of these islands, though it is likely that they existed in the later Hellenistic period. Testimonies from the Roman imperial period are comparatively rare.

Karia

Scattered but lean attestation for Sarapis and Isis in coastal cities of Karia such as Kaunos and Knidos confirm the arrival of the Egyptian gods in the early Hellenistic period.[57] The fact that coins from Myndos (at the western end of the Halikarnassos peninsula) from the second century BCE show Zeus with the hairstyle of Sarapis on the obverse and the *basileion* of Isis on the reverse may be evidence for the official introduction of the cult in the Hellenistic period.[58] A private dedication to Sarapis and Isis from Halikarnassos has been dated as early as the end of the fourth or the beginning of the third century BCE,[59] which may be the oldest appearance of the name outside Egypt.[60] The mention of a priest of Isis in an inscription from Halikarnassos of the late third or second century[61] testifies to the establishment of a sanctuary in the Hellenistic period. The expression Εῑσιδι, Σαράπιδι καὶ τῷ δήμῳ χαριστήριον ("a thank offering to Isis, Sara-

---

50. On the Egyptian inscriptions from Lesbos, see Dunand, *Culte d'Isis,* 97–99.

51. Vidman, *Sylloge,* no. 258.

52. Ibid., no. 259.

53. Ibid., no. 262.

54. Ibid., no. 260.

55. Ibid., no. 261.

56. Especially the title κυρά (= κυρία) is rarely used outside Egypt; see Dunand, *Culte d'Isis,* 99.

57. For Knidos see Vidman, *Sylloge,* no. 268 (2d century BCE); for Kaunos see Vidman, *Sylloge,* no. 267 (no certain date).

58. Dunand, *Culte d'Isis,* 35–36, 322 and plate XXI 2 and 3.

59. Vidman, *Sylloge,* no. 269

60. Dunand, *Culte d'Isis,* 34.

61. Vidman, *Sylloge,* no. 271.

pis, and the people") in an inscription from the early Roman period concerning a gymnasiarch[62] gives evidence for the continued existence of the Egyptian gods in a public cult in Halikarnassos.[63]

A very fragmentary inscription of the third century BCE from Bargylia[64] records the announcement by a prophet of Isis of the benefits brought by Isis, Sarapis, and Anubis[65] and their σύνναοι θεοί. This might refer to the establishment of a sanctuary, probably not under the influence from Rhodos, where the triad of the Egyptian gods is not attested.[66] For the neighboring Iasos, the establishment of the Egyptian cult is attested by coins from the Hellenistic period. More difficult is the interpretation and dating—late Hellenistic or early Roman—of the fragment of a sacred law from Iasos.[67] The law is recorded by the *neokoros* Menekrates, son of Menekrates, the Alexandrian, according to a command by Sarapis, Isis, and Anubis. The Alexandrian Menekrates may have introduced the cult in Iasos, or he may have renewed an existing older cult. The appearance of the same triad of the Egyptian gods as in neighboring Bargylia is perhaps not accidental.[68] No evidence for the continuation of the Egyptian cult in these cities exists for the Roman imperial period.[69]

Some significant evidence comes from the nearby city of Mylasa. An evidently important civic official in Mylasa of the late Hellenistic period is a priest of Isis;[70] and a table dedicated to Sarapis and Isis, mentioned in a very fragmentary inscription of the same period,[71] also points to a recognized official cult. A priest of Isis is also attested in an inscription of about 84 BCE that was found in Olymos, but it belonged originally to Mylasa.[72] The tomb inscription for a *neokoros* of Isis from the imperial period[73] confirms the continuation of this cult in Mylasa for the later period.

The only inland city of Karia in which more substantial evidence for the worship of the Egyptian gods has been found is Stratonikeia. All relevant inscriptions from this city belong to the second and/or third century of the Roman imperial period; coins from the late second or early first century BCE, however, show the *basileion* ("royal

---

62. Ibid., no. 272.

63. Dunand, *Culte d'Isis,* 35.

64. Vidman, *Sylloge,* no. 273.

65. It is not certain that this third Egyptian deity was in fact mentioned.

66. *Pace* Dunand, *Culte d'Isis,* 36, n. 2. Dunand refers to the domination of Bargylia and the neighboring Iasos by Rhodos in the 3d century BCE and thus assumes Rhodian influence in the establishment of this sanctuary.

67. Vidman, *Sylloge,* no. 274a. The date given by Vidman is *aetatis imperatoriae.* Dunand (*Culte d'Isis,* 39) assumes a Hellenistic date.

68. The traditional triad also appears in a dedication by members of a Thiasos from Herakleia sub Latmos (Vidman, *Sylloge,* no. 285). No date is given for this inscription. In any case, it does not indicate the existence of an official cult.

69. Only a private dedication from the Roman imperial period of an altar sanctified to Anubis and Isis Pelagia and Isis Boubastis has been found in a nearby village (Vidman, *Sylloge,* no. 274).

70. Vidman, *Sylloge,* no. 276.

71. Ibid., no. 275. On both inscriptions, see Dunand, *Culte d'Isis,* 37–38.

72. Vidman, *Sylloge,* no. 278. On the question of the origin of this inscription, see Dunand, *Culte d'Isis,* 39.

73. Vidman, *Sylloge,* no. 276.

diadem") of Isis.[74] While it may remain uncertain, though not unlikely, whether this attests an official cult of Isis for the Hellenistic period, it seems that the existence of such a cult should not be questioned for the second century CE.

Of the four inscriptions mentioning Egyptian deities, three were found on the inside of the wall[75] of the pronaos of a large temple in the center of the city, which was dedicated to the primary deity of the city, Zeus Panemerios.[76] A rough plan of the temple[77] shows a prostyle temple, measuring about 30 by 45 m., with six columns in front, four columns in the rear, and two more columns before the entrance to the cella, so that the pronaos occupies about half of the length of the structure and provides room for additional cultic installations. It is important to realize this because all inscriptions and perhaps some additional structures concern this pronaos.

One of the inscriptions is a votive dedicated to Ζεὺς Πανημέριος and Ἡλίῳ Διὶ Σεράπει ("Zeus Panemerios and the Sun God Sarapis") by four men, who had been saved from great wars and dangers at sea.[78] The close connection of Zeus Panemerios and Sarapis is also evident in the second inscription found in the pronaos. It is a decree concerning ceremonies for Zeus and Hekate that is to be set up ἐν τῷ προνάῳ τοῦ Σεραπίου ἐν τῇ παιδίκη ("in the pronaos of Sarapis in the place of the children").[79] Dunant assumes that the παιδίκη must be located within the pronaos of this temple, which is the most likely interpretation.[80] The third inscription from the pronaos of the temple of Zeus Panemerios, dated to between 253 and 268 CE, records an oracle of Zeus Panemerios that the city requested "upon the command of Sarapis" at the time of the Gothic invasion.[81] The close link between Zeus Panemerios and Sarapis appears in all three inscriptions. Zeus Panemerios, to be sure, remains the primary deity of the city; but clearly Sarapis had found a prominent place in Stratonikeia in the temple of this god during the Roman period.[82]

Although the *basileion* of Isis appeared on Hellenistic coins of Stratonikeia, according to the inscriptions discussed above she apparently does not have a share in the association of Sarapis with the main deity of the city. Isis, however, is mentioned in a fourth inscription found in this city. It is dated to the second century CE, perhaps to the time

---

74. Dunand, *Culte d'Isis*, 42. Other coins show a deity with a dog; but this is probably Hekate, not Isis (ibid., 43).

75. Vidman, *Sylloge*, no. 280 refers to the place, where these inscriptions were found as "in pariete Serapei."

76. The temple has never been thoroughly excavated and a definitive publication is still missing; see Wild, "Isis-Sarapis Sanctuaries," 1832; for literature on this temple, see Dunand, *Culte d'Isis*, 43, n. 1.

77. Wild, "Isis-Sarapis Sanctuaries," 1834.

78. Vidman, *Sylloge*, no. 280.

79. Ibid., no. 281.

80. Dunand, *Culte d'Isis*, 43. Wild ("Isis-Sarapis Sanctuaries," 1834) disagrees, arguing that this term does not necessarily refer to this structure. In any case, the inscription presupposes the existence of a Sarapeion.

81. Vidman, *Sylloge*, no. 282.

82. Wild's ("Isis-Sarapis Sanctuaries," 1832–34) skepticism is not justified. To the contrary, the association of Sarapis with Zeus may well reflect the tendency toward monotheism that one can observe throughout the 2d and 3d centuries CE.

of Marcus Aurelius.[83] In this inscription, addressed to Zeus Panemerios and Hera, a priest reports that he has dedicated Sarapis and Isis and their temple and altar (τὸν Σάραπιν καὶ τὴν Εἶσιν καὶ τὸν νεὼν αὐτῶν καὶ τὸν βώμον καθιέρωσαν). It is difficult to know, however, whether this refers to a separate structure or to a small chapel within the pronaos of the sanctuary of Zeus Panemerios.[84]

With respect to the cult of the Egyptian gods in Karia, the founding of sanctuaries in the Hellenistic period is limited to coastal or near-coastal cities like Mylasa. Further inland, only Stratonikeia shows that the cult became established, and indeed prominently established, during the Roman imperial period, especially in the second century CE, although an earlier existence of a private or even of an official cult cannot be excluded. While the establishment of the cult in the Hellenistic period may be due to Egyptian influence, this cannot be assumed for the Roman imperial period. For Stratonikea, at least, it is striking that the cult of Sarapis was joined with the long established cult of the primary local deity, Zeus Panemerios.

Ionia/Lydia/Mysia without Miletos and Ephesos

As in Karia, the arrival of the worship of the Egyptian gods in the Hellenistic period is attested in scattered pieces of evidence from the Hellenistic period in this geographical area. However, it is difficult, though not always impossible, to draw some conclusions about the official establishment of this cult during the Hellenistic period in these cities. The most tangible evidence for Ionia comes from Miletos and Ephesos. But as this evidence relates particularly to the Roman imperial period, I shall first give a brief survey of the extant materials from the other cities, especially concerning the Hellenistic period.

Priene boasted a small sanctuary of the Egyptian gods, namely, a *temenos*, measuring about 30 by 46 m., that yielded several inscriptions. The *temenos* is entered by a propylon and it encloses a large altar, but there was no temple. The oldest of the inscriptions, dated to the third century BCE, is a dedication to Isis, Sarapis, and Anubis.[85] A very lengthy inscription from about 200 BCE records a sacred law about the worship and sacrifices for the various Egyptian deities (Sarapis, Isis, and Apis).[86] An inscription from about 100 BCE adds Harpokrates and the invincible Herakles to the traditional triad Sarapis (now taking first place), Isis, and Anubis,[87] and Isis is mentioned alone in an inscription of uncertain date.[88] Evidence from the Roman period is missing.

---

83. Vidman, *Sylloge,* no. 279.

84. The place where this inscription was found is not clear. Vidman says, "in parva aedicula." Dunand (*Culte d'Isis,* 43) assumes that it also comes from the sanctuary of Zeus Panemerios, where she locates the small chapel to which this inscription belongs.

85. Vidman, *Sylloge,* no. 290.

86. Ibid., no. 291.

87. Ibid., no. 292.

88. Ibid., no. 293.

A sacred law from the second century BCE is preserved from Magnesia on the Meander.[89] It concerns the cult of Sarapis as an officially recognized cult that may have previously existed as a private cult. Isis is not mentioned here. There is no inscriptional or archaeological evidence for the continuation of the cult in the Roman imperial period. Roman coins from Magnesia, however, show Sarapis as well as Isis and/or her symbols.[90] This may indicate a continuous existence of the Egyptian cult into the Roman period. Tralles, further to the east in the valley of the Meander River, has yielded only one brief inscription, which is dated to the Roman period. It mentions a priest of Isis and Sarapis.[91] There are, however, Trallian cistophoric coins from the years 190 to 133 BCE that show the *basileion* of Isis above two crossed ears of wheat. But the conclusion that this is evidence for a cult of Isis in the Hellenistic period is not necessarily justified.[92] I have no dates for a small marble head of Sarapis and a head of Sarapis from a Medallion that were found in Tralles.[93]

A guild of Anubiasts is attested for Smyrna for the third century BCE in an inscription dedicated to Anubis in behalf of Queen Stratonike, daughter of Demetrios Poliorketes and wife of Seleukos I Nikator;[94] the dedication is followed by 25 lines listing the names of the members of the guild.[95] This is evidently a private cult. The only other inscription concerning the Egyptian deities from Smyrna can be dated to the time of Caracalla; it mentions the Lord Sarapis.[96] The scarcity of the inscriptional evidence, however, should not lead to the hasty conclusion that there was no established cult of the Egyptian gods in Smyrna. We must remember that only very little has been excavated in Smyrna. Sarapis appears as the representative of the city of Smyrna on the *homonoia* coins of Smyrna and Ephesos from the time of Nero and on the homonoia coins from the time of Antonius Pius.[97] This clearly indicates that Sarapis was one of the main deities of Smyrna in the Roman imperial period. Moreover, there are other finds from Smyrna representing Sarapis: a marble head of Sarapis (23 cm. high),[98] a headless bronze statuette of Sarapis enthroned,[99] numerous terra-cotta heads of Sarapis,[100] lead tessara with a bust of Sarapis,[101] and a bronze oval seal tablet stamped with the heads of

---

89. Ibid., no. 294.

90. Dunand, *Culte d'Isis,* 65–66.

91. Vidman, *Sylloge,* no. 295.

92. Dunand, *Culte d'Isis,* 78–79.

93. Kater-Sibbes, *Catalogue,* nos. 380 and 381. The latter is listed by Kater-Sibbes under "Tralles" with the note: "Formerly in the evangelical school at Smyrna. Perhaps from Aphrodisias. Lost."

94. Seleukos I later ceded Stratonike to his son Antiochos I. The Stratonike named in this inscription has also been identified with the wife of Eumenes II of Pergamon, which would date the inscription to the 2d century. See on this question the note in Vidman, *Sylloge,* ad no. 305.

95. Vidman, *Sylloge,* no. 305.

96. Vidman, *Sylloge,* no. 306. For the interpretation of this inscription that tells of the philosopher Papinios, who has made himself a "recluse for the Lord Sarapis" (ἐγκατοχήσας τῷ κυρίῳ Σαράπιδι), see ibid. and Dunand, *Culte d'Isis,* 74.

97. Dunand, *Culte d'Isis,* 74.

98. Kater-Sibbes, *Catalogue,* no. 402.

99. Ibid., no. 403; "his hand lowered a small distance above the Cerberus."

100. Ibid., nos. 404, 406–11.

101. Ibid., no. 412.

the emperor Philippus Arabs and his son and wife and Sarapis enthroned.[102] To be sure, Isis is missing here except for the single find of terra-cotta jugate busts of Sarapis and Isis.[103] Yet the several references in two orations of Aelius Aristeides to a temple of Isis in Smyrna seem to demand the conclusion that the absence of Isis in the archaeological record for Smyrna is accidental.[104] Moreover, a votive marble stele for Sarapis and Isis was found in Magnesia ad Sipylum. The inscription at the beginning, naming the two deities, is dated to the second century CE,[105] that is, to a time at which Magnesia was closely associated with Smyrna.[106]

Further to the north of Smyrna, the important Aeolian city of Kyme has yielded some evidence for the worship of Isis. The interpretation is, however, problematic and controversial.[107] In 1925 a Czech team under Antonin Salac found several inscriptions referring to Egyptian gods in a temple that seems to have been built in the fourth century BCE for Aphrodite. There has never been a full publication of this excavation. Apparently this temple was rededicated to Isis in the second century CE.[108] All inscriptions, including an Isis aretalogy, must be dated to the second and third centuries of the Roman imperial period. Coins from Kyme representing Isis on the reverse confirm this date; the earliest come from the time of Hadrian, while the latest are dated in the time of Valerian and Gallienus.[109] One of the inscriptions, as is well known, is an Isis aretalogy.[110] Two of the inscriptions are votives for Isis,[111] and one mentions Osiris.[112] While these inscriptions were published by the excavator,[113] bronze votive ears dedicated to Isis have been published later.[114]

---

102. Ibid., no. 413.

103. Ibid., no. 405.

104. Dunand, *Culte d'Isis,* 73–74.

105. Vidman, *Sylloge,* no. 307; the list of the names on the stele that follow the initial dedication was inscribed much later, probably in the 1st or 2d century BCE.

106. See the συμπολιτεία treaty between Smyrna and Magnesia.

107. See the discussions in Dunand, *Culte d'Isis,* 84–89, and Wild, "Isis-Sarapis Sanctuaries," 1767–70.

108. The excavator assigned a 2d-century BCE date to this transfer of the cult, and this date was accepted by Dunand. But this Hellenistic date has not been generally accepted; see the discussion in Wild, "Isis-Sarapis Sanctuaries," 1769.

109. See the descriptions and table in Dunand, *Culte d'Isis,* 88–89, also plates XXII 4–6, XXIII 1. Sarapis appears only once on the obverse of a coin from the 3d century CE.

110. See among others Jan Bergmann, *Ich bin Isis: Studien zum memphitischen Hintergrund der ägyptischen Isisaretalogien* (Acta Universitatis Upsaliensis. Historia Religionum 3; Uppsala, 1968); Yves Grandjean, *Une nouvelle arétalogie d'Isis à Maronée* (EPRO 49; Leiden: Brill, 1975).

111. Vidman, *Sylloge,* nos 308 and 310.

112. Ibid., no. 309; it is not certain whether also Isis was named on this small limestone base.

113. Antonin Salac, in *BCH* 49 (1925) 476–78 (summary in A. M. Woodward, "Archaeology in Greece. 1925–26," *JHS* 46 [1926] 249); idem, "Inscriptions de Kyme d'Eolide, de Phocé, de Tralles et de quelques autres villes d'Asie Mineure," *BCH* 51 (1927) 374–86.

114. Roman Haken, "Bronze Votive Ears Dedicated to Isis," in *Studia antiqua Antonio Salac septuagenario oblata* (Prague, 1955) 170–72 and plates xi–xii. All inscriptions have now been republished by Helmut Engelmann, *Die Inschriften von Kyme* (Inschriften griechischer Städte aus Kleinasien 5; Bonn: Habelt, 1976) 97–110, nos. 41–44, plates 11–14. Another find referring to the Egyptian cult are two ushabtis—small statue of a mummified dead with a hieroglyphic inscription—dating to the 6th century BCE. Is seems, however, that these statuettes were brought to Kyme no earlier than the Roman period; see Wild, "Isis-Sarapis Sanctuaries," 1769, n. 67.

The conclusion is thus warranted that several cities of this region must have established and officially recognized cults of the Egyptian gods in the Hellenistic period, possibly continuing into the Roman period. Unfortunately, the very limited excavations of ancient Smyrna make it impossible to judge the extent and significance of the cult of Sarapis in Smyrna in the Roman imperial period. One wonders whether more extensive excavations in this important Ionian city—if that were ever possible—would not yield evidence that could be compared to that of Pergamon, Miletos, and Ephesos. I shall now turn to the discussion of Miletos and Ephesos in the final section.

Miletos and Ephesos

The evidence for these two cities, though debated, is remarkable, especially for the second and third centuries of the Roman imperial period.

The evident close relationship of Miletos with Ptolemaic Egypt in the third century BCE should lead to the expectation of relevant finds from Miletos during the Hellenistic period. The evidence from Didyma yields only a private dedication to Sarapis, Isis, and Anubis, dated to 150–100 BCE,[115] while no inscriptions from the Hellenistic period have been found in Miletos. It is difficult to imagine, however, that the worship of the Egyptian gods was not known in Miletos during the Hellenistic period. The very frequent theophoric names of Milesian citizens, like Isogenes, Isodotos, Isidora, and others, seem to indicate that Isis was very popular in the Hellenistic period.[116]

As one encounters the archaeological evidence from the second and third centuries CE, however, the emergence of Sarapis and of his identification with Helios is striking. Sarapis appears, together with Phoebus and Nemesis, in an oracle of Didyma that is quoted in a Milesian inscription from the time of Hadrian.[117] A marble altar from the later imperial period, found in the Faustina Baths, is dedicated to Helios Sarapis.[118] Most important, however, is the discovery of a major building that doubtlessly served the worship of Sarapis. The inscription on the epistyle of the pronaos is dedicated to "Sarapis, who listens to prayer" (ἐπηκόῳ Σαράπιδι),[119] while the head of Sarapis Helios appears in the pediment above the inscription. The dedicator added this entrance structure as a votive to Sarapis and the "sweetest fatherland" in the third century CE to an older building, probably from the second century CE. This building is unusual; it does not resemble a temple of the usual type.[120] It is rather a three-isled basilica, measuring 12 by 22 m. on the inside, with two rows of five columns. A platform at the center of

---

115. Vidman, *Sylloge,* no. 289a.

116. Dunand, *Culte d'Isis,* 52. There is also a 2d-century BCE dedication of a Milesian to Isis on the island of Delos (ibid., 53).

117. Vidman, *Sylloge,* no. 286.

118. Ibid., no. 288.

119. Ibid., no. 287.

120. Wild, "Isis-Sarapis Sanctuaries," 1791–93. Wild's suggestion, however, that "some group, perhaps merchants from Alexandria, used this building for a combination of cultic and commercial purposes" (ibid., 1793), is unwarranted.

the northern end, opposite the entrance, does not seem to have been the base for a cult statue but rather an offering table, while the cult statue was probably placed in a niche higher in the north wall, which is suggested by the unusual thickness of the north wall (almost 1.5 m., as compared to only 80 cm. of the other walls). A close analogy can be found in the Roman-period temple of Isis from Thessalonike. In both instances, it is evident that this particular type of building was designed as an assembly hall for the worshipers, not as a house for the deity. In fact, this building is a predecessor of the later Christian basilica. We shall see that Ephesos presents an analogy to this type of "temple," not to speak of Pergamon.

The cult of the Egyptian deities was established in Ephesos[121] at the very beginning of the third century BCE. Sarapis is mentioned in a dedication to Ptolemy I and Arsinoe in the early third century BCE.[122] An inscription dated to the first half of the third century BCE relates that an altar was erected "for Sarapis, Isis, and Anubis, the temple-sharing gods (θεοὶ σύνναοι)."[123] This does not necessarily indicate the presence of a temple, and it is not certain that another inscription, dated to a time between 244 and 204 BCE, which reports the establishment of a sanctuary and of a temple "according to a command"[124]—no deity is named in the preserved text of this inscription—can be assigned to the Egyptian religion. It is not improbable, however, that both inscriptions refer to a temple of the Egyptian gods in the third century BCE.

An early date for cultic activities, however, is suggested by a fragment of an Egyptian water clock that was found in recent excavations near the West Hall of the Tetragonos Agora approximately 36 m. north of the agora's southwest corner.[125] The location of this find in the fill under the western drain of the Tetragonos Agora is significant for the location of the Hellenistic Sarapeion (see below).

The exterior of the water clock fragment shows parts of three ritual scenes with the gods of the months; each is located directly behind the month indicators of the interior. Between the scenes are vertical inscriptions. The one on the right has been restored as the name of Ptolemy II, who was co-regent from 285/284 BCE and sole ruler of Egypt 282–246 BCE. Since such a water clock is calibrated to solar movement, a rough approximation of the latitude for which it was made can be calculated. Furthermore, it is possible to discover the century in which it would have accurately measured the equinoxes and solstices. Although the workmanship

---

121. It was most recently discussed by James C. Walters, "Egyptian Religions in Ephesos," in Helmut Koester, ed., *Ephesos: Metropolis of Asia* (HTS 41; Valley Forge, Pa.: Trinity Press International, 1995) 281–309; see also Helmut Koester, ed., *The Cities of Paul: Images and Interpretations from the Harvard Archaeology Project* (Minneapolis: Fortress Press, 2004) [CD Rom].

122. Walters, "Egyptian Religions in Ephesos," 285 and n. 21.

123. Vidman, *Sylloge,* no. 296.

124. Ibid., no. 297.

125. It is now located in the museum of Selçuk. See Gerhard Langmann, "Die ägyptische Wasserauslaufuhr aus Ephesos. I. Fundgeschichte und Fundort," *JÖAI* 55 (1984) Sup 1–6; Maria G. Firneis, "Die ägyptische Wasserauslaufuhr aus Ephesos. II. Astronomische Bestimmung der geographischen Breite aus den Markierungen einer ägyptischen Wasseruhr," *JÖAI 55* (1984) Sup 7–20; Günter Hölbl, "Die ägyptische Wasseruhr aus Ephesos. III. Die ägyptische Wasseruhr Ptolemäos' II," *JÖAI* 55 (1984) Sup 21–68; Koester, *Cities of Paul.*

of the Ephesian example is not as precise as some others, it reflects the actual conditions of Middle Egypt around 300 BCE. This suggests Hermopolis as its place of origin, a supposition supported by the prominence of that city and by the appearance of its patron deity Thot on the clock fragment's ornamentation and in its inscription. A major adjustment of the Egyptian calendar, modifying the system used on the Ephesian clock, was enacted in approximately 280 BCE. Because of this, the clock's construction can be dated to the early part of the reign of Ptolemy II. The calendar reform soon made the water clock obsolete.[126]

Moreover, the place where this water clock was found affirms that the Sarapeion to which it belonged was not located in the old city of Ephesos at the foot of Mount Aya-soluk, but in the new city Arsinoea that had been founded by Lysimachos at the very beginning of the third century BCE.

Otherwise, there is only one other piece from the Hellenistic period, namely, a recently published stele erected for Sarapis and Isis.[127] Furthermore, a dedication to Sarapis (only the words Σαράπιδι ἀνέθηκεν are preserved) has been dated to the first century BCE.[128] There is more evidence, however, from the first century BCE: cistophoric coins struck in Ephesos between 88 and 48 BCE show the *basileion* of Isis on the reverse.[129]

All other inscriptions for the Egyptian religion are dated in the second and third centuries of the imperial period. An inscription dedicated to the Ephesian Artemis, the emperor Antoninus Pius, to the first and greatest metropolis of Asia, Ephesos, and to those who conduct business at the customs house for tolls on fishing reports the erection by a woman of a statue of Isis together with an altar.[130] From the same period comes an inscription that has been recorded by Cyriacus of Ancona and by Wood, but is now lost, that reports the dedication to Sarapis and Isis of a *phiale* bowl and a *spondeion* offering cup.[131] The two most interesting inscriptions are unfortunately difficult to interpret, but significant because of the place where they were found. One is an epistyle fragment, dated to the first or second century CE, found in the rubble of the propylon to the *temenos* of the large temple structure west of the Tetragonos Agora. The preserved letters ΙΣΤΟΛΟΣΚΑΙΝ have been reconstructed by Joseph Keil to ἀρχ]ιστόλος καὶ ν[εωκόρος = "keeper of the sacred vestments and temple warden."[132] If the explanation of the otherwise unattested term ἀρχιστόλος as an honorary title for a ἱερο-στόλος—a term well known in the context of the Egyptian cult—is correct, the place where this piece was found may be one of the clues to the identification of the Ephesian Sarapeion. A second fragmentary and almost illegible inscription on a statue

---

126. Friesen in Koester, *Cities of Paul*.

127. Published in *JÖAI* 62 (1993) 133.

128. Vidman, *Sylloge*, no. 298.

129. Walters, "Egyptian Religions in Ephesos," 288; Dunand, *Culte d'Isis*, 68.

130. Vidman, *Sylloge*, no. 301; for the interpretation of the phrase τοῖς ἐπὶ τὸ τελώνιον τῆς ἰχθυικῆς see ibid.; Walters, "Egyptian Religions in Ephesos," 291; Dunand, *Culte d'Isis*, 71.

131. Vidman, *Sylloge*, no. 302; Walters, "Egyptian Religions in Ephesos," 289–90.

132. Vidman, *Sylloge*, no. 298; for the interpretation of the term ἀρχιστόλος see Walters, "Egyptian Religions in Ephesos," 290–91.

base was found in the eastern stoa of the same *temenos*. It was dedicated to the emperor Caracalla by a certain "Ti(berius) Cl(audius) [Bith]ynos (with?) those who sacrifice to Sarapis in the presence of my Nile god" (Τι. Κλ. [Βί]θυνος ἐπὶ θεοῦ μου Νείλου Σεραπίδι θύουσι).[133]

Where was the temple of Isis and/or Sarapis in Ephesos?[134] After the excavation of the upper agora, the so-called State Market ("Staatsmarkt"), Wilhelm Alzinger identified the small peripteral temple in the western part of the district as a temple of Isis, built for the occasion of the visit of Marc Antony and Kleopatra.[135] Various other suggestions for the identification of this temple have been made,[136] but Alzinger's thesis has often been accepted, albeit with some hesitation.

There is, however, very little evidence to back this hypothesis. The few finds that might possibly point to Egyptian religion—and they are very few and problematic in their interpretation—have all been discovered above the destruction level of the temple. Moreover, this is the wrong place, the wrong part of the city, and the wrong time—if only by a few years—for a temple of Isis. The State Agora was developed early in the time of Augustus—not yet at the time of Marc Antony—as the new civic center of Ephesos, and the entire large rectangular place is not well designated as an "agora"; it is better understood as a large *temenos* for an important civic sanctuary, which was most likely "the temple that Octavian dedicated to the *conventus civium Romanorum* ('assembly of the Roman citizens') for Divus Julius and Dea Roma in 29 BCE, when Ephesos became the capital of Asia."[137]

The structure serving as the temple for the Egyptian religion is much more likely the large *temenos* and temple west of the Tetragonos Agora, where two of the imperial-period inscriptions concerning the cult of the Egyptian deities were found. Moreover, the fragment of the Egyptian water clock was discovered nearby, suggesting that also the Hellenistic sanctuary for the Egyptian gods was located in this area.[138] The *temenos* of the second-century CE sanctuary is 73 m. wide and 106 m. deep. It was entered through a propylon from the north from a street that was leading from the Tetragonos Agora to the harbor, and it was surrounded by porticos, 7 m. deep, on its eastern, northern, and

---

133. The reconstruction and translation is taken from Friesen in Koester, *Cities of Paul,* who used Joseph Keil's personal notes in order to improve the readings of the published text; see also Vidman, *Sylloge,* no. 303; Walters, "Egyptian Religions in Ephesos," 292.

134. For a detailed discussion, see Friesen in Koester, *Cities of Paul;* Walters, "Egyptian Religions in Ephesos," 293–304.

135. Wilhelm Alzinger, "Das Regierungsviertel," *JÖAI* 50 (1972–75) Sup 283–94.

136. See Peter Scherrer, "The City of Ephesos from the Roman Period to Late Antiquity," in Koester, ed., *Ephesos,* 4.

137. Ibid.; see Dio Cassius *Hist.* 51.20.6.

138. The identification was first suggested by Joseph Keil and further elaborated in his essay "Das Serapeion von Ephesos," in Türk Tarih Kurumu, ed., *Halil Edhem hatira kitabi* (2 vols.; Türk Tarih Kurumu Yayinlarindan 7.5; Ankara: Türk Tarih Kurumu Basimevi, 1947–48) 1.182–83. Keil's hypothesis was accepted by Dunand, *Culte d'Isis,* 68–72; and Salditt-Trappman, *Tempel der ägyptischen Götter,* but it was rejected by Wild, "Isis-Sarapis Sanctuaries," 1775–76. Convincing arguments confirming Keil's identification have been set forward by Friesen in Koester, ed., *Cities of Paul;* and Walters, "Egyptian Religions in Ephesos," 295–303. The following description summarizes the detailed descriptions given in these two publications.

western sides. The temple was approached by means of a monumental stairway. The front of the temple was formed by a pronaos with eight gigantic monolithic marble columns, 15 m. tall with a diameter of 1.6 m. The temple itself was entered through a door 5.3 m. wide and 12 m. high. The workmanship is of the highest quality throughout the building.

While the pronaos with its impressive columns gave the appearance of a regular Greek temple, the interior differed markedly from the canonical temple. It was a wide room, measuring 29 by 37 m., with a deep rectangular niche at its southern end. Six small rectangular niches were found in its eastern and western wall with water basins before each of these niches. There were also outer walls, thus creating two passageways, 1 m. wide with five rectangular niches each in the outer wall on the east and west; these passageways were leading to two staircases reaching two small platforms above the large central niche at the southern end of the temple, where the cult statue or statues must have been standing. I shall not speculate here about the purpose of these passageways, though they would be perfectly suited for nocturnal initiations. The most important feature of the building is its design as a large assembly hall that could accommodate a considerable number of worshipers.

Conclusion

The worship of the Egyptian deities in western Asia Minor began in many cities, especially those that were close to the coast and to commercial traffic, in the third century BCE. In many instances it was first established in the form of private dedications and organized in the form of religious associations. There is good evidence, however, that officially recognized cults were founded early in some cities, although nothing indicates that royal Ptolemaic protection or promotion played any role. While evidence for private and public cults is strongest in the second century BCE, comparatively little documentation can be found for their existence in the first century BCE and the first century CE.

The second century of the Roman imperial period, however, seems to witness an explosion of the cult of Sarapis and/or Isis. Major evidence for the Egyptian religion appears in two different forms, especially in some of the more important centers of the region. In Kyme and in Stratonike the cult of the Egyptian gods is closely associated with the major deity of the city, Zeus Panemerios and Aphrodite, respectively. In Miletos, Ephesos, and Pergamon, however, the worship of Sarapis and Isis—very little is in evidence for other Egyptian deities like Anubis and Harpokrates—is established in major sanctuaries that no longer conform to the traditional style of temple worship. Rather, "temples" have become assembly halls that could accommodate a large number of worshipers.

At the beginning of the second century CE, Pliny reports to Trajan that the Christians had made so many proselytes that even the regular worship in temples and their sacrifices had suffered seriously.[139] At the time of Marcus Aurelius, Bishop Polycarp of

---

139. Pliny *Epistularum libri decem* 10.96.

Smyrna was led before the Roman governor, while the people cried, "this is the teacher of Asia and the destroyer of our gods." It appears that the impressive expansion of the Egyptian religion in the major cities of western Asia Minor with large buildings, financed officially or even through imperial sponsorship, coincides with a remarkable missionary success of the Christian propaganda in exactly the same geographical area—and, *nota bene,* with the construction of major sanctuaries for the imperial cult, like the huge sanctuary for Hadrian Olympios in Ephesos and the Trajan-Hadrian temple in Pergamon. The causes for these developments still await explanation.

I may be permitted to go beyond my assigned topic with a concluding and perhaps speculative comment. The second century of the imperial period, as far as the evidence from the major cities of western Asia Minor suggests, witnesses a religious development that leads away from the locally established cults, like Artemis in Ephesos, to the worship of universal deities: Zeus Asklepios in Pergamon; Sarapis or Isis in Pergamon, Miletos, and Ephesos; and the Christian God in all these cities. At the same time, the worship of the Roman emperors, Trajan and Hadrian, is documented in such very impressive building projects as the vast complex of the Hadrian Olympios *temenos* in Ephesos and the Trajan/Hadrian temple in Pergamon—both visible from afar. These sites were designed to dominate each city's visual self-presentation as clearly as the Olympieion of Ephesos, for anyone who sailed into Ephesos or approached Pergamon by road.

14

ASSOCIATIONS OF THE EGYPTIAN CULT IN ASIA MINOR

I have to start with a disclaimer: this paper will not present any spectacular or worth-while insights. Rather, it can only point to a notorious difficulty. In the field of early Christian studies we have learned that there was no unity in the organization of Christian communities in the various regions of the Roman Empire. With respect to the Egyptian cults of the Hellenistic and Roman period, it is more than likely that regional differences existed and prevailed for a long time, perhaps throughout the entire period. Unfortunately, however, literary sources are very few—in fact nonexistent for the most part—and the inscriptional evidence is extremely uneven. Thus the effort of uncovering details about the organization of Egyptian cult communities in a particular area can be frustrating.

In his masterful book *Isis und Sarapis bei den Griechen und Römern* (1970),[1] Ladislav Vidman has presented a chapter entitled "Gläubige und Kultvereine."[2] Together with the chapter on "Priester und Priesterkollegien,"[3] it is no doubt an illuminating and comprehensive scrutiny of all available epigraphic evidence relating to the organization, offices, and the question of associations in the Egyptian cults. The following general picture emerges.

The worship of the Egyptian gods is often introduced by a "priest," who brings the cult image and the knowledge of cultic procedures from Egypt. Such a priest may serve for a longer period or even for life. As soon as an Egyptian cult is officially recognized and a temple established, however, the city will appoint the priest (ἱερεύς) or priestess (ἱερεία), who serves alone without colleagues, usually for just one year at a time. He or she may be assisted by a ζάκορος, who seems to have served for a longer period. Additional cult officials may be officially appointed, such as a temple warden (νεωκόρος) and a keeper of the keys (κλειδοῦχος). Lower-ranking cult servants are the ἱεροποίοι, who enact cultic procedures and sacrifices; the Pastophoroi, often called Hierophoroi, who carry the holy objects in processions; also a βωμοφόρος ("carrier of a small altar") and a carrier of the lights (λαμπτηροφόρος) are attested. Important also are the στολίσται, who care for the dress of the gods and goddess. Finally, a dream interpreter (ὀνειροκρίτης), in one instance also a female ὀνειροκρίτις, appears as well as an ἀρετάλογος. To be sure, not all these functionaries were present in every sanctu-

---

1. Ladislav Vidman, *Isis und Sarapis bei den Griechen und Römern: Epigraphische Studien zur Verbreitung und zu den Trägern des ägyptischen Kultes* (RVV 29; Berlin: de Gruyter, 1970).
2. Ibid., 66–92.
3. Ibid., 48–65.

ary of the Egyptian gods. Nevertheless, this is still a rich and complex number of priests and cult servants—not to mention musicians, singers, and dancers.

Much less rewarding is the information about the people who must have constituted the mass of worshipers of the Egyptian religion, whom Vidman calls "the believers" (*die Gläubigen*). That their number cannot have been very small, especially in the Roman imperial period, is evident in the construction of large assembly halls, such as in Miletos, Ephesos, and Pergamon (see the map on p. xvi). There is, of course, evidence for the formation of associations of worshipers of the Egyptian gods. Like the official appointment of priests and other officials, the formation of such associations is not an Egyptian heritage but a typical Greek, more specifically Hellenistic, phenomenon. Associations of Sarapiasts appear very early at the beginning of the Hellenistic period. Also associations of Isiasts are known. Whenever an association of Oseiriasts appears, more specific Egyptian influence can be assumed, because the worship of Osiris was not popular, at least not during the Hellenistic period; only in the Roman imperial period do we find more evidence for Osiris worship. Most striking is the formation of associations called the "Wearers of Black" (μελανηφόροι) and the "Servants of the Gods" (θεραπευταί). The former seems to have been the higher-ranking association because they are always named first whenever the two are named together. Sometimes the θεραπευταί, or some of them, are designated as those who have paid their contribution (οἱ συμβαλόμενοι). It remains unclear, however, what the distinction between the members of these associations and the general worshipers (called *die Gläubigen* by Vidman) may have been.

So far the summary of Vidman's impressive analysis of the available evidence. There are problems, however, with a generalization of this evidence. First of all, Vidman is heavily dependent upon the evidence from Delos. This is not surprising because there are 238 extant Delian inscriptions relating to the Egyptian religion. On the other hand, the number of inscriptions from all other regions and places amounts to 810 in Vidman's catalogue.[4] Moreover, all Delian inscriptions date from the Hellenistic period, which means that about half of all Hellenistic inscriptions have been found on Delos. As far as the area of western Asia Minor (Karia, Lydia, and Mysia) and the adjacent islands (Rhodos, Karpathos, Kos, Samos, Chios, Lesbos) are concerned, there are only a total of 137 inscriptions from both the Hellenistic and the Roman imperial periods, and of these just about half come from the island of Rhodos. Although there can be no question that centers of the Egyptian religion were well established on these islands and in many cities of this area, often as officially recognized cults, the total evidence is very slim.

When I wrote my study on the Egyptian cults in western Asia Minor,[5] I was intrigued by the occasional references to cultic associations. I shall present this evidence here, however inconclusive, and I shall abstain from interpolating conclusions from the Delian inscriptions. Delian evidence will be presented in my comparative survey at the end of this essay.

Inscriptions from the island of Rhodos, which are most numerous, show that the

---

4. Ladislaus Vidman, *Sylloge inscriptionum religionis Isiacae et Sarapiacae* (RVV 28; Berlin: de Gruyter, 1969).
5. See "The Cult of the Egyptian Deities in Asia Minor," chapter 13 in this volume.

Egyptian cults were firmly established as official cults in the cities of Rhodos, Lindos, and Kameiros as early as the beginning of the second century BCE. In the city of Rhodos a guild (κοινόν) of Isiasts is mentioned twice in inscriptions dating from the second and first centuries BCE.[6] But also a *koinon* of Sarapiasts existed in this city during the same period.[7] Lindos also boasts a guild of Sarapiasts that must have existed in the Hellenistic as well as in the early Roman period.[8] In inscriptions from Kameiros, lists of priests (ἱερεῖς and ἱερατεύσαντες) and cult supervisors (ἱεροποίοι) of the various divinities[9] often include toward the end a priest or priests of Sarapis,[10] but there is no evidence for a religious association in this city.

Also on Kos the cult of the Egyptian gods is officially recognized, perhaps as early as the late third century BCE—the possible date of an inscription that mentions a νεωκόρος.[11] Another Hellenistic inscription, dated to the second century BCE, lists the members of a guild (σύνοδος) of Oseiriasts.[12] This is rather unusual for the Hellenistic period and probably due to direct Egyptian influence. For the early Roman period, a guild of Isiasts is attested;[13] it was apparently a funerary association.[14] An inscription from Kardamina on Kos, also from the first century CE, mentions a gymnasiarch of an association of the Sarapiasts.[15] I am not sure whether this implies that the Sarapiasts owned a private gymnasium.

Lesbos (Mytilene) is the only other island of this area that has yielded evidence for an association in an inscription from Methymna of a guild of the Sarapiasts, who celebrate the "Great Serapeia";[16] Vidman assigns a late Hellenistic date to this inscription.[17]

With respect to the cities of Karia, Lydia, and Mysia—more or less the later Roman province of Asia—there is ample evidence in inscriptions and on coins for the existence of the Egyptian cult as a recognized religious establishment. This includes the cities of Kaunos, Knidos, Halikarnassos, Myndos, Bargylia, Iasos, Mylasa, Stratonikeia, and Herakleia sub Latmos in Karia, Priene, Magnesia on the Maeander, Tralles, Smyrna, Magnesia ad Sipylum, Kyme, Didyma, Miletos, Ephesos, and Pergamon in Lydia-Mysia-Ionia.[18] However, only very little is told in these inscriptions about religious associations.

Pergamon yields evidence on a mutilated marble plaque for the θεραπευταί, but the

---

6. Vidman, *Sylloge,* nos. 177, 178.

7. Ibid., no. 176 (2d century BCE); see also ibid., no. 181 (Hellenistic): ἱερατεύσαντες Σαράπι.

8. Ibid., nos. 237 (1st century BCE), 238 and 239 (both 10 CE).

9. Athena Polias and Zeus Polios usually stand at the head of these lists, followed by Apollo Pythios and Apollo Karneios, Asklepios, Dionysos and the Muses, and Aphrodite.

10. Vidman, *Sylloge,* nos. 182–94. These lists date from the mid-3d to the mid-2d century BCE.

11. Ibid., no. 247.

12. Ibid., no. 248.

13. Ibid., no. 250.

14. Françoise Dunand, *Le culte d'Isis dans le bassin oriental de la Méditerranée,* vol. 3: *Le culte d'Isis en Asie-Mineure* (EPRO 26; Leiden: Brill, 1973) 93–97; also 31–32.

15. Vidman, *Sylloge,* no. 251.

16. On the Egyptian inscriptions from Lesbos, see Dunand, *Culte d'Isis,* 97–99.

17. Vidman, *Sylloge,* no. 262.

18. For a more detailed discussion, see my article "The Cult of the Egyptian Deities in Asia Minor," chapter 13 in this volume.

name of the deity is not preserved, though Sarapis would fit the lacuna on the stone; the inscription dates from the first or second century CE.[19]

Θεραπευταί are mentioned once more in an inscription from Magnesia ad Sipylum. The inscription appears on a marble stele as "a votive for Sarapis and Isis"; following is a list of the donors: θεραπευταί· Εὔθηνος ἱερεύς, Τ. Φλάβιος Εὐάρεστος, Εὔθηνος Εὐθήνου Θεαίτητος ἱερός, Μενεκράτης β' ἱερὸς Κολλυβᾶς, five other names follow.[20] What is remarkable here is the listing at the beginning of the inscription of two of the members of the guild as ἱερός, a title that designates them as specially honored and distinguished members or leaders of the guild. Only the priest and eight members of the guild are listed on this inscription from the first or second century CE. Were these all the members of the association, or were only those listed who had made a financial contribution?

A guild of Anubiasts is attested in Smyrna in an inscription that can be dated as early as the third century BCE. The inscription is dedicated to Anubis in behalf of Queen Stratonike, daughter of Demetrios Poliorketes and wife of Seleukos I Nikator;[21] the dedication is followed by as many as 25 lines listing the names of the rather numerous members of this guild.[22] Guilds dedicated to the worship of Anubis are rare. As far as I know, there is only one other piece of evidence that comes from Thessalonike and dates to the Roman imperial period. It is an inscription for dining associations (οἱ ἱεραφόροι συνκλῖται) listing names that are typical for slaves and freedmen.[23]

A final piece of evidence for a religious association comes from Herakleia sub Latmus. It is a very fragmentary dedication to Sarapis, Isis, and Anubis of uncertain date that was made by a certain Nestor and the θιασῖται.[24] Unfortunately, any further information about this Thiasos is lost due to the mutilation of the stone.

It is difficult to draw final conclusions from this meager evidence. There are, however, some interesting features. The majority of these guilds are named after one of the Egyptian gods. There are Sarapiasts and Isiasts, also Oseiriasts, and surprisingly there is evidence from the very early Hellenistic period for a guild of Anubiasts. The ubiquitous θεραπευταί of the Delian inscriptions appear only twice, and the distinguished guild of the "Wearers of the Black Garments" (μελανηφόροι), so prominent in some of the Delian inscriptions, never appear. In any case, the evidence presented here argues against a general application of the Delian evidence for the description of associations of the Egyptian cult in other areas and places of the Hellenistic and Roman world. Further scrutiny of the evidence from other regions will probably show that there was considerable diversification in the organization of the Egyptian cults.

19. Max Fränkel, *Die Inschriften von Pergamon* (Berlin: W. Spemann, 1895) 249, no. 338; Vidman, *Sylloge,* no. 314.

20. Vidman, *Sylloge,* no. 307.

21. Seleukos I later ceded Stratonike to his son Antiochos I. The Stratonike named in this inscription has also been identified with the wife of Eumenes II of Pergamon, which would date the inscription to the 2d century BCE. See on this question the note in Vidman, *Sylloge,* ad no. 305.

22. Vidman, *Sylloge,* no. 305.

23. Ibid., no. 109; see also H. L. Hendrix, "Thessalonike," in H. L. Hendrix and Helmut Koester, eds., *Archaeological Resources for New Testament Studies,* vol. 1 (2d ed.; Valley Forge, Pa.: Trinity Press International, 1994) no. 15 = Koester, ed., *Cities of Paul: Thessalonike.*

24. Vidman, *Sylloge,* no. 285.

Comparative Survey of Associations
and Titles of Cult Officials

Associations, Officials

Pergamon

One is a mutilated marble plaque that mentions θερ-   θεραπευταί
απεύται but the name of the deity is not preserved.[25]
The other piece is a small marble altar, mentioning a
βωμοφόρος, that was found in the cisterns of the   βωμοφόρος
upper agora.[26]
This inscription[27] tells that Euphemos and Tullia
Spendousa, the ἱεροφόροι ("bearers of holy objects"),   ἱεροφόροι
gave to the gods a number of statues as the goddess
had commanded: "Sarapis, Isis, Harpokrates, Osiris,
Apis, Helios on a horse, . . . Ares, and the
Dioskouroi."[28]

Rhodos

Also a guild of Isiasts is mentioned several times.[29]   guild of Isiasts

Kameiros

In inscriptions from Kameiros and Lindos, Sarapis
appears as the principal god, while Isis took second
stage.[30] In inscriptions from Kameiros, lists of priests
(ἱερεῖς and ἱερατεύσαντες) and cult supervisors   ἱερεῖς and ἱερατεύσαντες
(ἱεροποίοι) of the various divinities[31] often include   ἱεροποίοι
toward the end of the list a priest or priests of
Sarapis.[32]
A guild of Sarapiasts is mentioned several times.[33]   Sarapiasts

---

25. Fränkel, *Inschriften von Pergamon*, 249, no. 338; Vidman, *Sylloge*, no. 314.
26. It was found by Hugo Hepding in 1911; see Vidman, *Sylloge*, no. 315.
27. Fränkel, *Inschriften von Pergamon*, 248, no. 336; Vidman, *Sylloge*, no. 313: Π. Εὔφημος [κ]αὶ [Τ]υλλία Σ[π]ένδο[υ]σ[α] οἱ ἱεραφόροι καθιέρωσαν | τοὺς θεούς, ὃν ὁ θεὸς ἐκέλευσε, Σάραπιν. Εἶσιν, Ἄνουβιν, Ἀρφο|κράτην, Ὄσειριν, Ἄπιν, Ἥλιον εφ᾿ ἵππῳ καὶ ἱκέτην παρὰ τῷ ἵππῳ, Ἄρη, Διοσ|κούρους, σίν-δονα, ἐν ᾗ ἐζωγράφηται ἡ θεὸς καὶ περὶ τὴν θεὸν ||| πάντα, ἄλλας σινδόνας λαμπρὰς τρεῖς, πέταλα χρυ-σέα ὀγδοήκοντα. Ἐπεσκεύασεν δὲ καὶ τὰ ἀκρόχειρα τῶν ἀγαλμάτων, συνδάλια, χαλκεία καὶ περιρραντήριον πρὸ τοῦ πυλῶνος.
28. On the evidence of this inscription for the not yet identified older sanctuary, see Dunand, *Culte d'Isis*, 93–97.
29. Vidman, *Sylloge*, nos. 177, 178. A koinon of Sarapiasts is mentioned ibid., no. 176 (2d century BCE); see also ibid., no. 181 (Hellenistic): ἱερατεύσαν]τες Σαράπι.
30. Dunand, *Culte d'Isis*, 24–27.
31. Athena Polias and Zeus Polios usually stand at the head of these lists, followed by Apollo Pythios and Apollo Karneios, Asklepios, Dionysos and the Muses, and Aphrodite.
32. Vidman, *Sylloge*, nos. 182–94. These lists date from the mid-3d to the mid-2d century BCE.
33. Ibid., nos. 195–97 (dated to the 2d and 1st century BCE).

Lindos

Lindos boasts a guild of Sarapiasts.[34]

Sarapiasts

Kos

Another Hellenistic inscription, dated to the 2d century BCE, lists the members of a guild (σύνοδος) of Osiriasts.[35] For the early Roman period, a guild of Isiasts is attested;[36] it was apparently a funerary association.[37] An inscription from Kardamina on Kos, perhaps also from the 1st century CE, mentions a gymnasiarch of an association of the Sarapiasts.[38]

guild (σύνοδος) of Osiriasts
guild of Isiasts

association of the Sarapiasts

Lesbos (Mytilene)[39]

The inscription from Methymna on Lesbos of a guild of the Sarapiasts, who celebrate the "Great Serapeia," is also given a late Hellenistic date.[40]

Sarapiasts

Smyrna

A guild of Anubiasts is attested for the 3d century BCE in an inscription dedicated to Anubis in behalf of Queen Stratonike, daughter of Demetrios Poliorketes and wife of Seleukos I Nikator;[41] the dedication is followed by 25 lines listing the names of the members of the guild.[42]

Anubiasts

Ephesos

One is an epistyle fragment, dated to the 1st or 2d century CE, found in the rubble of the propylon to the *temenos* of the large temple structure west of the Tetragonos Agora. The preserved letters ΙΣΤΟΛΟΣΚΑΙΝ have been reconstructed by Joseph Keil to ἀρχ]ιστόλος καὶ ν[εωκόρος = "keeper of the sacred vestments and temple warden."[43] If the

ἀρχ]ιστόλος καὶ
ν[εωκόρος

---

34. Ibid., nos. 237 (1st century BCE); 238 and 239 (both 10 CE).

35. Ibid., no. 248.

36. Ibid., no. 250.

37. Dunand, *Culte d'Isis*, 31–32.

38. Vidman, *Sylloge*, no. 251.

39. On the Egyptian inscriptions from Lesbos, see Dunand, *Culte d'Isis*, 97–99.

40. Vidman, *Sylloge*, no. 262.

41. Seleukos I later ceded Stratonike to his son Antiochos I. The Stratonike named in this inscription has also been identified with the wife of Eumenes II of Pergamon, which would date the inscription in to the 2d century. See on this question the note in Vidman, *Sylloge*, ad no. 305.

42. Ibid., no. 305.

43. Ibid., no. 298; for the interpretation of the term ἀρχιστόλος see James Walters, "Egyptian Religions

explanation of the otherwise unattested term ἀρχιστόλος as an honorary title for a ἱεροστόλος—a term
well known in the context of the Egyptian cult—is
correct, the place, where this piece was found, may be
one of the clues to the identification of the Ephesian
Sarapeion.

Magnesia ad Sipylum

Inscription on a marble stele "a votive for Sarapis and
Isis"; following is a list of the donors: θεραπευταί·   Θεραπευταί
Εὔθηνος ἱερεύς, Τ. Φλάβιος Εὐάρεστος, Εὔθηνος   ἱερός
Εὐθήνου Θεαίτητος ἱερός, Μενεκράτης β´ ἱερὸς
Κολλυβᾶς, five other names follow.[44]

Thessalonike

Dining association of Anubis.[45]   οἱ ἱεραφόροι/συνκλῖται

Delos

Sarapeion A, before 166 BCE
οἱ θεραπεύοντες ἐν τῷ ἱερῷ τούτῳ[46]   θεραπεύοντες

Sarapeion B, before 166 BCE   θεραπευταί
οἱ συμβαλόμενοι τῶν θεραπευτῶν[47]   ἐρανίσται
cultores ἐρανίσται appallati[48]   κοινὸν τῶν θεραπευτῶν
τὸ κοινὸν τῶν θεραπευτῶν, τὸ κοινὸν τῶν μελανη-   κοινὸν τῶν μελανηφόρων
φόρων, ὁ θίασος ὁ τῶν Σεραπιαστῶν[49]   θίασος ὁ τῶν Σεραπια-
                                                         στῶν
τὸ κοινὸν τῶν ἐνατιστῶν[50]   κοινὸν τῶν ἐνατιστῶν

Sarapeion C, before 166 BCE
Ὑπὲρ ... Δημητρίου οἱ θεραπευταὶ οἱ ὑπ᾽ αὐτὸν   θεραπευταί
ταττόμενοι[51]
οἱ θεραπευταί οἱ ὑπ᾽ αὐτὸν ταττόμενοι[52]   θεραπευταί

---

in Ephesos," in Helmut Koester, ed., *Ephesos: Metropolis of Asia* (HTS 41; Cambridge: Harvard University Press, 2004) 290–91.

44. Vidman, *Sylloge,* no. 307.

45. Charles Edson, *Inscriptiones Graecae Epiri, Macedoniae, Thraciae, Scythiae,* Pars 1: *Inscriptiones Macedoniae,* Fasciculum 1: *Inscriptiones Thessalonicae et viciniae* (Berlin: de Gruyter, 1972) no. 58. The date of this inscription is debated (1st or 2d century CE).

46. Vidman, *Sylloge,* p. 63; *IG* IX 4, 1217.

47. Vidman, *Sylloge,* p. 63; *IG* IX 4, 1290.

48. Vidman, *Sylloge,* p. 64; *IG* IX 4, 1223.

49. Vidman, *Sylloge,* pp. 64–65; *IG* IX 4, 1226.

50. Vidman, *Sylloge,* p. 65; *IG* IX 4, 1228.

51. Vidman, *Sylloge,* p. 66; *IG* IX 4, 1215.

52. Vidman, *Sylloge,* p. 66; *IG* IX 4, 1062.

οἱ συμβαλόμενοι[53]	συμβαλόμενοι
οἱ συμβαλόμενοι εἰς τὸν βωμὸν κατὰ τὸ πρόσταγμα τοῦ θεοῦ[54]	συμβαλόμενοι
Σαραπίσται . . . οὓς συνήγαγεν Μόνιμος ὁ ἱερεύς[55]	Σαραπίσται
Ἀπολλώνιος . . . σινδονοφόρος κατὰ πρόσταγμα τοῦ θεοῦ[56]	σινδονοφόρος
μελανηφόρος[57]	μελανηφόρος
ἀρετάλογος[58]	ἀρετάλογος

Sarapeion C, after 166 BCE

ὀνειροκρίτης[59]	ὀνειροκρίτης
Ἡ σύνοδος ἡ τῶν μελανηφόρων[60]	σύνοδος τῶν μελανηφόρων
οἱ μελανηφόροι[61]	μελανηφόροι
daughter of a priest as κανηφορήσασα[62]	κανηφορήσασα
οἱ μελανηφόροι καὶ οἱ θεραπευταί[63]	μελανηφόροι, θεραπευταί
οἱ μελανηφόροι καὶ οἱ θεραπευταί[64]	μελανηφόροι, θεραπευταί
ὀνειροκρίτης καὶ ἀρετάλογος[65]	ὀνειροκρίτης, ἀρετάλογος
μελανηφόρος[66]	μελανηφόρος
οἱ μελανηφόροι καὶ οἱ θεραπευταί[67]	μελανηφόροι, θεραπευταί
ἀνέγραψεν τοὺς συνβεβλημένους τῶν θεραπευτῶν[68]	θεραπευταί
λαμπτηροφόρος, . . . ὀνειροκρίτις[69]	λαμπτηροφόρος, ὀνειροκρίτις
θεραπευταί[70]	θεραπευταί

53. Vidman, *Sylloge,* p. 66; *IG* IX 4, 1224.
54. Vidman, *Sylloge,* p. 66; *IG* IX 4, 1225.
55. Vidman, *Sylloge,* p. 66; *IG* IX 4, 1343.
56. Vidman, *Sylloge,* p. 66; *IG* IX 4, 1253.
57. Vidman, *Sylloge,* p. 67; *IG* IX 4, 1249.
58. Vidman, *Sylloge,* p. 67; *IG* IX 4, 1263.
59. Vidman, *Sylloge,* p. 68; Pierre Roussel, *Inscriptions de Délos* (Paris: H. Champion, 1937) no. 2120.
60. Vidman, *Sylloge,* p. 69; *Inscr. Délos* 2075.
61. Vidman, *Sylloge,* p. 69; *Inscr. Délos* 2076.
62. Vidman, *Sylloge,* p. 70; *Inscr. Délos* 2055; cf. also *Inscr. Délos* 2039.
63. Vidman, *Sylloge,* p. 70; *Inscr. Délos* 2078.
64. Vidman, *Sylloge,* pp. 70–71; *Inscr. Délos* 2079.
65. Vidman, *Sylloge,* p. 71; *Inscr. Délos* 2027.
66. Vidman, *Sylloge,* p. 71; *Inscr. Délos* 2085.
67. Vidman, *Sylloge,* p. 73; *Inscr. Délos* 2080.
68. Vidman, *Sylloge,* p. 75; *Inscr. Délos* 2617.
69. Vidman, *Sylloge,* p. 75; *Inscr. Délos* 2619.
70. Vidman, *Sylloge,* p. 75; *Inscr. Délos* 2620.

15

THE RED HALL IN PERGAMON

Pergamon, in the northeastern part of the Roman province of Asia, was once the proud capital of the wealthy Hellenistic kingdom of the Attalids. During the Roman imperial period it was in competition with Ephesos, which had become the capital of the province, for the title of "the first city of Asia." Indeed, Pergamon had received the first imperial neocorate, the title of "warden of the temple for the worship of the emperor," in the province of Asia,[1] well over a hundred years before Ephesos. The latter did not achieve this honor until the reign of Domitian at the end of the first century CE, and it had to wait for Hadrian to achieve a second neocorate. Pergamon was granted its second imperial neocorate under Trajan (98–117 CE). The temple of Trajan on the acropolis of Pergamon was a large peripteral podium temple surrounded by stoas on three sides and was completed during Hadrian's reign (117–138 CE).[2] However, this was by no means the only major building that was erected in Pergamon at that time. The Asklepieion, situated 2 km. west of the city, was rebuilt according to a completely new general design. The plan incorporated stoas surrounding a large square measuring 120 m. by 90 m., with a propylon, theater, library, and a large round temple for Zeus-Asklepios, modeled on Hadrian's Pantheon in Rome.[3] It also seems that the theater in the lower city, the amphitheater, and the stadium were built, or completed, during Hadrian's reign.[4]

While all these major constructions were under way, another monumental building project was undertaken in the lower city of Pergamon—a sanctuary for the worship of the Egyptian gods. It is one of the most impressive structures in the Greek world from the Roman period. The central building, which is still standing to a height of 19 m., is known as the "Red Hall" (often erroneously called the "Red Basilica").[5] This enormous structure, however, is only the central part of a much larger sanctuary complex, which in its dimensions dwarfs even the Jupiter temple of Baalbek. Unfortunately, this sanctuary is still not fully excavated and published, and its interpretation remains a conundrum.[6] Some badly needed repairs have been made in the main building, and the

---

1. The temple serving this first provincial cult in Asia, built during the time of Augustus, has not yet been found or identified. See Wolfgang Radt, *Pergamon: Geschichte und Bauten, Funde und Erforschung einer antiken Metropole* (DuMont Dokumente; Cologne: DuMont, 1988) 46–47.

2. Ibid., 239–50; for bibliography see pp. 376–77.

3. Ibid., 250–71; Oskar Ziegenaus and Gioai de Luca, *Das Asklepieion* (Altertümer von Pergamon 9.1–4; Berlin: de Gruyter, 1968–84).

4. Radt, *Pergamon*, 292–95.

5. See plate 17.

6. Radt, *Pergamon*, 228–39, bibliography, 275–76. A brief but problematic discussion, including a rather unsatisfactory map, can be found in Regina Salditt-Trapmann, *Tempel der ägyptischen Götter in Griechenland und an der Westküste Kleinasiens* (EPRO 15; Leiden: Brill, 1970), 15–22.

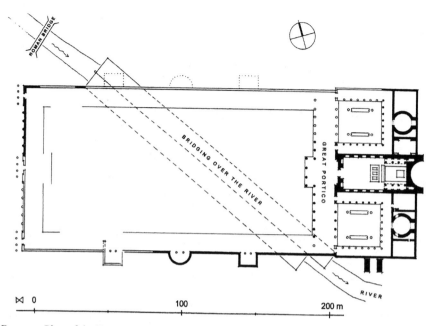

PLATE 17. Plan of the Temenos of the Red Hall (from Nohlen in *Pergamon: Citadel of the Gods*)

German Archaeological Institute conducted a thorough architectural survey shortly before World War II. Yet the results of this survey were never published. This is unfortunate, because this sanctuary at Pergamon is testimony to the great popularity of the Egyptian cult in a region where also the new Christian religion was rapidly expanding and becoming established during the same period. In the following discussion I will introduce the results of the preliminary investigations into the discussion of the religions of the early Christian period.

The *Temenos*

The Red Hall is the central temple structure of a much larger sanctuary.[7] It was flanked by two round temples on its northern and southern sides. These three temples stood at the eastern end of the monumental *temenos* (sacred precinct/enclosure), and the Red Hall sits on its main axis, against its eastern wall. Most of the central and western parts

---

7. The following discussion is to some extent based on the description provided by Radt (*Pergamon*, 228–39) and for the most part on on-site inspections under the guidance of Professor Dr. Klaus Nohlen of Wiesbaden, the architect of the German Archaeological Institute in Pergamon, who has also read a draft of this paper and to whom I wish to express my gratitude for all that I have learned during my visits. The plates are drawn from the article of Klaus Nohlen, "The 'Red Hall' (Kizil Avlu) in Pergamon," in Helmut Koester, ed., *Pergamon, Citadel of the Gods: Archaeological Record, Literary Description, and Religious Development* (HTS 46; Harrisburg: Trinity Press International, 1998) 77–110.

of the *temenos* are now occupied by houses of the modern city of Bergama. However, of the *temenos* wall the northwestern corner and parts of the western and southern side are still standing to a height of 13 m. The entire *temenos* measures about 270 m. from east to west and about 100 m. from north to south. The *temenos* wall was built of small rectangular blocks to a height of at least 13 m. The western *temenos* wall contained the entrances to the sanctuary, consisting of one large central door and two narrower doors close to its northern and southern end. This triportal western façade, of which portions are preserved, must have provided a magnificent sight. It was entirely faced with marble revetments; the three entrance gates were built of marble blocks. In front of this western wall stood a row of columns that were joined with the wall's protruding joists and, according to some recent finds, must have been constructed of gray granite. The central door opened onto a central *dromos,* which proceeded some 200 m. to the *propylon* of the Red Hall with its 14-m. high columns.

In order to create the necessary space for this immense sanctuary, the Selinus River had to be channeled into two vaulted tunnels, over which the *temenos* was built. After passing under a Roman bridge, which is fully preserved today (and is used even by automobile traffic), the Selinus River passes diagonally underneath the *temenos* from northwest to southeast for a distance of about 150 m. The reason for the construction of these water tunnels is most likely that the sponsor of the building wanted to situate the sanctuary in the center of the city rather than in an outlying district. Using the area over the river would also reduce the number of houses that had to be torn down in order to create the space needed for this gigantic project. The building of the tunnels is an example of the ingenuity of Roman engineering; the tunnels still function perfectly today as they drain without any difficulties the large amounts of water that swell the Selinus River during winter and spring rains.

There were probably three protruding *exedras* in the north and south walls of the *temenos;* the eastern and western *exedras* seem to have been rectangular, the central *exedras* semicircular. But there is no definitive evidence for the existence of these *exedras* (the northern *exedras* are not featured on the plan). It is likely that porches surrounded the open western interior area of the *temenos,* and that a *dromos* ran from the central gate of the western *temenos* wall to the *propylon* of the Red Hall.

At the eastern end of the *temenos* stood the three temples, a rectangular temple in the center, namely, the Red Hall, flanked by two round structures. The spaces in front of the two round structures were occupied by square colonnaded courts. It seems that a colonnaded portico, running from north to south, with a central *propylon* in front of the entrance to the Red Hall, separated these structures from the central and western parts of the *temenos.*

The Red Hall

The central rectangular structure, the Red Hall, measures 60 m. from east to west and 26 m. from north to south.[8] Its southern, western, and northern walls are preserved up

---

8. See plate 18.

PLATE 18. View of the Red Hall from southwest

to a height of 19 m. The eastern wall was destroyed when the building was remodeled into a Christian basilica with an eastern apse. Nonetheless, the foundations of the eastern wall that are preserved demonstrate that this wall was originally curved so as to form an apse on the outside. It is not possible to say definitively whether there were windows in this eastern wall; however, this may have been the case in order to provide special effects from the light of the rising sun.

The building is not a basilica, but a huge hall that was covered by a wooden roof without any interior support or colonnade.[9] The walls were constructed entirely of brick—a feature that has no parallel anywhere in Anatolia but is typical of buildings of this period in Rome and Italy. All its walls, inside and out, were covered with marble revetments in various colors. Important structural parts, like the frames of the door and the gable of the building, were constructed of solid marble blocks.

Stoas were attached on the outer long walls of the Red Hall (see below). Above the roofs of these stoas narrow balconies ran along the entire length of the building, probably serving for the maintenance of the roofs and windows, which were situated in the uppermost parts of the long wall above these balconies. There were five windows on each side in the western half of the building. In the eastern part the row of windows is continued on the outside by three arched niches on each side, which are in fact false windows. Thus the eastern portion of the Red Hall did not receive any natural light, unless there were windows in the eastern wall, which is not preserved.

---

9. For its later Christian use, the building was changed into a basilica by the construction of the two inner colonnades, of which the foundations are still preserved.

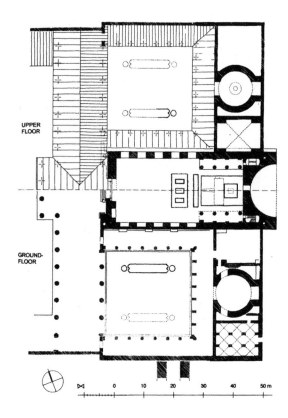

UPPER
FLOOR

GROUND-
FLOOR

0   10   20   30   40   50 m

PLATE 19. Plan of eastern part of
the temenos (from Nohlen in
Pergamon: Citadel of the Gods)

The door in the center of the west side of the Red Hall was more than 7 m. wide and approximately 14 m. high. The preserved doorsill was constructed of one large marble monolith, weighing approximately 30 tons. There are cuttings for the bronze pins for the hinges of the huge wings of the door. In front of these a second set of cuttings indicates the presence of an iron grating. The doors themselves must have been kept open all the time because no traces of rollers for the door have been found. Access to the interior was probably controlled by a gate in the iron grating in front of the doors.

The interior of the Red Hall is divided into two sections of approximately equal length, which are separated by a water channel (1.40 m. wide and 1.37 m. deep) extending from the north wall to the south wall.[10] The floor and walls of the channel are revetted with Egyptian alabaster. A water pipe ends in the center of the eastern wall of the channel. The western part of the hall was lit by the windows in the upper story of the north and south walls and was accessible to the public; the eastern part was reserved for the monumental cult statue and for the attending priests.

In the western part of the Red Hall five arched niches are preserved in the inside of the north and south walls, situated below the upper-story windows. In addition there

10. See plate 19.

are two niches on the inside of the western wall, flanking the door, for a total of twelve niches. The niches begin 2.70 m. above the floor; each one is 3.12 m. wide and about 6 m. high. They probably served for the placement of statues of deities. The pillars between the niches, measuring 2.55 m. in width and 2.25 m. in depth, together with the massive pillars at the four corners are the most important structural elements of the building. The floor consisted of plates of red Rhodian and green Indian marble and black Egyptian granite. At the point of the fourth window the floor was interrupted by a shallow basin, 22 cm. deep, extending 5.20 m. west to east. Three rectangular tubs were standing in this basin, placed parallel to one another.

The eastern part of the Red Hall behind the water channel is dominated by a podium. It begins abruptly behind the water channel, rises 1.50 m. above the floor, and is 8.82 m. wide. The base for the temple statue rises another meter above the podium and measures 4.60 m. square. One can estimate that the statue was at least 10 m. high. A central well in the base for the statue, measuring 1.5 m. square, indicates that the statue was hollow and could be accessed from the inside. A staircase 2.8 m. north of the podium gave access to a passageway that leads to the opening underneath the inside of the statue[11] and connects to the tunnel system of the sanctuary complex. This tunnel system could also be reached from a staircase outside the southern wall of the Red Hall, in the southern court.[12]

Two massive towers form the eastern end of the north and south walls. These towers contain staircases that lead to narrow balconies that protruded from the walls right and left of the temple statue. The original east wall of the Red Hall is not preserved because it was replaced by an apsidal wall when the building became a Christian basilica. But the foundations show that it originally formed an inverted apse straight on the inside and open to the outside—a strange feature for a wall that also served as part of the eastern terminating wall of the entire *temenos*.

The Two Courts and Their Temples

The spaces north and south of the Red Hall were occupied by two courts measuring about 35 m. square. The courts were surrounded on all sides by stoas, 5 m. deep, with eight columns on each side. It appears that marble benches and intervening pedestals were placed in the northern, eastern, and southern stoas as some remains have been found along the outside of the southern wall of the Red Hall. The stoas on the western sides of the two courts opened onto the portico that connected to the *propylon* in

---

11. Thus priests were able to climb, probably by means of a wooden ladder, into the inside of the statue and issue statements as if coming from the mouth of the deity.

12. The plan on plate 19 does not try to present the entire tunnel system; they need to be investigated once more. The tunnels shown on the map of Salditt-Trapmann (*Tempel der ägyptischen Götter*) are confusing because they fail to distinguish between the higher and wider access tunnels, connecting the interior of the three temples and linking up with the staircase outside the south wall of the Red Hall, and the narrower drainage tunnels that were designed to channel the water from the roofs of the buildings into the Selinus River.

front of the Red Hall. Together with this *propylon,* the portico served at the same time as the eastern boundary of the large western courtyard of the *temenos.*

Many of the low bases for the columns have been found in situ; the corner bases measure 2.25 m.; the others are 1.60 m. square. Caryatids and atlantes, of which many parts and fragments have survived, served instead of columns on the eastern stoas of the two courts. Each consisted of two figures, sometimes a male and a female, sometimes two females, which stood back to back on a 2-m.-high square pedestal that was set on a low square base. On their high Egyptian headdress they carried a capital that was shaped like a chalice but was flat in front and in back. The dressed parts of the figures along with the pedestal and capital were of white marble, but the faces, arms, hands, and feet were made of a dark gray marble. The dark-colored marble of the naked parts of these figures undoubtedly indicates that they represented Egyptians. The lowest course of the architrave was curved downward between each of these double figures, giving the appearance of hanging garlands. The points at which the beams of the roof of the stoas were joined to the walls of the Red Hall demonstrate that their total height (column bases, caryatids, capitals, entablature, and roof) was 14.5 m.

There were water basins in the two courts, of which several are preserved. They were not situated in the center of the courts, but at a distance of 5.6 m. from the colonnades of the northern and southern stoas. They are 11.5 m. long, 2.5 m. wide, and .85 m. deep. At each end of these basins are smaller round basins of 1.75 m. diameter.

Two round temples, flanking the Red Hall on the north and on the south, were set in the center behind the eastern stoas of the courts against the eastern back wall of the *temenos.* Both temples are well preserved; the one in the northern court now serves as a mosque. The inner diameter of these round temples is 12 m., and their height rivals that of the Red Hall; the domed roof begins at a height of 16 m.; the doors are 11.5 m. high.

Conclusion

This impressive building complex, one of the largest from the entire Roman period, was certainly a sanctuary of the Egyptian gods. An inscription referring to this sanctuary tells that Euphemos and Tullia Spendousa, the ἱεροφόροι ("bearers of holy objects"), gave to the gods what the goddess had commanded: "Sarapis, Isis, Harpokrates, Osiris, Apis, Helios on a horse . . . Ares, and the Dioskouroi."[13] Another inscription from Pergamon mentions Sarapis,[14] and a small terra-cotta head of Isis with sun disk and horns was found in the area of the *temenos.*

It is difficult, however, to assign the three temples to any of the particular Egyptian deities. The main temple—that is, the Red Hall—must have been dedicated to either Sarapis or Isis. Sarapis appears on two coins from Pergamon from the periods of Antoninus Pius and Commodus. *Oxyrhynchus Papyrus* 1380 calls Isis ἐν Περγάμῳ δεσπότις

---

13. *Die Inschriften von Pergamon,* ed. Reinhold Merkelbach, et al. (Bonn: Habelt, 1979–83) no. 336.

14. Ibid., no. 337.

("mistress [or she who rules] in Pergamon"). The two round temples may have been dedicated to Horus and Anubis.

The complexity of the buildings, the underground passageways, and the water installations invite hypotheses about cult, ritual, and procedures of initiation. It is difficult to use Apuleius's description (*Metamorphoses* 11) as a guide for the interpretation, but some of the architectural features can be interpreted. Most important is that this Egyptian temple does not follow the classical pattern of a Greek temple, according to which the temple itself is strictly the house of the deity. Rather, the place for the deity is restricted to the eastern part of the building, whereas the western part provides space for the worshiping community. This has analogies in the Sarapeion of Ephesos,[15] the Sarapeion of Miletos,[16] and the Isis temple of Thessalonike. The *temenos* of the Egyptian sanctuary of Pergamon was surrounded by very high walls, which did not allow outsiders to witness activities or rituals inside the *temenos*. Such enclosures of a *temenos* are otherwise found only in Greek mystery sanctuaries, such as Eleusis.

The western two-thirds of the *temenos*, about 200 m. long, would certainly have featured a central *dromos*, to be used by the procession leading from the central entrance in the west *temenos* wall to the *propylon* of the Red Hall. The twelve niches in the western part of the Red Hall may have contained images of the twelve gods of the zodiac, representing the universe.[17] Access to the underground passages by a staircase outside of the Red Hall gave the opportunity to lead an initiand to the interior of the Red Hall and of the two round temples. The initiand could then, at the end of the initiation, emerge inside the eastern part of the main temple and be presented to the worshipers, standing on the podium in front of the statue of the god or goddess,[18] but separated from the crowd by the deep water channel that divided the hall into a public and a sacred area. At the same time, the public western space of the Red Hall was large enough to provide room for hundreds of worshipers who came to witness the presentation of the person who had just been initiated. Water basins inside the hall gave the opportunity for generally accessible purification rituals, while the water basins in the courtyards may have been purely decorative. However, the pedestals between the benches in the stoas of the two courtyards allowed for the placement of votive offerings.

There can be no question about the incredible wealth and economic power of the city of Pergamon at that time. The building techniques of the Red Hall and the style of the sculptures indicate a date in the first half of the second century CE. However, the use

---

15. The large structure west of the commercial agora of Ephesos, erected in the first half of the 2d century, is commonly identified as the temple of the Egyptian gods. However, this identification is not certain.

16. This is a three-aisled basilica that dates from the 2d century; a *propylon* with an architrave inscription that mentions Sarapis was added in the 3d century.

17. The two passageways inside the north and south wall of the Sarapeion of Ephesos also featured a total of twelve niches. See also the report in Apuleius (*Metamorphoses* 11.23.8): "Deos inferos et deos superos accessi coram et adoravi de proxumo" ("I saw the gods infernal and the gods celestial, before whom I presented myself and worshiped").

18. Ibid., 11.24.2: "Namque in ipso aedis sacrae meitullo ante deae simulacrum constitutum tribunal ligneum" ("There in the middle of this sacred temple before the image of the goddess I was made to stand on a wooden pulpit").

of brick for the erection of such an immense structure is a unique feature of the architecture of Anatolia in the imperial period. It must be assumed, therefore, that the emperor himself, most likely Hadrian, dispatched a Roman architect and workshops of brick masons to Pergamon to accomplish this task.[19] The sanctuary of the Red Hall is thus important evidence for the Hadrianic sponsorship and patronage of the Egyptian cult. The same emperor who issued the rescript regarding the treatment of Christians to Minucius Fundanus,[20] the proconsul of Asia, also lavishly provided money and sent Italian masons, skilled in large brick structures, for the building of this Egyptian sanctuary in the venerable royal city of Pergamon, whose mistress—as the Egyptian papyrus says—was Isis, the queen of the universe.

---

19. Cf. Trajan's answer to Pliny's request that an architect from Rome be sent to him in Bithynia: "I do not even have a sufficient number of architects for the buildings that are erected in Rome and its vicinity" (Pliny *Epistulae* 10.18).

20. Justin *1 Apology* 68.3–10; Eusebius *Hist. eccl.* 4.8.7–4.9.3.

16

LEFKOPETRA

Inscriptions from the Sanctuary of the Mother of the Gods

In 1965 a temple of the mother of the gods was discovered at a place called Lefkopetra in the mountains west of Verria (ancient Beroia) in Macedonia near a road leading from Verria to Kozane. The temple itself as well as most of the inscriptions remain unpublished to the best of my knowledge. The numerous marble fragments bearing inscriptions (pieces of marble walls, columns, etc.) were at the time of my visit accessible in the courtyard of the museum in Verria. Only three inscriptions cut in the side of a marble support for a table, about 1 m. high, have been published.[1]

These three inscriptions are reproduced here on the basis of the original publications and of my own careful inspection on site and of two photographs that I took during the visit to Verria. The English translations are my own. The inscriptions have been dated to the period between 169 and 362 CE.

Inscription I

    Ἀγαθὴ Τύχη
    Μητρὶ Θεῶν Αὐτόχθονι
    Μαρσίδια Μαρμαρὶς εὐξα-
    μένη ἐχαρισάμην κοράσιν
    ὀνόματι Τυχικὴν σὺν τοῖς
    ἐπιγεννωμένοις ὑπερετοῦ-
    σαν τῇ θεῷ καὶ τὴν ἐξουσίαν ἐ-
    χούσης τῆς θεοῦ ἀνύβριστα
      Ἔτους αἰς Σεβαστοῦ
        τοῦ κὲ ζτκ.

Translation:

    For good Fortune.
To the Aboriginal Mother of the Gods:
I, Marsidia Mamaris, according to a vow,
have given a woman
by the name of Tychike with any

---

1. F. M. Petsas, "Χρονικά Ἀρχαιολογικά," *Makedonika* 7 (1966/67) 343–45; idem, *Deltion* 21 (1966) 352–54.

offspring, which may be born to her, to serve
the goddess, and the goddess shall have
power over her that shall not be violated.[2]
In the year 211 of Augustus
which is also 327.[3]

Inscription II

Πετρωνία Ἀμίλλα ἐχαρισάμην Μητρὶ Θεῶν Αὐτόχθονι κοράσιον Σανβατίδα. Μηδένα
κυριώτερον εἶναι ἢ τὴν θεόν. Ἐπιμελουμένου Κλαυδίου Σωτῆρος.

Translation:

I, Petronia Hamilla, have given to the Aboriginal
Mother of the Gods the young girl Sanbatis. No one
shall have more authority (over her) than the deity.
While Claudius Soter was curator.

Inscription III

Ἀντίγονος Παραμόν-
ου ἐχαρισάμην πε-
δάριον ὀνόματι Ἀλέ-
ξανδρον, τὸ καὶ ἠγόρασα,
Μητρὶ Θεῶν Αὐτό-
χθονι, ἱερομένου
Ἰλιανοῦ Δημη-
τρί[ου], ἐπιμελουμένου
Αὐρηλίου Ἀμυντια-
νοῦ.

Translation:

I, Antigonos, son of Paramo-
monos, have given a young
boy by the name of Alex-
ander, whom I have also bought,

---

2. The Greek term ἀνύβριστα is difficult to translate. One could perhaps render "no violence to be done (to the woman)."

3. The dates on this inscription synchronize the era beginning with the battle of Actium (31 or 32 BCE) with the Macedonian era beginning with the year, in which Macedonia became a Roman province (148 BCE). Thus the inscription must be dated in the year 180 CE. Cf. Alan E. Samuel, *Greek and Roman Chronology* (Munich: Beck, 1972) 246–47.

to the Aboriginal Mother of the
Gods, under the priesthood
of Ioulianos, son of Demetrios, under the curatorship
of Aurelios Amyntia-
nos.

The first inscription tells of the dedication of a person, according to the name "Tychike" apparently a slave, into factual temple slavery—unless the language is wholly figurative. But εὐξαμένη ("according to a vow") is a typical formula of dedication. This inscription is clearly an ex-voto.

The second and third inscriptions are possibly documents of manumission, the freeing of slaves by transfer of ownership to the goddess. As freedmen such persons would be nominally slaves of the deity. This would be an interesting parallel to 1 Cor 7:22, where Paul says that those called as slaves are freedmen of Christ and those called as free persons are slaves of Christ.

A study of the various names occurring in these inscriptions could prove interesting. While most of the names are Greek, the names of the curators are Roman.

17

MELIKERTES AT ISTHMIA

A Roman Mystery Cult

Solutions of problems in the interpretation of ancient materials are not always readily available. Abraham Malherbe, the scholar and friend in honor of whom this essay was written, has demonstrated that the careful presentations and evaluations of materials from the world of the New Testament always have their merits. Thus I am offering here a discussion of an Isthmian cult without any claim to a final solution, but in the hope that the discussion of this important Corinthian sanctuary will interest those who want to learn about the world of the apostle Paul. After all, a reference to the Isthmian Games seems to appear in 1 Cor 9:24–25: "Do you not know that in a race all runners compete, but only one receives the prize? . . . They do it to receive a perishable wreath."

Isthmia and Poseidon

The ancient sanctuary of Isthmia[1] is situated near the Saronic Gulf in the eastern part of the Isthmus of Corinth, the narrow strip of land that connects the Peloponnesus with the Greek mainland. This sanctuary was the site of the Isthmian Games, which were conducted there every two years in honor of the god Poseidon. The center of the sanctuary was the temple of Poseidon. The classical temple of Poseidon that replaced an archaic structure was a Doric peripteros with 6 columns on the eastern and western sides and 13 columns on the north and south on a stylobate that measured 23 by 53 m. In dimensions and plan, it was very similar to the temple of Zeus in Olympia and was probably built at the same time (468–460 BCE).[2] Partially destroyed during the sack of Corinth by Mummius in 146 BCE, it was restored in its original form after the refounding of Corinth as a Roman colony a hundred years later.

The altar of Poseidon, situated 9 m. east of the temple and centered on its eastern entrance, measured 40 m. from north to south. One of the largest altars of the Greek

---

1. See plate 20.
2. On the temple of Poseidon in Isthmia, see Oscar Broneer, *Isthmia: Excavations by the University of Chicago under the Auspices of the American School of Classical Studies at Athens* (3 vols.; Princeton: American School of Classical Studies, 1971–77) 1.3–55; idem, "Isthmia Excavations, 1952," *Hesperia* 22 (1953) 111–17. For Broneer's first detailed presentation of the similarities of the classical temple at Isthmia with the temple of Olympia, see his "The Temple of Poseidon at Isthmia," in Χαριστήριον εἰς Ἀναστάσιον Κ. Ὀρλάνδον III (Athens: Βιβλιοθήκη τῆς ἐν Ἀθήναις Ἀρχαιολογικῆς Ἑταιρείας 54, 1966).

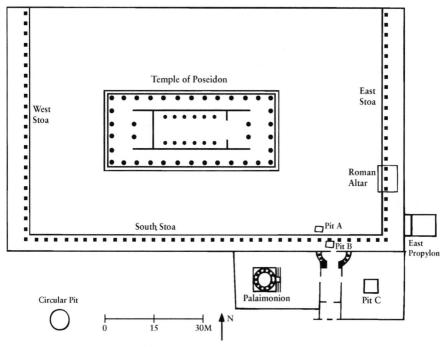

PLATE 20. Plan of the Sanctuary of Poseidon in Corinth

world, it was destroyed during the sack of Corinth by Mummius in 146 BCE and never rebuilt.[3]

Building activities surrounding the temple of Poseidon in the Roman period include a structure measuring about 8 by 10 m., of which the foundations and the two lower steps are preserved.[4] This may have been the later altar of Poseidon, built in the Julio-Claudian period, although it lies about 20 m. to the southeast of the temple of Poseidon and is not centered on its east entrance. In the Antonine period stoas were built on the eastern, southern, and western side of the temple of Poseidon; the steep slope to the north prevented the construction of the stoa on that side. The Roman altar southeast of the temple was dismantled at that time: the Antonine east stoa runs across the altar foundations.[5] Nothing is known about an altar of Poseidon after that period.

Poseidon, to be sure, together with his traditional consort Amphitrite, continued to be the primary deity of Isthmia. It was these two deities to whom Herodes Atticus gave a new gold and ivory statue group in the middle of the second century CE that Pausanias saw in the temple.

---

3. Broneer, *Isthmia* 1.98–101.

4. On this Roman altar foundation see ibid., 2.73–75. The exact measurements are 10 m. north to south, 8.2 m. east to west at the foundation level, 9 m. by 7.61 m. at the first course.

5. The Antonine stoas are described in Broneer, *Isthmia* 2.75–85.

Melikertes–Palaimon in the Classical Period

Other archaeological finds from the Roman period seem to suggest that the worship in liturgy, ritual, and sacrifice emphasized the presence of another deity: Melikertes-Palaimon. He may already have been associated with Isthmia in the classical period.[6] In a fragment from an *Isthmian Ode* of Pindar, the Nereïds request of Sisyphus to establish games in honor of Melikertes: "They commanded Sisyphus, the Aeolid, to determine a widely visible honor for the dead child Melikertes."[7] Another Pindar fragment recalls the myth of Ino, who, fleeing the madness of her husband, threw herself and her son into the sea: "Ino snatched the child out of the fire and threw him into the waves where she joined the fifty daughters of full-bosomed Doris."[8]

But the information remains very scanty. Unfortunately that is also true with respect to the archaeological record. Professor Elizabeth R. Gebhard has suggested that an enclosure just south of the classical temple of Poseidon may mark the place where Melikertes-Palaimon was worshiped in the classical period.[9] But she also points out that, without further excavation, "the best support at present for the identification of this enclosure as the classical temenos of Melikertes-Palaimon is its resemblance to the shrine of Opheltes-Archemoros at Nemea," another cult for a dead child that was associated with the Nemean Games. The use of wild celery in the victory crown of both Nemea and Isthmia[10] may also be evidence for the worship of Melikertes in the classical period: wild celery is worn as a sign of mourning for a dead person.[11]

Otherwise, there is very meager literary information from the classical period about Melikertes-Palaimon. We know the story of Ino's jump into the sea with her son, as she was fleeing from her husband Athamas, who had been stricken with madness by Hera.[12] The identification of Ino with the sea goddess Leukothea occurs as early as Homer's

---

6. All ancient materials related to Melikertes are listed in J. G. Frazer, *Pausanias's Description of Greece* (New York: Biblo and Tannen, 1965) 2.549.

7. Pindar, frg. 5 Snell; frg. 4 Tusculum.

8. Pindar, frg. 128d Snell; frg. 104 Tusculum. Frg. 128e Snell (= frg. 105 Tusculum) speaks of Leukothea (Ino) and requests that the dirge be sounded aloud.

9. Orally and in a paper presented at the Corinth Symposium, January 22, 1987: "The Early Sanctuary of Poseidon at Isthmia." In this paper, Professor Gebhard says: "The *temenos* is located immediately south of the Classical Temple of Poseidon and west of the early Stadium. The use of blocks from the Archaic Temple securely places the construction after the temple fire and the *temenos* wall is so close to the south pteron of the temple as to suggest that the two are contemporary. The size and the finish of the blocks also point to a 5th c. date."

10. The victory crown is discussed by Oscar Broneer, "The Isthmian Victory Crown," *AJA* 66 (1962) 259–63. For a marble head of an orator crowned with pine, ca. 2d century CE (Isthmia Museum inv. number 15351), see Mary C. Sturgeon, *Isthmia N: Sculpture* 1. 1952–1967 (Princeton: American School of Classical Studies, 1987) 131–32, no. 56, plate 61A; idem, *Mind and Body: Athletic Contests in Ancient Greece* (Athens: Ministry of Culture, 1989) 236, no. 127. Broneer also remarks that the use of wild celery, which withers quickly, may have prompted Paul to speak of "a perishable wreath" in 1 Cor 9:25. Apparently, at the end of the 1st century CE a change took place: victory crowns were henceforth made of pine branches, but celery crowns were still also used.

11. Suggested by Professor Gebhard, "Early Sanctuary."

12. See the Pindar fragment quoted above.

Odyssey (5.333–34).[13] Euripides speaks of the "Lord Palaimon, son of the goddess Leukothea" (both sea divinities); but he does not connect Leukothea with Ino.[14] Nowhere in classical literature is Palaimon connected or identified with "Melikertes"— a name that appears only once, that is, in the Pindar fragment quoted above. On the other hand, Palaimon is related to Herakles in several passages. Lycophron (3d century BCE) says of the "hero" Palaimon of Tenedos: "And now Palaimon to whom babes are slain beholds [the Greek ships sailing in from Troy]" (*Alexandra* 229). In another passage (*Alexandra* 663) he identifies Palaimon with Herakles: "And he shall see the remnant that was spared by the arrows of Keramynthes (= Herakles Alexikakos) Paukeus Palaimon." An association of these two divinities appears in Plautus *(Rudens* 160): "[At the sight of two girls drifting in the sea:] O Palaemon, sancte Neptuni comes, qui Herculis socius esse diceris [O Palaemon, holy friend of Neptune, you who are said to be a companion of Hercules]."

Although there can be little doubt that Melikertes-Palaimon was somehow connected to the Isthmian Games and its rituals, at least as early as the fifth century BCE, the figure remains elusive, and even the attestation of his story is so fragmentary that it would be impossible to reconstruct it solely on the basis of the surviving classical evidence. In stark contrast, the evidence for Melikertes-Palaimon and for his cult is overwhelming as soon as one enters the Roman period. This is true of the literary as well as the archaeological materials.

Archaeological Evidence for Melikertes-Palaimon from the Roman Period

During the excavations of Isthmia by Oscar Broneer, three pits for the burning of sacrificial animals were discovered.[15] All three are situated 20 to 40 m. to the southeast of the temple of Poseidon. The oldest of these pits is roughly rectangular and measures 3.70 by 2.00 m. and 1.30 m. deep. The north side was lined with rough stones, which were cracked from intense heat. The pit was surrounded by an enclosure wall, measuring about 9 m. square. When the pit was found, it was filled with ashes, animal bones, pottery, and lamps. According to the date of the pottery, the pit must have been in use during the first half of the first century CE; it was closed half a century later. The animal bones from this pit, as well as in the other two pits, have been identified as those of bulls. A second burning pit, slightly larger than the first, was built 3 m. to the southeast. A new enclosure wall with sides measuring between 16 and 19 m. surrounded both the first and second burning pits.

---

13. Homer says that the sea goddess Leukothea, "Ino, Kadmos's daughter," was once a human woman but was now receiving divine honors in the sea.

14. Euripides *Iph. Taur.* 270–71: "Son of Leukothea, guardian of ships, lord of the sea Palaimon, be merciful to us."

15. Oscar Broneer, "Excavations at Isthmia, Fourth Campaign, 1957–1958," *Hesperia* 28 (1959) 312–17; idem, *Isthmia,* 2.100–106.

A third burning pit was built 15 m. to the southeast of the second pit. It is the largest of the three, measuring 4.05 m. from east to west and 3.57 m. from north to south. Its preserved height is 1.10 m. All stones lining its walls were blackened and had partially disintegrated from intense heat. This points to a long period of use. Also this pit was filled with ashes, animal bones, and a very large quantity of lamps to a depth of 0.75 m. It was probably built at the beginning of the second century CE and may have been in use for as long as a hundred years.

Together with many lamps of various ordinary shapes, a large quantity of lamps of an unusual form have been found in and near the three burning pits. They are round bowls with a high funnel in the center that served to hold the wick, and they vary in size from 10 to 25 cm. in diameter. The excavator Oscar Broneer dated these lamps into the early first to the late second century CE. Lamps of this type have not been found anywhere else in Greece.

To the west of this third burning pit, but like it just outside of the southeastern corner of the stoas surrounding the temple of Poseidon in the Antonine period, the concrete core of the foundations of a structure from the early second century CE was discovered.[16] It is 2 m. high and almost square, measuring 8 m. from north to south and 8.8 m. from east to west. There is a passage in the center of the foundations, which is the end of a water channel, that brought water from a reservoir lying to the west. The passage is now 1.70 m. wide; but it was originally lined with poros blocks on both sides of which the lowest course is preserved, leaving a passage that was only 0.73 m. wide. At the eastern end was a door with a threshold 1 m. above the floor of the channel. There are no traces of any steps leading down into the channel from the threshold. The walls and the bottom of the channel were lined with thick waterproof stucco to the northwestern end, where it is joined to the older Greek stucco of a channel that was originally built for the supply of water for the basins of the archaic stadium. The new function of this water channel is difficult to explain.

Two bronze coins minted in Corinth in the second century CE show a *monopteros* (a structure of circular columns) standing on a podium with several steps leading up to the floor level of the temple. There is a door in the center of the steps to the podium. One coin shows a bull standing to the left of the temple: a pine tree is visible behind the animal.[17] The other coin shows, between the columns of the temple, the sculpture of a dolphin with a figure lying prostrate on its back, and a pine tree on either side of the temple.[18] A variant of this coin shows Melikertes on the dolphin in a monopteros with the pine tree behind.[19]

The preserved foundations and the evidence provided by the coins make it possible to reconstruct the temple that stood on these foundations.[20] It was a monopteros

---

16. Oscar Broneer, "Excavations at Isthmia, Third Campaign, 1955–1956," *Hesperia* 26 (1957) 15–17; idem, "Fourth Campaign," 317–19; idem, *Isthmia,* 2.106–12.

17. Coin of Corinth, Marcus Aurelius; B.V. Head, *Catalogue of Greek Coins: Corinth, Corinthian Colonies, etc.* (London: Trustees of the British Museum, 1889) 78, no. 613, plate 20 no. 14; *Sylloge Nummerum Graecorum Copenhagen: Corinth* (Copenhagen: Einar Munksgaard, 1944) no. 360, plate 8. See plate 21 here.

18. Coin of Corinth, Lucius Verus; Head, *Catalogue,* 80, no. 623; plate XX no. 22.

19. *Sylloge Nummerum Graecorum Copenhagen: Corinth,* no. 342, plate 7.

20. See plate 22.

PLATE 21. Coin of the Palaimonion with bull and pine tree.

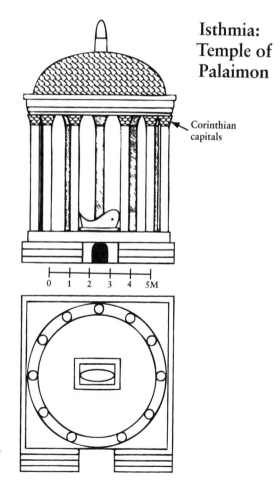

Isthmia: Temple of Palaimon

Corinthian capitals

PLATE 22. Reconstruction of the Palaimonion

without walls and with eleven Corinthian columns and a domed roof, standing on a square foundation that is typical for Roman podium temples with stairs leading up to the stylobate from the east. Pausanias (2.2.1), describing his visit to Isthmia, speaks of this structure as "a temple of Palaimon with images in it of Poseidon, Leukothea, and Palaimon himself." The last is most likely the figure lying on the back of the dolphin as depicted by the coin. When the temple of Palaimon was built, the western rectangle of the earlier enclosure for the third burning pit, lying to the east of the temple, was enlarged, and the enclosure walls were raised to the height of several meters and reinforced by strong buttresses. On the northern side, the back wall of the new southern stoa of the temple of Poseidon now served as the enclosure wall for this district. Thus the entire area—the temple of Melikertes-Palaimon, as well as the third, large burning pit—was surrounded by high walls that would have made it impossible for anyone outside to witness the rituals performed inside.

There is also epigraphic evidence for the building activities at the Palaimon temple in the Roman period. An inscribed statue base, found in Isthmia during the excavation of the site (now in the Corinth Museum), carried a statue of "Iuventianus, the Priest."[21] The date of the inscription is the early second century CE. This Iuventianus is known from another inscription (now in the Museo Lapidario in Verona; *IG* IV, 203). This latter inscription gives the full title of Iuventianus and lists his benefactions as follows (my translation):

To the ancestral gods and to the fatherland. Poplius Licinius, son of Poplius, Aemiklia Priscus Iuventianus, high priest for life, has constructed the guest lodgings for the athletes who come from all over the world to the Isthmian Games. The same also made out of his own funds the Palaimonion with its decorations and the place for the offerings for the dead (ἐναγιστήριον) and the sacred entryway and the altars for the ancestral gods with their enclosing walls and the pronaos and the houses for the examination of the athletes and the temple of Helios and the statue in it and the enclosing walls of the sacred grove and the temples of Demeter and Kore and Dionysus and Artemis in it with their statues and decorations and pronaoi; and he reconstructed the temples of [Demeter] Eueteria and Kore and the Ploutoneion and the passageways and their substructures which had been weakened by earthquakes and age. When he held the office of Agoranomos he also erected the stoa at the stadium with the vaulted chambers and decorations.

Another priest from Isthmia is mentioned in a third inscription that has since disappeared. It was reported by Johann Joachim Winckelmann over two hundred years ago, in 1764, in his famous *Geschichte der Kunst des Altertums* (2.383):

A large and beautiful statue of Neptune, which together with a Juno, so-called, was excavated about twelve years ago at Corinth, was probably executed either

---

21. Oscar Broneer, "Third Campaign," 15–17; idem, "Fourth Campaign," 317–19; idem, *Isthmia* 2.106–12.

in the time of Julius Caesar or not long afterwards. The style of the workmanship also points to about this time, and from it, though more from the shape of the letters in a Greek inscription on the head of a dolphin at the feet of the statue, it can be proved that it was not made before the destruction of the city. The inscription tells that the statue was erected by Publius Licinius Priscus, a priest of Neptune. It is as follows: "P. LIKINIOS PRISKOS IEREUS."[22]

Winckelmann is describing an entire statue group from Isthmia. It is unlikely that this group, although apparently monumental, came from the temple of Poseidon, because some of the statues from the temple of Poseidon appear to have been found in the recent Isthmian excavations. The torso of a monumental female marble statue, found in a trench at the west end of the temple of Poseidon,[23] is most likely part of the statue of Amphitrite that Pausanias (2.1.7) saw in the pronaos of the temple of Poseidon, where it was standing next to a statue of Poseidon. These statues must have been the original temple statues of the naos of the temple of Poseidon, which were moved into the pronaos when Herodes Atticus dedicated new gold and ivory statues of Poseidon and Amphitrite. Pausanias (2.1.7–8) describes this later group as a four-horse chariot (the bodies of the horses gilded except for the hooves, which were made of ivory), with two tritons beside the horses and Poseidon and Amphitrite standing in the chariot. Pausanias also says that the boy Melikertes, standing upright, was part of the group depicted in this new temple statuary that Herodes Atticus dedicated. Thus the statues that Winckelmann saw in Rome must be the group mentioned by Pausanias: Poseidon, Leukothea, and Palaimon on the dolphin from the Temple of Palaimon.

Literary Evidence for Melikertes-Palaimon from the Roman Period

Roman writers of the Augustan time were quite familiar with the story of Ino and Melikertes. Virgil, in the *Georgica* (436–37), mentions both deities: "And the sailors, safe in port, shall pay their vows on the shore to Glaucus and to Panopea and to Melicerta, Ino's son." Horace refers to the "tearful Ino" (*Ino flebilis; Ep.* 2.3 = *Ars poetica* 123).

The myth about Ino and Melikertes is recorded in full for the first time by Ovid in his *Metamorphoses* (416–542). He tells of Juno's wrath against Ino, because she had nursed her sister Semele's infant Bacchus, and of Ino's flight and mad jump into the sea from a high rock together with her son Melicerta. But Venus requests Neptune to change the two into sea gods. Neptune complies, stripping away their mortality and renewing them, changing both form and name: "And he called the new god Palaemon, and his goddess mother Leucothoe."

In his *Fasti* (6.485–550)—written in 8 CE, just before the exile and about a year after

---

22. ET: Johann Joachim Winckelmann, *History of Ancient Art* (2 vols.; New York: Unger, 1968) 2.280–81.

23. Broneer, "Isthmia Excavations, 1952," 189–91. Definitive publication by Mary C. Sturgeon, *Isthmia IV,* cat. no. 17 A: pp. 83–99 (discussion), 99–100 (catalogue entry), plates 34–40.

the completion of the *Metamorphoses*—Ovid adds that Ino and her son Melicerta, whom she had snatched from the cradle, are brought to Italy to the mouth of the Tiber, where Hercules rescues them from the Maenads. On their flight, they encounter a Tegean priestess, who prophesies to them their future divine status:

> "You will be a goddess of the ocean; your son, too, will have his home in the sea. While Hellas calls you Leucathea, our people call you Matuta; your son rules over the harbors, whom we call Portunus, in his own language Palaemon. . . . Their suffering ends, he is a god, she a goddess." (*Fasti* 6.543–550; translation mine)

In the *Fasti* (6.495–96) it is also clear that the sanctuary in which the two are worshiped is situated on the narrows of the Isthmus: "A land there is, shrunk with narrow limits, which repels twin seas and, single in itself, is lashed by twofold waters."

The relationship of Melikertes and Isthmia is explicit also in Ps.-Apollodoros *Bibliotheca* 3.4.3, a mythography probably written in the first century CE; however, here it is presumed that Melikertes was already dead when Ino jumped into the sea:

> Ino threw Melikertes into a boiling cauldron, then carrying it with the dead child she sprang into the deep. She is called Leukothea, and the boy is called Palaimon—this is what they are called by the sailors, because they help those who are tossed by a storm. The Isthmian Games were instituted in honor of Melikertes by Sisyphus.

In the second century CE, the mythographer Hyginus (*Fabulae* 2) gives a full account of the story. He tells how Ino had parched the grain in order to make it infertile; how Athamas, stricken with madness, sacrificed Ino's older son, Phrixus; how Ino, saved by Liber, threw herself into the sea together with her younger son. Hyginus concludes the story with a reference to the Roman identification of Leukothea as Mater Matuta and of Melicerta-Palaemon as Portunus.

The fuller accounts of the myth by Roman writers may be related to the renewal of the Isthmian cult when Caesar had refounded Corinth and returned the control of the Isthmian Games to the new colony—the games had been held at Sikyon during the hundred years in which Corinth lay in ashes. These accounts also seem to confirm the archaeological record, that is, that the cult of Melikertes-Palaimon had moved to center stage in Isthmia. Very little can be learned from these accounts about the cult itself. But it seems clear that the Isthmian Games were understood as games in honor of Melikertes-Palaimon. That is also evident in Pausanias's report about his travel from Megara along the coast of the Saronic Gulf from Athens: "Further on the pine still grew by the shore at the time of my visit, and there was an altar of Melikertes. At this place, they say the boy was brought ashore by a dolphin; Sisyphus found him lying and gave him burial in the Isthmus, establishing the Isthmian Games in his honor" (2.1.3).

This dating of the founding of the games to the legendary Corinthian king Sisyphus is confirmed by an archaeological find. A statue base, found at the site and dated to the second century CE, bears the inscription "Sisyphus" both on the front and on the back of the base.[24] Thus the statue that stood on this base must have been displayed prominently somewhere within the precinct of the temple of Palaimon.

The Mystery Cult of Melikertes-Palaimon

Pausanias, however, also gives some indication of the character of the cult of this deity. After having described the temple of Palaimon and its statues, he goes on to say this: "There is also another what is called secret holy place (ἄδυτον) and an underground descent leading into it, where they say that Palaimon is concealed. Whoever, whether Corinthian or stranger, swears falsely here, can by no means escape from the oath" (2.2.1). The excavations, however, have not brought to light anything that could be identified with this "adyton." It is possible that Pausanias associated it with the door in the middle of the staircase leading up to the temple. But the water channel that ended behind this door is very narrow and not easily accessible from the threshold lying about 1 m. above the floor of the channel (see above). Pausanias says nothing about the rituals in honor of Palaimon; he mentions only the swearing of oaths—hardly the oaths that the athletes had to swear before the games.

That the rituals were secret is clearly stated by Plutarch (*Theseus* 25). He reports Theseus's arrival on the isthmus after killing the giant Skeiron, and says that Theseus founded the Isthmian Games in honor of Poseidon, emulating Herakles, who had founded the Olympian Games for Zeus. Then Plutarch continues: "But what is dedicated to Melikertes in that place is performed at night, and its order involves a mystical rite (τελετή) rather than a public festival and celebration." Although the character of the ritual is clearly designated as a secret rite, no other details are given.[25]

More detailed information comes from Philostratus in his description of a picture entitled "Palaimon," whom he also calls Melikertes (*Imagines* 2.16). He describes the people of Corinth sacrificing on the isthmus, the king—"we will think that it is Sisyphus"—and the sacred grove of Poseidon in which the pine needles whisper the story of Ino and Palaimon. Whereas Ino-Leukothea is not pictured, though her story is told briefly, the painting apparently includes the scene of Palaimon arriving asleep (not dead) on the back of a dolphin who is obedient to his will; Poseidon announces the child's coming. Then Philostratus continues his description of the painting:

For him who arrives, a sanctuary (ἄδυτον) breaks forth on the Isthmus as the earth splits open on Poseidon's command; it seems to me that Poseidon has also foretold to Sisyphus here the arrival of the boy and that it would be necessary to sacrifice to him. He [Sisyphus] sacrifices a black bull—I think that he took it from the herd of Poseidon. The meaning of the sacrifice, the garb worn by those who conducted it, the offerings (ἐναγίσματα), my child, and the method of

---

24. Broneer, "Third Campaign," 22–23.
25. The terms τελετή and ὀργιασμός are also used by Aelius Aristides, p. 375 (Keil), for the cult of Palaimon.

slaughtering (τὸ σφάττειν) must remain hidden for the rites (ὄργια) of Palaimon, for the doctrine is holy and altogether secret, as the wise Sisyphus has clothed them in mystical language (ἀποθειώσαντος).

In agreement with Pausanias, Philostratus calls the sanctuary an "adyton" and, like Plutarch, he points to the secrecy of the rites. The unusually high *temenos* walls of the Palaimonion testify to the exclusion of the public. The sacrificing of a bull is confirmed by the excavation of the burning pits. Ἐναγίσματα and/or σφάγια are sacrifices to the dead, to heroes, and to chthonic deities; in a σφάγιον, the blood is poured into a bothros, and nothing of the sacrificed animal is eaten.[26] But there is no indication in Philostratus's description that the bull was meant to become a whole burnt offering.

There can be no doubt about the mystery character of the cult of Melikertes-Palaimon in the Roman period. The secret rites of offerings to a hero are affirmed in several sources and borne out by the archaeological finds. Closely related is the renewed propagation of the story—the cult myth—among writers of the Roman period. About the third element constituting a mystery cult, the community that celebrated this cult, nothing is known. This community was possibly related to the celebration of the Isthmian Games, but that must remain speculation.

It is difficult to determine whether, and in which way, this Roman mystery cult of Melikertes-Palaimon was related to any classical cult for this hero. Neither the full cult myth nor the ritual is attested in the classical period, although tantalizing fragments of this myth appear in several writers. The burning of whole large animals in pits was apparently not practiced in classical times; rather, the animals were cut up and burned piece by piece in small pits. It is possible that there was no direct connection to whatever Palaimon cult existed in the classical period and also that the cult rituals for Melikertes-Palaimon, as they are evidenced by writers and archaeological finds, were created in the Roman period, once Corinth was reestablished by Caesar.

It is not possible, however, to explain this Roman cult or the name Melikertes as a completely novel creation of that time. To be sure, the name Melikertes (which possibly means "honey cutter") is a strange Greek name and not otherwise attested. It is also not possible to find an explanation for the identification of Palaimon with Melikertes.[27] The attempt has been made to explain Melikertes as Greek transcription of the Syrian god Melqart,[28] who was associated very early with Herakles.[29] Since Herakles is Παλαιμώνιος as well as Μέλκαθρος (Melqart),[30] the identification of Palaimon with

---

26. See Martin P. Nilsson, *Geschichte der griechischen Religion* (2d ed.; 2 vols.: HAW 5.2; Munich: Beck, 1955) 1.186–87: Paul Stengel, *Opferbräuche der Griechen* (Darmstadt: Wissenschaftliche Buchgesellschaft, 1972) 92–104.

27. Cf. Albin Lesky in PW 29 (1931) 514–21.

28. A full statement of this hypothesis and a listing of older literature can be found in John G. Hawthorne, "The Myth of Palaemon," *TAPA* 89 (1958) 92–98.

29. See Karl Preisendanz in PW Sup 6.293–97.

30. Μέλκαθρος is the usual Greek transcription of Melqart. That the Thassian Herakles came from Tyre in Syria is already stated by Herodotus 2.44.

Melikertes would find a natural explanation.[31] However, all this must remain idle speculation because of the attestation of the name Melikertes in the Pindar fragment quoted above. This name, its association with Palaimon, and an older cult for this hero in Isthmia clearly predates the reorganization of the cult in the Roman period.

However, the Roman mystery cult of Melikertes-Palaimon deserves attention. The classical period knew of the child who was tragically killed by his mother's mad jump into the sea. In the later versions, the child is once dead and buried in his adyton (Pausanias), once sleeping on the dolphin (Philostratus), once standing upright with Poseidon and Amphitrite as they ride the sea (the statue group in the temple of Poseidon as described by Pausanias), a hero who was once dead and rose to new life. What was the significance of the nocturnal rites, illuminated by strange lamps, in which bulls were sacrificed in a secret ritual and burned in a pit? What did the worshiper experience, and what was the meaning of this ritual? We may never know the answers, but we should continue to discuss the hero Melikertes-Palaimon and his cult in the context of the mystery religions of the Roman period and—last but not least—in the context of Paul's stay in Corinth.

31. I have discussed this thesis in more detail in my essay, "The History-of-Religions School, Gnosis, and the Gospel of John," *ST* 40 (1986) 123–26 (to be reprinted in a second volume of my essays). I acknowledge gratefully the helpful criticisms of Professor Elizabeth R. Gebhard, and I have revised my presentation accordingly.

III

READING EARLY CHRISTIANITY

18

THOMAS JEFFERSON, RALPH WALDO EMERSON, THE *GOSPEL OF THOMAS*, AND THE APOSTLE PAUL

An essay recently published in *Harper's Magazine* about Thomas Jefferson and the *Gospel of Thomas*[1] moved me to reflect further on this question. It occurred to me that Ralph Waldo Emerson should be included in my considerations; he is mentioned only in passing in that essay.

Thomas Jefferson, born in 1743, coauthor of the American Constitution and of the Bill of Rights, served as secretary of state under George Washington, was vice president under Washington's successor John Adams, and became the third president of the United States of America from 1801 to 1809. He may have been the most educated and most cultured president of the United States, but was also an unerring advocate of the democratic principles and of the rights of all people without any regard of status and class in the society.[2] Jefferson had been reading the literature of the Age of Enlightenment extensively, was interested in all disciplines of scholarship, from geography, agriculture, botany, and medicine to the arts of literature and languages (he had a command of Greek, Latin, French, Italian, and Anglo-Saxon), and was also an accomplished violin player. Like other signers of the Declaration of Independence, the Constitution, and the Bill of Rights, Jefferson was an avowed Deist. It was enlightened Deism that inspired the separation of church and state in the American Constitution, which was closely related to concepts developed by John Locke, the pioneer of the Enlightenment in the English-speaking world. The more recent claim that the American Constitution was based upon conservative Christian principles is pure legend. Enlightenment and Deism were the fathers of the American Constitution. For Jefferson, religion belonged to the realm of individual education of moral character, of which he deemed capable even the lowliest farmer.

In his leisure hours, Thomas Jefferson worked on a new edition of the message of Jesus. Unfortunately, nothing is said about that in all the bulky thirty-six volumes of the recently completed German *Theologische Realenzyklopädie*.[3] During the years of his presidency he had composed a simplified Gospel from the sayings of Jesus, in which he included only the moral teachings of Jesus but no miracle stories and nothing about the

---

1. Eric Reece, "Jesus without the Miracles," *Harper's Magazine* 311, 1867 (2005) 33–41.
2. It must be noted, however, that Jefferson owned slaves and, although he was not quite comfortable with their inferior status, he did not include the slaves in his vision of the equality of all human beings.
3. Ed. Gerhard Krause and Gerhard Müller (Berlin: de Gruyter, 1977–2002).

virgin birth and the resurrection. Later, in a rather laborious effort, he produced a revised text of Jesus' purified message, which he composed in four parallel columns of the Greek, Latin, French, and English versions of those sayings of Jesus he deemed to be genuine. A facsimile of this work was published only many decades after Jefferson's death by his grandson, subsidized by a grant of the American Congress.[4]

In a letter to John Adams, Jefferson wrote in 1813: "[I have excerpted] the very words only of Jesus, paring off the amphibologisms into which [the Evangelists] have been led, by forgetting often, or not understanding, what had fallen from him, by giving their own misconceptions as his dicta, and expressing unintelligibly for others what they had not understood themselves."[5] To his friend Charles Clay he wrote in 1815: "Probably you have heard me say I had taken the four Evangelists, had cut out from them every text they had recorded of the moral precepts of Jesus, and arranged them in a certain order, and although they appeared but as fragments, yet fragments of the most sublime edifice of morality which had ever been exhibited to man."

Jefferson's selections of the sayings of Jesus from the first three Gospels resemble closely those chosen as genuine words of Jesus by Reimarus, published several decades earlier by Gotthold Ephraim Lessing in the *Wolfenbüttel Fragments*.[6] But a direct dependence of Jefferson upon Reimarus is very unlikely; German was one of the languages that Jefferson did not control. But both Reimarus and Jefferson were Deists and thus brothers in spirit. This explains the similarities of their selections.

Devoted to Enlightenment thinking, Jefferson was a moralist and a rationalist. Education in morality and for the formation of individual character was for him the foundation of the young U.S. democracy. Religious communities and churches might contribute; but Jefferson considered them more as a necessary evil than as an ally. The emphasis of the churches' sermons upon the life and the redeeming suffering and death of the divine Son was for Jefferson a fatal obfuscation of the clear moral message of the human Jesus. For Jefferson the education of the people in the universities, which would provide access for all citizens to a humanistic and democratic education, was more important than the church. Everybody could learn here what the message of Jesus proclaimed: a righteousness that grew out of the heart, to respect others as one would like to be respected, to find peaceful solutions of conflicts, to be generous without expecting rewards, and to lead a simple life. In his last years, Jefferson devoted most of his energies to the founding of the university of his home state, Virginia.

At the same time, Jefferson believed that only the farmer, who was bound to the soil, was destined to the freedom of Jesus' morality, because only he was able to recognize in the rhythm of nature the moral laws that would result in righteous actions toward one's neighbors and fellow citizens. In contrast to his influential colleague and political opponent Alexander Hamilton, whose political philosophy was later adopted by the Republican Party, Jefferson rejected industrialization. Thus Jefferson's reception of Jesus'

---

4. Thomas Jefferson, *The Life and Morals of Jesus of Nazareth* (Washington, D.C.: United States Congress, 1904).

5. This and the following citation are quoted from the "Introduction" to the *Jefferson Bible* by Cyrus Adler (Jefferson, *Life and Morals,* 15).

6. ET published by Charles H. Talbert, *Reimarus: Fragments* (Philadelphia: Fortress Press, 1974).

message of a rationalistic morality is bound up with an almost romantic and—as future developments would soon demonstrate—unrealistic view of the "natural" world of the farmer, where he sees the environment in which the moral laws of Jesus could be fully realized. This understanding of the message of Jesus therefore found little acceptance in the rapidly developing industrialization and commercialization of American society.

The author of the essay in *Harper's Magazine* was fascinated by the parallels between the *Jefferson Bible* and the *Gospel of Thomas*. But he succeeded in this by choosing from the *Gospel of Thomas* only those sayings that seemed to proclaim an individualistic morality. It was for him, the son of an evangelical Baptist preacher, a liberating experience to realize that the *Gospel of Thomas* did not contain any narrative of Jesus' death and resurrection, which redeemed the sinful human being with God. Compared to the narrow-minded evangelical Christianity that still today dominates many American churches, he saw in the *Gospel of Thomas* and in the *Jefferson Bible*, that is, in the words of Jesus, the right gospel for the United States.

This, of course, does not fully comprehend the message of the *Gospel of Thomas*. A real affinity to this message does not yet appear in Jefferson but only a few decades later with Ralph Waldo Emerson. Emerson, born in 1803 as the son of a minister of a Congregationalist church in Boston, studied theology at the Theological Faculty of Harvard University. After the conclusion of his studies he became minister of the Second Church Unitarian of Boston, which he served from 1828 to 1832. But he left this ministry because of his criticism of the celebration of the Lord's Supper by the Unitarians, who at that time were still committed to a strict biblicism. Emerson then retreated to Concord, a suburb of Boston, where he continued to live as a wealthy private scholar and lecturer.

In Concord he soon became the leading spirit of a small but very influential circle of progressive intellectuals, to which also belonged the celebrated poet Nathaniel Hawthorne and Henry David Thoreau, who would become famous through his book *Walden,* for which he became known as the "American Rousseau." Throughout the thirties, forties, and fifties of the nineteenth century Concord became the intellectual center of progressive thinking in America. Because of their interest in Immanuel Kant and German idealism this circle of philosophers, poets, and theologians became known as the "Transcendentalists."

Emerson had familiarized himself with Kant and especially with Johann Wolfgang Goethe, inspired by the Unitarian minister William Ellery Channing, who had studied in Göttingen and is known as the forerunner of Transcendentalism. In addition, Emerson studied Swedenborg and became an enthusiastic student of Plotinus and Neoplatonism. In 1838 he was invited by the graduating class of Harvard Divinity School as their commencement speaker. In this commencement address, which dealt with the topic "Make Yourself Acquainted with Deity," he met with the bitter criticism of the professors of the theological faculty, which then was fully committed to a formalistic Unitarianism. The result was that Emerson was banned from the premises of Harvard University for quite a few years. Today Emerson is one of the saints of the Unitarian-Universalist Church, which established a major endowment gift at Harvard University in this very year 2006 for a new professorship in religion honoring Emerson.

Emerson's "Divinity School Address" contains passages of biting criticism of the cold and formalistic worship services of the Unitarians, which at that time held sway over much of the religious life of New England. The Unitarians, an offspring of the Congregationalists that were founded by the Pilgrim fathers, also controlled the influential Harvard University. They rejected the doctrine of the Trinity, but were otherwise strictly bound to the study of the Bible. At that time, the curriculum of Harvard Divinity School, designed primarily by Unitarian churches, required that two-thirds of all classes had to be devoted to the study of the Bible, biblical preaching, and learning Greek and Hebrew. This biblical orientation demonstrated that the Unitarians at that time were bound to the belief in the redemption through Jesus' suffering and death, which characterized most of the American churches, all transplanted from Europe to the new continent.

Emerson's critique of this biblical tradition, however, is not simply a rejection of the cold formalism of the services and of bad preaching. He and his friends in the Concord circle of poets, writers, and philosophers had a much loftier goal, which was the second liberation of the United States from the fetters of European domination. The American War of Independence had brought freedom from British rule and was written into history by the American Constitution. The second liberation should free the American spirit and American religion from the shackles of Europe. These were for Emerson most evident in the structures of Christian faith and religious services that were bound to the story of Jesus and to his death and resurrection. Once British rule had held the settlers of the new world captive as obedient subjects of the British crown. But still now the Christian churches held the human being, born to spiritual freedom, captive as born in original sin and thus dependent upon the means of grace, administered by the churches, in order to obtain salvation.

For Emerson, freedom could not come from the churches, which were bound to the story of Jesus and his redeeming suffering and death. It could come only through the separation of the message of Jesus from the story of the suffering Son of God, upon which the institution of the church was founded. God could not be found in this story but only in Jesus' immortal words. Jesus was God because he had found God in his own soul and in his own mind. It is this divine presence that Jesus proclaims in his words. Illumination can come only through the words of Jesus, but not in the attempt to understand his story, his miracles, and his suffering and death. The words of Jesus reveal that he was divine:

> Jesus belonged to the true race of prophets. He saw with open eye the mystery of the soul. Drawn by its severe harmony, ravished by its beauty, he lived in it, and had his being there. One man was true to what is in you and me. Alone in all history he estimated the greatness of man. He saw that God incarnates himself in man. . . . He said in this jubilee of sublime emotion "I am divine. Through me God acts, through me God speaks." (259–70)[7]

---

7. The line numbers refer to the edition of the Divinity School Address in Kenneth Walter Cameron, *Emerson at the Divinity School: His Address of 1838 and Its Significance* (Hartford: Transcendental Books, 1994).

But listening to Jesus' words, a human being is no longer dependent upon Jesus. Rather, these words inspire human beings to discover the Deity also in their own soul:

> Meantime, whilst the doors of the temple stand open, night and day, before every man, and the oracles of this truth cease never, it is guarded by one stern condition; this, namely: it is an intuition. It cannot be received at second hand. Truly speaking, it is not instruction, but provocation, that I cannot receive from another soul. What he announces, I must find true in me, or reject.

Whoever translates this provocation into just action has therefore found entrance into the region of the Deity:

> He who does a good deed is instantly ennobled. . . . If a man is at heart just, then insofar he is God, the safety of God, the immortality of God, the majesty of God do enter into that man with justice. (91–97)

The human soul is the place where salvation and renovation take place, while the church is denied the ability to mediate salvation:

> We have contrasted the Church with the Soul. In the soul then let the redemption be sought. Wherever a man comes, there comes revolution. The old is for slaves. When a man comes, all books are legible, all things are transparent, all religions are forms. He is religious. Man is the wonderworker. (674–80)

Everything external, including the entire business of the churches, has no share in the communication of divinity. On the contrary, it blocks access to divine inspiration:

> Yourself a newborn bard of the Holy Ghost, cast behind you all conformity, and acquaint men first hand with Deity. Look to it first and only, that fashion, custom, authority, pleasure, and money, are nothing to you,—are but bandages over your eyes, that you cannot see,—but live with the privilege of the immeasurable mind! (730–37)

On the other hand, Emerson sees in the observation of nature a path to find God. Nature itself, however, is not divine. Ultimately, also the natural world is not real but only a mirror of the Deity because in it one can discover the eternal laws of God:

> But when the mind opens and reveals the laws which traverse the universe and make things what they are, then shrinks the great world at once into a mere illustration and fable of the mind. What am I? and What is? asks the human spirit with a curiosity newly kindled, but never to be quenched. (31–37)

Not harmony with nature as such but rather the recognition of the eternal divine laws, which penetrate all nature, leads to the recognition of oneself and makes the human being divine:

The dawn of the sentiment of virtue on the heart, gives and is the assurance that the Law is sovereign over all natures; and the world, times, space, and eternity do seem to break out in joy. This sentiment is divine and deifying. It is the beatitude of man. It makes him illimitable. Through it the soul first knows itself. (165–72)

The individualism of Emerson's piety is evident. To be sure, in Emerson's understanding righteous action contributes to the well-being of society, although it is interesting that the concept of love does not play a role in his theological reflections. The righteous individual is for him the farmer, who is closely connected to nature. His views here are close to those of Jefferson. Emerson encouraged his younger friend Henry David Thoreau to engage in his experiment of living alone in a small self-constructed hut on Walden Pond near Concord, where he spent two years, summer and winter, eating only fruits and vegetables that he had raised himself. Thoreau was a naturalist; but Emerson was a transcendentalist and remained the fairly wealthy country squire, whose well-furnished house can still be visited today. Only later in his life did Emerson engage in social questions and take a position with respect to the question of slavery, which, admittedly, played a smaller role in New England. Emerson's fascination with the divinity of the human soul allowed him to develop an understanding of human existence that was ultimately independent of all powers of the world and of the society and its institutions.

Similar to Jefferson and Emerson, also the *Gospel of Thomas* presents a proclamation of Jesus without the miracles of Jesus and without a story of his suffering and death. The words of Jesus alone proclaim salvation, and only those who understand these words will receive immortality (*Gos. Thom.* 1).[8] But while Jefferson might have included the moral maxims of the *Gospel of Thomas* in his Bible, he would not have had any use for the mystic sayings of this Gospel. But Emerson would have found an affinity of ideas exactly in those mystic sayings of the *Gospel of Thomas.* Also this Gospel challenges the readers to discover the divinity in themselves:

When you come to know yourselves, then you will become known, and you will realize that it is you who are the sons of the living father. But if you will not know yourselves, you dwell in poverty and it is you who are that poverty. (3b)

Only those who have recognized themselves as children of the divine Father, in whom they have their origin, will be able to proceed without hindrance on the way on which they return to the repose in their heavenly home:

If they say to you, "Where did you come from?", say to them, "We come from the light, the place where the light came into being on its own accord and established itself. . . ." If they say to you, "Is it you?", say, "We are its children and we are the elect of the living father." If they ask you, "What is the sign of your father in you?", say to them, "It is movement and repose." (50)

---

8. The numbers refer to the numbering of the sayings of Jesus in most editions of the *Gospel of Thomas.* All quotations in the following present the translation of Thomas O. Lambdin in Bentley Layton, ed., *Nag Hammadi Codex II,2–7* (2 vols.; NHS 20; Leiden: Brill, 1989) 1.52–93.

The source of this revelation is Jesus in his words. Jesus is God, and all who receive the revelation through his words have a share in his divinity:

> Jesus said, "It is I who am the light which is above them all. It is I who am the all. From me did the all come forth, and unto me did the all extend." (77a)

> Jesus said, "He who will drink from my mouth will become like me. I shall become he, and the things that are hidden will become revealed to him." (108)

Nevertheless, the human being thus enlightened is not necessarily bound to Jesus but bears the divinity and the divine light in himself:

> His disciples said to him, "Show us the place where you are, since it is necessary for us to seek it." He said to them, ". . . There is light within a man of light and he lights the whole world. If he does not shine, he is darkness." (24)

> [If someone is like God]⁹ he will be filled with light, but if he is divided he will be filled with darkness. (61)

An interesting parallel to Emerson's distinction between rational knowledge and transcendental inspiration of the mind appears in another saying of the *Gospel of Thomas:*

> If someone knows all things but is still deficient of one thing, he is completely deficient. (67)¹⁰

Like Emerson also the *Gospel of Thomas* rejects the teachings of the church that all human beings are trapped in Adam's sin; true human existence and thus human divinity is superior to the concept that all human beings are heirs of original sin:

> Adam came into being from a great power and a great wealth, but he did not become worthy of you. For had he been worthy, he would not have experienced death. (85)

Closely related is the rejection of the religious institutions and of their recognized representatives:

> The Pharisees and the scribes have taken the keys of knowledge and have hidden them. They themselves have not entered nor have they allowed to enter those who wish to. (39)

> His disciples said to him, "Is circumcision beneficial or not?" He said to them, "If it were beneficial, their father would beget them already circumcised from their mother. Rather, the true circumcision in spirit has become completely profitable." (53)

---

9. Translation uncertain.
10. Translation modified.

As the Gospel of Matthew and the *Didache* show, the early Christian churches had continued the customary Jewish pious practices of fasting, praying, and almsgiving. The *Gospel of Thomas*, however, rejects this submission to conventional piety:

> His disciples questioned him and said to him, "Do you want us to fast? How shall we pray? Shall we give alms? What diet shall we observe?" Jesus said, "Do not tell lies and do not do what you hate, for all things are plain in the sight of heaven." (6)

> Jesus said to them, "If you fast, you will give rise to sin for yourselves; and if you pray, you will be condemned; and if you give alms, you will do harm to your spirits." (14)

The community has no meaning whatsoever. It is the solitary one who will enter the kingdom of God:

> Jesus said, "Many are standing at the door, but it is the solitary who will enter the bridal chamber." (75)

> Blessed are the solitary and elect, for you will find the kingdom. For you are from it and to it you will return. (49)

At first glance it might seem as if the *Gospel of Thomas* completely rejects the tangible earthly world altogether:

> Whoever has come to understand the world has found a corpse. (56)

> Whoever finds the world and becomes rich, let him renounce the world. (110)

But the relationship to the world appears as more multifaceted in other sayings of the *Gospel of Thomas*. The kingdom of the Father is also present in this world. In Emerson's theology, nature is not in itself divine and ultimately not real. Only the recognition of the divine laws, which order the visible world, provides access to the Deity. Similarly, in the *Gospel of Thomas* what is really divine is also present in the world, but it can be recognized only by the one who is truly enlightened. God's kingdom is not only present within the human being, it is also everywhere on earth:

> Jesus said, "If those who lead you say to you, 'See, the kingdom is in the sky,' then the birds of the sky will precede you. If they say to you, 'It is in the sea,' then the fish will precede you. Rather, the kingdom is inside of you and it is outside of you." (3)

> His disciples said to him, "When will the kingdom come?" Jesus said, "It will not come by waiting for it. It will not be a matter of saying, 'Here it is,' or 'There it is.' Rather, the kingdom of the father is spread out upon the earth, and men do not see it." (113)

The similarities between the *Gospel of Thomas* and Emerson are probably not accidental. Using Hans Jonas's comprehensive definition of the concept of "Gnosis," it is possible to assign the *Gospel of Thomas* to the same intellectual movement that also includes Plotinus's "philosophical Gnosticism," with which Emerson was familiar. But my purpose is not to characterize the tradition and the interpretation of the words of Jesus as "Gnostic." Rather, what connects Jefferson, Emerson, and the *Gospel of Thomas* is their interpretation of the words of Jesus in relation to individualistic concepts of salvation, piety, and righteousness, which in turn implies a clear rejection of the piety that is present in organized churches.

Such an individualistic understanding of piety and redemption is indeed not restricted to the interpretation of Jesus' words. It dominates broadly also the piety of many churches, though here it is bound to religious communities that function as institutions for personal salvation. But it is interesting that the protest against such institutionalized piety makes recourse to the words of Jesus, that is, to a gospel without miracles and without the story of Jesus' redemptive suffering and death. Such protest finds a liberating message in the *Gospel of Thomas*. It sees especially in the evangelical circles of churches only servility, degrading dependence, and outworn morality and self-righteousness. But in the liberating words of Jesus, this protest against traditional church piety finds only the freedom of individuals, which provides them with responsible free decisions in moral questions and just judgments about questions of life, occasionally also with mystical experiences of the Divine. What is missing is a vision of a new community that is built upon new moral criteria that make justice for all people possible.

The apostle Paul, like no other person, has dealt with this very question. In the tradition of the churches, however, especially through the lens of the deutero-Pauline letters, Paul has been transformed into a preacher of an individualistic and moralistic piety. But that does not do justice to a critical interpretation of his genuine letters. Especially the First Letter to the Corinthians but also the Letter to the Galatians provide a window into a radical distinction: on the one side stands individual piety and righteousness, and on the other side stands a vision of a community of justice that is founded upon freedom and love.

In Paul's writings, the words of Jesus play only a secondary role. In no way are they considered as capable of providing salvation. Rather, for Paul the proclamation of salvation is a story, namely the narrative of Jesus' suffering, cross, and resurrection, to which he points right at the beginning of his controversy with the Corinthians (1 Cor 1:17–18) and which he quotes in 1 Corinthians 15 in a short formula as the "gospel." The introduction to the words of institution of the Lord's Supper, "[the Lord] in the night in which he was handed over" (11:23), demonstrates that Paul knew an orally transmitted story of the suffering and death of Jesus. Moreover, it is evident that this story was closely connected with the ritual of the Lord's Supper. In Israel the narrative of the exodus together with the celebration of the Passover meal were the story and the ritual that established Israel as the unified people of God; in an analogous way, in early Christianity and in the churches of Paul, the narrative of the passion together with the celebration of the Lord's Supper constitute story and ritual through which the believers become the new people of God.

The contrast between story and ritual on the one hand and individual piety on the other hand dominates the controversy of Paul with the Corinthians. Paul was forced here to come to terms with believers who claimed for themselves the possession of divine perfection, inspired by words of Jesus, which were similar to those preserved in the *Gospel of Thomas*. They had recognized the wisdom of salvation in themselves, were already participants of the eternal life and therefore liberated from all responsibilities relating to life on earth. Thus anything was permitted to them as long as it did not impair their religious perfection. They demonstrated their superiority in spirit-inspired speaking in tongues and other spiritual displays, perhaps also in immoral sexual liberalism (1 Cor 6:15–18) or in extreme asceticism (7:25–39). In all these experiences, the Corinthian Christians had achieved the consciousness that they had discovered their own divinity.

Paul himself knows about such spirit-inspired experiences in his own religious life. But Jesus' suffering, cross, and resurrection did not happen in order to bring about personal experiences of piety. Rather, they were God's acting for the founding of a new people of God. Therefore Paul attaches little value to demonstrations of personal piety and inspiration as compared to that which builds the eschatological community and alone represents the presence of eternity, namely, love. Through love all members are bound together into the new community. In the ranking of spiritual gifts, love takes the first place. Everything that documents the discovery of the divine self of human beings, like inspiration, intuition, speaking in tongues, and asceticism, is relegated to second place. Instead of a club of religiously inspired individuals, Paul wants the new community to be an inclusive fellowship that it bound together through mutual love. In this fellowship of the new community all are welcome, be they Jews or Greeks, poor or wealthy, free or slaves, men or women.

Righteousness of God is for Paul not present in the righteousness, morality, and piety of the individual but in the community, in which justice and equity becomes a reality for all. In Emerson's transcendentalism and in the Gnosticism of the *Gospel of Thomas* the future of God becomes present in the recognition of one's divinity. For Paul, it is the new community in which the eschatological future becomes a reality. The people of God envisioned as the eschatological fulfillment is a utopia, but as the body of Christ it is already a present reality, instituted through the participation in the one bread and the one cup of the new covenant. All who eat from the one bread and drink from the one cup are thus one body (1 Cor 10:16–17).

In the celebration of this common meal all participants should honor and receive each other as brothers and sisters. The Corinthians are criticized by Paul because as pious people they recognized the sacredness of bread and cup but they let the poor go away hungry. They do not recognize that the community of the church is the body of Christ (1 Cor 11:29). As the body of Christ, the church is in the following chapter (1 Cor 12) not described in spiritual categories. Rather, Paul employs an image that he has drawn from the Greco-Roman world, in which the mutual responsibility of all members of a political community is illustrated through the cooperation of all members to the benefit of the entire body.

The bond of the mutual responsibility is the commandment of love. Thus the chapter of the letter that follows upon the chapter that describes the body of Christ in sociopolitical categories is an exposition of the commandment of love, often falsely called a hymn to love (1 Cor 13). It is rather a didactic poem, in which the actions of love are juxtaposed to actions that demonstrate religious fulfillment. Speaking in tongues, prophecy, miracles of faith, and even radical asceticism are meaningless if there is no love. Only in the actions of love the divine reality is present in the midst of the realities of this world. Only in love are the people of God made real as they have been constituted through the common meal that remembers Jesus' suffering and death. Only love will remain, while all other religious phenomena of inspiration and piety have no eternal value.

It is only consistent that Paul rejects the discovery of individual divinity in an anticipation of the resurrection (1 Cor 15). In this life and its world, Christian action remains bound to this world and cannot be determined on the basis of an imagined experience of a present resurrection and the discovery of one's own divinity. Until the return of Christ the believers are still bound to the first Adam created from the dust of the earth. Christian existence in this life is and remains a life in history; it is eschatological only insofar as Christian actions are determined by the commandment of love.

The commandment of love is also the end of the law. It cannot be replaced by moral and lawful actions. When Paul calls the commandment of love the fulfillment of the entire law (Rom 13:8) he does not say that all the prescriptions of law have now gained a new validity. On the contrary, wherever the law erects boundaries in the relationships of human beings to each other these boundaries are abolished by the commandment of love. To be sure, such things as murder, theft, and adultery remain outlawed. But legal boundaries as those between Jews and Gentiles or those that demand subordinate positions for slaves and for women have no longer any validity. The list of Gal 3:28 could be expanded today. Does the commandment of love permit policies that make Christians and Muslims into enemies? Or does it permit legislation that makes people of a different sexual orientation into second-rate citizens? Paul never explains the commandment of love as the sum total of all sorts of legal prescriptions. Righteousness obtained by the fulfillment of moral commandments is excluded. The fruit of the Spirit is defined as love, joy, peace, patience, kindness, faithfulness, gentleness, and self-control (Gal 5:23).

Today our Western societies, especially in the United States, suffer from a self-righteousness that is based upon individualistic piety and morality. Among evangelical Christians, the story of Jesus has been reduced to the "blood of the Lamb" that grants personal forgiveness and righteousness; the Lord's Supper often plays only a minor role, as also in many Protestant churches, and in most cases it is not understood as a meal that celebrates an inclusive and nondiscriminating community. Instead discriminating barriers are erected with reference to often misinterpreted biblical commandments in order to document the self-righteousness of the individual. Such self-righteousness is then translated in a frightful fashion into the superiority of a powerful Christian nation.

Whoever rejects such Christian moralism does not gain anything through the flight into the words of Jesus and into the piety of Emerson and the *Gospel of Thomas*. The result of such flight is nothing more than a consciousness of divine freedom for the individual. But there is no vision of a new community of justice for all, equality, acceptance of those who are different, and loving endurance of those who do not agree with us. The apostle Paul has been able to translate the story of Jesus, not Jesus' words, into a vision of a new community. It is time for New Testament scholarship to liberate Paul from the traditional interpretation. "Righteousness of God" is in Paul's writings not the grace of God that makes the individual sinner into a righteous person. Rather, in Paul's understanding what matters is God's creation of justice in this world through the suffering and cross of his Son, which opens up for all people the freedom to break down all barriers and to create a new community through fulfilling the commandment of love. This new community is founded on the basis of the story of the self-sacrifice of God in Jesus' suffering and death and becomes a reality in the unity of the body of Christ that is symbolized in the Lord's Supper and in the commandment of love that unites all people.

19

WRITINGS AND THE SPIRIT

Authority and Politics in Ancient Christianity

The Authority of the Spirit

"Spirit" in antiquity was seen as the uncontrollable, dynamic, and numinous presence of divine power. It had no relation to rationality, nor were human beings masters of this spirit. On the contrary, it was thoroughly irrational and entirely the agent of the gods. When the spirit was present in human beings, its manifestations were poetry, prophecy, visions, ecstasy, and speaking in tongues.[1]

The early Christian communities began as churches of this divine spirit. The story of Pentecost in its present form, as it is presented in the Acts of the Apostles (2:1–13), does not describe the ecstatic phenomenon of speaking in tongues but reports a speaking in different languages. This description, however, is the result of much later rationalistic interpretation.[2] The older tradition of this story leaves no doubt that Pentecost was an experience of overwhelming divine presence—so overwhelming that those who were thus inspired knew that the end of the ages had come. This experience resulted in irrational glossolalia and inspired prophecy. Acts 2:17–21 appropriately quotes the prophecy of the book of Joel that seemed to be fulfilled in this event:

And in the last days it shall be, God declares,
that I will pour out my spirit upon all flesh,
and your sons and daughters shall prophesy,
and your young men shall see visions,
and your old men shall dream dreams;
and on my menservants and my maidservants in those days
I will pour out my spirit, and they shall prophesy.
And I will show wonders in the heavens above
and signs on the earth beneath. (Joel 2:28–30 = Acts 2:17–19)

---

1. The classic work on this subject remains Hermann Gunkel, *Die Wirkungen des heiligen Geistes nach der populären Anschauung der apostolischen Zeit und der Lehre des Apostels Paulus* (3d ed.; Göttingen: Vandenhoeck & Ruprecht, 1909). For the entire discussion and bibliography, see Hermann Kleinknecht, "πνεῦμα, πνευματικός," *TDNT* 6 (1968) 339–52.

2. Luke used a report of a mass ecstasy, which he interpreted as the miracle of speaking in different languages; see Eduard Lohse, "πεντεκοστή," *TDNT* 6 (1968) 50–52. For the discussion of other interpretations, see Hans Conzelmann, *Acts of the Apostles: A Commentary on the Acts of the Apostles,* trans. James Limburg, et al. (Hermeneia; Philadelphia: Fortress Press, 1987) 15–17.

The experience of the gift of the spirit became closely related to the rite of entrance into the new eschatological community. Baptism conveyed the spirit to every new member. "For by one spirit," says the apostle Paul, "we were all baptized into one body—Jews or Greeks, slaves or free—and all were made to drink of one spirit" (1 Cor 12:13).

According to the letters of Paul, all activities in these new communities were seen as gifts of the spirit:

> To each is given the manifestation of the spirit for the common good. To one is given through the spirit the utterance of wisdom, and to another the utterance of knowledge according to the same spirit, to another faith by the same spirit, to another gifts of healing by the same spirit, to another the working of miracles, to another the ability to distinguish between spirits, to another various kinds of tongues, to another the interpretation of tongues. (1 Cor 12:7–10)

This same passage clarifies another important aspect: since the spirit was understood as a common possession of all members of the community, hierarchical structures of community organization were no longer possible. Possession of the spirit could not be claimed as the privilege of a special class of priests or prophets. That everyone experienced the gift of the spirit implied that the spirit functioned as a principle of democratization.

Spirit and Ecclesiastical Office

It has often been argued that the development of the ecclesiastical offices—namely, those of bishops, presbyters, and deacons—in the postapostolic period signified the end of the spirit-empowered democratic understanding of the Christian communities. Furthermore, this development initiated an age in which the authority of the institutional officeholder took precedence over the inspired activities of members of the communities. Ignatius, bishop of Antioch in the beginning of the second century, is the person who is primarily cited for having developed the concept of a hierarchy of ecclesiastical offices opposed to the free activity of the divine spirit. This interpretation, however, cannot be substantiated from the letters of Ignatius.[3] Ignatius never makes recourse to ordination through an ecclesiastical agency, nor does he ever refer to any written authority. On the contrary, his authority rests in his familiarity with spiritual things: "Not because I am in bonds and am able to know heavenly things, both the angelic locations and the archontic formations, things both visible and invisible, am I already a disciple."[4]

---

3. For discussion of this question, see Hans von Campenhausen, *Ecclesiastical Authority and Spiritual Power in the Church of the First Three Centuries,* trans. J. A. Baker (Stanford: Stanford University Press, 1969) 97–106; William R. Schoedel, *Ignatius of Antioch: A Commentary on the Letters of Ignatius of Antioch* (Hermeneia; Philadelphia: Fortress Press, 1985).

4. Ignatius *Trall.* 5.2. See also the reference to the bishop of the Magnesians, whose "reckoning is not with flesh, but with God, who knows the secret things" (*Magn.* 3.2).

His regular self-designation is "Theophoros" (θεοφόρος), "the one who bears God,"[5] never "bishop," nor does he call Polycarp a "bishop." Rather, he refers to Polycarp's "godly mind" (ἡ ἐν θεῷ γνώμη) and to the "[divine] grace (χάρις), in which he is dressed."[6] When Ignatius wants to emphasize his authority, he refers to his inspired speech: "Yet the spirit, which is from God, is not deceived; for it knows whence it comes and where it goes, and it exposes hidden things. I cried out while among you, I spoke with a voice, the voice of God. . . . I did not learn it from a human being. It was the spirit who made proclamation."[7]

Only in the course of the developments of the second and third centuries did the understanding of the authority of the bishop find new foundations in the doctrine of the apostolic succession, the claim to the possession of the power of the keys for the forgiving of sins, and the concept of the unity of the church.[8] However, these nonspiritual justifications for ecclesiastical authority cannot be understood without the instrument that enabled these foundations to function in the actual practice of the life of the ancient Christian churches, that is, the use of the medium of writing, especially the letter.

The Letter as Rational Political Instrument

Writing plays a negligible role in the organization and practice of all the vibrant propaganda religions of the Hellenistic and Roman periods. To be sure, there are occasional inscriptions that record the rules of some religious association, or the decrees by which the establishment of a religion is recognized and regulated, or a miraculous event that confirmed the legitimacy of a new cult. There are also occasional references to the use of written materials in the ritual itself. The wall paintings of the Villa dei Misteri in Pompeii depict a boy reading from a scroll. It is no accident, however, that we do not possess extensive records of either authoritative scriptures or correspondence by which these religions legitimized and regulated their affairs. Judaism and Christianity are noteworthy exceptions.

The writing of letters characterizes the activities of Christian communities from the very beginning.[9] In the Roman period, two types of letter were common, and both were of a distinctly secular character.[10] The private letter was written by members of a

---

5. For the explanation of this self-designation, see Schoedel, *Ignatius*, 36.

6. Ignatius *Pol.* 1.1–2. Even Polycarp himself (*Phil.* inscr.) does not call himself "bishop." The sender is simply identified as "Polycarp and the elders with him."

7. Ignatius *Phld.* 7.1–2 (trans. Schoedel, *Ignatius*, 204).

8. For these developments see von Campenhausen, *Ecclesiastical Authority*, 163–69 and passim.

9. Whether the writing of letters played a significant role in the organization of Jewish Diaspora communities is not clear.

10. Some basic works on the writing of letters in antiquity are Francis Xavier J. Exler, *The Form of the Ancient Letter: A Study in Greek Epistolography* (Washington, D.C.: Catholic University of America Press, 1923); Heikki Koskenniemi, *Studien zur Idee und Phraseologie des griechischen Briefes bis 400 n. Chr.* (Annales Academiae Scientiarum Fennica B, 102,2; Helsinki: Suomalainen Tiedeakatemia, 1956); John Lee White, *The Form and Function of the Body of the Greek Letter: A Study of the Letter-Body in the Non-Literary Papyri and in Paul the Apostle* (SBLDS 2; Missoula, Mont.: Scholars Press, 1972).

family who were absent from home, by business associates, or by friends who had been separated. Hundreds of such letters have been discovered among the papyri from Egypt.[11] In the published correspondence of educated writers like Cicero, the private letter appears as a highly developed form of literary art.[12] An extension of this private letter is its use for the dissemination of philosophical teachings to a wider audience, such as the letters of Epicurus[13] and the Cynic Epistles of Pseudo-Heraclitus.[14]

The other type is the official letter. The Hellenistic rulers as well as the Roman emperors corresponded extensively with their local governors and other officials. Excellent examples are preserved among the published letters of the Younger Pliny. Among these is the famous letter that reports to the emperor Trajan the measures that the author had taken in order to control the dangerous expansion of the sect of the Christians, as well as the rescript from the emperor to Pliny.[15] In the context of the Roman imperial administration, correspondence was the most important instrument for the regulation and adjudication of the affairs of the vast and often distant provinces. The secretary *ab epistulis* ("for correspondence") was one of the three or four most important cabinet officials in the Roman imperial administration. Without this correspondence, unity would not have been possible in the Roman realm.

The oldest Christian documents that are preserved are letters, namely, the letters of the apostle Paul, which were written in the first generation of the Christian missionary activity. They are directed to communities that understood themselves as founded by the activity of the spirit, as is especially evident in 1 Corinthians. These letters, however, are not witnesses of inspired communication and edification; rather, they are political instruments designed to organize and maintain the social fabric and financial affairs of these communities. It is not difficult to classify these letters within the traditional categories of ancient epistolography. These early Christian letters are neither private correspondence nor writings in which the letter format is used for the dissemination of philosophical or theological ideas to a wider public. Their format reveals that they belong to the genre of the administrative and official letter, that is, the most secular genre of the epistolary literature.

Paul, as the writer of these letters, often identifies himself not only by his name but also by the title of his office, "apostle."[16] The addressee is normally a community, and

---

11. Excellent examples of such letters and a discussion of the way in which they were "mailed" were more recently presented by Eldon Jay Epp, "New Testament Papyrus Manuscripts and Letter Carrying in Greco-Roman Times," in Birger A. Pearson, ed., *The Future of Early Christianity: Essays in Honor of Helmut Koester* (Minneapolis: Fortress Press, 1991) 35–56.

12. I shall not discuss in this context the pseudepigraphical school letter. The writing of such letters under the name of famous ancient philosophers or other historical figures belonged to the fundamentals of rhetorical education.

13. P. van der Mühll, ed., *Epicurus: Epistulae tres et Ratae sententiae a Laertio Diogene servatae* (Stuttgart: Teubner, 1922).

14. Harold W. Attridge, ed., *First-Century Cynicism in the Epistles of Heraclitus* (HTS 29; Missoula, Mont.: Scholars Press, 1976).

15. Pliny the Younger, *Letters and Panegyricus*, trans. Betty Radice (2 vols.; LCL; Cambridge: Harvard University Press, 1969) 10.96, 97.

16. Exceptions are 1 Thessalonians, the oldest letter of the Pauline corpus that was jointly written by Paul, Timothy, and Silvanus; Philippians, which names as the senders "Paul and Timothy, servants of Christ Jesus";

that community is called ἐκκλησία,[17] that is, the political assembly of all voting members.[18] The proem of the letter does not simply deal with personal matters but relates the personal situation of the sender to the affairs of the addressed community as a whole. Greetings are not designed to confirm purely personal relationships but to bind certain explicitly named functionaries in the communities to their assigned or chosen tasks and duties.

The content of these letters confirms their political character. They address such matters as the legitimacy of the inclusion of the Gentiles into the new Israel,[19] the relationship of various groups in a Christian community,[20] the question of authority that was raised by the arrival and activity of other Christian missionaries,[21] the regulation of affairs relating to the procedures during the actual meeting of the members,[22] and the financial transactions regarding the collection for Jerusalem—a topic to which large portions of these letters are devoted.[23] Indeed, it has been observed that no ancient author talks as much about money as the apostle Paul.[24]

These issues are not, of course, presented in the form of authoritarian instruction, but often with elaborate justifications and theological arguments. Paul was not in a position that would have given him the means to enforce commands. Furthermore, the idea that the apostle could rule as an authoritarian leader would have been contrary to Paul's understanding of the apostle's role and his concept of the church, which excluded a hierarchical structure. The building of the community remained the responsibility of the community itself. The apostle could influence this process only through argument and persuasion. The theological arguments of Paul's letters do not intend to serve any explicit spiritual or religious purposes but to bolster the persuasive undergirding of the advice communicated in the letters. It is therefore characteristic that in his letters Paul uses the established methods of ancient rhetoric that were developed in the political

---

and Philemon, a private letter written to an individual. On 1 Thessalonians see my article "First Thessalonians: An Experiment in Christian Writing," chapter 2 in this volume.

17. 1 and 2 Corinthians, Galatians, 1 Thessalonians; Philemon names "the ἐκκλησία in your house" together with Philemon, Apphia, and Archippus. The Epistle to the Romans is addressed "to all the beloved of God who are in Rome, called saints" (Rom 1:7), Philippians "to all the saints in Christ Jesus who are in Philippi" (Phil 1:1).

18. Erik Peterson (*Die Kirche* [Munich: Beck, 1929] 19) had once argued that the term ἐκκλησία should be understood in analogy to the Greek political usage: "that the λαός of the Christian ἐκκλησία is the successor of the ancient δῆμος" (quoted from Karl Ludwig Schmidt, "καλέω, κτλ.· ἐκκλησία," *TDNT* 3 [1965] 513 n. 27; the original was not accessible). However, the rejection of this interpretation by the influential article of Karl Ludwig Schmidt ("καλέω, κτλ.· ἐκκλησία," 506–36) has resulted in a general acceptance of the derivation of the term from the LXX, where קָהָל is usually translated by ἐκκλησία. It must be noted, however, that ancient Judaism preferred the term συναγωγή, and that in the Greek world the term ἐκκλησία is used exclusively in the political realm. It never occurs as a designation for a religious association; see Schmidt, "καλέω, κτλ.· ἐκκλησία," 513–17.

19. Galatians.

20. 1 Cor 1–4.

21. Especially 2 Cor 10–13; see also Phil 3.

22. 1 Cor 11; 14.

23. Gal 2:10; 1 Cor 16:1–4; 2 Cor 8 and 9; Rom 15:25–30.

24. Professor Dieter Georgi, conversation. See also the discussion of financial matters in 1 Cor 9:13–18; Phil 4:10–20; 2 Cor 12:13–18.

arena of the Greco-Roman world.[25] The so-called theology of Paul's letters must therefore be understood as secondary when compared to the political intent of the letters.

One other element makes these letters eminently political: although Paul does not urge uniformity in all his churches, he has a vital interest in the continuing coherence and unanimity of the churches he had founded. The ἐκκλησία, that is, the assembly of the people in one particular city, is always seen as part of a universal commonwealth of the faithful that also includes the Jewish Christians in Jerusalem.[26] The collection for Jerusalem was specifically designed to establish concretely that members of all churches, Gentile Christians as well as Jewish Christians, are bound into one and the same universal new people or nation "in Christ," in which the past distinctions between Jew and Gentile, male and female, and slave and free no longer apply. No central organization or administration held together the proliferating Christian movement. In addition to travels, the sending of messengers, and personal visits, the letter was the primary political instrument that enabled the building and maintenance of this universal community.

From the Letters of Paul to Letters of Bishops

The first step in the utilization of the letter was the collection of the Pauline correspondence, which must have happened well before the end of the first century. The question has been asked repeatedly: Why were the letters of Paul collected and distributed, not only among the churches that Paul had founded, but also elsewhere? The purpose was certainly not the creation of a theological authority. In fact, there is little evidence that the theology of Paul had much influence after his death. New letters written in his name, perhaps in the context of the collecting and editing of his letters, show at best a modified use of his theological insights, but demonstrate that Paul's letters were seen as instruments of the organization of the churches. Church order, the refutation of controversial practice (such as the observation of circumcision, the Jewish calendar, and ritual),[27] and interest in the unity of the churches were the predominant factors. The latest set of letters in Paul's name, the Pastoral Epistles (1 and 2 Timothy and Titus), were written in the first half of the second century and consist primarily of church order materials, while their theology is quite different from that of the genuine Pauline letters.

In the postapostolic and later periods of Christianity, the writing of letters continued to serve as the primary vehicle of communication not only regulating the life of individual churches but also creating the unity of the universal church. A famous example is the *First Epistle of Clement,* written by the scribe of the church of Rome to the church at Corinth at the end of the first century. The rather lengthy epistle directs the

---

25. This has been demonstrated most persuasively with respect to the Epistle to the Galatians by Hans Dieter Betz, *Galatians: A Commentary on Paul's Letter to the Churches in Galatia* (Hermeneia; Philadelphia: Fortress Press, 1979), especially 14–25.

26. The singular ἐκκλησία is never used for the "church universal," but always designates the Christian assembly in one city.

27. This is evident in the earliest of the deutero-Pauline letters, the Epistle to the Colossians.

church in Corinth to settle a dispute between younger members of the community and the elders of the church. Its themes are entirely practical: obedience to the laws of God, respect for the chosen leaders, honor to the elders. In this context a multitude of Christian virtues are remembered and explained in order to establish the entire framework in which the well-being of the community can be maintained. It is interesting to observe that *1 Clement* appeals to many of the virtues that were traditionally considered necessary for the building of the ideal commonwealth of the city.[28] As in the letters of Paul, theological arguments serve to make the church order persuasive.

The letters of Ignatius, written by the imprisoned bishop of Antioch at the very beginning of the second century to five different churches in western Asia Minor, to Bishop Polycarp of Smyrna, and to Rome, are concerned primarily with the strengthening of the authority of the bishop in each of these churches. However, this is only one aspect of a political program. The presupposition for the unity of the church universal under Christ is the unity of the local congregation, and this unity is guaranteed only by a central organization in each city, held together by the bishop who presides over the Eucharist:

> Let no one do anything apart from the bishop that has to do with the church. Let that be regarded as valid Eucharist which is held under the bishop or to whomever he entrusts it. Wherever the bishop appears, there let the congregation (πλῆθος) be; just as wherever Jesus Christ is, there is the whole church (ἡ καθολικὴ ἐκκλησία).[29]

The unity of the local congregation is here paralleled by the unity of the universal church under Christ.[30] Christianity does not appear as a new religion but as a political utopia, the building of a new empire that was, like the Roman Empire, understood as an alliance of cities. Constitutive were the assemblies of the people of each city, the local ἐκκλησίαι, each held together by one local bishop and one Eucharist. The office of the one bishop in each city guarantees the integrity of the local assembly, and the church universal is thus seen as an alliance of the ἐκκλησίαι of these cities—a concept analogous to that of the Roman Empire as an alliance of cities. Dissensions in the local church threatened the very constitution of the church universal.

In this new empire no human being takes the place of the supreme ruler, the emperor. Rather, the universal ruler is none other than Christ himself. This implies that the unity of the church universal had to rely upon the communication of the local

---

28. Barbara Ellen Bowe, *A Church in Crisis: Ecclesiology and Paraenesis in Clement of Rome* (HDR 23; Minneapolis: Fortress Press, 1988).

29. Ignatius *Smyrn.* 8.1–2 (trans. Schoedel, *Ignatius,* 238); the term ἡ καθολικὴ ἐκκλησία appears for the first time in this letter of Ignatius. Schoedel (*Ignatius,* 243–44) has argued persuasively that the term καθολική cannot be understood as meaning "orthodox." Rather, because of references to unauthorized assemblies in the context of the quoted passage, the term "carries with it an idea of organic unity or completeness" (p. 243).

30. "The local congregation (πλῆθος) for Ignatius is an organic unity under the bishop just as the universal church is an organic unity under Christ" (Schoedel, *Ignatius,* 244).

congregations with one another. The primary instrument was the letter. While in the Roman Empire the edicts issued by the central and superior authority of the emperor guaranteed unity, the exchange of letters among Christian congregations was a nonauthoritarian but a no less effective way for the building of unity. While controversies and disagreements were unavoidable, practical questions dominated. That a leader of one church would write to a congregation in another city was not rare. Polycarp of Smyrna dispatched a letter to Philippi giving advice with respect to a presbyter who seems to have embezzled funds.[31] Irenaeus, bishop of Lyons, wrote to Bishop Victor of Rome, who was about to excommunicate the churches of Asia Minor in the Quartodeciman controversy, advising him that the churches should be able to live in the agreement of faith although they might disagree about the days of the Easter fast.[32]

Typical is the apparently extensive correspondence of Dionysius, bishop of Corinth (mid-2d century CE), of which some fragments are preserved.[33] The correspondence ranged over a wide geographical area; Eusebius mentions in his *Historia ecclesiastica* letters not only to the nearby communities of Sparta and Athens but also to Nicomedia and Amastris in northern Asia Minor, to Gortyna and Cnossos on Crete, and to Rome. That such letters were at times critically received can be seen in the summary of one of these letters:

> To this list has been added another epistle to Cnossus in which he exhorts Pinytus, the bishop of the diocese, not to put on the brothers and sisters a heavy compulsory burden concerning chastity and to consider the weakness of the many. To this Pinytus replied that he admired and welcomed Dionysius, but exhorted him in turn to provide at some time more solid food, and to nourish the people under him with another more advanced letter, so that they might not be fed continually on milky words, and be caught unaware by old age while still treated as children.[34]

Here, as also in the following report of Eusebius, the practical orientation of such correspondence is clear:

> He also wrote to the church sojourning in Amastris. . . . He gave them many exhortations about marriage and chastity, and orders them to receive those who are converted from any backsliding, whether of conduct or heretical error. [35]

A quotation from Dionysius's letter to the Romans shows that mutual financial support continued to be an important bond of the church universal:

---

31. Polycarp *Phil.* 11. Note also the reference to the letters that Paul had once written to the Philippians (*Phil.* 3.2).

32. Eusebius *(Hist. eccl.* 5.24.11–17) has preserved portions of this letter in which Irenaeus also mentions the earlier visit of Bishop Polycarp of Smyrna with Anicetus of Rome, reporting that Anicetus yielded the celebration of the Eucharist to Polycarp although they continued to disagree.

33. In Eusebius *Hist. eccl.* 4.23.1–13.

34. Ibid., 4.23.7–8 (this and the following translations are from Kirsopp Lake, *Eusebius: The Ecclesiastical History* [2 vols.; LCL; Cambridge: Harvard University Press, 1959]).

35. Ibid., 4.23.6.

This has been your custom from the beginning, to do good in manifold ways to all Christians, and to send contributions to the many churches in every city, in some places relieving the poverty of the needy, and ministering to the Christians in the mines, by the contribution which you have sent from the beginning, preserving the ancestral custom of the Romans, true Romans as you are.[36]

It is quite possible that the mention of "the ancestral custom of the Romans" implies that the contributions to other churches from the church of Rome parallel the benefactions of the Roman emperor to the cities of the empire.

There is ample evidence from the third century for the continuing use of the letter as a political instrument for the organization and unification of the Christian churches. This is most clearly visible in the well-preserved correspondence of Cyprian, bishop of Carthage (249–258 CE).[37] His contemporary, Dionysius, bishop of Alexandria (248–265 CE), also developed a truly ecumenical correspondence. Unfortunately, almost all these letters have been lost.[38] Concerning the letters that Dionysius wrote about the question of repentance and readmission of those who had lapsed in the persecution, Eusebius, who had access to a collection of Dionysius's correspondence, writes as follows:

He wrote also to the Egyptians a letter On Repentance, in which he set forth his opinions with reference to those who had fallen, outlining degrees of failures. And to Colon (he was bishop of the community of the Hermopolitans[39]) a personal letter of his is extant On Repentance, and another in the nature of a rebuke to his flock in Alexandria. Among these there is also a letter written to Origen On Martyrdom, and to the brothers and sisters at Laodicea[40] over whom Telymidres presided as bishop; and he wrote to those in Armenia, likewise On Repentance, whose bishop was Meruzanes. In addition to all these he wrote also to Cornelius of Rome. . . . Next to this there is also another extant, a "diaconic" letter of Dionysius to those in Rome through Hippolytus.[41]

In all instances, the practical purpose of the letters is evident. There is little appeal to inspiration, and theological themes are secondary.

---

36. Ibid., 4.23.10.

37. The collection of his preserved correspondence comprises a total of 81 letters. Of these, 65 are written by Cyprian, and 16 are addressed to him or to the church in Carthage. For an English translation, see *St. Cyprian: Letters (1–81)*, Fathers of the Church 51 (Washington, D.C.: Catholic University of America Press, 1964).

38. In addition to several fragments, only three letters are more fully preserved by Eusebius: his letter to Novatian of Rome (*Hist. eccl.* 6.45), his letter to Hierax (*Hist. eccl.* 7.21), and a letter about the persecution and the plague that followed upon it (*Hist. eccl.* 7.22–23).

39. Hermopolis is a city in Upper Egypt.

40. There are several cities of this name; the seaport in northern Syria is probably meant here.

41. Eusebius *Hist. eccl.* 6.46.1–3, 5 (trans. Kirsopp Lake, LCL, modified). Later (*Hist. eccl.* 7.26.1–2) Eusebius says: "in addition to these letters of Dionysius there are extant also many others, as for example those against Sabellius to Ammon bishop of the church at Bernice, and that to Telesphorus, and that to Euphranor and Ammon again and Euporos. . . . And we have many letters of his besides these."

While Christian letters from the apostolic and postapostolic period were widely used and indeed preserved to be read again even after many decades,[42] they did not claim either inspiration or canonical status. At the same time, the spiritual prophetic authority of the early Christian church began to claim the written medium for its own purposes. The oldest witness is the book of the Revelation of John. The author introduces his vision saying, "I was in the spirit" (ἐγενόμην ἐν πεύματι, 1:10),[43] and the book begins with letters to the seven churches, each letter concluding with the phrase, "The one who has ears should listen to what the spirit says to the churches (τί τὸ πνεῦμα λέγει ταῖς ἐκκλησίαις)."[44] Thus these letters are products of the spirit and stand in contradistinction to the correspondence of Paul and to episcopal letters like those of Ignatius, Polycarp, and others. Such prophetic writing under the authority of the spirit continues in the second century[45] and finds its culmination in the literary productions of the Montanist movement. Inspired activity was not immediately rejected by the organized churches. Even Irenaeus at the end of the second century does not reject the Montanist movement as heretical. Tertullian welcomes the renewal of the early Christian prophetic spirit that is documented in these writings. The dissemination of such literature, however, increased skepticism with respect to the criterion of inspiration in the process of the formation of a Christian canon of Holy Scripture. As a result, inspired prophetic books such as the *Shepherd of Hermas* and the *Apocalypse of Peter* did not become part of the New Testament canon, and even the Revelation of John was not easily accepted in the developing canon of the New Testament.

Christian Writings as Holy Scripture

The impulse for the creation of a Christian book of Holy Scripture came from a different quarter. Throughout the first hundred years of early Christian history, the recognized Holy Scripture was the Bible of Israel, the law of Moses and the books of the prophets, as they were collected in the Greek translation of the Hebrew Bible, the Septuagint.[46] Jewish authors had already claimed that this translation into Greek was inspired.[47] Christian writers assumed that either "the Lord," that is, Christ, or the spirit spoke in these writings. Justin Martyr designates the entire Bible of Israel as oracles of "the prophetic spirit" (τὸ προφητικὸν πνεῦμα).[48] At the same time, the moral legisla-

---

42. See the remark of Dionysius of Corinth in his letter to Rome that the letter sent to Corinth from Rome through Clement half a century earlier was still being read.

43. The phrase occurs again in Rev 4:2; and compare 17:3.

44. Rev 2:7, 11, 17, 29; 3:6, 13, 22.

45. *Hermas* (*Vis.* 1.1.3) begins with the report that the prophet was transported by the spirit to another place (καὶ πνεῦμά με ἔλαβεν καὶ ἀπήνεγκέν με); see also *Hermas Vis.* 2.1.1.

46. Hans von Campenhausen, "Das Alte Testament als Bibel der Kirche vom Ausgang des Urchristentums bis zur Entstehung des Neuen Testaments," in *Aus der Frühzeit des Christentums: Studien zur Kirchengeschichte des ersten und zweiten Jahrhunderts* (Tübingen: Mohr/Siebeck, 1963) 152–96. A brief survey can be found in Lee Martin McDonald, *The Formation of the Christian Biblical Canon* (2d ed.; Nashville: Abingdon, 1995) 25–133.

47. On this question see Naomi Janowitz, "The Rhetoric of Translation: Three Early Perspectives on Translating Torah," *HTR* 84 (1991) 129–40.

48. Justin *1 Apol.* 31.1. In this context, Justin repeats the story of the translation of the Bible from

tion of the books of Moses and the ethical instructions of the Hellenistic-Jewish synagogue had become very influential in Christian attempts to establish rules for a Christian life and for the organization of the churches.[49] Moreover, an interpretation that viewed these Scriptures as inspired had become an important factor in the development of Christian theology.

The protest against this development came from a scholar and church leader who rejected such Judaizing tendencies and despised spiritual interpretation of anything, most of all the Scriptures of Israel: the wealthy merchant and shipowner Marcion of Pontus, who came to Rome sometime around 130 CE.[50] Marcion had grown up in the tradition of the Pauline churches; and he was, first of all, a scholar. Rejecting the Holy Scriptures of Israel as the work of an inferior deity who was just but not merciful, Marcion wanted to use exclusively scholarly principles for the establishment of a new book of Christian Scriptures. The starting point for his work was the collection of the letters of Paul. He set out according to scholarly principles to purify these letters of all assumed secondary Jewish additions. Marcion found the "gospel" that Paul had used in his teachings in the Gospel of Luke. From this he excluded whatever appeared to him as secondary Judaizing contamination. This gospel of Jesus had authority because it contradicted in every point the inferior legislation of Moses. Thus the first collection of authoritative Christian writings came into existence.

The church rejected Marcion's experiment; Marcion was excommunicated by the Roman church and organized his own churches, which survived for several centuries. However, Marcion's attack upon the authority of what was later called the Old Testament left the church in Rome rather perplexed. The apologist Justin, Marcion's Roman contemporary, made a threefold response: he asserted once more the authority of the Scriptures of Israel as inspired prophetic writings; he avoided any reference to the corpus of the Pauline writings; he sought to establish a new understanding of the writings that later became known as the Gospels.

Until then, the events of Christ's coming, suffering, death, and resurrection had been understood as the fulfillment of prophecy. These events constituted the life-giving proclamation of the Christian churches. No evidence was required to prove the legitimacy of the oral or written story about these events. The belief of the hearers was their verification. Justin made a decisive step in a new direction. He introduced written documents, which he usually called the "Remembrances of the Apostles" and sometimes also "Gospels," as the proof for the truth of the Christian kerygma. For Justin, these writings were reliable because they presented a historical record that was written by firsthand witnesses. These books recorded the exact fulfillment of the prophecies of the

Hebrew into Greek under King Ptolemy; however, he does not ascribe inspiration to the translation (*1 Apol.* 31.2–5).

49. The most important evidence is the acceptance of the Jewish teachings of the "Two Ways" in the *Didache* and *Barnabas.*

50. The basic monograph on Marcion remains Adolf von Harnack, *Marcion: Das Evangelium vom fremden Gott* (2d ed.; TU 45; 1924; repr. Darmstadt: Wissenschaftliche Buchgesellschaft, 1960). Also important is John Knox, *Marcion and the New Testament: An Essay on the Early History of the Canon* (Chicago: University of Chicago Press, 1942); see further the treatment of Marcion in Hans von Campenhausen, *The Formation of the Christian Bible,* trans. J. A. Baker (Philadelphia: Fortress Press, 1972) 147–68.

books of Moses and of the prophets of Israel. Indeed, as these writings were taking the place of the Christian proclamation, they could themselves be called "Gospels." He may have learned this designation from Marcion. That these Gospels could be inspired writings never occurred to Justin. Inspiration properly characterized prophetic books. The Gospels were historical records, not inspired writings.

The Authority of the New Testament Gospels

These Gospels of the New Testament have been acclaimed in the later Christian churches as inspired documents. This claim, however, has no basis in their actual origin, composition, and usage. The status and usage of these gospel writings in the time before Marcion and Justin Martyr is unclear. It seems that they were used and read, and that they, like early Christian letters, served as instruments for the organization of the early Christian communities. It is unlikely, however, that these writings were called "Gospels" before the time of Justin Martyr, that is, in the mid-second century.[51] The Christian churches did not equate these writings with the "gospel," the saving message that created and sustained Christian faith.

The history and development of this literature has become clear in modern scholarship. All Gospels of the New Testament are composite documents. They employ in their composition various and often contradictory sources and traditions about Jesus that had been used in the propaganda and instruction of the early churches. The Gospels of Matthew and Luke are the most striking examples. Both writings combined two very different sources: the Gospel of Mark, which proclaimed Jesus as the crucified and risen Lord; and the Synoptic Sayings Source, which made no reference to Jesus' death but announced Jesus as the teacher of wisdom and as the eschatological prophet. These are two very different christological concepts, the first based on the Pauline kerygma of Christ's resurrection as the turning point of the ages, the second oriented to the interpretation of the sayings tradition that eventually resulted in a heretical Gnostic understanding of salvation through Jesus' words.[52] How could these two different christological concepts be combined into one single writing? This combination cannot be viewed primarily as a successful theological experiment; rather, it is an accomplishment of ecclesiastical politics. By incorporating the traditions of two very different Christian communities into one single document, both traditions were recognized as legitimate in spite of their theological disagreements. Such gospel writings were useful, not because they dispensed information about doctrine and theology, but because they provided a handbook for the order of the church and the conduct of the life of the members of the community. This is most clearly evident in Matthew, whose "speeches" of Jesus are essentially catechisms and church orders.

This argument, however, does not explain why these four Gospels eventually became

---

51. For this question as well as the following, see Helmut Koester, *Ancient Christian Gospels: Their History and Development* (Philadelphia: Trinity Press International, 1990).

52. Such interpretation of Jesus' sayings appeared very early. It must be presupposed for the development of the Johannine discourses and dialogues, is perhaps visible in 1 Cor 1–4, and is clearly evident in the *Gospel of Thomas*.

the first part of the canon of the New Testament. The Christian churches had their inspired Holy Scriptures, namely the Greek Bible that was later called the Old Testament. They also possessed a still growing and as yet undefined collection of apostolic letters. But why should these writings about Jesus become the fundamental core of a new scripture? Only the Gnostics thought that books with the records of the words of Jesus were inspired. When Marcion had elevated one of these writings, the Gospel of Luke, to a kind of canonical status, Justin Martyr had answered Marcion's challenge by exploiting the usefulness of three of these writings, Matthew, Mark, and Luke, as reliable historical records that were capable of proving the fulfillment of prophecy. This rationalist apologetic argument, however, hardly qualifies as the cause for the eventual canonization of such literature.

The arguments of ancient church theologians for the acceptance of all four of these Gospels were based not on artificial proofs for their theological unity, or on the evidence of their historical reliability, or on the claim that they were inspired writings, but on the tradition of their early usage in the process through which churches were maintained and developed. The building of the churches is again a political rather than a spiritual argument. In this respect, the development of the gospel literature was a process that is analogous to the establishment of the authority of Christian epistolary literature.

With respect to the Gospels, however, it is necessary to explore further the argument of early usage insofar as it is related to the political process of the building of community. At this point, I can suggest no more than the outline for a model that may be helpful but still needs to be documented and argued in more detail.[53] The oldest Gospels are built around the narratives of the passion and death of Jesus.[54] The formation of this story in the first decades of Christian history must be located in the reenactment of the memory of this event, which had three important components: first, the resumption of the ritual meal consisting of bread and wine or, more accurately, the bread that was broken and shared and the cup; second, recitation[55] of scriptural passages about the suffering righteous and prophets; third, the telling of the story of Jesus' passion and death in analogy to the traditional story of the suffering righteous.[56] Literary fixation of these stories must have been casual at first. There may have been different sets of stories, just as there were different developing liturgies of the eucharistic meal. These are still visible

---

53. I want to acknowledge my indebtedness to Gregory Nagy, *Pindar's Homer: The Lyric Possession of an Epic Past* (Baltimore: Johns Hopkins University Press, 1990). In this book Nagy has constructed a model for the textual fixation of Homeric poetry in the context of Panhellenism and the Greek "polis"; see especially pp. 52–53. I am aware of the hazards involved in the construction of an analogous model that could explain what is known as the process of the canonization of the Christian Gospels. However, several analogies exist.

54. That the oldest Gospel, Mark, is a passion narrative with an extended biographical introduction has become a commonplace in NT scholarship.

55. I am using the term "recitation" to include the reading and telling of passages from the prophets as well as the singing of psalms.

56. It is important to distinguish this earliest process of the formation of narratives in analogy to the Psalms and the stories of the suffering prophet or Servant of God (especially from Deutero-Isaiah) from the later attempts to provide scriptural proof (visible in Matthew and Justin Martyr); see Koester, *Ancient Christian Gospels,* 220–40. It is my opinion that there was never anything that could be called a historical report or memory that was independent of the recitation of the fate of the suffering righteous in the Scriptures of Israel.

in the differences between the Markan and the Johannine chronology of the passion narrative, the latter related to the Quartodeciman practice of Asia Minor, the former connected to the more common "Roman" calendar of Easter.

The written passion narratives that were circulated, as well as later the writings that became Gospels, reveal a political interest, namely, to disseminate a narrative that would unite different communities that shared the same eucharistic liturgy. The increasing intercommunication of Christian communities, also visible in the development of the epistolary literature, called for the creation of both a common ritual and a common story.[57] I suggest that one should call this the development of Panchristianity[58] and discard the prejudiced terms "(early) catholicism" and "orthodoxy." The uniting of the Gospel of John and the Synoptic Gospels into one commonly accepted record of the Panchristian narrative is a major political achievement and was not accomplished without considerable controversy.[59] What was ultimately at stake was the unity of the Asian and Western churches. This unity had already been threatened by the controversy about the Easter date, known as the Quartodeciman controversy.[60] When Irenaeus, an Asian who had become bishop of a church in Gaul, accepted the difference in the date for the Easter fast but argued for the inclusion of the Gospel of John, he assigned the highest priority to the creation of a Panchristian narrative. Those who shared neither the common rite nor the common story—Gnostic sects and the Jewish-Christian churches—remained on the margins and were eventually excluded as heretics.

Common ritual and story were formative political and social forces. As early as 1 Corinthians 10–12, the "body" of Christ in the Eucharist is the "body" of the church, a commonwealth with obligations of mutual support and respect regardless of social status. The line of development from here to the establishment of the canon of the four Gospels at the end of the second century is continuous. What Irenaeus says in defense of the four-Gospel canon is merely a rationalization of the reenactment of ritual and the recitation of a story that together had already become the central paradigm of Panchristianity. One might argue that his contemporary Tatian accomplished the creation of the written canon of this story even more radically in his composition of the Gospel harmony known as the *Diatessaron,* while Irenaeus created the less perfect "Four-Gospel Canon," which was one narrative in four versions. In any case, the latter became the literary fixation of the Panchristian narrative for the "sacrament" (μυστήριον) of the new political entity of the ecumenical church (καθολικὴ ἐκκλησία).

Criteria for Canonization

The success of the canon can be understood only if seen against this background. Artificial arguments, such as authorship by one of the twelve original apostles, are evidently

---

57. See above the discussion of the function of the Christian letter. See also Nagy, *Pindar's Homer,* 52, concerning the intensified intercommunication of the city-states of Hellas.

58. Nagy (*Pindar's Homer,* 52) uses the term "Panhellenism" for the analogous process in the preclassical period of Greece.

59. See von Campenhausen, *Formation of the Christian Bible,* 237–43.

60. See above on Irenaeus's letter to Victor of Rome.

secondary. Paul did not belong to this group anyway, and of the four Gospels of the New Testament neither Mark nor Luke could claim apostolic authorship. In fact, the authority of this canon had to be defended against the claim to both spiritual authority and apostolic authorship that was put forward by heretical groups in order to establish the legitimacy of their own literature. The production of a large number of such writings testifies to the prominence that authority in written form of whatever kind had achieved in the early Christian movement. In circles that were later excluded as heretical, the claim that their literature was either inspired or apostolic or both became common. These writings claimed that they were based upon a direct revelation, that they had the dignity of a spiritual interpretation of Jesus' words, or that they transmitted a secret tradition handed down from the apostles. However, according to the defenders of the ritual and narrative of the churches that shared in the Panchristian intercommunication, they could not prove that their literature had been effective in the building and organization of communities from the beginning. This became the ultimate criterion in the development of what later appeared as the "canon of New Testament writings."

The Canon of the New Testament and the Spirit

At the end of the second century, most of the Christian churches in East and West had accepted the letters of the Pauline corpus and a selection from the literature under the title "Gospel" because these were found to be approved resources for the organization of religious ritual and social and individual morality in the circle of developing Panchristianity. Marcion's attack upon the validity of the Scriptures of Israel had been rejected. These Scriptures had been reinstated as the inspired prophetic Holy Scripture of the church. Parallel to this inspired ancient corpus of literature, now increasingly called "the Old Testament," stood a "New Testament,"[61] the record of the history of salvation that was at the same time the Panchristian narrative. Because there was no need for it, a clearly delimited "canon" of the New Testament had not yet developed. Whatever attested the events of salvation and told the shared story and whatever proved to be useful for the building of communities was acceptable. Apart from the four Gospels (or the *Diatessaron* in the Eastern churches) and the corpus of the Pauline writings, it was not clear which writings should be included and which rejected. Nor was there any attempt to draw up definitive lists of canonical and rejected literature.[62] In the Corinthian church of Bishop Dionysius, the letter of the Romans written by Clement (generally called *1 Clement*) was read in the Sunday assembly of the congregation. That it was not written by an apostle did not matter. The letter was not inspired, but it was useful.

Why then did there come to be a clearly delimited canon of Christian writings? No later than the beginning of the second century, and perhaps even earlier, the *Gospel*

---

61. Or sometimes, as in Tertullian's writings, called the *Vetus instrumentum* and *Novum instrumentum*.

62. The *Canon Muratori* must be dated in the 4th century, not ca. 200 CE as is often argued; see Albert Sundberg, "Canon Muratori: A Fourth-Century List," *HTR* 66 (1973) 1–41.

of Thomas presented the "Secret Words of Jesus" as a writing that could claim apostolic authority and would give life to those who could find its hidden meaning. Here was a new concept: a writing whose interpretation would accomplish the same task as the proclamation of the kerygma that was preached by Christian missionaries. In order that writing could function in this way what was needed at this point was the application of a sophisticated method of inspired interpretation to Christian writings. "Inspiration" no longer implied that the writing in question was prophetic but that it contained deep wisdom that could be unlocked and thus convey a significant saving message.

Philo of Alexandria had learned the allegorical method from the Stoic interpretation of Homer and had applied it to the books of Moses. Clement of Alexandria had adopted this Philonic method and used it with respect to all sorts of writings, including the writings of the Greek philosophers, whom he could also call prophetic and inspired.[63] Clement, however, did not see any reason to restrict this allegorical method to the definition of a Christian canon. Only on occasion, as in his letter concerning the *Secret Gospel of Mark* that was used by the Carpocratians, did he make a distinction.[64]

The shift that was taking place with Clement of Alexandria and, subsequently, with the great Alexandrian theologian Origen is most significant. Until then, only the Old Testament, as an inspired and prophetic document, called for a spiritual and allegorical interpretation that was capable of uncovering its hidden truths insofar as they referred to the events of salvation. Only Gnostic circles had found that the sayings of Jesus were also secret revelations that required an interpretation accessible exclusively to those who were initiated into the circle of the truly elect. The Alexandrian theologians, especially Origen, adopted this Gnostic principle and extended the concept of inspiration to the Gospels and to the letters of Paul, that is, to the literature that formed the nucleus of the Christian canon developed by Irenaeus and Tertullian.[65] All these writings now became the bearers of religious truths that were mysteriously hidden in the words of these writings and accessible only to the inspired interpreter. This implied that the apostles who had produced these writings were themselves inspired; they were no longer witnesses of the most important moment in the history of salvation but communicators of deep religious wisdom and doctrine. This provided "the rational basis for regarding the Canon [comprising both the Old and the New Testament] as unified, infallible, and inexhaustible."[66] Because deep meaning could be found in even the smallest word of Scripture, the doctrine of verbal inspiration of the entire Scripture came into existence.

As a consequence, the limits of the canon needed to be defined more precisely. If these writings were to become the infallible source for all doctrine of the church and for its theology, other writings that could be used for the falsification of this truth had

---

63. On Clement's concepts of inspiration and allegorical interpretation, see von Campenhausen, *Formation of the Christian Bible,* 296–300.

64. See Koester, *Ancient Christian Gospels,* 293–95.

65. However, for Clement of Alexandria, only the four Gospels form a clearly defined corpus, while it is not clear what other Christian writings can claim a similar status; see von Campenhausen, *Formation of the Christian Bible,* 294–96.

66. Ibid., 324.

to be excluded. Hitherto, the formation of a body of authoritative Christian writings had been guided by the principle of inclusiveness: all writings that had contributed to the creation of Panchristianity were considered worthy of inclusion, whether or not they had been written by an apostle. On the basis of Origen's new view of the Christian canonical writings as inspired, however, exclusivity became the standard for the definition of the canon.

The most radical shift is evident in the relocation of the activity of the Holy Spirit in the church. The Spirit was now bound into a canon of Christian writings, written by inspired apostles, and was no longer seen as the miraculous power of the continuing divine action in the world. Christianity became a religion of a sacred and inspired book, and its doctrine and teaching had to be justified in the interpretation of this Holy Scripture. Moreover, the interpretation of these Holy Scriptures eventually became a function that could be controlled by ecclesiastical authority. Liberation of the early Christian writings from their usage as inspired sources of doctrine and authoritarian control is the most dignified task of scriptural scholarship. Critical interpretation of these writings must recognize their original function: they are bearers of a story of salvation and witnesses to a political vision of a new ecumenical community.

20

THE APOSTOLIC TRADITION AND THE ORIGINS OF GNOSTICISM

The Traditional View

How were the apostles and apostolic authority established at the beginnings of Christianity? The traditional response to this question is well known: Jesus called the "twelve apostles," who were the eyewitnesses of his holy ministry, of his words and his acts, as well as of his crucifixion and his resurrection. Those who hold this point of view usually refer to the Acts of the Apostles. Luke wished to ensure that in fact the circle of these twelve apostles was the only and exclusive link between Jesus and the young catholic church: when Judas disappeared from this circle, a special election had to be held in order to restore the group to its original number; and in the book of Acts even the ministry of Paul was conceived in such a way as to become dependent upon these original twelve apostles.[1] But what is not generally recognized is that Luke himself did not make use of this conception in order to establish enduring apostolic authority.

In later attempts to establish apostolic authority, Luke's conceptions were used to justify the claim of the catholic church to be the true heir of the tradition of Jesus and of, so to speak, the apostolic age. The three pillars of this claim were (1) the apostolic canon of the texts of the New Testament, (2) the apostolic creed, (3) the legitimacy of the bishop, whose authority was invested by the theory of uninterrupted apostolic succession. These three factors became the pillars of the organization of the early catholic churches and their authority.[2]

From this point of view, every other pretension to hold apostolic authority came to appear as a secondary and illegitimate utilization of this authority. Thus texts attributed to an apostle yet not included in the apostolic canon of the church (i.e., the New Testament), especially the Gnostic Gospels, must have appeared to be deliberate attempts at falsification and perversion of authentic apostolic texts that the church possessed. Such, indeed, was the argument of the first catholic fathers, Irenaeus, Tertullian, and Hippolytus, against the Gnostics; these fathers affirmed that only they possessed the

---

1. For older literature see A. Medebielle, "Apostolat," *Dictionnaire de la Bible Supplément* 1 (1928) 533–88; extensive literature in J. Roloff, G. G. Blum, and F. Mildenberger, "Apostel/Apostolat/Apostolizität: I. Neues Testament, II. Alte Kirche, III. Systematisch-theologisch," *TRE* 3 (1978) 430–77; cf. Harald Riesenfeld, "Apostel," *RGG* (3rd ed.) 1.497–99.

2. With respect to these assumptions see Hans von Campenhausen, *The Formation of the Christian Bible* (Philadelphia: Fortress Press, 1972). For this article I owe much to this masterful work. See also idem, *Ecclesiastical Authority and Spiritual Power* (Stanford: Stanford University Press, 1968).

true apostolic texts and that only they held the right to apostolic succession. Tertullian, in his *De praescriptione haereticorum*, formulated the anti-Gnostic position in its classic form: only the church can claim the prescribed law, since it alone holds the authority of the apostles from the start—the Gnostics entered into the scene only much later.

Historical research, of course, has established for a long time the impossibility of confirming these affirmations of the first early catholic fathers. The so-called Apostolic Creed was certainly not formulated until toward the end of the second century, and neither apostolic origin nor authority was ever claimed for creedal formulations more ancient than that which is found later in the developed Apostolic Creed. Moreover, it is undeniable that all the lists purporting to demonstrate apostolic succession for the principal episcopal sees are fictitious; they were created during the second half of the second century, and, in each case, one cannot attribute any historical authenticity whatsoever to the names of the first successors of the apostles. Indeed, the bishops of the first half of the second century that we know, for example, Ignatius of Antioch and Polycarp of Smyrna, claim no apostolic succession.

I shall deal here primarily with the texts that later constituted the apostolic canon of the New Testament. The question of their claim of apostolic origin is complex. The most ancient texts of the canon are the writings of the apostle Paul; at least, a certain number of these texts are generally recognized as having been written by Paul himself. Paul was of course an "apostle"—in fact, the most important and well known of the first generation of Christianity. But he was neither a disciple of Jesus nor one of the "Twelve." Moreover, even if many names belonging to the circle presumed to be the "Twelve" are adduced as authors of New Testament writings (John, Peter, Matthew), all historical critics and even a great number of more conservative historians agree that none of these texts was authored by one of the first disciples of Jesus.

The task of historical research that examines the first development of apostolic authority is not facilitated by attempts to salvage at least some scraps of historicity to support the claim to hold such authority, a claim that is, on the whole, poorly founded. Historical research demands, on the contrary, to reconstruct in a critical inquiry based on the available sources, including noncanonical sources, the emergence of the notion of apostolic authority at the outset of Christianity. What then was "apostolic authority" at the beginning, and how did it function?

The Function of Apostolic Authority in the Earliest Period

During the whole apostolic period, that is, the epoch of the mission of Paul (and some other early Christian missionary activities), the three expressions, "the Twelve," "apostles," and "disciples of Jesus," designated three different groups. This last, "disciples of Jesus," that is, disciples of the historical Jesus, was not a fixed and precise designation. It never appeared in the correspondence of Paul; some older materials in the Gospels (e.g., Mark 2:18) show that it was used in the church of the first period for every person who followed the teachings of Jesus;[3] and it was used with a specific meaning for the first

---

3. In general, the "disciples" of Jesus in the Synoptic Gospels provide the model for following Jesus, that

time in the Gospel of Mark (and in the other Gospels following him) for the "twelve disciples" of Jesus. The term "the Twelve" is used only one time by Paul (in 1 Cor 15:5) to designate a definite group of persons, those to whom the Lord appeared before appearing to "all the apostles." It is possible that it concerns a group chosen by Jesus himself; but if this was the case, it does not seem that these twelve were chosen so much because they were missionaries, namely apostles, but rather as representatives of the twelve tribes of Israel.[4] (That does not exclude, of course, the possibility that certain persons issued from the circle of the Twelve would also be commissioned to missionary activities, as was certainly the case with Peter.)

By contrast, the term "apostle" designates all the Christian missionaries of the time of Paul. This circle of apostles was certainly much larger than the group of "the Twelve" and the use of this term by Paul indicates that an "apostle" was any person who was committed to missionary activities. Paul himself conferred this title without any hesitation to himself, and he has furnished clear indications that allow us to assume that the missionaries who opposed him in Galatia and elsewhere were and also called themselves "apostles." Among those referred to as apostles by Paul one finds the names of Barnabas (1 Cor 9:6), who was evidently not one of the Twelve, and even of a woman, Junia (Rom 16:7). The criterion for the legitimate use of this term was "to have seen the Lord" (1 Cor 9:1; cf. 1 Cor 15:9; Gal 1:17). Paul himself based the legitimacy for his missionary activities directly on such an apparition of the Lord: he was an "apostle called by Jesus Christ."

This use of the term "apostle" continues even after Paul. The *Didache*, although it presents itself as the work of the "Twelve Apostles," speaks of many itinerant missionaries who claim this title (*Did.* 11.3–6); and Rev 2:2 speaks of persons who claim this title "apostles" for themselves. The function of these "apostles" consists in preaching the gospel and instructing the converts in the new faith. The letters of Paul, which were all written in the context of his apostolic activity, give a vivid impression of the work required of these apostles: preacher, teacher, advisor, traveler and visitor, sender of messengers and writer of letters. For Paul, and certainly also for the other apostles of his times (although this was not the case for all his opponents), the foundation and the preservation of such communities is evidently the principal task of the apostolic function. That is why he writes to the Corinthians (1 Cor 9:1–2): "Are not you my workmanship in the Lord? If to others I am not an apostle, at least I am to you; for you are the seal of my apostleship in the Lord."

This apostolic activity was recognized and honored, as well as remunerated. Just as

---

is, they show exemplary Christian conduct. In the Gospel according to John and in the Acts of the Apostles, the term "disciple" is, in general, synonymous with "believer." Cf. Karl Heinrich Rengstorf, "Μαθητής," *TDNT* 4 (1967) 415–60. While this term does not appear in the epistles of the NT, Ignatius of Antioch uses it to designate those who have acquired a special level of allegiance to Jesus Christ (*Eph.* 1.2; *Magn.* 9.1; especially *Rom.* 4.2). In Papias (in Eusebius, *Hist. eccl.* 3.39) the "disciples of the Lord" are those who followed Jesus during his earthly life.

4. Cf. Karl Heinrich Rengstorf, "Δώδεκα," *TDNT* 2 (1964) 321–28; see also the literature in *ThWNT* 10,2 (1978) 1061–62.

for the "divine man," well known in the religious marketplace of the epoch, the authority of this function could be reinforced by the accomplishment of acts of power, such as miracles, exorcisms, skillful preaching or other acts that demonstrated the possession of the divine spirit. Although acts of this type could sometimes lead to public acclamation of the apostle as a god revealed, as the story of Barnabas and Paul in Lystra (Acts 14:8–13) demonstrates, it does not seem that the name of the apostle as such had a particular authority. On the contrary, the apostles exercised their divine power "in the name of the Lord" or "in the name of Christ," even as Alexander of Abonoteichus says that he was Glykon, that is the revelation of Asklepios.[5]

For Paul himself, special traditions transmitted to the believers were legitimated not by the name of an apostle but by Christ as the initiator of these traditions; this is most clearly evident in the introduction to the words of institution of the Eucharist (1 Cor 11:23). There is, however, in the epistles of Paul an example indicating that the apostles could guarantee by their own name that which was transmitted to their disciples: 1 Corinthians demonstrates, indeed, that certain persons in Corinth were boasting that their possession of a special wisdom entitled them to claim that they "belonged" to the one, from whom they had received such wisdom: "I belong to Paul," "I belong to Apollos," "I belong to Cephas," or again, "I belong to Christ" (1:12). The passage in which Paul cites these affirmations is considered, in general, as a proof of the existence of Corinthian "parties." It is, however, not a question of parties that each had political points of view or different theologies. Paul critiques all parties for one reason alone: they claim to hold a special wisdom that is transmitted and guaranteed by a particular name; that, says Paul, "reduces to nothing the cross of Christ" (1:18), and, moreover, divides the church into two groups: those who can claim to be entitled by some such name and by the possession of a special wisdom, and those who cannot.

One must note that Paul says with insistence, in this context, that he has baptized very few persons in Corinth (1 Cor 1:14–17). Thus the transmission of this special wisdom was attached to the name of the person from whom it had been received, and also, but not necessarily, the person who had baptized the beneficiary of this wisdom. But one can ask if the fact of remembering the name of the baptizer, that is, the mystagogue, was the principal element. As the first chapters of 1 Corinthians indicate, the central question is not baptism, but the possession of a special wisdom. By consequence, the question consists in knowing the character of this wisdom and determining its rapport with the names of certain specific apostolic authorities.

Religious wisdom, in Judaism as well as in early Christianity, was transmitted in the form of sayings. By all evidence, it is not by accident that Paul, in 1 Corinthians, refers to the sayings of Jesus much more often than in any other of his letters.[6] Additionally, the language of Paul in 1 Corinthians 1–4 is rather particular. These chapters, and these chapters alone in all the Pauline epistles, contain a certain number of terms that have very close parallels with the wisdom sayings of the Synoptic Gospels and, as we are

---

5. Lucian *Alexander* 18 and 39.

6. David L. Dungan, *The Sayings of Jesus in the Churches of Paul* (Philadelphia: Fortress Press, 1971) 3–25, 83–99.

going to see, with such works as the *Gospel of Thomas*.[7] It is true that Paul calls this wisdom, which the Corinthians claim to possess, "wisdom of this world" (1 Cor 1:20). But for the Corinthians these words contain a salvific wisdom bestowing eternal life, filling the beneficiaries with a divine wisdom, and leading them to the kingdom. Indeed, Paul speaks of the Corinthians with irony, paraphrasing their pretensions: "Already you are satisfied! Already you have become rich! Quite apart from us you have become kings!" (4:8). We can also suppose that such sayings were understood to communicate "knowledge" (*gnosis*); 1 Corinthians 8 confirms explicitly that certain persons in Corinth claimed to have "knowledge."

If traditions of such wisdom sayings were really known in Corinth, we can deduce from it that the Corinthians had an understanding of apostolic authority different from the concept that Paul had of his role as an apostle of Jesus Christ. For Paul, apostolic authority is the authority of the founder in his rapport with the community. The foundations on which this authority is established are the cross of Christ and the resurrection, and the apostle is commissioned to proclaim this "gospel." Baptism is for everyone an act of incorporation into this community, and each receives the Holy Spirit by this rite of initiation (1 Cor 12:13). For certain Christians in Corinth, on the contrary, apostolic authority, and also the authority of Christ himself, is aligned with a tradition of wisdom sayings transmitted under the authority of a name (Paul, Apollos, etc.) and communicated in the act of baptism: one receives salvation through the "knowledge" of these sayings.

Can these people from Corinth who oppose Paul be called "Gnostics"?[8] This is a question that historians have debated for a long time. One cannot doubt that *gnosis*, that is, salvific knowledge, and *sophia*, wisdom, came to play a central role in the Corinthians' understanding of salvation. The question is whether this knowledge must be understood by analogy to the concept of *gnosis* as it appears in the Gnostic sects of the second century. Happily, this question can be settled. The discovery of the Nag Hammadi Library attests the existence of a conception of the sayings of Jesus that has very striking resemblances with the beliefs of the Corinthians, in that these sayings were transmitted under the apostolic authority and communicate "knowledge" of eternal life.

The Words of Jesus Placed under the Cover of Apostolic Authority

The best-known text of the Nag Hammadi Library is the *Gospel of Thomas*, a collection of more than one hundred sayings of Jesus, of which each is introduced, quite simply, by the words "Jesus says." A number of these sayings are known also in the Synoptic

---

7. Cf. Helmut Koester, "Gnostic Writings as Witnesses for the Development of the Sayings Tradition," in Bentley Layton, ed., *The Rediscovery of Gnosticism* (2 vols.; Numen Sup 41; Leiden: Brill, 1980) 1.244–50.

8. See on this subject Hans Conzelmann, *1 Corinthians: A Commentary on the First Epistle to the Corinthians,* trans. James W. Leitch (Hermeneia; Philadelphia: Fortress Press, 1975) 14–15.

Gospels, others remain unattested to this day or exist only in other noncanonical sources. In order to determine the age of the *Gospel of Thomas*, it is important to note that the sayings of this Gospel do not depend, by all evidence, upon their canonical parallels. As a consequence, one must suppose that the *Gospel of Thomas*, at least in its original form, is an independent collection of the sayings of Jesus that was composed in the first century.

That these sayings have been transmitted under the cover of apostolic authority is evident if one considers the introduction to the *Gospel of Thomas*: "These are the secret sayings that the living Jesus spoke and Didymos Judas Thomas recorded. And he said, 'Whoever discovers the interpretation of these sayings will not taste death.'"[9] It is quite remarkable to find such an introduction to a Gospel.[10] None of the canonical Gospels has any such introduction that names an apostolic author. Quite to the contrary, as the Gospel according to Mark demonstrates clearly, the canonical Gospels are supposed to be the Gospels of Jesus Christ, and they have no need of supplementary apostolic legitimating. We find thus in the *Gospel of Thomas* a conception of apostolic authority that is completely absent from the Gospels of the New Testament. This conception, however, corresponds to that which the Corinthians make of the wisdom sayings placed under the authority of an apostle.

It is interesting to remark that there exist also a number of close parallels between the *Gospel of Thomas* and the discussions of Paul about the wisdom teaching at Corinth. The second saying of this Gospel says: "Jesus said, 'Let one who seeks not stop seeking until one finds. When one finds, one will be disturbed. When one is disturbed, one will marvel, and will reign over all.'" In 1 Cor 4:8 Paul makes reference to the Corinthians as to those who reign already and who have already become kings. Additionally, in 2:9 Paul cites as "scripture" what appears in *Gospel of Thomas* 17 as a saying of Jesus: "Jesus said, 'I shall give you what no eye has seen, what no ear has heard, what no hand has touched, what has not arisen in the human heart.'" Other indications in the new Gnostic texts show that the words of Jesus were transmitted under the cover of the authority of certain apostles who are explicitly named. In the *Apocryphon of James* (= *Epistula Jacobi apocrypha*), the words of Jesus and their interpretation are introduced in the following way: "the twelve disciples [were] all sitting together and recalling what the Savior had said to each one of them, whether in secret or openly, and [putting it] in books. [But I] was writing that which was in [my book] . . . lo, the Savior. . . ."[11] The *Apocryphon of James* treats also the question: how can one obtain *gnosis* and life thanks to the interpretation of the sayings of Jesus, especially the parables? As in the *Gospel of Thomas*, such a tradition of sayings of Jesus is legitimated by the name of an apostle, in this instance by James.

---

9. The translations of the *Gospel of Thomas* are by John S. Kloppenborg, *Q Thomas Reader* (Santa Rosa, Calif.: Polebridge, 1990).

10. This introduction must be distinguished from the colophon, added by later scribes in order to separate one document from another in a manuscript.

11. *Apoc. James* 2.7–17. Translation by Francis E. Williams in James M. Robinson, ed., *The Nag Hammadi Library in English* (3d ed.; San Francisco: HarperSanFrancisco, 1990) 30.

Such references to the words of Jesus are in no way limited to Gnostic documents. One finds them also in mainline Christian circles, as shown by the fragments of a text written by the bishop Papias of Hierapolis, who lived at the beginning of the second century, and which is preserved by Eusebius. In one of the fragments of *Interpretation of the Oracles of the Lord*, Papias says this:

> I shall not hesitate to append to the interpretations all that I ever learnt well from the presbyters and remember well, for of their truth I am confident. For unlike most I did not rejoice in them who say much, but in them who teach the truth, nor in them who recount the commandments of others, but in them who repeated those given by the Lord and derived from truth itself; but if ever anyone came who had followed the presbyters, I inquired into the words of the presbyters, what Andrew or Peter or Philip or Thomas or James or John or Matthew, or any other of the Lord's disciples had said, and what Aristion and the presbyter John, the Lord's disciples, were saying.[12]

Papias refers also to texts of the gospel, and his references are to the Gospel according to Mark and to the "sayings" (λόγια = oracles) embedded in the writing by Matthew. These are the first references to the written Gospels that we know. Noteworthy is not only the somewhat negative opinion of Papias regarding the written Gospels, in relation to his very positive evaluation of the oral tradition, but also the fact that he mentions that these Gospels are written under the authority of an apostle (Matthew) or under the name of a disciple of an apostle (Mark, who was the secretary of Peter).

In all these witnesses, from the Corinthians to the Gnostic Gospels and Papias of Hierapolis, one finds the same specific structure:

1. Sayings (of Jesus) that transmit wisdom and truth.

2. Sayings are aligned to the authority of a particular apostle.

3. Their possession and/or even their interpretation transmit knowledge (*gnosis*) that is necessary to life and salvation.

4. These sayings are finally reassembled in the books that are supposed to have the apostles as authors and that claim explicitly a specific apostolic authority.

Interpretation of the Sayings and the Gnostic Gospel

In the *Gospel of Thomas* one finds a concept of salvation by Jesus entirely different from that according to which salvation is attained by faith in the proclamation of the death and resurrection of Jesus, which are salvific events. Jesus is not the one who died and came back to life, but he is "the living one," living always in these wisdom sayings. Paul must have met the same teachings in Corinth. So he underlines the salvific power of the cross of Jesus as the only divine offer of salvation: "For myself, brothers, when I

---

12. Eusebius, *Hist. eccl.* 3.39.3-4. Translation by Kirsopp Lake in LCL.

came to you, I did not come proclaiming the mystery[13] of God to you in lofty words or wisdom. For I decided to know nothing among you except Jesus Christ, and him crucified" (1 Cor 2:1–2). For Paul, salvation is the eschatological event of the presence of the cross of Christ in the proclamation. It is realized in the community of believers and will be consummated in the advent of Christ. Once the task of the apostle is accomplished—to found and organize churches—there remains no more authority in his office; and there exists no more, either, a rapport of apostolic authority with the interpretation made of the sayings of Jesus. These interpretations can function as rules for the community (with a limited authority! cf. 1 Cor 7:8–10); but analyzing or interpreting these words adds nothing to the power of salvation possessed by the gospel of the cross of Jesus and his resurrection; and such interpretation is not the business that occupies the apostle.

But where the words of Jesus are the principal instruments for the communication of salvation, two new elements appear that are aligned with each other: (1) "the gospel" becomes the interpretation of the words of Jesus, and (2) the apostle is established as an enduring authority.

1. If the sayings give access to the knowledge of eternal life, one must analyze and interpret them. In this process, the words of Jesus become mysteries, that is, the words that only the person possessing the divine Spirit can penetrate in order to provide a living interpretation. It is not by accident that Paul, in refuting the wisdom teaching of the Corinthians, speaks of his own proclamation by making use of the term "mystery of God" (1 Cor 2:1)—a term that he uses in no other place in order to designate the gospel—and that right afterward he mentions "the Spirit" that "searches everything, even the depths of God" (2:10).

2. The apostle assumes the role of guarantor of the tradition and he becomes the inspired interpreter of sayings. Although the sayings are the words of Jesus, the apostle, for his part, must be a personal disciple of Jesus; this is another element that does not play any role in the Pauline concept of the function of the apostle. But when the sayings were considered as "gospel," one must realize that the earthly Jesus is no longer physically present among the disciples; interpretations are then added to the sayings of Jesus and become subsequently an integral part of the life-giving tradition of Jesus' sayings.

The New Testament itself contains some examples of such understanding of Jesus' words. In Mark 4:10–12 the parable of Jesus about the sower is designated explicitly as a "mystery of the kingdom of God" for which an interpretation is required. The interpretation that follows—without doubt an addition to the original parable—is presented as an instruction that Jesus himself gives to his disciples in private (4:13–20).

An analogous phenomenon is the construction of discourses based on the traditional sayings or even dialogues in which questions are posed about the significance of the sayings, questions to which Jesus responds. Dialogues and discourses of this type are well known in the Gospel according to John. A manifest example is the dialogue with

---

13. The original reading is μυστήριον (with NA[26]) instead of μαρτύριον. Cf. Günther Bornkamm, "μυστήριον," *TDNT* 4 (1967) 802–28; Conzelmann, *1 Corinthians*, 53.

Nicodemus in John 3. The first declaration of Jesus: "Truly, truly, I say to you, except by being born anew, no one can see the kingdom of God," is a variant of a traditional saying, conserved in a more original form by Justin *1 Apol.* 61.4: "Except by being reborn (ἀναγεννηθῆναι), no one can enter into the kingdom of God." John introduces some changes that are characteristic: "to be born anew" (γεννεθῆναι ἄνωθεν) replaces the more original "reborn" (ἀναγεννηθῆναι), because this new formulation can be interpreted also as "to be born from above," which John explains two verses later as "born of water and spirit." In the development of the dialogue that follows, other traditional materials are used. When Jesus says (in the first person plural!): "We speak of that which we know and we attest that which we have seen" (John 3:11), he cites two phrases of a declaration of faith of the community of John. Furthermore, a christological interpretation of Num 21:9 is added: "As Moses elevated the serpent in the desert, so must the Son of Man be elevated, so that everyone who believes should have by him eternal life" (John 3:14–15).

The best example in the library of Nag Hammadi of the development of the dialogues and discourses of this genre is the *Dialogue of the Savior.* This text, which in its extant form was composed during the course of the second century, preserves a much more ancient dialogue, where the Lord speaks with his disciples Judas, Matthew, and Mary, and where several aspects of the words of Jesus are explored. Indeed, it seems that this more ancient dialogue may be a systematic elaboration of the saying of Jesus that is cited at the beginning of the *Gospel of Thomas:* "Let the one who seeks not stop seeking until he finds, and, when he finds, he will be amazed, and when he is amazed, he will rule, and when he rules, he will rest."[14] The first part of the dialogue source used by the author of the *Dialogue of the Savior* explores the topic of "seeking":

His [disciples said: "Lord,] who is it who seeks and [who] reveals?"

[The Lord said]: "He who seeks [is also the one] who reveals."

Matthew said: "Lord, when I [seek] and when I speak, who [. . .] is it who listens?"

The Lord said: "It is the one speaks who also [listens], and it is the one who can see who also reveals."[15]

This passage of dialogue seeks to establish the role of the disciple as one who listens to the sayings of Jesus and who becomes thus, in turn, the one who reveals wisdom to others, because he or she can "see," that is, understand, the words of Jesus. Additionally, in

---

14. This translation is based on the Greek version cited by Clement of Alexandria *Strom.* 5.14, §96, and attributed by him to the *Gospel of the Hebrews* (*Strom.* 2.9, §45). I believe that this is the original text of the saying found in the *Gospel of Thomas* or at least the version known by the author of the *Dialogue of the Savior.*

15. *Dial. Sav.* 9–12 (p. 126, 6–16). The translations are based on those of Stephen Emmel in idem, Helmut Koester, and Elaine Pagels, *Nag Hammadi Codex III,5: The Dialogue of the Savior* (NHS 26; Leiden: Brill, 1984) 53.

the dialogues of the Nag Hammadi Library, material originating from other sources is included in the interpretation of the words of Jesus, material that becomes thus an integral part of these sayings. In the *Dialogue of the Savior*, for example, one finds first of all a fragment of a myth of creation; second, a traditional list of sapiential character about the elements of the world (the heaven and the earth, light and darkness, fire, wind, and water to which remarks on baptism are added); and finally, a vision of an elevated place and of the abyss that Jesus explains to the disciples.[16]

The role and the authority of the disciple/apostle are important during the whole development of these texts. The disciples are not only those who pose questions, but it happens sometimes also that they are praised for their perspicuity: "Mary said, 'Thus with respect to "the wickedness of each day" and "the laborer is worthy of his food" and "the disciple resembles his teacher."' She uttered this as a woman who had understood completely."[17] But what is most important is that the disciple/apostle appears rather regularly as author of these texts, at the same time as he/she can play a certain role in the texts themselves. This is a characteristic of the Gnostic Gospels that distinguishes them from the three first Gospels of the New Testament, which do not try to establish an apostle as author, either in the title or in the narrative or in the discourses.

The only notable exception to this rule in the New Testament is the Gospel of John. Although there is no introduction referring to the authority of an apostle, the disciple "whom Jesus loved"—a mysterious figure apparently designating the author—reappears in several decisive passages of the text of the Gospel (John 13:23; 19:26; 20:2); and this figure is introduced again explicitly in the additional chapter placed at the end of the text (John 21), where the truthfulness of the testimony of this apostle is once more underlined: "This is the apostle who testifies to these facts and who has written them and we know that his testimony is true" (21:24).

While such a claim to possess apostolic authority is rare in the early catholic apostolic tradition, it represents the rule in the tradition and in the interpretation of the sayings of Jesus within those circles of Christians that one calls "Gnostic." What Ptolemy, the student of Valentinus, says at the end of his *Letter to Flora* is characteristic of the persistence of this Gnostic claim to possess apostolic authority: "For, God permitting, you will next learn about both the first principle and the generation of these two other gods, if you are deemed worthy of the apostolic tradition, which even we have received by succession; and along with this you will learn how to test all the propositions by means of our savior's teaching."[18]

The Catholic Church and the Gnostic Apostolic Gospel

How did the churches, which became later the "catholic churches," respond to the claim presented by the Gnostic disciples of Jesus to be in possession of authentic

---

16. This analysis is presented in detail in ibid., 1–15.

17. *Dial. Sav.* 53 (p. 139, 9–13).

18. *Ptolemy's Epistle to Flora* 33.7.9, translated by Bentley Layton, *The Gnostic Scriptures* (New York: Doubleday, 1987) 314.

interpretations of the sayings of Jesus, guaranteed by the authority of the inspired apostles?

The concept that the early catholic church had of apostolic authority had nothing to do with the production of some type of literature and certainly not apostolic literature containing interpretations of the sayings of Jesus. Assuredly, one preserved the memory of the apostles, especially Paul and Peter, and they were honored. But one remembered them as founders of churches and as martyrs. That is the way in which they appeared in the *First Epistle of Clement* and in the *Letters* of Ignatius of Antioch, written around the year 100. To be sure, the apostle Paul had written letters, which were widely accepted toward the end of the first century. But when they are cited and referred to, they have not yet acquired the status of apostolic authority. *First Clement* makes reference in a rather fortuitous way to things written by Paul. Ignatius frequently uses terms and locutions from the epistles of Paul, and he holds them in high estimation; nevertheless, if Paul is an apostle, that is because of his martyrdom, not thanks to any apostolic status of his letters.[19] One could also make use of other letters, not written by an apostle, for the edification of the churches: Bishop Dionysius of Corinth, writing to the Romans toward the middle of the second century, speaks thus of the *Epistle of Clement of Rome to the Corinthians*: "Today we observed the holy day of the Lord and read out your letter, which we shall continue to read from time to time for our admonition, as we do with that which was formerly sent to us through Clement."[20]

One supposes that, for the early catholic churches, the authority of each of the apostles was established by the fact that the episcopal office was based on this very specific authority. But Ignatius of Antioch carried a vital interest in reinforcing the episcopal office; however, his frequent references to apostles are limited to general remarks, designating them as "*presbyterion* of the church" (*Phld.* 5.1). A direct rapport between the authority of an apostle and an ecclesiastical office is never established. Even the famous passage *1 Clement* 42 on the bishops and deacons, who were named by the apostles among the firstborn, cannot be understood as the institution of an office with apostolic succession. The accent is placed on an apostolic office consisting of preaching the gospel, rather than on taking the helm or on exercising a disciplinary authority. Thus this passage does not tell more than does the reference to bishops and to deacons in Phil 1:1, a prologue to an epistle in which Paul treats the continuation of the preaching of the gospel after his departure. Neither *1 Clement* nor Philippians 1 recommends a structure for the transmission of apostolic authority to future generations.

Another striking proof of early catholic churches' inability to establish some authority of apostolic succession for its tradition can be found in the Acts of the Apostles. When one considers the pain that Luke takes to establish the circle of "twelve apostles," and also his description of activities endowed with the divine power of these apostles, especially of Paul, one is struck that Luke does not seek to make their authority a foundation, whether it be for ecclesiastical offices or for written documents. That Luke does not even mention the epistles of Paul is well known.

---

19. Ignatius *Eph.* 12.2; *Rom.* 4.3; cf. also *1 Clem.* 5.5.
20. Eusebius *Hist. eccl.* 4.23.11, translated by Kirsopp Lake (LCL).

The first reference to an enduring apostolic authority relates not to an office, but rather to a tradition: "You are Peter and upon this rock I will build my church" (Matt 16:18). It is impossible to interpret this passage as the institution of an ecclesiastical office, since there is no mention of a successor, and since final ecclesiastical authority is seen in Matthew as being devolved upon the assembly of the entire community (18:15–18). To be sure, Matthew claims the authority of apostolic tradition for his Gospel; this is, however, not his own authority that he claims but that of Peter, whose missionary activities in Syria seem to be maintained in the Matthean church. That Matthew utilized traditions under the authority of Peter is indicated, moreover, by the striking parallels between his Gospel and the *Gospel of Peter,* which also originated in Syria.

The only Gospel of the New Testament that explicitly draws from the authority of the apostles of the church and its interpretations of the ministry of Jesus is the Gospel of John. The discourses of this Gospel, which in their structure are very close to the development of the literature of the Gnostic Gospels, belonged without doubt to the interpretation that sees the living sayings of Jesus as the center of the Christian message. In several refrains these speeches resort to the conception according to which salvation is obtained in accepting and understanding the words of Jesus:

Jesus says, "It is the spirit that gives life, the flesh is of no avail; the words that I have spoken to you are spirit and life." (6:63)

When Jesus asks his disciples if they wish to leave also, Peter responds:

Lord, to whom shall we go? You have the words of eternal life. (6:69)

In a formulation that is analogous to the introduction of the *Gospel of Thomas,* Jesus says:

Truly, truly, I say to you, if any one keeps my word, he will never see death. (John 8:51)

And in another passage:

If you continue in my word, you are truly my disciples, and you will know the truth, and the truth will make you free. (8:31–32)

At the same time, the Gospel of John invests the apostles with a special authority. The Paraclete, the Spirit of truth (15:26), is sent to them after Jesus' departure. This Spirit will lead the disciples to the entire truth and will explain to them what Jesus has said (14:25–26; 16:7–11). When Jesus speaks to them of his return as the Spirit of Truth, the disciples understand that Jesus does not speak to them any longer in a mysterious discourse (παροιμία) but in a clear language (παρρησία, 16:29). The interpretation of his sayings through the Spirit is thus the revelation for future generations, his authority resides in the disciples who possess this Spirit, and 20:22 tells explicitly that Jesus confers the Holy Spirit upon the disciples after his resurrection. The appendix to the Gospel (John 21) confirms this apostolic authority and claims it precisely for the disciple who guarantees the truth of this Gospel (21:24).

The emergence of this conception of apostolic authority originates in the Gnostic tradition of the interpretation of the words of Jesus, adapted by the author of the Gospel of John by skillful particulars. He has sought to reconcile this Gnostic tradition of sayings with the proclamation of the cross, so that the Jesus who possessed the living sayings was the same Jesus who was glorified on the cross. But it does not seem that the Gospel of John directly influenced the development of apostolic authority in the catholic church. During the second century, it was especially the Gnostics who made use of it and it was the Gnostic theologians who, first of all, wrote commentaries on this Gospel.

The progressive emergence of the conception of apostolic authority was made in the tradition of the churches of Paul. In this case also one can maintain the very close rapport with Gnostic theology and perhaps even with the Gnostic interpretation of Paul as the apostolic authority for the texts transmitted under his name. The beginnings of this development are visible in the Epistle to the Ephesians. Its author makes use of Gnostic terminology, which designates the Christian message as "mystery" (μυστήριον) but the term "mystery" does not designate the sayings of Jesus. It is rather the gospel of Paul that is designated thus:

> For surely you have already heard of the commission of God's grace that was given me for you, and how the mystery was made known to me by revelation, as I wrote above in a few words, a reading of which will enable you to perceive my understanding of the mystery of Christ … as it has now been revealed to his holy apostles and prophets by the Spirit. (Eph 3:2–5)

All the elements of the Gnostic conception of apostolic authority are present here: mediation through revelation, the binding of the written texts (the epistles of Paul), the penetration into the mysteries of Christ, and the interpretation by the apostles who are in possession of the Spirit. The later development of this transfer of the conception of apostolic authority to the epistles of Paul cannot be elaborated further here. But the Epistle to the Ephesians marks the beginning of the establishment of the only and unique apostolic authority, tangible for the early catholic churches, that is, the collection of the epistles of Paul. The term "the apostle," as it is used in the second century, means: Paul and his epistles. The first attempt to establish a canon of written documents under the apostolic authority—the canon of Marcion—is based on this conception of the epistles of Paul; and if the Gospel of Luke was included in this canon of Marcion, that is only because it corresponded to the gospel of Paul. In itself the Gospel of Luke did not have apostolic authority.

The keystone in the final canonization of the New Testament once more was the authority established by "the apostle," that is, the collection of the epistles of Paul, which gave a legitimacy to the inclusion of other Gospels and other texts, primarily Hebrews, of which it was thought that Paul was the author, then the Catholic Epistles, of which each was supposed to have been written by an "apostle." It was during this epoch only, at the end of the second century, that apostolic authority was also established for the episcopal office through the compilation of lists of succession for the major episcopal sees. But the concept of apostolic authority that was then applied to the canon and to the offices of the early catholic church was owed, in the final analysis, to the interpretation of the sayings of Jesus under apostolic authority in the first stages of Gnostic theology.

21

THE THEOLOGICAL ASPECTS OF EARLY CHRISTIAN HERESY

The Present Situation of the Debate

Time and time again, students of Rudolf Bultmann find themselves turning to the problem of heresy in primitive Christianity;[1] it seems to be quite a characteristic interest of those whose work has been associated with that great scholar and teacher. All their work on this problem has likewise been influenced by Walter Bauer's pioneering monograph *Rechtgläubigkeit und Ketzerei im ältesten Christentum,* which appeared in 1934.[2]

Walter Bauer tried to refute the long-standing theory that heresy, both in essence and in its historical appearance, was the later adulteration of a more original orthodox belief. Indeed, Bauer claimed, we cannot deny that there was "heresy" in the apostolic age itself, nor can we show that "orthodox" belief had universal priority. Bauer's theses were developed still further by the scholars to whom I have just referred. Above all, Bauer tried to determine more closely the nature of heresies in the New Testament age and thus to form a clearer conception of the theology expressed in New Testament literature.

After one has taken stock of the present state of the discussion, one must deal with a number of problems. One might begin by undertaking detailed studies of more extra-

---

1. The following bibliography is by no means exhaustive; it only suggests the work done in the last few years on our topic by the writers to whom I have referred. On 1 and 2 Corinthians: Günther Bornkamm, "Herrenmahl und Kirche bei Paulus," in *Studien zu Antike und Urchristentum* (Munich: Kaiser, 1963) 138–76; ET: "Lord's Supper and Church in Paul," in *Early Christian Experience* (New York: Harper & Row, 1969) 123–60; Walther Schmithals, *Die Gnosis in Korinth* (FRLANT 66; Göttingen: Vandenhoeck & Ruprecht, 1956); ET: *Gnosticism in Corinth: An Investigation of the Letters to the Corinthians* (Nashville: Abingdon, 1971); Ulrich Wilckens, *Weisheit und Torheit* (BhTh 26; Tübingen: Mohr/Siebeck, 1959). On 2 Corinthians alone: Ernst Käsemann, "Die Legitimität des Apostels," *ZNW* 47 (1942) 33–71; Dieter Georgi, *Die Gegner des Paulus im 2. Korintherbrief* (WMANT 11; Tübingen: Mohr/Siebeck, 1964); ET: *The Opponents of Paul in Second Corinthians: A Study in Religious Propaganda in Late Antiquity* (Philadelphia: Fortress Press, 1986). On Colossians: Günther Bornkamm, "Die Häresie des Kolosserbriefes," in *Das Ende des Gesetzes* (BevTh 16; Munich: Kaiser, 1958) 139–56. On Philippians: Walther Schmithals, "Die Irrlehrer des Philipperbriefes," *ZThK* 54 (1957) 297–341; Helmut Koester, "The Purpose of the Polemic of a Pauline Fragment," *NTS* 8 (1961/62) 317–32. On the Johannine Epistles: Ernst Käsemann, "Ketzer und Zeuge," *ZThK* 48 (1951) 292–311 (= idem, *Exegetische Versuche und Besinnungen* [Göttingen: Vandenhoeck & Ruprecht, 1965] 1.168–86). Generally: Helmut Koester, "Häretiker im Urchristentum," *RGG* (3rd ed.) 3.17–21; Walther Schmithals, "Zur Sammlung und Abfassung der ältesten Paulusbriefe," *ZNW* 51 (1960) 225–45.

2. 2d ed.; BhTh 10; Tübingen Mohr/Siebeck, 1964; ET: *Orthodoxy and Heresy in Earliest Christianity* (Philadelphia: Fortress Press, 1971).

canonical writings that are related to the topic at hand—there is certainly a need for this.[3] The most important question, however, concerns the rise of early Christian heresy and the history-of-religions problem. By now Bultmann and his students have received at least their fair share of the blows exchanged over this controversial question—one can only hope that the controversy has not degenerated once and for all into an uncontrollable polemic.[4] Whether the discussion will continue at such a level is now simply a question of one's dignity. But without a doubt, we can no longer ignore the need for a new look at the history-of-religions problem, even though such a task will not be undertaken in this paper.[5]

My main concern here is to raise once more the theological aspects of the heresy problem and only its theological aspects—since, as I suspect, our problem is very deeply a theological one, and not just the purely descriptive task of the historian of religion. The situation facing us is not simply that on the basis of new research we must now date the appearance of heresy a few decades earlier than we had previously supposed, and that the beginning of Christian Gnosticism now dates perhaps from the time of Paul and not just from the time of Ignatius or Justin. Were this the only point of our discussion, the critic would be just as shortsighted as his opponents. For the criteria for determining "right" and "wrong" belief, which were worked out toward the end of the second century by the anti-Gnostic fathers, have no validity when we consider the theological problems and relationships of the first Christian generations. Therefore the question is not whether we may rightly label the opponents of Paul as Gnostic heretics, or whether in Paul's time there was yet even such a thing as Gnostic heresy.[6] The danger of putting the question this way is clear; for one would only succeed in casting the theological problems of the Pauline age in the categories of second- and third-century controversy. One would make it appear either that Paul was orthodox and had Gnostic opponents, or that he had no Gnostic opponents but only Judaizing ones, or perhaps none at all. In any case, one would assume that he was "orthodox," and thus naturally that he was "finally" or "essentially" or "properly understood" in agreement with the Pastoral Epistles.

---

3. Under Rudolf Bultmann's influence, a few such studies have already been undertaken; cf. Heinrich Schlier, *Religionsgeschichtliche Untersuchungen zu den Ignatiusbriefen* (BZNW 8: Giessen: Töpelmann, 1929); Günther Bornkamm, *Mythos und Legende in den apokryphen Thomasakten* (FRLANT 49; Göttingen: Vandenhoeck & Ruprecht, 1933).

4. Cf. the following words, for example: "The author of this book lacks historical training," "a striking proof of the decline of exegetic research since the thirties" (Johannes Munck, "The New Testament and Gnosticism," *ST* 15 [1961] 187); cf. also the rather condescending judgments of Robert M. Grant, "Hermeneutics and Tradition in Ignatius of Antioch," *Archivio di Philosophia* 1–2 (1963) 183–201. It is unfortunate that in this kind of polemic the arguments of one's opponents are rarely reproduced with great accuracy, a fact that makes further discussion all the more difficult.

5. The reader will observe that within the so-called Bultmann School quite a bit of sharp critical observation has been made in this regard; e.g., Dieter Georgi's excellent review (*VuF* 13 [1960] 90–96) of Walther Schmithals, *Die Gnosis in Korinth*; or my review (*Gnomon* 33 [1961] 590–95) of Ulrich Wilckens, *Weisheit und Torheit*; ET printed as "Wisdom and Folly in Corinth," chapter 8 in this volume.

6. The question of when "Gnosticism" had its beginning is, of course, open to debate, although in my opinion one simply cannot explain many early Christian and extra-Christian phenomena without accepting the existence of a pre-Christian Gnosis.

Yet we must not forget that Bultmann, in his *Theology of the New Testament,* preceded the treatment of Paul with a chapter on "Gnostic Motifs." If Paul's thought was already determined by motifs that appeared to be objectionable heresy to the later church, Paul himself stands in the twilight zone of heresy. In other words, we are forced to redefine the traditional standards of "heretical" and "orthodox."[7] So it appears that we cannot base our research upon the expectation that in the end these labels will fit Paul and his contemporary opponents, as previous generations of scholarship argued. The need to redefine the terms "heretical" and "orthodox" if we are going to use them of Paul's time is obvious when one notes that although Paul is fighting Gnostic opponents in 1 Corinthians, it is *Gnostic* arguments that he himself uses in 2 Corinthians to combat Jewish pneumatics.[8]

A Critique of the Search for New Criteria for Defining Heresy

Can we attain any new criteria for defining heresy by studying the beginnings of Christianity? How to answer this question is made difficult by the fact that the church later invented such criteria and read them back into its origins, adroitly translating orthodox teaching and its authority back into the time of the very earliest beginnings. This was accomplished not only by the establishment of the New Testament canon, but also within the canon by three concepts in particular: the authority of the apostles (which, as it was later conceived, had precedence over that of Paul), the early Christian kerygma, and, above all, the life and teaching of Jesus.

From the canon per se, no *new* standards can be derived; what then should we take as a guide? To what extent does critical investigation open up new points of view? Or does theology in the end have no other alternative than subjecting itself to tradition and the criteria fixed by it?

In its day, the history-of-religions school offered a solution that is still widely accepted, namely, that the standard of genuine Christianity is piety, religiosity, and intensity, especially of cultic experience. What is opposed to this standard, and hence heretical, is doctrine abstracted from life, whether it appears as Jewish legalism or as Hellenistic speculation. With this presupposition, the conception of Ferdinand Christian Baur could simply be continued without modification. Consequently there arose the rule of thumb widely current even today, namely, that the two fundamental errors of Christianity were Judaism or Hellenism, legalism or speculation, apocalyptic fanaticism or Gnostic mysticism. It is within such a conceptual framework that much scholarly discussion of this problem still moves—and not only scholarly discussion but its less scholarly counterpart in the church at large as well.

---

7. One cannot simply give them up, even though the technical terminology is not to be found in the NT. Historians must carry out their responsibility to see primitive Christianity for what it actually is, namely a movement struggling over the theological question of the right or wrong understanding of its revelation.

8. See Georgi, *Opponents of Paul.*

In such a discussion, however, the fact is overlooked that "orthodoxy," standing midway between legalism and speculation, is defined only in formal terms, as "religiousness"; as a result a vacuum arises, not defined further, a linguistic void between the two extremes of false doctrine. The source of error is that in establishing a set of propositions that lie outside the realm of theological discourse, one still cannot escape language and the realm of language. Otherwise, one enters upon a fatal path of error: thinking that the thing that has to be expressed in terms of the supposedly "unexpressible" can be actualized in cultic gesture, sign, and symbol. This line of thinking is a complete misunderstanding of the real character of cultic and liturgical actions. For these actions are in their true intention meant to condense and concentrate religious language, not to overcome it (when this is not the case, cult has been degraded to pure mysticism). Furthermore, to interpret the central criterion of orthodoxy psychologically as "the experience of faith" or to reduce theological standards to ethical attitudes is simply to propose second-rate substitutes for theological discourse.

The history-of-religions approach brought to light yet another thesis, in this case one that must be maintained under all circumstances: primitive Christianity was a totally syncretistic phenomenon—not just those forms that were judged heretical. When one recognizes this, one traditional criterion for the identification of heresy falls by the wayside, namely, tracing the heresies of one's opponents back to the foreign influences of heathen piety and Greek philosophy. The search for extra-Christian origins of heretical views has not yet been freed from the untenable prejudices of the ancient Christian opponents of heresy. Naturally it remains true that the motifs, myths, and cultic conceptions noted in history-of-religions studies could and did migrate from place to place. Likewise one religio-cultural milieu can more or less strongly influence another. Yet cognizance of this fact does not explain the phenomenon of early Christian heresy. This has been finally confirmed by the uncontestable fact that Christianity as such is syncretistic, not just those forms that were later condemned as heretical. The Gnostic *Gospel of Truth* that we now possess, thanks to the Nag Hammadi find, is neither more nor less a product of syncretistic religious development than the contemporary Roman document *The Shepherd of Hermas* or, for that matter, the theology of Paul. In view of this, it is quite hard to understand the common zeal for attributing to New Testament writings a greater theological trustworthiness by citing Old Testament, Jewish apocalyptic, and rabbinic parallels. For it cannot be doubted that Judaism itself was already a product of oriental syncretism. Indeed, the Christian Gnostic writings of the second century are just as strongly rooted in Jewish theology as are their "orthodox" counterparts.

The thesis of the history-of-religions school that primitive Christianity is itself syncretistic may be of great lasting value, and, as I have said, sheer piety is no longer a satisfactory criterion for distinguishing orthodox belief. For the question of orthodoxy must be decided not by the most ancient witnesses to religious experience, but by the verbal content of the early Christian message.

For this reason, the attempt to orient oneself to the language of the New Testament might seem more promising. Such an attempt presupposes that the unity of the New Testament is a unity of language. If evidence to support this presupposition could be adduced, then an impressive criterion for the distinction of orthodoxy would have been found. Here the names Hermann Cremer and Julius Kögel come to mind, for their work along these lines was widely influential.[9] It is well known that their fundamental distinction between biblical and secular Greek decisively influenced that great project, the *Theologisches Wörterbuch zum Neuen Testament,* edited by Gerhard Kittel and Gerhard Friedrich (translated into English as the *Theological Dictionary of the New Testament*).[10] Of course today we no longer have to fight the tendency to make this distinction, for to a greater and greater extent this work itself has led us to realize that New Testament Greek is intimately related to the secular Greek of New Testament times.[11] It was precisely philological investigation that showed that the New Testament cannot be considered sui generis as a linguistic phenomenon. Clearly, the Greek of the New Testament is not classical Greek; but there is quite a strong resemblance, to say the least, between Hellenistic Greek and the Greek of the New Testament, both in structure and in vocabulary. Reliance upon the methods of philology can lead only to the conclusion that the language of the New Testament is neither unique nor uniform. However interesting and informative we may find philological investigations of biblical language and its characteristics, these investigations cannot provide us with a standard to separate the heretical from the orthodox.

Another attempt to work out the linguistic characteristics of orthodox theological discourse pretends to proceed upon certain philosophical presuppositions about the nature of language. I should like to indicate how hopeless it is to search for new criteria through such an endeavor by making a few critical observations on T. Bonhoeffer's article on theological language in the third edition of *Die Religion in Geschichte und Gegenwart*.[12] Perhaps we need not spend too much time evaluating Bonhoeffer's surely profound proposition: "the noun 'speech' is derived from the verb 'to speak.'"[13] It is quite obvious that Bonhoeffer attempts to make the word "God" or, more precisely, the use of the phonetic unit "god," into the measuring stick of orthodox theological discourse. When Judaism replaced the Old Testament word for "God" (Yahweh) with the substitute "Adonai," that was plainly the theological fall of Judaism in Bonhoeffer's estimation. On the other hand, he says, in the proclamation of Jesus, "the word 'God' lays a mighty claim upon the language of justice and thereby gives 'freedom to the word.'"[14] Accordingly, it is supposed to be the word "God" that holds together the various fundamental theological concepts like "kingdom" (Jesus), "justification" (Paul), and "witness" (John).

---

9. *Biblisch-Theologisches Wörterbuch* (1866; 11th ed.; Gotha: Perthes, 1923).

10. Trans. G. W. Bromiley, *Theological Dictionary of the New Testament,* 1964–76. Selected articles translated by J. R. Coates, et al. in *Bible Key Words* (3 vols.; London: Black; New York: Harper, 1951–61).

11. For this reason the violent attacks of James Barr, *The Semantics of Biblical Language* (Oxford: Oxford University Press, 1961); and idem, *Biblical Words for Time* (SBT 1/33; Naperville, Ill.: Allenson, 1962) are not really justifiable; decisive though they be, his remarks are aimed at a few articles of the *Theologisches Wörterbuch* that are hardly convincing anyway; likewise he attacks such authors as Thorlief Boman and Thomas F. Torrance.

12. "Sprache. IV. Theologisch," *RGG* 6.272–82.

13. Ibid., 272.

14. Ibid., 278.

But should we not expect God to be the source as well as the object of discourse in the New Testament? Is not the problem actually that except for the word "God" the theological vocabulary is different in every case? Hence it is not immediately clear, for example, how what Paul says about justification is simply the continuation of what Jesus says about the kingdom of God. If by "talk of God" we simply mean the *subject matter* that holds together the entire New Testament, we perhaps can agree. But the problem that faces us is that this subject matter does not appear in one uniform language, but in a variety of languages. Our conscientiousness as historians demands that we consider the linguistic diversity of the New Testament to be characteristic of all primitive Christian proclamation.[15] We must learn to grasp the nature of this diversity, and indeed, we must do so through the methods of philology and the history of religions. Thus one must begin not by assuming the unity of New Testament language, but rather with the observation of its syncretistic character. This point now deserves further elaboration.

The Language of the New Testament as a Syncretistic Phenomenon

First, the language of the New Testament is syncretistic inasmuch as there is simply no peculiarly biblical language. There are no words, concepts, forms, or sentences that the philologist and historian of religion can consider typical for the "New Testament" and upon which they can base the pronouncement of orthodoxy. Proof of this was brought to light long ago by exegetical work on the New Testament—a glance at the critical commentaries, dictionaries, and handbooks makes that immediately clear. Parallels between the language of the New Testament world and the New Testament itself, discovered by philological and history-of-religions research, are so overwhelmingly convincing that one does not assume there is any sentence in the New Testament that has not been found—or not yet or at least could not be found—outside early Christianity.

Second, in all the diverse layers of New Testament tradition there are no exceptions to this rule. The language spoken by Jesus had the same syncretistic nature as the language of the New Testament; thus it does not precede the latter as "not yet syncretistic."[16] There is no support for the assertion that certain forms of discourse used by Jesus, that is, analogy, antithesis, and parable, are "ur-Christian" and so have no parallels.

---

15. Admittedly in asserting this I have plainly (and confidently) allied myself with those whose "historical conscientiousness is ungodliness" (Bonhoeffer, ibid., 279), especially "the ungodliness of the language of those who have called the Gospel a paradox and have allowed it to stand dogmatically as foolishness." I will also cheerfully admit that to me the gospel, which preaches the foolishness of the cross, seems to be a paradox; but in my opinion this confession is a virtue of faith and not a sign of ungodliness.

16. It seems to me that on these grounds Ernst Käsemann's theses must be revised: the assertion that Jesus' proclamation was not yet apocalyptic seems to set off the language of Jesus from that of the rest of the NT as a phenomenon sui generis, unless we understand Käsemann to mean that the language of Jesus was indeed apocalyptic, but that this apocalyptic language was interpreted so radically in the case of Jesus that it lost its apocalyptic implications. Cf. Ernst Käsemann, "Zum Thema der urchristliche Apokalyptik," *ZThK* 59 (1962) 257–84 (= idem, *Exegetische Versuche und Besinnungen* [Göttingen: Vandenhoeck & Ruprecht, 1964] 105–31); ET: *New Testament Questions of Today* (London: SCM, 1969) 108–37.

Admittedly there are some striking dissimilarities in the way such forms of discourse are used here and in the language of apocalypticism, but they are significant only because they result from an interpretation of this same apocalyptic language; hence we can see their profile only against the contrast of their historical background—which it is our task to reconstruct. A good illustration of this may be found in the parables of Jesus, which by and large correspond to rabbinic and apocalyptic parables. To be sure, they are distinguished from them by the complete absence of allegory. Yet there are parallels for this in the Old Testament (cf. Nathan's parable in 2 Sam 12).

Third, likewise, there was never an original Christian kerygma not yet subject to the syncretistic nature, as it were, of the language of the New Testament. To designate the proclamation of the resurrection of Jesus as such an "ur-kerygma" would be unfortunate.[17] Without question, talk of the resurrection belongs primarily to Jewish apocalypticism both from a linguistic and a theological point of view. Through proclamation in the Christian kerygma of Jesus' resurrection, fulfillment of apocalyptic expectation is "given verbal expression" (*zur Sprache gebracht*) in the figure of Jesus. Only within the linguistic conceptions of apocalyptic expectation does it make sense to put the revelation in Jesus into words in such a way.[18] Outside this realm of discourse, either one cannot understand what is meant by "the resurrection of Jesus," or one misunderstands the Jewish hope for resurrection, within which context alone talk of the resurrection of Jesus is meaningful. Persuasive evidence of this point may be found in 1 Corinthians 15 and 2 Tim 2:18. But other Christians, for whom the language of Jewish apocalypticism was incomprehensible, proclaimed Jesus not as the Resurrected One but as the Exalted One (Phil 2; Hebrews).

Fourth, nevertheless, the possibilities for any historically given language are not simply formal, for the language of Christian proclamation (which Christianity did not create) has its own peculiar content as well. In using a traditional language one cannot strip away the old content and substitute a new one. Rather, the alteration of a historically given linguistic complex takes place so that the traditional contents are reunderstood in a way corresponding to a new situation, that is, so that they are interpreted and demythologized. On the other hand, the content inherent in a given language contributes to the understanding or misunderstanding of the contemporary historical situation and of the experiences that are determined by it.

This becomes clear in the case of apocalyptic language, which was for Jesus, and to a certain extent for primitive Christianity, the language of proclamation. Jesus did not simply confirm or contest the correctness of certain apocalyptic expectations in his preaching, but rather he announced their fulfillment. In the same way, the early Christian proclamation asserted that certain apocalyptic expectations (such as the resurrection and the gift of the Spirit) had been fulfilled with the coming of Jesus, but that

---

17. Still more unfortunate is the desire to treat the resurrection of Jesus as a historical fact preceding such a configuration of problems. For the "resurrection of Jesus" is by no means an objective historical event; rather it is nothing but a phenomenon of primitive Christian language. First of all one must speak of the kerygma and only then of the resurrection of Jesus—not vice versa.

18. See T. Bonhoeffer's article (cited above); cf. also James M. Robinson, *The New Quest of the Historical Jesus* (SBT 1/25; London: SCM, 1959).

others were still awaited (e.g., the parousia). Jesus and early Christianity were oriented to the given structure of apocalyptic expectation to such an extent that they could define the place and time at which they themselves stood in the course of apocalyptic events. The sect of the Essenes acted in a very similar way.

Yet in both cases there arises a conflict that has its roots in the mythological content of the given language. Apocalypticism is in essence mythological, since it speaks of a future salvation through which the worldly, historical existence of human beings is to be abolished. The coming of the Messiah, the resurrection, the gift of the Spirit, the messianic banquet, and the last judgment are completely mythological concepts. All these concepts are now part of the Christian preaching, though in a somewhat altered form. To be sure, Christian preaching can still relate itself to the future even today, and thus carry on the traditional and mythological language uncritically. But what is original about this preaching is its assertion of the present historical reality of that salvation which was originally conceived of in mythical, futuristic terms. In this way the mythical terminology receives a new meaning. It appears in a peculiar relationship to a historical event and is thus lifted outside the realm of history and made nonmythological, sometimes radically (as in John) and sometimes only partially (as in 1 Peter). The extent to which that happens at any given time, and to what degree *rightly,* are questions that one must ask in interpreting each individual text. The texts themselves pose this problem. For they are first-rate witnesses to the fact that what was at stake in early Christianity was the understanding of a given linguistic content within a new historical situation. Has only the first resurrection occurred, or have all now experienced resurrection? Has the Messiah come, or only a prophet who proclaimed his advent? So far the question of orthodox language apparently revolves only around the announcement of the time, the time within the given apocalyptic timetable. But much more is really at stake. For that which has been fulfilled has become a part of history. The Spirit as an eschatological gift is the real historical possession of a corporate body. Does that mean that this congregation understands itself unhistorically—as the congregation of the eschatological age, already removed from this world—and that it withdraws from its historical, that is, its political and social, responsibility? Or is possession of the Spirit the power of a new moral change? In the answer to these questions lies the difference between orthodoxy and heresy.

The Historical Jesus as Source of the Problem of Orthodoxy and Heresy

The task of Christian proclamation and theology, then, is not the repetition of a fixed religious content and mode of expression but the reinterpretation of traditional linguistic contexts. The critical standard for this task is given in the fact that Christian proclamation is intimately related to the historical revelation in Jesus. Without such an intimate relationship to the historical source, there would be no problem of heresy in this sense. The problem of doctrinal differences or the question of orthopraxy can arise in every religious context. But only in Christianity (and in Judaism) must the historical origin continually be reappropriated and presented anew. This task is indispensable for the self-understanding of the faith, and heresy is the failure to accomplish it.

The question of the historical Jesus is thus a quite valid question to raise. But one must not ask this question unhistorically or uncritically. Below the surface of the *unhistorical* way of putting the question lies a fundamental lack of interest in the work and proclamation of Jesus. It amounts to looking merely for a historical support for the content of the faith and the teaching of the church, support in the sense of a historical causality, and in so doing it presupposes that the known content of the faith can be found once more in the historical Jesus. Such an inquiry is carried on as though a statement of one's theological convictions could in this way become more "true" (a word that usually has no comparative degree), more true because one could substantiate it directly or indirectly by knowledge of the historical Jesus. We are adopting an "unhistorical" procedure when we make Jesus, his life, and his preaching, even critically interpreted, the standard of orthodox belief. On this basis heresy would seem to be nothing more than frivolous or malevolent misinterpretation and falsification of the originally unadulterated teaching of Jesus; and it would not make any difference whether one dated such a "fall" from the time of Paul or from the time of Marcion.

The reorientation of Christian proclamation toward its historical origin is no mere formal problem, but concerns the subject matter itself. "Bridges" between the theology of the church and the historical Jesus, all of which are artificially constructed, are finally of no consequence. This holds true of hypothetical linguistic relationships of the reconstruction of an original kerygma or even of talk about the resurrection, which like a deus ex machina subsequently raises Jesus into a sphere from which an orthodox church can directly trace its doctrine. But actually in its historical reality the earliest community found the connection between its faith and its historical origin to be a stumbling block that could be overcome only with difficulty; it was by no means a joyfully welcomed religious advantage. Historically speaking, this problem became a burning issue right at the hour of Christianity's birth, with respect to the death of Jesus on the cross; it is still crucial. That this has been the case historically is demonstrated by the manifold attempts to remove the offense of this historical event and to incorporate the cross into the traditional systems of religious expectation as a "necessary element." The prophetic proof texts exemplify these attempts, as does the Gnostic interpretation of the cross in the *Gospel of Truth*.[19]

This does not mean that the heretical position is characterized by abandonment of the historical Jesus as the foundation of faith. For indeed this Jesus had a central and leading place in the thinking of Paul's opponents, whether as renewer of the law (Galatians), as teacher of wisdom (1 Corinthians), as model of the *homo religiosus* (2 Corinthians), or as guide to perfection (Philippians). Paul never reproaches his opponents for deliberate ignorance of Christ. His criticism is rather that they do not make the cross of Christ the critical standard for reinterpreting traditional theological language (including the language of Jesus!). Of course, Paul does not think of "the cross" as simply an especially powerful religious symbol; for him it is the critical yardstick of the historical event, "Jesus," by which it is shown whether the believers' existence is understood in a

---

19. 20.10ff., especially 20.25ff.

radical historical way, or whether the traditional mythical content of the language ulti-mately remains the yardstick. In themselves the life and teaching of Jesus alone have no value as such a standard. They have value only as part of the preaching of the crucifix-ion of Jesus through which the paradox and offense of the historical revelation of God were first made manifest.

Heresy arises, then, when the radical nature of the historical dimensions of the new existence are not recognized, when the crucifixion of the Revealer is not seriously taken as the shattering, that is, the demythologizing, of that security which is the attempt to escape through religiosity, piety, and theology from existence within history. True belief never lies in "overcoming the paradox of the cross," for example, through belief in resurrection, rather in the courage to affirm a theology that dares to understand the content of the believers' historical existence on the basis of the proclamation that this historical event was the revelation of God. In orthodoxy the offense of the cross is not, as it were, theologically overcome, not even through preaching of the resurrection. As we can see in Pauline theology, the resurrection of Jesus is the basis for the believer's hope for the future; through that hope it creates a place in the present for a historical understanding of faith that corresponds to the cross.

Admittedly, once such an understanding of faith has been attained, it cannot be used as a new standard for the further distinction of heresy and orthodoxy. In itself it is valid only in any unrepeatable historical situation in which it arises from the critical con-frontation of the preaching of the cross to the mythological language associated with it. Naturally the historian and the theologian have much to learn from the latter. But faith remains bound to its source, the historical cross of Jesus, which from time to time in a new situation and in a different language must be reappropriated as the critical standard of faith. This task may or may not succeed. But appealing to the orthodoxy of an age that is past is no protection against failure; for it gives no guarantee that we can thus rediscover the historical origin of faith in our interpretation of tradition and of the language of our own world.

The cross of Jesus is of interest not because it offers formal proof for the historical reality of revelation, nor because it once led the disciples into a doubt that they could overcome in some miraculous way for the benefit of all later generations. Rather in the cross of Jesus theological security is shattered, the security that is implied by the inten-tion of traditional language and thus by the traditional self-understanding (Christian though it may be).[20] The way in which this is done is never certain in advance, because the origin of the proclamation is this historical event, which is always bound to the ambiguity of concrete historical phenomena, including even the historical Jesus.

Early Christian Heresy as the Failure to Demythologize

We cannot now undertake to reclassify Christian writings according to the criterion of the cross. The standard of the cross is not available to us as a scholarly tool but must be

---

20. If this is understood as one possible result of the renewed quest for the historical Jesus, then to that extent the quest is justified.

worked out in each specific case. In the attempt to reunderstand Christian existence within the framework of language, given to us by tradition, the interpreter does not know in advance how this criterion will apply to a certain writing. The interpreter can decide what the criterion is only case by case, in the interpretation of primary sources. At the same time, once a linguistic manifestation of heresy or orthodoxy has been identified, it cannot simply be carried over as a standard from one document to another one that arose in a different historical situation. What is the language of heresy in one case can be the language of orthodoxy in another. While the common predicates "Jewish," "apocalyptic," "Hellenistic," and "Gnostic" have a certain correctness from the history-of-religions viewpoint, they are quite useless for the identification of heresy, especially when they are used in opposition to the concept "Christian."

One can proceed methodically, however, first investigating the background[21] behind the mythological intention of the language that was used (since there is indeed a mythological content in the language of the primitive Christian writings). Then one can ask whether the demythologization succeeded, or whether the decisive criteria were taken from the mythological content of the traditional language instead of being oriented toward the *skandalon* of the historical origin of revelation. In fact, apocalyptic and Gnostic mythology often influenced early Christianity toward the latter, mythological criteria.

Thus, for example, apocalyptic thought understands the present from the standpoint of a strictly future (and therefore unhistorical) divine act of salvation. At most, this salvation is a present possibility only as a kind of enthusiastic anticipation. But as a rule the present is determined by legalistic rigorism as a preparation for the coming salvation. If God's act of revelation in Jesus is uncritically inserted into this apocalyptic framework, then the traditional words of Jesus may be made into law. The idea of a covenant that is stamped by apocalypticism and thus mythically conceived (since salvation is not identical with the covenant as such but only corresponds to the supposedly future blessing) makes this a necessary consequence.

In such Judaizing heresy the tradition concerning the revelation in Christ, to the extent that it is not of a legalistic nature, is a matter of apocalyptic prophecy; history itself is no longer a problem. For the law, demanding obedience is just as unambiguous and leads just as directly to divinely ordered perfection as that awaited future event which will unambiguously put an end to the realm of history.

Such an understanding can be noted within early Christianity, for example, in Paul's opponents at Galatia, who by requiring circumcision attempt to define membership in the chosen people of the end time on the basis of the law. A second example is the *Shepherd of Hermas,* where we find that one can attain membership in the people of God (to whom God's promise applies) by simply leading a perfect life after the second and final repentance that has now been made possible.

In Gnosticism the dissolution of the ambiguities of history likewise arises out of late Jewish mythology. The expected eschaton, however, is understood here as being radically present, and the corresponding consequences are drawn only for the individual. If

---

21. As the history-of-religions school has done.

events that transcend the realm of history are the possession of the present, history has been suspended. What the believers need is a teaching about the "way" by means of which they can escape from the historical constraints of the here and now.

From this standpoint the essential characteristic of Gnosticism is not a specific redeemer myth, but rather a teaching concerning the present situation of humanity and the possibilities of freeing oneself from the constraining powers of this world and of history. In this way, Christ the Redeemer[22] can simply become the bringer of the message—although naturally he is also the primal model of the Gnostic who not only knows the way personally, but follows it as well.[23]

Within the context of this problem, namely, the unhistorical purposes for which traditional language may be used, orthodoxy is not a teaching formulated once and for all that neatly avoids every danger of either left or right. Nor—considering the possible misunderstanding of the historical dimensions of Christian revelation and in view of the claim within history that it makes upon human beings—is orthodoxy identical with a theory that stays clear of all those terminologies through which such misunderstandings necessarily emerge. In the case of Paul, for example, it would seem that his orthodoxy consists in doing two things: it maintains the historical dimensions of the present by holding to the hope of certain mythological apocalyptic events (like parousia and resurrection). But it achieves such understanding of the present existence of the believer not directly from this future hope, but from the paradox of the historical act of God in the foolishness of the cross.

Of course the point of our reflections has not been to reassign the labels "heretical" and "orthodox." If, on the one hand, "orthodoxy" is the venture of a theology that has learned from the crucified Jesus and that wants to speak of the latter suitably in a language that it cannot choose for itself, then the real alternative to orthodoxy is not heresy in the traditional sense, but heresy as the uncritical continued use of traditional language, whether the latter be of "Christian" or of "secular" origin: it is the escape into tradition. Such an escape might seem to be completely safe, since it does not expose one to the possibility of new heresies; for tradition repeats only what earlier generations have already accepted. But merely repeating tradition does not create an "orthodox" theology, for no orthodoxy originates in tradition. Rather it is only codified and set up as a sign in tradition, indeed as a sign that needs to be interpreted. Here we can find the voices of former debates, now become past history, and their attempts to answer the problem. But these answers have lost their present historical actuality and acuteness the moment they are accepted as valid tradition; indeed, tradition as such becomes heresy

---

22. A christology is certainly not indispensable to Gnosticism. As the new finds from Nag Hammadi show, we can by no means presuppose the existence everywhere of a redeemer myth in Gnosticism in the traditional sense. Apparently one should also be more careful in treating Paul's opponents in this regard.

23. The Gnostic understanding, just like the apocalyptic one, corresponds to one aspect of late Judaism. Jewish wisdom already brought the heavenly message to the wise, and this message gives individuals the possibility of freeing themselves from the adversities of existence within the realm of history and of anticipating eschatological endowments. In Jewish wisdom speculation, as in Christian *gnosis,* the historical revelation is irrelevant. It is knowledge of primeval time, of the *Urzeit,* that is revealed to the wise, and it is revealed at the end of time and not in God's activity within history.

as soon as one attempts to use it as if the historical context had not changed since it was formulated.

Yet there is something to be learned from the history of orthodoxy and heresy in primitive Christianity. One cannot learn *what* orthodox theology must say. But one can learn that the historical dimensions of revelation demand to give one's own expression to one's own theological existence, while undertaking the venture necessarily proposed anew in every age, namely, courageously grappling with the problems offered by the mythologies of one's *own* age, even at the risk of heresy.

22

EPHESOS IN EARLY
CHRISTIAN LITERATURE

Ephesos in the Letters of Paul

In order to assess the information about Ephesos in early Christian literature, it is important to begin with the genuine letters of Paul and not with the well-known story of the riot of the silversmiths in Acts 19.

Paul mentions Ephesos for the first time in 1 Corinthians, written early in his stay at Ephesos, which, according to Acts 19:8–10, lasted two years and three months. The probable dates for this stay are from the fall of 52 to the spring of 55 CE, that is, after Paul's missionary activity in Macedonia, Corinth, and Achaia. Reconstructing the sequence of the letters that Paul wrote from Ephesos, as well as interpreting some parts of these letters, is problematic. There is no question, however, that these were turbulent and difficult years for Paul's ministry, not only with respect to events in Ephesos, but also with regard to his controversy with the newly founded church in Corinth.

Paul's Letter to the Galatians may have been the first letter[1] written from Ephesos,[2] but nothing about his stay in that city can be learned from this letter. 1 Corinthians, however, was certainly written from Ephesos,[3] and contains several remarks that seem to reveal something about Paul's experience there. In 1 Cor 15:32 Paul remarks, "If after the manner of human beings I fought with beasts in Ephesos, what benefit is it to me?" This phrase has been interpreted either as a reference to an actual fight with wild beasts in the stadium[4] or as a metaphor for controversies with opponents.[5] While the former interpretation is unlikely, the latter is possible and would reveal that Paul had encountered serious challenges to his missionary activity. The phrase can also be inter-

---

1. Apart from the generally accepted fact that Galatians was written before Romans, it is impossible to be certain about the time of the writing of Galatians relative to 1 and 2 Corinthians. See Hans Dieter Betz, *Galatians: A Commentary on Paul's Letter to the Churches in Galatia* (Hermeneia; Philadelphia: Fortress Press, 1979) 11–12. 1 Cor 16:1 indicates that Paul had written to the Galatians before writing 1 Corinthians ("Now concerning the collection for the saints: you should follow the directions I gave to the churches of Galatia").

2. Most scholars think that this is the most likely place of origin; however, "there is not the slightest hint in Galatians itself as to the place from which it was sent" (Betz, *Galatians*, 12).

3. Ephesos is mentioned explicitly in 1 Cor 16:8 as the city in which Paul stayed while he was writing the letter; see below.

4. *Acts of Paul* 7 developed the story of Paul's fight with the wild beasts in the stadium on the basis of this remark.

5. Hans Conzelmann, *1 Corinthians: A Commentary on the First Letter to the Corinthians,* trans. James W. Leitch (Hermeneia; Philadelphia: Fortress Press, 1975) 264, 277–78.

preted in the context of the language of popular philosophy; here it is used in order to describe the struggle of the wise man against his desires and emotions.[6]

At the end of the letter, Paul discusses his travel plans, indicating that he intends to come to Corinth for a longer stay, traveling by way of Macedonia (1 Cor 16:5–7), but wants to remain in Ephesos until Pentecost (16:8). If Paul arrived in Ephesos in the fall of 52 CE, it is unlikely that he was already planning to leave in the following spring; 1 Corinthians is therefore better dated to the spring of 54. As the reason for the continuation of his stay in Ephesos, Paul points to further opportunities for missionary work, as well as considerable resistance: "a great and effectual opportunity[7] has opened to me and there are many adversaries" (16:9). It is not possible to discern whether this resistance arose from Jews or Gentiles, or was caused by opposition within the newly founded Christian community. Other remarks in 1 Corinthians 16 reveal that the staff of the Ephesos campaign was sizable. Timothy, who was with Paul, was apparently sent to Corinth along with this letter (16:10), Apollos, formerly active in Corinth,[8] was in Ephesos (16:12), and Aquila and Prisca as well as Stephanas,[9] Fortunatos, and Achaïkos (16:17) had come from Corinth to Ephesos (16:19). Moreover, that Paul sends greetings "from the churches of Asia" (16:19) demonstrates that other churches had been founded in the province of which Ephesos was the capital.

Paul was not able to carry out his plan to leave Ephesos for Corinth after Pentecost of that year. The correspondence that is now preserved in 2 Corinthians must be dated in the period between the intended departure from Ephesos in the spring of 54 and Paul's actual departure for Corinth a year later. 2 Corinthians is a composition of several of Paul's shorter letters, written over a longer period of time.[10]

During the year after the writing of 1 Corinthians, a new opposition to Paul had arisen in Corinth, instigated by foreign missionaries who had invaded the Corinthian church.[11] This forced Paul to write a letter to Corinth in defense of his own ministry, which letter is preserved in 2 Cor 2:4–7:4; he also visited Corinth briefly—crossing the Aegean Sea by boat—in the summer of 54. A second letter, written shortly after this visit and preserved in 2 Corinthians 10–13, indicates that the personal visit only increased the tensions with the Corinthian church. The remainder of the correspondence contained in this composite letter is made up of several brief letters (1:1–2:13 and 7:5–16; 8:1–24; 9:1–15) written from Macedonia in the summer of 55, after Paul had left Ephesos.

These later letters give evidence that Paul had meanwhile been in serious trouble (θλῖψις) "in Asia," and had even given up hope to escape with his life (2 Cor 1:8; ὥστε

---

6. Abraham Malherbe, "The Beasts at Ephesus," *JBL* 87 (1968) 71–80.

7. The Greek term for "opportunity" is θύρα, a term that Paul uses in the same way in 2 Cor 2:12. In both instances Paul speaks of an opportunity for the proclamation of the gospel.

8. 1 Cor 1:12; 3:4–6; 4:6. On Apollos, see also below.

9. Stephanas is called "the firstborn of Achaia," who now has a house in Ephesos (1 Cor 16:15).

10. Gerhard Dautzenberg, "Der Zweite Korintherbrief als Briefsammlung: Zur Frage der literarischen Einheitlichkeit und des theologischen Gefüges von 2 Kor 1–8," *ANRW* 2.25.4 (1987) 3045–66.

11. See Dieter Georgi, *The Opponents of Paul in 2 Corinthians: A Study in Religious Propaganda in Late Antiquity* (Philadelphia: Fortress Press, 1985).

ἐξαπορηθῆναι ἡμᾶς καὶ τοῦ ζῆν). This implies that he had been imprisoned for a longer period during the winter of 54/55. Many recent scholars agree that this remark refers to an Ephesian imprisonment,[12] during which Paul also wrote the Letter to the Philippians—or several letters,[13] occasioned by the arrival of Epaphroditos, who had come from Philippi bringing financial support, and by the delay of his return caused by a longer illness. At this time he also wrote the letter to Philemon, whose house was in Colossae. The physical proximity of Philippi and Colossae to Ephesos and the exchange of messengers make it likely that these letters were written from an imprisonment in Ephesos rather than Rome. Philippians and Philemon thus provide more information about the imprisonment in Ephesos.

Ephesos stands out as the place from which most of the Pauline correspondence originated—1 Corinthians, Philippians, Galatians, Philemon, and the major parts of 2 Corinthians. The remaining two genuine Pauline letters, namely his first letter (1 Thessalonians) and his last letter (Romans), were written in Corinth. There is no further mention of Ephesos in Paul's letters after his departure from the city. It is possible, however, that a letter survives that Paul wrote in Corinth to the church in Ephesos. This is certainly not the letter known as Ephesians[14] but a letter to Ephesos that has survived as chapter 16 of Romans.[15] Here Paul sends greetings to Prisca and Aquila (Rom 16:4), his old associates from Corinth who had gone to Ephesos, according to 1 Cor 16:19 and Acts 18:18; a greeting to Epainetos, whom Paul calls the firstborn of Asia (Rom 16:5), follows. Moreover, Rom 16:6–15 contains greetings to as many as twenty-three of Paul's fellow workers and personal acquaintances, who must have been located in Ephesos rather than in Rome, unless one assumes that there was a mass immigration of Ephesian Christians to Rome within less than a year after Paul's departure from that city. If Romans 16 was indeed a letter written to Ephesos, most likely as a cover letter for a copy of Romans that Paul sent to Ephesos, a wealth of additional information about the early Christian community in Ephesos is available. Not only are twenty-six names of individual Christians listed—there is no other early Christian church for which such information is available—but details about the Ephesian community also are included. There was a house church in the home of Prisca and Aquila (16:5a). As the first person converted, Epainetos obviously occupied a prominent position (16:5b). The first fellow worker mentioned after Epainetos is a woman named Maria (16:6). Next Junia and

---

12. This thesis was first convincingly argued by George Simpson Duncan, *Paul's Ephesian Ministry: A Reconstruction with Special Reference to the Ephesian Origin of the Imprisonment Epistles* (New York: Scribner's, 1929).

13. Wolfgang Schenk, "Der Philipperbrief in der neueren Forschung (1945–1985)," *ANRW* 2.25.4 (1987) 3280–3313; Helmut Koester, "The Purpose of the Polemic of a Pauline Fragment (Phil III)," *NTS* 8 (1961/62) 317–32; Lukas Bormann, *Stadt und Christengemeinde zur Zeit des Paulus* (NovTSup 78; Leiden: Brill, 1995) 109–18.

14. The Letter to the Ephesians is not a genuine letter of Paul's. Moreover, the address of this letter (ἐν Ἐφέσῳ) is missing in the manuscript witnesses; see below.

15. See, among others, J. J. MacDonald, "Was Romans xvi a Separate Letter?" *NTS* 16 (1969/70) 369–72; Wolf-Henning Ollrog, "Die Abfassungsverhältnisse von Rom 16," in Dieter Lührmann and Georg Strecker, eds., *Kirche: Festschrift für Günther Bornkamm zum 75. Geburtstag* (Tübingen: Mohr/Siebeck, 1980) 221–44.

Andronikos, two fellow prisoners of Paul's, who hold the rank of apostle, are mentioned (16:7); this is also an important piece of evidence for the existence of a female apostle. A number of other persons are designated as engaged in some work as ministers of the church, among them again several women (Tryphaina, Tryphosa, Persis, and Julia). Of the twenty-six names, one is Semitic (Maria), nineteen are Greek, and six Latin; of these six Latin names, however, three belong to people who are certainly Jews (Prisca, Aquila, and Junia), while only two of the Greek names designate Jews (Andronikos and Herodion).[16] The fact that only a total of six persons named can be identified as Jews—two of these were Paul's fellow workers from Corinth, and another two identified as "apostles before me"—points to a largely Greek, Gentile constituency of the church in Ephesos.[17] Since all of these names appear in their simple form, without praenomina and cognomina, it is almost impossible to draw any conclusions with respect to their social status and citizenship. I believe that it is unlikely that those mentioned held Roman citizenship, and those who had come to Ephesos only recently were not even Ephesian citizens.

Ephesos in the Deutero-Pauline Letters

Ephesos appears in the prescript of Ephesians. It is certain, however, that this letter was neither written by Paul nor addressed to Ephesos. The letter is addressed to "the saints and faithful in Christ Jesus";[18] but the designation "in Ephesos" is missing in the oldest and most valuable textual witnesses.[19] What is generally called the Letter to the Ephesians is actually a letter directed to all churches, written at the end of the first century CE. Its place of origin is unknown.[20]

Ephesos is mentioned again several times in the Pastoral Epistles, 1 and 2 Timothy and Titus. These three deutero-Pauline letters were composed not earlier than the end of the first century, but probably as late as the fourth or fifth decade of the second century. Although all names of places and persons in these letters may be fictional, the author may have relied upon a tradition about Paul's activities in Greece, Macedonia, and Asia after his Roman imprisonment.[21] Traditionally, Rome claimed Paul as its mar-

---

16. Paul calls them συγγενεῖς μου, which cannot mean "relatives," but rather designates people of the same ethnic origin.

17. For the analysis of names in Pauline letters and a comparison with the fishermen's inscription from Ephesos (*IvE* I 20) see G. H. R. Horsley, *New Documents Illustrating Early Christianity* (6 vols.; North Ryde, NSW: Ancient History Documentary Research Centre, Macquarie University, 1989) 5.95–114.

18. Eph 1:1; Παῦλος ἀπόστολος Χριστοῦ Ἰησοῦ διὰ θελήματος θεοῦ τοῖς ἁγίοις τοῖς ἐν Ἐφέσῳ καὶ πιστοῖς ἐν Χριστῷ Ἰησοῦ.

19. MSS 𝔓⁴⁶ ℵ* B* 6. 1739 Marcion.

20. A number of manuscripts have a subscriptio that informs the reader that the letter was written from Rome. This only reflects the later assumption that all so-called imprisonment letters of Paul were written from Rome.

21. It is true that the Pastoral Epistles do not mention an earlier imprisonment in Rome. This cannot be used, however, as an argument against the existence of a tradition that reported later activity of Paul in the East. Whether this tradition is based upon historically reliable information is another matter.

tyr, but this claim can be questioned, and the information about places and persons contained in these letters—although the letters themselves are pseudepigraphical—could be valuable if it points to a tradition about a second stay of Paul in the East after his Roman imprisonment. The question of the situations assumed in the Pastoral Epistles, however, is extremely complex and cannot be discussed in this context.[22]

For the purposes of this study, one can say with certainty that 1 and 2 Timothy presuppose that Timothy is staying in Ephesos: "I have asked you to remain in Ephesos, as I did when I traveled to Macedonia" (1 Tim 1:3). It is also assumed that Onesiphoros and his house are in Ephesos and that he has provided useful services there for the church (2 Tim 1:16–18). Alexander, a coppersmith in Ephesos, is mentioned in this context as one who had done much harm to Paul and against whom Timothy is asked to be on his guard (2 Tim 4:14–15); an Alexander is also mentioned in Acts 19:33, a Jew who is informed about the riot of the silversmiths and prepares to give a speech, but never actually opens his mouth.[23] Finally, Paul says that he had sent Tychikos to Ephesos, and that Timothy should bring the coat and the books and parchments that Paul had left in Troas (2 Tim 4:12–13)—a request that would make sense if Paul was thought to be imprisoned in Philippi at the time of the composition of this letter.[24] In any case, whatever is said in the Pastoral Epistles about Ephesos reveals that at the beginning of the second century a Pauline tradition connected with Timothy existed in Ephesos. In the Pastoral Epistles, Timothy functions as a superior church leader who is passing the Pauline tradition to other churches and church leaders.[25] It is not impossible that the Pastoral Epistles already know of the tradition of Timothy as bishop of Ephesos; this, however, is explicitly mentioned for the first time by Eusebius.[26]

Ephesos in the Acts of the Apostles

Luke, the author of Acts, intended to write the chapter about Paul's activity in Ephesos (Acts 18:18–20:1) as the last and most splendid event in the missionary activity of the apostle. His sources presented formidable obstacles, however, because they reported that a Christian community had already been founded in Ephesos by Apollos and that there was also a group of followers of John the Baptist in that city—two reports that Luke felt he could not ignore. The result is a rather complex composition.

---

22. See Martin Dibelius and Hans Conzelmann, *The Pastoral Epistles,* trans. Philip Buttolph and Adela Yarbro (Hermeneia; Philadelphia: Fortress Press, 1972) 1–5, 126–28.

23. It is unclear why Luke inserted this episode. On this problematic passage, see Ernst Haenchen, *The Acts of the Apostles: A Commentary,* trans. rev. R. McL. Wilson (Philadelphia: Westminster, 1971) ad loc.

24. On the question of Paul's imprisonment and martyrdom in Philippi, see "Paul and Philippi: The Evidence from Early Christian Literature," chapter 7 in this volume.

25. 1 Tim 4:14 presents Timothy as one who has received his office through the laying on of hands by the presbytery; in 2 Tim 1:6 it is Paul himself who has ordained Timothy. On the laying on of hands, see Dibelius and Conzelmann, *Pastoral Epistles,* 70–71.

26. "Timothy is related to have been the first appointed bishop of the diocese of Ephesos" (Eusebius *Hist. eccl.* 3.4.5). Eusebius continues by naming Titus as the first bishop of Crete, however, suggesting that this information is dependent upon the Pastoral Epistles.

The report about the activities of the learned Alexandrian Jew Apollos (Acts 18:24–28) may rely on trustworthy information that was perhaps advertised by a group of Apollos's followers at the time of Luke. The references to Apollos in 1 Corinthians[27] suggest that Apollos later appeared in Corinth,[28] probably coming from Ephesos; he must have returned to Ephesos when Paul wrote 1 Corinthians, because Paul says at the end of the letter that he had urged him repeatedly to travel to Corinth (1 Cor 16:12).[29] Paul does not denigrate the work of Apollos and recognizes him as a Christian teacher in his own right, but it is also clear from Paul's remarks that rivalry existed between Apollos and him. Luke's report in Acts reveals that there was already a Christian community in Ephesos, founded by Apollos, before Paul began his missionary activity there.

It is difficult to find corroborating evidence for Luke's report of a group of followers of John the Baptist in Ephesos. Rivalry between the disciples of John and the disciples of Jesus probably existed in Palestine at an early date and is confirmed in a number of stories about John the Baptist in the Synoptic Gospels.[30] The Gospel of John, written at the end of the first century CE, includes several polemical passages that argue against the belief that John the Baptist was the Messiah.[31] Such a sect may well have existed in Ephesos at Luke's time, if not as early as the arrival Paul.[32]

Using a lost composition that described Paul's activities in Ephesos, Luke begins with a travel report of Paul's trip from Corinth to Syria and Caesarea (Acts 18:18–21); Paul, together with Priscilla and Aquila, sails from Kenchreae in order to go to Syria (Acts 18:18). Their first stop is in Ephesos. The source Luke used here must have reported that Paul left Priscilla and Aquila in Ephesos (Acts 18:19) and continued to sail to Caesarea. Luke, however, inserted a brief report about Paul's visit to the synagogue and his preaching to the Jews[33]—a typical Lukan feature. They ask Paul to stay, but he declines and promises to return (Acts 18:20–21). In this way, Luke was able to present Paul as the first preacher in Ephesos, only later including the report about the presence of Apollos and the disciples of John the Baptist.

---

27. 1 Cor 1:12; 3:4–6, 22; 4:6.

28. This is also attested in Acts 19:1 ("while Apollos was in Corinth").

29. On the problems of the expression "but it was not the will (for him to come to Corinth)," see Conzelmann, *1 Corinthians*, on 1 Cor 16:12. Does this formulation and the fact that Apollos is not mentioned in the greetings of 16:19–21 imply that Apollos was not present when 1 Corinthians was written?

30. Mark 2:18–22 // Matt 9:14–17 // Luke 5:33–38; see also the materials used in the discussion about John the Baptist in Matt 11:7–19; Luke 7:24–35. See especially Walter Wink, *John the Baptist in the Gospel Tradition* (SNTSMS 7; Cambridge: Cambridge University Press, 1968).

31. John 1:15, 19–34; 3:25–30; 4:1; 5:33–35.

32. The historicity of the report about disciples of John the Baptist in Ephesos is debated; see Haenchen, *Acts*; Hans Conzelmann, *Acts of the Apostles*, trans. James Limburg, et al. (Hermeneia; Philadelphia: Fortress Press, 1987), on Acts 19:1–7; Ernst Käsemann, "The Disciples of John the Baptist in Ephesus," in *Essays on New Testament Themes*, trans. W. J. Montague (SBT 1/41; London: SCM, 1964) 136–48.

33. This is evident from the fact that the text first, following the source, reports that Paul left Priscilla and Aquila "there" (Acts 18:19a); but then Luke inserts that Paul went to the synagogue (18:19b–21a; κατήντησαν δὲ εἰς Ἔφεσον, κἀκείνους κατέλιπεν αὐτοῦ, αὐτὸς δὲ εἰσελθὼν εἰς τὴν συναγωγὴν διελέξατο τοῖς Ἰουδαίοις). Acts 18:21b–22 resumes the source with "and he set sail from Ephesos; and he came to Caesarea." Because of this insertion by the author of Acts, the "there" (αὐτοῦ) of v. 19b is left dangling; it now suggests the impossible scenario that Priscilla and Aquila stayed at the port while Paul went to the synagogue. See Conzelmann, *Acts*, on 18:19–21.

In reproducing information about Apollos from his source, Luke reports faithfully that Apollos was teaching correctly about Jesus, but he adds the historically unlikely note that he knew only the "baptism of John" (Acts 18:25c), thus connecting the information about Apollos with that about the disciples of John. Conveniently, Priscilla and Aquila are already there to correct this error.[34] Duly instructed about correct Christian preaching, Apollos is dispatched to Achaia (Acts 18:24–28).[35] Once more, Luke reveals unwittingly that a Christian community founded by Apollos existed in Ephesos before Paul's missionary activity in that city, but he then eagerly adds that "when [Apollos] wished to go to Achaia, the brothers and sisters encouraged him" (Acts 18:27).[36]

Luke now has to deal with the problem of the presence of a sect of John the Baptist in Ephesos. Apollos is safely in Corinth (Acts 19:1a); and Paul, arriving in Ephesos, learns that there are some disciples who had not received the Holy Spirit, because they had only been baptized with the baptism of John. Paul rebaptizes them without delay and the Holy Spirit immediately comes upon them so that they speak in tongues (19:1b–7). A concluding note, saying that they were only about a dozen people, assures the reader that this rival sect was so small that it did not pose any real threat.

Luke's next imperative is to create the space needed for a description of Paul's successful ministry in the capital of Asia. Little historical information, however, can be gleaned from Luke's narrative. The duration of Paul's activity—three months in the synagogue (Acts 19:8) and two years in the hall of Tyrannos (19:9–10)—may have come from Luke's source. Everything else is either legend or a reflection of the situation in Ephesos in Luke's time, that is, approximately 100 CE. Luke projected the separation from the synagogue and the hostility of the Jews, both accomplished facts at his own time, back to the time of Paul. Paul understood his apostolic mission as one to the Gentiles, and there is no indication in his letters that he always preached first in the synagogues and left them for mission to the Gentiles only after hostilities arose. Moreover, the letter to the Ephesians preserved in Romans 16[37] argues for a largely Gentile Ephesian community, although here as elsewhere Paul has Jewish apostles and fellow workers, and there were Jewish members of the communities he founded. The existence of two rival religious organizations—the Jewish synagogues and the Christian churches—is characteristic of Luke's time, one or two generations later than the time of Paul.

Furthermore, three episodes are recounted that describe Paul's ministry: first, Paul's miracle working, healing diseases even through his aprons and handkerchiefs (Acts 19:11–12); second, rivaling magicians, the sons of the Jewish high priest Skevas, fail when they try to use Jesus' and Paul's name for their exorcism (19:13–17); third, the

---

34. Acts 18:25c, together with v. 26, in which Priscilla and Aquila instruct Apollos in "the way of God," are evidently Lukan insertions; see Käsemann, "Disciples of John in Ephesos," 144. The note about Apollos knowing only about the baptism of John is secondary. Unlike the report about the disciples of John the Baptist (see below), nothing is said about a baptism of Apollos with the Spirit, as this would have been awkward after the description of Apollos as a man "fervent with the Spirit" (18:25a; ζέων τῷ πνεύματι). See Conzelmann, *Acts*, on 18:25.

35. "Luke avoids a meeting between Apollos and Paul (but contrast 1 Cor 16:12)" (Conzelmann, *Acts*, on 18:27).

36. Ibid.

37. See the discussion of Rom 16 above.

newly won believers and even some of the magicians bring and burn their magical books (19:18–20). All three episodes are typical stories of the competition in the religious marketplace. They do not characterize either the situation in Ephesos[38] or the methods of Paul's missionary practices. Contrary to his self-presentation in his letters, Paul is here the stereotype of the successful magician or divine man. It is unlikely that the case of the seven exorcist sons of the Jewish high priest Skevas rests on local traditions, neither is there any high priest of that name attested, nor is it probable that seven sons of a Jerusalem high priest could be found in Ephesos.

The story of the riot of the silversmiths (Acts 19:23–40), in contrast, reflects the milieu of Ephesos and attests to Luke's knowledge of the Ephesian political and religious situation. The cult of the Ephesian Artemis, because of which the city proudly called itself the "temple keeper" (19:35, νεωκόρος),[39] the production of small silver *naiskoi* (= "small temples") with the statue of Artemis for sale to visitors of the famous temple (19:24),[40] the existence of the office of asiarch (19:31),[41] and the mention of the "scribe of the *dēmos*" (19:35) as the most powerful Ephesian official[42] are typical Ephesian features. This, however, does not prove that the story is historical. On the contrary, Paul's own letters reveal that he was in mortal danger at the end of his Ephesian stay, indeed imprisoned for some time and fearing for his life. Luke says nothing about that because the information is of no interest to his story. While Luke knows that Paul intended to depart for Macedonia (19:21–22), his primary interest is in the description of the serious threat that the Christian mission poses to the pagan cult, not at the time of Paul but at his own time. Pliny's letter to Trajan about the Christians, written in the year 112 CE, demonstrates that the spread of the Christian faith began to constitute a serious threat to the regular temple cult and ritual: sacrifices at the temples had been neglected and the sacrificial meat found no buyers.[43] It is not unlikely that Luke, who wrote at about the same time, knew about analogous threats to the normal performance of the cult of Artemis in Ephesos and to the sale of religious paraphernalia. This may have been the basis for the development of this narrative, which is fictional as far as Paul's ministry in Ephesos is concerned, but related to the actual situation at Luke's own time. Moreover, Pliny's let-

---

38. The reference to magic in Ephesos reveals some local color, however; see Conzelmann, *Acts*, 157, and the literature he cites in n. 3.

39. This term is regularly used for cities that were host to a provincial temple for the cult of the Roman emperors, but it was used in Ephesos also with respect to the cult of Artemis; see Steven J. Friesen, *Twice Neokoros* (New York: Brill, 1993) 55–57.

40. It is unlikely that the designation "silver shrines" (ναοὶ ἀργυρεῖς) for the products of the silversmiths refers to small-scale models of the entire temple of Artemis; rather, the silversmith probably produced statues of Artemis standing in a simple, small *naiskos*.

41. The office of the asiarchs is widely attested in Ephesian inscriptions, but its function is not quite clear. The asiarchs were not connected with the cult of Artemis, but perhaps with the cult of the emperors and/or with the supervision of games. See Conzelmann, *Acts*, on 19:31.

42. The "scribe" (γραμματεύς) mentioned here is the "scribe of the assembly of the people (*dēmos*)" (γραμματεὺς τοῦ δήμου) because the theater was the place for this assembly. A "scribe of the council" (γραμματεὺς τῆς βουλῆς) is attested for Ephesos, but it seems to have been a peculiarity of Ephesos that the scribe of the *dēmos* held a higher rank than the scribe of the council.

43. Plinius Secundus *Epistularum libri decem* 10.96.

ter reveals the Roman administration's increasing interest in the case of the Christians at the time Acts was written. Concern with the Roman reaction to a riot informs the speech of the scribe at the end of the story (19:40). Luke wants to demonstrate that the Christians are not the cause of such rioting and to encourage local officials to enforce law and order in such a way that their responsibility to protect Christians is also upheld.

There is no relationship between this story—where Paul departs unscathed—and Paul's actual experiences in Ephesos—a long imprisonment and a trial that might have resulted in capital punishment. He must have become such a notorious troublemaker in this city that he did not dare to show his face there again, a fact reflected in the source used by Luke in Acts 20:14–17. On his return trip from Macedonia to Jerusalem, Paul did not dare to stop at Ephesos but sailed from Assos to Mitylene, and from there to Miletos by way of Chios and Samos, bypassing Ephesos (20:15). Luke explains that Paul's reason was his haste; he did not want to lose time since he wanted to be in Jerusalem on Pentecost (20:16). This is a poor explanation; waiting in Miletos for the Ephesian presbyters (20:17) would certainly have consumed more time than a quick stop in Ephesos.

Acts therefore does not reveal much about Paul's stay in Ephesos. Interesting information emerges, however, about the beginnings of Christianity in this city: the Jewish-Christian missionary Apollos, competing with disciples of John the Baptist, had begun a successful mission there before Paul's arrival. Luke also provides some insights into the formidable threat that the Ephesian Christian community presented to the established cult of Artemis in his own time. At the same time, Luke suppresses information about the diversity of the Christian community, although a number of competing Christian groups must have existed in the city by the turn of the first century, as Revelation, which was written in Patmos at about the same time, confirms.

Ephesos in the Book of Revelation

The author of Revelation includes Ephesos in the seven churches of Asia (Ephesos, Smyrna, Pergamon, Thyateira, Sardeis, Philadelphia, and Laodikeia) to which he is commanded (Rev 1:11) to address individual letters (2:1–3:22). The book was written by a prophet named John on the island of Patmos, to which he was exiled. His work is not pseudepigraphical; there is no reason to doubt that John was the real name of the author, and his home city may well have been Ephesos. This prophet John, however, is certainly not identical with Jesus' disciple John, whose name later appears as the apostolic author of the Fourth Gospel and the three Johannine letters of the New Testament. The majority of scholars today date Revelation to the time of the emperor Domitian, although older materials may well have been incorporated into the text.[44]

The letter written to the church at Ephesos is the first of these seven letters (Rev 2:1–7). On the whole, it is full of praise for the church's labor and steadfastness and its rejection of false apostles, and sees the church as unified except for the presence of a

---

44. For a survey of scholarship, see Otto Böcher, "Die Johannes-Apokalypse in der neueren Forschung," *ANRW* 2.25.5 (1988) 3850–98.

group the author calls the Nikolaites (2:6). This same group is referred to in the letter to the church in Pergamon (2:15). The author provides no further information about the character of this group. Later writers, beginning with Irenaeus and Clement of Alexandria, ascribe to the Nikolaites a heretical Gnostic teaching and name as its founder the Nikolaos who appears on the list of deacons in Acts 6:5 and who is there characterized as a proselyte from Antioch.[45] Justin Martyr, however, who came to Rome from Ephesos, says nothing about this sect;[46] thus all later information is probably speculative.

John's letter to Ephesos is revealing for another reason. The language, theology, and spirituality of Revelation are completely different from that of Paul (and presumably Apollos), and John lives in a world of thought and language that differs markedly from that of the author of Luke-Acts. Paul, on the one hand, is a skilled writer, well versed in the style of the Greek diatribe; his theology is eschatological, but he refrains from apocalyptic speculations. Luke, on the other hand, writes a fairly elegant Greek and his biblical language and knowledge is that of the Septuagint, the Greek translation of the Hebrew Scriptures; moreover, nothing in Luke's writings indicates that he is expecting an imminent cataclysmic eschatological event. The author of Revelation, however, uses a rather clumsy Greek that is heavily dependent upon Aramaic and often reflects the text of the Hebrew Scriptures; his thought and theology are deeply steeped in the apocalypticism of postexilic Judaism.[47] It is difficult to imagine that he was addressing the same Greek-speaking, Gentile, Christian church of Ephesos that Apollos and Paul had founded and that Luke—a contemporary of the prophet John—knew.

In his description of the Pauline mission in Ephesos, Luke makes an effort to present the church of Ephesos as a united Christian group. Acts 18:24–20:1 suggests that the real situation was very different. At the end of the first century, a variety of groups and sects existed in Ephesos: disciples of John the Baptist, a circle of Christians that claimed allegiance to Apollos, a church that derived its origin from Paul. To these groups one should add a prophetic conventicle, to which the prophet John sent his book from Patmos, and a sect called the Nikolaites. The congregation that Paul founded and that held on to the tradition of its founder is mentioned in the letter of Ignatius of Antioch to the Ephesians, but this congregation does not seem to have been the only—and perhaps not even the dominating—group of Christians in Ephesos.

Ignatius of Antioch and the Ephesian Christians

Some time during the reign of Trajan, only a few years after the writing of Acts, Bishop Ignatius of Antioch was traveling as a prisoner through Asia Minor on his way to

---

45. See Adolf Hilgenfeld, *Die Ketzergeschichte des Urchristentums* (Darmstadt: Wissenschaftliche Buchgesellschaft, 1963) 49–50.

46. Irenaeus probably did not find his information about the Nikolaites (*Adv. haer.* 1.26.3) in Justin's lost *Syntagma.*

47. For the Jewish and Christian apocalyptic tradition of language and thought in Revelation, see Adela Yarbro Collins, "Early Christian Apocalyptic Literature," *ANRW* 2.25.6 (1988) 4665–4711.

Rome.[48] In Philadelphia he had the opportunity to meet with Christians, and from there he seems to have dispatched messengers to the churches of Ephesos, Magnesia, and Tralles with the request to send delegations to Smyrna for a meeting there. After he had met these delegates, he wrote a letter to each of these communities. The letter to the Ephesian church is the longest of Ignatius's letters. It reveals that the Ephesian delegation to Smyrna was led by their bishop Onesimos—hardly the same person on whose behalf Paul had written to Philemon fifty years earlier[49]—whom Ignatius saw as the representative of the entire Ephesian church.

The governance of the Christian church of Ephesos by a bishop was a new phenomenon; Luke knew only of Ephesian presbyters. It is impossible to say to what degree the bishop controlled all Christian groups in Ephesos. Repeated admonitions in the letter to establish and preserve unity[50] seem to reveal that Ignatius had been informed of divisions; Ignatius also requests that the addressees be on their guard against false teachers.[51] He assumes, however, that the church in Ephesos knows about Paul and honors him, calling them "fellow initiates of Paul" and reminding them that Paul "had remembered them in every letter."[52] Ignatius takes for granted that Pauline teaching is normative for all the churches to which he writes.

Together with the church in Smyrna and its bishop, Polycarp, the Ephesian church gave material support to Ignatius and also sent one of their members, Burrhos, to work as Ignatius's assistant and accompany him as far as Troas. Ignatius mentions the Ephesians explicitly in his letters to the churches in Magnesia, Tralles, Philadelphia, Smyrna, and Rome.[53] The support of the church in the capital of Asia was evidently significant to him.

The Apostle John and Ephesos

While Ignatius assumed that Paul was a recognized authority in Ephesos, there is no hint of the presence of the apostle John in Ignatius's letter to the Ephesians, nor is there any indication of the apocalyptic message of the prophet John who wrote Revelation. The absence of reference to either of these Johannine traditions in western Asia Minor is also striking in the letters of Polycarp, bishop of Smyrna during the period from Ignatius's visit at the time of Trajan until his martyrdom under Marcus Aurelius. Polycarp is a church leader in the tradition of Paul, to whom he referred explicitly[54] and whose

---

48. On the date and the chronology of Ignatius's journey and letters, see William R. Schoedel, *Ignatius of Antioch: A Commentary on the Letters of Ignatius of Antioch* (Hermeneia; Philadelphia: Fortress Press, 1985) 5 and passim.

49. Onesimos is mentioned in Ignatius *Eph.* 1.3; 2.1; 6.2. Since Onesimos was a common name, there is little chance that this was the Onesimos of Paul's Letter to Philemon; see Schoedel, *Ignatius*, 43–44.

50. Admonitions to unity are found, for example, in Ignatius *Eph.* 3.2; 4; 5.

51. See ibid., 6–7; 9; 16.2.

52. Ibid., 12.2. There are also several allusions to Paul's letters and quotations from them.

53. Ignatius *Magn.* 15.1: Ἀσπάζονται ὑμᾶς Ἐφέσιοι ἀπὸ Σμύρνης, ὅθεν καὶ γράφω ὑμῖν; *Trall.* 13.1: Ἀσπάζονται ὑμᾶς ἡ ἀγάπη Σμυρναίων καὶ Ἐφεσίων; *Rom.* 10.1: Γράφω δὲ ὑμῖν ταῦτα ἀπὸ Σμύρνης δι' Ἐφεσίων τῶν ἀξιομακαρίστων; *Phld.* 11.2: ἐν Τρωάδι, ὅθεν καὶ γράφω ὑμῖν διὰ Βούρρου πεμφθέντος ἅμα ἐμοὶ ἀπὸ Ἐφεσίων καὶ Σμυρναίων εἰς λόγον τιμῆς; *Smyrn.* 12.1: ὅθεν καὶ γράφω ὑμῖν διὰ Βούρρου, ὃν ἀπεστείλατε μετ' ἐμοῦ ἅμα Ἐφεσίοις, τοῖς ἀδελφοῖς, ὃς κατὰ πάντα με ἀνέπαυσεν.

54. Polycarp *Phil.* 3.2; 9.1.

tradition he interpreted in a manner closely related to that of the Pastoral Epistles.[55] While it is likely that Polycarp knew the Gospels of Matthew and Luke,[56] it is certain that he did not know the Gospel of John. This lack of knowledge is especially signifi- cant if one considers P. N. Harrison's thesis that most of the *Letter of Polycarp* was not written until about 140 CE.[57]

The apologist Justin Martyr seems to have stayed in Ephesos sometime before the middle of the second century. In his writings, he never refers to John or to the Gospel attributed to him, while he uses Matthew and Luke frequently and also knows of Mark.[58]

The testimony of Papias, the bishop of Hierapolis during the first half of the second century,[59] is ambiguous. Papias does not reveal any knowledge of the Gospel of John, although the quotations from his writings that are preserved in Eusebius[60] demonstrate that he was familiar with Mark and Matthew.[61] Although unable to find any reference to the Fourth Gospel in Papias's writings, Eusebius reports that Papias "used quotations from the First Letter of John."[62] Moreover, Eusebius says that Papias also "expounds a story about a woman who was accused before the Lord of many sins," a story that Euse- bius does not attribute to John, where it is found in later manuscripts (John 7:53– 8:11),[63] but to the *Gospel according to the Hebrews*.[64] Since no church father before the end of the fourth century attributed this story to John, Papias's knowledge of this story must arise from the apocryphal tradition of narratives about Jesus. Eusebius's comments about the "two Johns" whom Papias knew are intriguing.[65] These comments refer to a passage from Papias that Eusebius quoted verbatim:

If ever anyone came who had followed the presbyters (τοῖς πρεσβυτέροις), I inquired into the words of the presbyters, what Andrew or Peter or Philip or Thomas or James or John or Matthew, or any other of the Lord's disciples (τῶν τοῦ κυρίου μαθητῶν) had said, and what Aristion and the presbyter (ὁ πρεσβύ- τερος) John, the Lord's disciples (τοῦ κυρίου μαθηταί), were saying.[66]

---

55. Hans von Campenhausen, "Polykarp von Smyrna und die Pastoralbriefe," in *Aus der Frühzeit des Christentums* (Tübingen: Mohr/Siebeck, 1963) 197–252.

56. See Helmut Koester, *Ancient Christian Gospels: Their History and Development* (Philadelphia: Trinity Press International, 1990) 19–20; idem, *Synoptische Überlieferung bei den Apostolischen Vätern* (TU 65; Berlin: Akademie-Verlag, 1957) 114–20.

57. P. N. Harrison, *Polycarp's Two Epistles to the Philippians* (Cambridge: Cambridge University Press, 1936).

58. Koester, *Ancient Christian Gospels*, 360–402.

59. The exact date of Papias's writings cannot be determined.

60. Eusebius *Hist. eccl.* 3.39.1–17.

61. It is not clear, however, whether Papias's reference to Matthew, "who composed the sayings (τὰ λογία)," refers to the extant Gospel of Matthew or to the Synoptic sayings source, Q; see Koester, *Ancient Christian Gospels*, 166, 316.

62. Eusebius *Hist. eccl.* 3.39.17; Κέχρηται δ᾽ ὁ αὐτὸς μαρτυρίας ἀπὸ τῆς Ἰωάννου προτέρας ἐπιστολῆς.

63. MS D, some Latin MSS, and the majority of the Byzantine MSS. It is missing in 𝔓[66.75] ℵ B C L N T W Y 0141. 0211. 33. 565. 1241. 133. 1424. 2768 sy sa.

64. Eusebius *Hist. eccl.* 3.39.17.

65. Ibid. 3.39.5–6 (trans. Kirsopp Lake; LCL; 2 vols.; Cambridge: Harvard University Press, 1959) 1.293.

66. Ibid., 3.39.4; ET 1.293.

Regarding the first John, Eusebius says that Papias "reckons him with Peter and James and Matthew and the other Apostles, clearly meaning the evangelist."[67] This John is doubtlessly the one who appears in the list of the apostles, which Papias could have drawn from Mark or Matthew or from oral tradition. Eusebius's remark, "clearly meaning the evangelist," is unwarranted, because Papias does not name this John as one of the evangelists together with Mark and Matthew, but as one of the Lord's disciples. The second John, Eusebius comments, is named by Papias "outside the number of the Apostles, putting Aristion before him and clearly calling him a presbyter."[68] Then follows a remark that Eusebius does not draw from Papias:

This confirms the truth of the story of those who have said that there were two of the same name in Asia, and that there are two tombs at Ephesus both still called John's. This calls for attention: for it is probable that the second (unless anyone prefer the former) saw the revelation which passes under the name of John.[69]

Moreover, Eusebius claims that Papias had actually heard Aristion and the presbyter John, an assertion not necessarily implied in the passage from Papias that Eusebius had quoted. A connection between Papias and John, the author of Revelation, may indeed exist, however: both are chiliasts, expecting the thousand-year kingdom of Christ, "set up in material form here on this earth."[70] Although Papias does not connect the presbyter John explicitly with Ephesos, one can reasonably assume that this John was indeed the author of Revelation.

Some memory of a John of Ephesos may have survived in the story that Clement of Alexandria tells about a young man whom this John entrusted to the bishop (or a presbyter) of Smyrna and who then became the leader of a band of brigands.[71] There is no indication in Clement's report that this John was the evangelist;[72] moreover, the story may be based on an old tradition because there is no reference to Polycarp of Smyrna, and the designation "bishop" of Smyrna could be Eusebius's interpretation of the original designation "presbyter" of Smyrna, that is, the story may come from a time before Polycarp became bishop of that city. If this is the case, the John of the old story was probably the prophet John who wrote Revelation.

Evidence therefore exists for a historical person, John of Ephesos, who was the author of Revelation. How did the apostle John, the assumed author of the Fourth Gospel, come to Ephesos as a second John of Ephesos; or how did he come to be identified with the original John of Ephesos? It seems to me that this identification is due to a fiction that Bishop Irenaeus of Lyon created. There is no trace of knowledge of this Gospel in

---

67. Ibid., 3.39.5; ET 1.293.

68. Ibid.

69. Ibid., 3.39.6; ET 1.293.

70. Ibid., 3.39.11. For the expectation of the thousand-year kingdom in Revelation, see Rev 20:2–7. Eusebius considers such belief and the traditions connected with it as "strange (ξέναι) parables and teachings of the Saviour and . . . more mythical (μυθικώτερα) accounts" (3.39.11; ET 1.295).

71. Clement of Alexandria *Quis div. salv.* 42; quoted in Eusebius *Hist. eccl.* 3.23.5–19.

72. In Clement's story he is simply called "John the Apostle." In his introduction to the story, Eusebius quotes Irenaeus in order to make sure that this John is understood to be the "apostle and evangelist."

western Asia Minor. Neither Papias nor Polycarp reveals any acquaintance with it. The Gospel of John must have been written elsewhere, most likely in Syria or Palestine; it was brought to Egypt early in the second century, where Gnostic theologians, especially the Valentinians, who later wrote the first commentaries on this Gospel, used it extensively. By the mid-second century, however, this Gospel must have reached Asia Minor, where Irenaeus, a native of the area, became acquainted with it and took it to Lyon when he became bishop of the church in that city. Irenaeus was primarily responsible for introducing and defending the four-Gospel canon of the New Testament. In order to lend greater authority to the Fourth Gospel, he identified its author with the well-known John of Ephesos and ascribed both the Fourth Gospel and Revelation to him.[73] This identification was even more important in view of the Quartodeciman controversy, as the Asian Christians could quote the Fourth Gospel in support of their special Easter praxis, which differed from the Roman dating of Easter. In this context, Irenaeus, describing Polycarp's visit in Rome, states that Polycarp continued in his praxis "inasmuch as he had always done so in company with John the disciple of our Lord and the other apostles with whom he had associated."[74] It is evident that a personal association of Polycarp with any apostle is impossible, since according to Eusebius, Polycarp suffered martyrdom as late as 167 CE at the age of 84; if this is the case, he would have been born in 83. If Polycarp met any of the several Johns, it must have been the prophet John of Ephesos who wrote Revelation. One must then also associate this prophet John with the story of the John who met the heretic Kerinthos in a bathhouse.[75]

The fictional identification of the author of the Fourth Gospel with the prophet John of Ephesos was successful, however. At the end of the second century, Bishop Polykrates of Ephesos, in his letter to Bishop Victor of Rome, speaks about "John, who leaned on the Lord's breast, . . . martyr and teacher, who sleeps at Ephesos."[76] By this time, there is no doubt that the church of Ephesos claimed that the tomb of John in their city was that of the author of the Fourth Gospel.

The *Acts of John*, written at the end of the second century, also adopted this fiction. John arrives in Ephesos, coming from Miletos. He stays there and performs many miracles, even destroying the temple of Artemis. He is then called to Smyrna, makes a long journey through many regions of Asia,[77] and finally returns to Ephesos for another stay. After a final worship service with his disciples, he goes outside the city, where a grave is dug for him, and lying down in the grave, he dies. According to the *Acts of Paul*, Paul makes only a very brief visit to Ephesos. It seems that even the author of the *Acts of Paul* knew that Ephesos had now become the city of John, apostle and evangelist.[78]

---

73. Irenaeus *Adv. haer.* 2.22.5; 3.3.4; 5.30.3.
74. Eusebius *Hist. eccl.* 5.24.16; see also 5.20.6.
75. Irenaeus *Adv. haer.* 3.3.4, which Eusebius quotes twice (*Hist. eccl.* 3.28.6; 4.14.6).
76. Eusebius *Hist. eccl.* 3.31.3.
77. Most of the report of this travel is lost.
78. There is no indication that this tradition of John, disciple and apostle, as it was brought to Ephesos, was in any way connected with a tradition of Mary the mother of Jesus. The tradition of the ancient church is almost unanimous in the assumption that Mary stayed in Jerusalem, where she died.

Conclusion

From its very beginning in the middle of the first century, the Christian community of Ephesos exhibits a remarkable diversity. Literary testimonies demonstrate that this diversity continued well into the second century, spanning the entire spectrum from a prophetic-apocalyptic enthusiasm (witnessed in the Revelation of John) to the sacramental orientation of an episcopal church (advocated in the letter of Ignatius of Antioch). Only two church leaders can be associated with Ephesos with absolute certainty: the apostle Paul and the prophet John, the author of Revelation. Indirect testimonies, however, suggest that the Alexandrian teacher Apollos was also one of Ephesos's earliest missionaries and that Paul's associate Timothy later occupied a leading position in this city after Paul's departure.

In his Acts of the Apostles, Luke first attempted to establish a particular Christian tradition as the single legitimate authority for Ephesos. Contrary to the information provided by his sources, he elevated Paul to the rank of founding apostle; Ignatius's letter to the Ephesians confirms that an appeal to Paul would find positive response in at least one of the several groups of Ephesian Christians. All known early Christian leaders who were active in Ephesos, however, were finally overshadowed by the authority of an apostle who had never been in that city and whose tradition did not arrive there until the second half of the second century: John the evangelist. Once the Gospel of John had become known in western Asia Minor, it proved to be a powerful weapon for the Asian Christians in the Easter controversy. The prominence that Ephesos had achieved in the second century made it natural that the tomb of John would be located in the metropolis of Asia.

23

THE DESIGNATION OF
JAMES AS ᾽ΩΒΛΙΑΣ

In a fragment of Hegesippus quoted by Eusebius (*Hist eccl.* 2.23.7) appears the follow-ing much debated sentence about Jesus' brother James: διὰ γέ τοι τὴν ὑπερβολὴν τῆς δικαιοσύνης αὐτοῦ ἐκαλεῖτο ὁ δίκαιος καὶ ὠβλίας, ὅ ἐστιν Ἑλληνιστὶ περιοχὴ τοῦ λαοῦ, καὶ δικαιοσύνη, ὡς οἱ προφῆται δηλοῦσιν περὶ αὐτοῦ ("Because of the excess of his righteousness he was called the Righteous and the *Ōblias*, which is trans-lated into Greek 'Fortress of the People,' and 'Righteousness,' as also the prophets reveal about him").

The difficulties of this sentence are the following: (1) How should one understand the designation of James as ὠβλίας ("Oblias")? (2) Why does Hegesippus translate ὠβλίας ("Oblias") into Greek as περιοχὴ τοῦ λαοῦ ("Fortress of the People")? (3) Why does Hegesippus refer to this interpretation as one that had been revealed by the prophets?

The word ᾽Ωβλίας ("Oblias") is not attested anywhere else and is unintelligible.[1] C. C. Torrey has suggested reading ᾽ΩΒΔΙΑΣ instead of ᾽ΩΒΛΙΑΣ.[2] The name ᾽Ωβδίας appears in Josephus in the form ᾽Ωβεδίας as a transcription of the Hebrew name עֹבַדְיָ(הו), which is otherwise usually transcribed as ᾽Αβδίας. The change from α and ο into ω in the transcription of Hebrew names is not rare.[3] Thus ᾽Ωβδίας ("Obdias") cor-responds to the Hebrew name עֹבַדְיָה Obadiah.

The LXX normally uses περιοχή to translate מְצוּדָה and related Hebrew terms (1 Sam 22:4; 1 Par 11:16 and elsewhere). In Obad 1, however, the Greek phrase of the LXX καὶ περιοχὴν εἰς τὰ ἔθνη ἐξαπέστειλέν σε translates Hebrew וְצִיר בַּגּוֹיִם שֻׁלָּח. περιοχὴ εἰς τὰ ἔθνη corresponds to περιοχὴ τοῦ λαοῦ in the Hegesippus fragment. Thus the relation of "Obadiah" and the phrase περιοχὴ τοῦ λαοῦ is evident. At the same time, it becomes clear why Hegesippus remarks that this designation has been revealed by the prophets (ὡς οἱ προφῆται δηλοῦσιν περὶ αὐτοῦ).

The result is that James the Just had the surname "Obadiah." This raises the ques-tion whether it is possible to establish a connection to the prescript of the Epistle of James, considering that Obadiah means עֶבֶד יְהֹוָה = "Servant of God." This corresponds to the Greek δοῦλος θεοῦ = "Servant of God" of Jas 1:1.

---

1. For the various attempts at an understanding see Hans-Joachim Schoeps, *Aus frühchristlicher Zeit* (Tübin-gen: Mohr, 1950) 120–25.

2. Charles C. Torrey, "James the Just, and His Name 'Oblias'," *JBL* 63 (1944) 93–98; see in his article also other examples for scribal mistakes of Δ and Λ: ΙΩΒΕΛ in B א syˢ in Luke 3:32 for ΙΩΒΗΔ; cf. Judg 9:20 in A and B.

3. See ibid. Cf. also ᾽Ωβεθ in 2 Esdr 8:6 for עֶבֶד and ᾽Αβδεδομ in 1 Par (= Chron) 15:25 for עֶבֶד אֱדֹום.

24

EARLY CHRISTIANITY FROM THE PERSPECTIVE OF THE HISTORY OF RELIGIONS

Rudolf Bultmann's Contribution

I

Few would doubt that Rudolf Bultmann's most lasting accomplishment is his *Theology of the New Testament*. It will remain as the twentieth century's most perceptive and enlightening theological interpretation of Christianity's basic document. In my opinion, however, what guided Bultmann on his path to the completion of this work was several decades of study devoted to the investigation of the religious environment of the New Testament in the tradition of the history-of-religions school. It appears to me that much of this scholarly work of Bultmann either has simply been taken for granted or was not even mentioned in the process of the ongoing debate about the theological significance of his contribution.

Let me begin to illustrate this with a few reminiscences about my experience as a student of theology in the years immediately following World War II. Even after several semesters in Bultmann's lectures and seminars, if someone had asked me, "Who are the history-of-religions scholars at the University of Marburg?" I would not have named Bultmann. There were two students of Rudolf Otto on the faculty, both teaching systematic theology. And there was Friedrich Heiler, though he was then a member of the arts-and-sciences faculty (until 1948). But Bultmann? No.

There are several reasons for this negative answer:

1. To judge from the lecture courses that Bultmann offered, there could be no doubt that he was a New Testament scholar and theologian. His lectures were on John's Gospel, Romans, 1 Corinthians, 2 Corinthians, New Testament theology—and then the cycle of his courses began again with John's Gospel. They were exegetical and theological lectures with minute exegetical detail, which were difficult to understand without the *Novum Testamentum Graece* in front of each student in class. There were explanations of crucial terms with references to other biblical and nonbiblical materials: Greek philosophy, Stoic moralists, Gnostic texts. Then came the great moments in class when the student's patience was rewarded with these crystal-clear summaries of the meaning of the text, its theological significance, and the consequences for the understanding of Christian faith and life. It was for this reason that hundreds of students came to Bult-

mann's classes in these last years before his retirement, including large numbers from other faculties.

2. At that time Bultmann was publishing his *Theology of the New Testament*.[1] In the year of the appearance of the first fascicle of this work (1948), the volume of collected essays *Glauben und Verstehen*[2] also became available again in the bookstores.[3] There are no examples of Bultmann's history-of-religions works among the articles of this volume, nor in any of the subsequent volumes of *Glauben und Verstehen*.[4] Unfortunately, there is no preface to any of these volumes of collected essays. Bultmann does not tell us why these particular essays were chosen rather than any of the more exegetical and historical articles of the earlier period of his scholarly endeavors. The dust jacket of volume 3 of *Glauben und Verstehen* says that these essays allow the reader to have a look "into the workshop of an important theological thinker," and the dust jacket of volume 4 reveals: "In all these contributions of Rudolf Bultmann the same theme is dealt with: what it means to live historically as a human being, i.e., to exist while one lives on the basis of decisions."

In this way Bultmann was presented at that time—not as a history-of-religions scholar. The *Theologie des Neuen Testaments* and *Glauben und Verstehen* were the works that were available and these were the works that students read first of all at that time.

The impression that Bultmann was primarily a theologian, albeit a biblical theologian, was further reinforced by the "Demythologizing Debate" that was occupying everyone in the late forties and early fifties. Scholars from many theological disciplines became involved in this debate, even philosophers. But, aside from some discussion of Bultmann's use of the term "myth," perspectives of the history-of-religions school did not play any role in this debate. Even exegetical details were not discussed very much, although Bultmann's major exegetical works were soon reprinted, often with a supplement volume (*Ergänzungsheft*). But it took almost another twenty years before Bultmann's most important earlier essays on Hellenistic history of religion were also reprinted in a volume of collected essays: *Exegetica*, edited by Erich Dinkler.[5]

II

It is interesting to note that many of Bultmann's works became available in the English-speaking world in exactly the opposite sequence of their original publication, his later works appearing first. To be sure, an English translation of the small volume *Die Erforschung der synoptischen Evangelien* (1930) was published as early as 1934,[6] and the

---

1. *Theologie des Neuen Testaments* (Tübingen: Mohr/Siebeck, 1st fascicle 1948, 2d fascicle 1951, 3d fascicle 1953).

2. First published: Tübingen: Mohr/Siebeck, 1933; later reprinted as *Glauben und Verstehen I*.

3. During the first years after the war almost none of the previously published books was available in any of the bookstores.

4. Vol. 2 was published in 1952, vol. 3 in 1960, and vol. 4 in 1965; all volumes were published in Tübingen by Mohr/Siebeck.

5. Rudolf Bultmann, *Exegetica: Aufsätze zur Erforschung des Neuen Testaments*, selected, introduced, and edited by Erich Dinkler (Tübingen: Mohr/Siebeck, 1967).

6. Rudolf Bultmann and Karl Kundsin, *Form Criticism: Two Essays on New Testament Research,* trans. Frederick C. Grant (1934; repr. New York: Harper, 1962).

same year witnessed the English publication of Bultmann's *Jesus*.[7] But the real impact of Bultmann's work on the English-speaking world began in 1951 with the publication of his *Theology of the New Testament*.[8] In the year of the publication of volume 2 of his *Theology of the New Testament* the second volume of *Glauben und Verstehen* appeared as *Essays, Philosophical and Theological*.[9] Two years later Bultmann's Gifford Lectures were published in England under the title *History and Eschatology*[10] and in the United States under the title *The Presence of Eternity*.[11] In the following year the Shaffer Lectures *Jesus Christ and Mythology*, delivered in 1951 at Yale Divinity School, appeared in the United States.[12] It is not surprising that the collection of essays in English translation that Schubert Ogden published in 1960 under the title *Existence and Faith*[13] had the explicit intention to introduce Bultmann as a theological thinker, not primarily as an exegete and historian of religion. This volume does include two of the exegetical articles that have never been reprinted in the German volumes of *Glauben und Verstehen* ("Romans 7 and the Anthropology of Paul," and "Ignatius and Paul"), but the insightful introduction of the editor barely mentions Bultmann's significance as an interpreter of ancient texts. Schubert Ogden writes, "In Bultmann's case . . . what constitutes the inner integrity of all that he really intends to say is his affirmation of the 'infinite qualitative difference' between time and eternity in its several negative and positive implications."[14] One would hardly suspect that these words characterize the leading New Testament scholar of the twentieth century.

The major exegetical works of Bultmann, though written before the publication of his *Theologie des Neuen Testaments*, appeared in English translation only after the English translations of his theological and philosophical writings, namely, *The History of the Synoptic Tradition* in 1963,[15] and the *Commentary on the Gospel of John* in 1971.[16] However, the collected essays *Exegetica* that Dinkler published in 1967 have not yet been translated into English. Yet in particular the essays dealing with the background of the Gospel of John, originally published in 1923,[17] 1925,[18] and 1928–30,[19] Bultmann's response to Ernst Percy[20] of

---

7. *Jesus and the Word,* trans. Louise Pettibone Smith (New York: Scribner's, 1934).

8. Trans. Kendrick Grobel (New York: Scribner's, vol. 1, 1951; vol. 2, 1955).

9. Trans. James C. G. Greig (London: SCM, 1955).

10. Edinburgh: University Press, 1957.

11. New York: Harper, 1957; in this case, the German edition, *Geschichte und Eschatologie* (Tübingen: Mohr/Siebeck, 1958), was published a year after the English edition.

12. New York: Scribner's, 1958; the German edition, *Jesus Christus und die Mythologie,* was not published until 1964.

13. New York: Meridian, 1960.

14. In Bultmann, *Existence and Faith*, 14.

15. Trans. J. Marsh (Oxford: Blackwell).

16. Trans. G. R. Beasley-Murray (Philadelphia: Westminster).

17. "Der religionsgeschichtliche Hintergrund des Prologs zum Johannes-Evangelium," in ΕΥΧΑΡΙΣΤΗΡΙΟΝ: *Hermann Gunkel zum 60. Geburtstag* (2 vols.; FRLANT 36; Göttingen: Vandenhoeck & Ruprecht, 1923) 2.3–26 = *Exegetica*, 10–35.

18. "Die Bedeutung der neuerschlossenen mandäischen und manichäischen Quellen für das Verständnis des Johannesevangeliums," *ZNW* 24 (1925) 100–146 = *Exegetica*, 55–104.

19. "Untersuchungen zum Johannesevangelium," *ZNW* 27 (1928) 113–63; *ZNW* 29 (1930) 169–92 = *Exegetica*, 124–97.

20. *Untersuchungen über den Ursprung der johanneischen Theologie: Zugleich ein Beitrag zur Frage nach der Entstehung des Gnostizismus* (Lund: Gleerup, 1939).

1940,[21] and his review of Karl Holl's *Urchristentum und Religionsgeschichte*,[22] are works that have become increasingly significant in the present situation of scholarship, especially in the United States with its large number of scholars who are involved in the publication, translation, and interpretation of the Gnostic documents of the Nag Hammadi Library, and where the instruction in the history, phenomenology, and sociology of religion has become such an important part of the curriculum of colleges, universities, and theological schools.

These essays and reviews, after rereading them now, more than half a century after their original publication, strike me as methodologically extremely significant and well worth a critical reconsideration. In this context, one should also reconsider the history-of-religions works that Bultmann inspired among his doctoral students of those early years of his teaching career at Marburg, although I shall not deal with them in this essay.

III

In his autobiographical reflections, Bultmann names as his most influential theological teachers the church historian Karl Müller in Tübingen, Hermann Gunkel and Adolf von Harnack in Berlin, and Adolf Jülicher, Johannes Weiss, and Wilhelm Herrmann in Marburg. It was Johannes Weiss who inspired Bultmann's dissertation *Der Stil der paulinischen Predigt und die kynisch-stoische Diatribe*.[23] By the time Bultmann had completed his dissertation, Weiss had left Marburg to occupy a chair in Heidelberg, and his successor, Wilhelm Heitmüller, accepted the dissertation in the year 1910.

Both Weiss and Heitmüller belonged to what had come to be called the *Religionsgeschichtliche Schule*; indeed, Weiss must be considered as one of its founders. It is doubtful, however, whether one should really use the term "school" in its technical sense. Rather, it was a new beginning in a circle of young students and scholars at the University of Göttingen in the last two decades of the nineteenth century, all students of Albrecht Ritschl, the most towering figure of liberal theology in the second half of the nineteenth century. In his work *Die christliche Lehre von der Rechtfertigung und Versöhnung*,[24] Ritschl had created the classical writing of German liberal theology with its central evolutionary concept that the kingdom of God, as it was proclaimed by Jesus, is the divine design that would find its fulfillment through the establishment of moral law among humankind. An impressive number of leading theologians of the following generation were deeply influenced by Ritschl (Adolf von Harnack, Wilhelm Herrmann, Emil Schürer, Martin Rade, and others).

But several members of this circle of younger scholars in Göttingen made discover-

---

21. "Johanneische Schriften und Gnosis," *Orientalische Literaturzeitung* 43 (1940) 150–75 = *Exegetica*, 230–54. One essay that appeared much later, published after World War II but probably written earlier, should probably be added to the list of Bultmann's history-of-religions works: "Zur Geschichte der Lichtsymbolik im Altertum," *Philologus* 97 (1948) 1–36 = *Exegetica*, 323–55.

22. *ThR*, NF 4 (1932) 1–21; not included in *Exegetica*.

23. FRLANT 13; Göttingen: Vandenhoeck & Ruprecht, 1910.

24. 3 vols.; Bonn: Marcus, 1870–74; ET: *The Christian Doctrine of Justification and Reconciliation* (2nd ed.; Edinburgh: T. & T. Clark, 1902).

ies, primarily through their work in biblical exegesis, that were to present a fundamental challenge to Ritschl's understanding of the Bible in general, and in particular to his interpretation of Jesus' preaching of the kingdom of God. Later, these younger scholars became known as the *Religionsgeschichtliche Schule*: Hermann Gunkel (born 1862, in Göttingen until 1889), William Wrede (born 1859, in Göttingen until 1893), Wilhelm Bousset (born 1865, remained in Göttingen as *Privatdozent* until the time of World War I), Ernst Troeltsch (born 1865, in Göttingen until 1892), and Johannes Weiss (born 1863, in Göttingen until 1895). Weiss, who was Ritschl's son-in-law, in his book *Die Predigt Jesu vom Reiche Gottes* (published 1892, three years after Ritschl's death), presented the most direct attack upon the biblical basis of the theology of his teacher and father-in-law: Jesus' preaching of the kingdom of God was eschatological; Jesus expected the kingdom as divine miracle of the future that had no relationship to the moral perfection of humankind.

What the "members" of the *Religionsgeschichtliche Schule* had discovered would change the direction of biblical studies fundamentally. Other scholars were soon drawn into the sphere of influence of the initial discovery: Ulrich von Wilamowitz-Moellendorff (he taught in Göttingen 1882–97), Julius Wellhausen (came to Göttingen in 1892),[25] Rudolf Otto (came to Göttingen in 1897), and elsewhere Albrecht Dieterich (1866–1908), student of the classical philologian Hermann Usener (1834–1905)[26] in Bonn, forcefully promoted the history-of-religions investigation of Hellenistic materials.

It may be useful to summarize briefly the new insights of these scholars, in order to evaluate Bultmann's work as a scholar of the history of religions. They can be briefly characterized as follows:

1. The concepts of the Bible are not moral and intellectual, but mythical and eschatological.

2. Religion, and especially early Christianity, is syncretistic in character.

3. Cult and liturgy are the center of the religious experience of people (not literature and theological concepts).

4. Folklore and oral traditions are the instruments of the transmission of religious knowledge.

5. The central religious experience is essentially irrational.

6. The quest for the understanding of "religion" must transcend the limitations of any specific religion or theology.

When Bultmann was a student in the first decade of the twentieth century, the new insights of the *Religionsgeschichtliche Schule* had already been widely publicized, but its founders were still occupying important teaching positions in several universities, and

---

25. He had been in Göttingen as a student in 1862–65 and as a *Privatdozent* in 1870–72—well before the beginnings of the *Religionsgeschichtliche Schule*.

26. Usener was one of the first scholars in Germany to offer lectures on *Allgemeine Religionsgeschichte*.

Bultmann had studied under more than one of these scholars. But he had also been exposed to the liberal theology of Ritschl's students and friends (Herrmann and von Harnack). When he was in Marburg as a _Privatdozent_ until 1916,[27] he had established a close association with Ritschl's student Martin Rade, the editor of the leading journal of liberal theology, _Die Christliche Welt_, and he himself became a member of the group "Freunde der christlichen Welt." When he returned to teach in Marburg in 1921, after several years at the University of Breslau (where he was a colleague of Rudolf Otto) and a year at the University of Giessen as the successor of Wilhelm Bousset (1920–21), he followed his _Doktorvater_, Wilhelm Heitmüller, who had accepted a call to Bonn. In the following year, his teacher Wilhelm Herrmann died and Rudolf Otto became his successor as professor of systematic theology. Adolf Jülicher retired a year later (1923). But in the year 1922, Martin Heidegger had moved to Marburg, and it seems that the association between Bultmann and Heidegger was established very quickly. This is the time in which Bultmann began to write his most important essays on the history-of-religions background of the New Testament.

In the earlier period, the influence of the _Religionsgeschichtliche Schule_ is mostly visible in the works devoted to the investigations of nonliterary patterns of communication and transmission. This is, of course, first evident in Bultmann's dissertation on the style of Pauline preaching and its relationship to the rhetorical style of the Cynic preacher.[28] But Bultmann's major work that fulfills this part of the program of the _Religionsgeschichtliche Schule_ is his fundamental work on the form criticism of the Synoptic Gospels, _Die Geschichte der synoptischen Tradition_.[29] This book was written during Bultmann's years in Breslau (1916–20) and is dedicated to Heitmüller.

Bultmann was never actively involved in pursuing the more universalistic ambitions of the history-of-religions program, that is, searching for the underlying common denominator of all specific religions and theologies. Nor did he accept any definition of the religious experience as fundamentally irrational. Of course, he knew that there are irrational, ecstatic, and mystical religious phenomena; but he would never allow these to govern the definition of Christian faith. There are numerous reflections of Bultmann on this subject. A statement from his "Autobiographical Reflections" summarizes his position well: "It seemed to me that in this new theological movement [dialectical theology] it was rightly recognized . . . that the Christian faith is not a phenomenon of the history of religion, that it does not rest on a 'religious _a priori_' (Troeltsch), and that therefore theology does not have to look upon it as a phenomenon of religious or cultural history."[30] It is clear that there could be no common ground with Bultmann's colleague Rudolf Otto, who had come to Marburg as the successor of Herrmann shortly after Bultmann's move from Giessen to Marburg. In his "Autobiographical Reflections," Bultmann mentions the "oppositions" within the theological

---

27. He had written his _Habilitationsschrift_, submitted in 1912, under the supervision of the liberal historical-critical NT scholar and church historian Adolf Jülicher on "Die Exegese des Theodor von Mopsuestia."

28. _Stil der paulinischen Predigt;_ see above at n. 23.

29. FRLANT 29; Göttingen: Vandenhoeck & Ruprecht, 1921; 2d ed., 1931; further editions followed in 1957, 1958, and 1962; for the ET see above, n. 16.

30. _Existence and Faith_, 287–88.

faculty at Marburg, "especially the tension between Rudolf Otto and myself, . . . (which) stirred even the students and led to lively discussions."[31]

But Bultmann was fascinated by the history-of-religions discovery of the predominance of myth and mythological language in the New Testament and of the syncretistic character of early Christianity. As he began to prepare his commentary on the Gospel of John, the relationship of the message of this Gospel to its syncretistic environment and, more specifically, to Gnostic mythology became the agenda for a series of publications in which Bultmann most clearly demonstrates that he was a student of the *Religionsgeschichtliche Schule*. This period of Bultmann's work also generated a renewed interest in the study of the religious environment of early Christianity among his students. Several dissertations written at Marburg during these years deal with this question, particularly with Gnosticism: Heinrich Schlier, *Religionsgeschichtliche Untersuchungen zu den Ignatiusbriefen;*[32] Ernst Käsemann, *Leib und Leib Christi;*[33] Günther Bornkamm, *Mythos und Legende in den apokryphen Thomasakten;*[34] and finally Hans Jonas, *Gnosis und spätantiker Geist.*[35]

In the first of these essays on the history-of-religions background of the Johannine prologue,[36] the text of John 1 sets the stage for the inquiry. The problem is defined on the basis of peculiar features of this text, as compared to other texts from the early Christian period. In the case of the Fourth Gospel, of course, comparison with the Synoptic Gospels often serves the purpose of recognizing Johannine peculiarities more clearly. In this respect, Bultmann differs from Richard Reitzenstein, who begins his *Hellenistic Mystery Religions* with a general assessment of the topic.[37] Bultmann is, therefore, much more closely allied to Eduard Norden, whose works formulate the topic and problematic of the investigation on the basis of a particular text, namely Acts 17 and Virgil's *Fourth Eclogue*, respectively.[38] It is only consistent with this starting point that Bultmann's comparative material is the reconstruction of a text, originally "Gnostic" in his opinion, for which he can adduce numerous parallels, primarily from Jewish wisdom literature.

Bultmann's essay of 1925 on the relevance of the new Mandaean and Manichaean texts for the interpretation of the Gospel of John is also primarily text-oriented.[39] It

---

31. Ibid., 286.

32. BZNW 8; Giessen: Töpelmann, 1929; see also his *Habilitationsschrift, Christus und die Kirche im Epheserbrief* (BhTh 6; Tübingen: Mohr/Siebeck, 1930).

33. BhTh 9; Tübingen: Mohr-Siebeck, 1933; see also idem, *Das wandernde Gottesvolk* (FRLANT 55; Göttingen: Vandenhoeck & Ruprecht, 1933); ET: *The Wandering People of God: An Investigation of the Letter to the Hebrews* (Eugene, OR: Wipf and Stock, 2002).

34. FRLANT 49; Göttingen: Vandenhoeck & Ruprecht, 1933.

35. Vol. 1 (FRLANT 51; Göttingen: Vandenhoeck & Ruprecht, 1934); vol. 2 was set in type in 1934–35, but published only twenty years later (FRLANT 63; Göttingen: Vandenhoeck & Ruprecht, 1954).

36. *Exegetica*, 10–35; originally published in 1923.

37. Pittsburgh Theological Monograph Series 15; Pittsburgh: Pickwick, 1978; ET of *Die hellenistischen Mysterienreligionen nach ihren Grundgedanken und Wirkungen* (3d ed. 1927; repr. Darmstadt: Wissenschaftliche Buchgesellschaht, 1956).

38. *Agnostos Theos: Untersuchungen zur Formengeschichte religiöser Rede* (1913; Darmstadt: Wissenschaftliche Buchgesellschaft, 1956); idem, *Die Geburt des Kindes: Geschichte einer religiösen Idee* (1930; Darmstadt: Wissenschaftliche Buchgesellschaft, 1958).

39. See above, n. 18.

makes the "riddle of the Gospel of John" the primary topic of the investigation. Specific texts from the Gospel of John set the stage for the detailed comparison with equally specific parallels from Mandaean and other literatures. It is clear that Bultmann works primarily as an exegete. The result of his investigation is the call for the reconstruction of the source that the author of the Gospel of John must have used in the construction of his discourses. As is well known, Bultmann's interpretation of these parts of the Gospel of John in his later commentary[40] depends on the assumption that such a source existed, and Bultmann's student Heinz Becker has indeed produced a very interesting reconstruction of this hypothetical source.[41]

Although some problems begin to appear in this second essay, I do not think that these problems must be seen primarily in the widely criticized hypothesis of this Johannine *Redenquelle*. On the contrary, new texts, such as the *Dialogue of the Savior* from the Nag Hammadi Library, may indeed lead us back to Bultmann's original assumption that the Johannine discourses and dialogues rested on some kind of written source (or sources). Moreover, this source was most probably a Gnostic document. The real problem with Bultmann's approach is, in my opinion, a different one.

Bultmann departs to a certain degree from a strictly textual approach. After briefly reporting the result of Reitzenstein's reconstruction of the redeemer myth of the primordial man, Bultmann introduces his own investigation by saying, "I will now demonstrate that this myth lies at the base of the Gospel of John."[42] To what degree the investigation is now determined by the general construct of this redeemer myth, and to what degree it is actually informed by the exegetical investigation of these Mandaean and Manichaean texts, is therefore not always clear. The dilemma is not that the source for the Johannine discourses is reconstructed from materials that have been composed several centuries later. Bultmann is, of course, quite aware of this, and he is capable of adducing impressive evidence from earlier sources, such as the *Odes of Solomon*, in order to support credibly the existence of the hypothetical source at a much earlier date. But the leading principle of the textual reconstruction is a theoretical construct that can be seriously criticized.[43]

That Bultmann uses this myth only as a general concept of the religious milieu at the time of early Christianity has some further consequences that become visible if one considers the interpretation of the Gospel of John itself: the question of the *Sitz im Leben* is not posed in sufficient specificity. We do not learn much about the particular function and purpose of the hypothetical source in which this myth has found its

---

40. Rudolf Bultmann, *Das Evangelium des Johannes* (KEK; Göttingen: Vandenhoeck & Ruprecht, 1941); for the ET see above at n. 16.

41. *Die Reden des Johannesevangeliums und der Stil der gnostischen Offenbarungsrede* (FRLANT 68; Göttingen: Vandenhoeck & Ruprecht, 1956).

42. *Exegetica*, 55.

43. See, e.g., Carsten Colpe, *Die religionsgeschichtliche Schule: Darstellung und Kritik ihres Bildes vom gnostischen Erlösermythus* (FRLANT 78; Göttingen: Vandenhoeck & Ruprecht, 1961). Bultmann's essay of 1925 is explicitly discussed in Colpe's critical treatment, also the 1923 essay on the history-of-religions background. It is noteworthy, however, that Colpe never refers to any of the later essays and reviews of Bultmann on this topic (see above, nn. 19–22).

expression. Rather, the interpretation of its meaning does not go beyond the reflections about the more general religious ideas that dominate this type of mythical thinking: the fate of the divine soul, the call from beyond, and the redemption and the return of the soul to its heavenly origin. Since Bultmann correctly recognizes that the author of the Fourth Gospel is critical of the mythical description of the soul's fate in this process of fall and redemption, the reinterpretation of this mythical material becomes radically reduced to the "that" (*dass*) of the revelation. There is hardly any alternative as long as the function of this mythical Gnostic source is understood only in such general terms. But the quest for the *Sitz im Leben* must reconstruct not only the mythical-religious dimension of the Gnostic source, but also its political, social, and communal function. It is possible to be more specific: the source must have been the bearer of a Gnostic message that was very much alive in Palestinian and Syrian Judaism; and it was used by the author of the Fourth Gospel at a time when his own community was trying to answer the question of its place in Judaism (or Israel)—quite likely also a political problem. What role does the critical interpretation of a Gnostic-Jewish document play in that particular historical situation?

If the more recent efforts of the interpretation of the texts from Nag Hammadi simply lead us to the substitution of a better, while ostensibly older, Gnostic source, we shall have failed the test of this question. It is not enough to point to Jewish baptist sects in Syria and Palestine in general as the place of origin for this source. The interpretation of this source by the author of the Gospel of John puts this Gospel in a close companionship with such circles and their political as well as religious ambitions. Thus we must discuss the specifics of the historical situation to which both the source and the Gospel of John belong.

IV

Bultmann's history-of-religions work is characterized by an impressive thoroughness and comprehensiveness that also includes detailed and careful consideration of philological questions. This is particularly evident in the essay published in two parts in 1928 and 1930 entitled "Investigations in the Gospel of John."[44] The first part studies the term ἀλήθεια ("truth"); the second part considers the phrase θεὸν οὐδεὶς ἑώρακεν πώποτε ("nobody has ever seen God," John 1:18). In these investigations, it is clear that Bultmann does not isolate the questions of Gnosticism and Gnostic terminology from their larger context. His patient observation of minute detail as well as his grasp of the larger contexts is committed to the whole of Greek philosophy and religion as well as to the Old Testament and Judaism. The clarity in which the relevant materials are presented still calls forth admiration. But one may also ask: What is the price that he had to pay to achieve this clarity?

The first part of this essay, as is well known, became the basis for Bultmann's article "ἀλήθεια" in the *Theologisches Wörterbuch zum Neuen Testament*, which was published five

---

44. "Untersuchungen zum Johannesevangelium," *Exegetica*, 124–97.

years later.[45] It may well have been one of the essays that set the stage for, and determined the structure of, much of the scholarly study contributed to this monumental work. But Bultmann did not, in this essay, follow the typical and often-criticized schema of the articles in the *Theologisches Wörterbuch* that begins with Greek usage, then moves to Hellenism, Old Testament, Judaism, and the New Testament. Rather, in his essay of 1928, Bultmann begins with the Old Testament and Judaism, then moves to the New Testament writers whose usage is related to this latter background. After the conclusion of this section, the author discusses the Greek and Hellenistic literature, in which he also includes the *Odes of Solomon* and the *Corpus Hermeticum*, but not Christian writings.

Bultmann's strength in this essay is obvious. He can show the striking difference in the understanding of the term "truth" in the Greek world from Plato to Plotinus as compared to its usage in the Old Testament and in the literature of Judaism. The New Testament's use of the term appears as a continuation of the Old Testament concept, and other Christian authors are missing altogether. The Alexandrian theologians Clement and Origen do not appear (although Plotinus is discussed), and Philo of Alexandria is treated as part of the chapter on Hellenism. This one-sided but fascinating and richly documented presentation of a topic in its Greek understanding is equally evident in Bultmann's essay on the history of the symbolism of light in antiquity.[46] The essay begins with an extensive treatment of the classical Greek tragedies, Pindar, and Hesiod, discusses Plato and Aristotle, presents the striking changes that took place in the Hellenistic period (the Stoics, Philo, and the mystery religions are mentioned), and concludes with Plotinus. But no lines are drawn to the Christian literature of the period, nor does Bultmann consider how Christian usage may have influenced the mystery religions and Plotinus. But it remains somewhat ambiguous where the Christian writings really belong in this context. The evidence is divided along some traditional lines, which do not quite reflect the actual historical relationships. In terms of word study, this may be justified; however, it is no longer possible to see the interaction among Jewish, Hellenistic, and Christian concepts in the understanding of existence in a particular historical moment as it is reflected in such terminology.

Analogous questions could be asked with respect to the last of these history-of-religions essays, Bultmann's response to the book of Ernst Percy on the origin of Johannine theology.[47] Bultmann criticizes Percy's statements about certain terms that simply fix these terms in a general theoretical system, and he rejects the abstract differentiations of details of a concept. He requests that the interpreter should not be satisfied with the claim that a certain concept agrees with its understanding in a particular "background." Just to say, for example, that the concept of "world" in the Gospel of John agrees with the concept of "world" in the Old Testament does not reveal anything. Rather, the interpreter must explain what it means that human beings express the understanding of their own existence through the use of such concepts, "how world is experienced." This emphasis is persistent. Bultmann defines such "meaning" usually in terms of a gen-

---

45. *ThWNT* 1 (1933) 239–51; ET: *TDNT* 1 (1964) 232–51.

46. "Zur Geschichte der Lichtsymbolik im Altertum," *Exegetica*, 323–55; see above, n. 21.

47. "Johanneische Schriften und Gnosis," *Exegetica*, 230–54.

eral phenomenology of religion, that is, the world can be experienced as "hostile," or as "fallen," or as a realm for education. Or Bultmann refers to the understanding of existence that is expressed in various concepts.[48] But he does not go beyond this inter-pretation to an explanation of the political and social factors that determine such expe-rience of existence in a particular historical situation.

Moreover, it does not become clear how the Christian authors share with those authors who belong to the "background" of the New Testament the ambiguities and agonies of the understanding of existence in a particular historical moment. The New Testament authors, and by all means Paul and the author of the Gospel of John, remain phenomena sui generis, isolated from the rest. They are shining examples of a true exis-tential, that is, eschatological, understanding of life in faith. Indeed, this happens despite Bultmann's better methodological insights, and against his inclination to understand the New Testament as a document of Hellenistic syncretism, and notwithstanding his ability of treating non-Christian documents with unbiased care and considerable empa-thy.

Nevertheless, the New Testament ultimately appears as a special kind of document—separated from its non-Christian context and isolated from other early Christian liter-ature. This is the consequence of elevating the principle of interpretation, the understanding of existence, into an abstract philosophical principle. Because true escha-tological understanding is present only in John and Paul, they cease to be historical phenomena. At this point, Bultmann is a Christian apologist rather than a scholar of the history of religions.

V

Further work with the Gnostic documents from Nag Hammadi will most likely con-firm Bultmann's hypothesis of the existence of a pre-Christian Jewish Gnosticism. Thus his most controversial hypothesis about the history-of-religions background of the New Testament will be confirmed. But it is our task to treat these documents no longer as "background." To be sure, the hypothesis that the Gnostic movement is a secondary aberration from Christianity still operates with the assumption of an original and unique Christian truth, "naturally" developed by John and later perverted by the Gnostics. In this respect, nothing can be added to Bultmann's arguments against Percy.[49] But our renewed efforts to investigate the relationship between Gnosticism and Christianity must not be limited to the tracing of concepts, mythological metaphors, and religious practices, thus producing much in terms of the detailed observation, however necessary, and little in terms of understanding. Considering both the claim of an original Christian

---

48. With explicit reference to the work of Hans Jonas, *Gnosis und spätantiker Geist,* vol. 1: *Die mythologis-che Gnosis* (FRLANT 51; Göttingen: Vandenhoeck & Ruprecht, 1934; 2d ed. 1954): Percy "reproduces the Gnostic mythology as if it were a kind of dogmatics, instead of interpreting it from the understanding of exis-tence that is expressed in it, although the book of Hans Jonas that he quotes repeatedly offered him the best methodical introduction" (*Exegetica,* 232; cf. 253).

49. "Johanneische Schriften und Gnosis," *Exegetica,* 230–54.

uniqueness and the retreat into the technicalities of so-called objective scholarship, Bultmann's work as a history-of-religions scholar offers challenging alternatives.

Some of the principles that Bultmann has accepted from the history-of-religions school and further refined in his work remain important guides for further investigations. Following Bultmann's essay of 1940 in which he defends his work against the criticisms of Percy, those principles can be summarized as follows:

1. The question of early Christianity's relationship to its religious environment must not be reduced to specific terms and concepts, but must be seen as a problem of the entire language world that Christian and non-Christian authors share.

2. Technical definitions of certain concepts, such as "light" or "world," as more "materialistic" or "religious-ethical" or "spiritual" are meaningless; rather, one must ask for the understanding of human existence that is evident in the use and interpretation of such concepts in specific historical situations.

3. Theological statements about the presence of salvation in Jesus or about the uniqueness of Christianity cannot be used as arguments against the total dependence of Christian soteriological language upon its non-Christian environment. On the contrary—and here Bultmann refers once more to the work of Jonas[50]— the early Christian understanding of Jesus is totally determined by the developed soteriologies of its time, particularly by the soteriology of the Gnostic religion.

It is our task to develop these insights further with respect to their specific historical ramifications. We must learn that early Christianity shares not only the language world of the religions of the late Hellenistic period, but also their agonies, predicaments, and failures. New sociological investigations into the religious world of that time will serve to deepen these insights, while games with new literary methods will tend to obscure the critical burden of the task. The important challenge of Christian apologetic theology is obviously more difficult and more frustrating than even Bultmann realized.

---

50. *Exegetica*, 253.

25

INSIGHTS FROM A CAREER
OF INTERPRETATION

The essays collected in this volume and a second volume to be published in the near future represent half a century of the development of my efforts to understand the New Testament and early Christianity in their historical development and contemporary environment. It has been a long way, and along its path the changes of time have challenged me to turn to new topics and endeavors I did not fathom when I began. But in order to understand what these challenges were, I must begin at a time well before my first publication.

Confirmation by a Lutheran minister, who belonged to the Confessing Church (the group of Protestant churches in Germany that had opposed the National Socialist political and religious ideology), active in the Hitler youth movement, two years in the German armed forces, half a year as prisoner of war—all this cumulated in the conviction that I wanted to become a Lutheran minister. Thus, not yet 19 years old and not knowing where I should go after my release from the American POW camp in Marburg on October 31, 1945 (my family was still living in the Russian occupation zone), on the next day I applied for admission as a student in the Faculty of Theology of the University of Marburg, and a week later I was admitted to begin my studies.

To describe the conditions under which we began our studies in November 1945 would take a separate chapter. We were all poor, hungry most of the time, studying in unheated libraries and seminar rooms, stuffing our pipes with horrible home-grown tobacco seasoned with chesterfield aroma, unable to buy new shoes and clothing, laundering what we had in cold water, and for years generally deprived of all the amenities of a normal life. The only lights in the darkness were CARE packages and gifts of clothing from students of Union Theological Seminary in New York. At the same time, these were very exciting years. A whole world of German and American literature and culture that was forbidden in the Nazi years, in which we had grown up, began to open. German authors of the early decades of the twentieth century, especially Jewish authors, and French and American literature, Thomas Mann, Thornton Wilder, Jean-Paul Sartre, Franz Kafka, to name only a few, were devoured, and it was the first time in my life that I could listen to music by Felix Mendelsohn and Stravinsky. But that is another chapter yet to be written.

Uncertainty about my theological place in the post–World War II Christianity in Germany was resolved by the advice of my first New Testament teacher, Dr. Ernst Fuchs, to whom I am forever grateful, to enroll in the seminar of Rudolf Bultmann. It was fascinating and it was very tough. One did not want to be caught in a mistake of a translation from Hebrew or Greek! It was merciless. But what I learned was close attention to the details of the texts, textual variants, analysis of terms, work with the Greek and Hebrew concordances, and "interpretation" of findings. In the years of my study at the University of Marburg I never missed a lecture course or a seminar that Bultmann offered.

Demythologizing, Karl Barth (of course, all of us devoured the first volume of his *Dogmatik*), Dietrich Bonhoeffer, Ernst Troeltsch—all these dominated the discussions among us. As far as specific New Testament literature was concerned, the works of the scholars of the so-called history-of-religions school dominated, together with works of Bultmann's older students, most of all the work of Hans Jonas (*Gnosis und spätantiker Geist*). To be sure, I learned much from other teachers of the University of Marburg. But Bultmann was the dominating teacher for most of us. I was particularly fortunate as, together with a friend, I was invited for lunch at Bultmann's home once every week during the academic year 1947/48. It remains the most precious memory of the years at Marburg, because it provided the opportunity to experience personally the unerring human integrity, humility, and piety of my beloved teacher.

It was a matter of course that, after the successful completion of my academic studies in 1950, I asked Bultmann whether he would be willing to supervise my dissertation, which he agreed to do. But there were at that time no such things as dissertation fellowships, and positions as research and teaching assistants were almost nonexistent. In any case, I wanted to become a Lutheran minister and therefore left Marburg to enter into the service of my home church, the Evangelical Lutheran Church of Hannover, serving for the better part of three years as a *Vikar* (a kind of combination of intern and assistant minister), in order to qualify for ordination (after a "second examination" conducted by the church).

By the spring of 1954, the dissertation was accepted, I passed the *Rigorosum* (the final examination after acceptance of the dissertation)[1] and also the church examination, thus qualifying for ordination, and waited for the assignment to my first parish. But a phone call from Professor Günther Bornkamm in Heidelberg changed all my own expectations. He needed a teaching and research assistant, someone who had already received his doctoral degree, because eventually a full-time teaching position for a *Dozent* (Assistant Professor) in New Testament would be open at his university, in order to replace Hans Conzelmann,[2] who would soon follow a call as a professor at another university. Since Bornkamm's own most advanced student, Dieter Georgi,[3] would not be ready for this position, Bornkamm had called his former teacher Bultmann and asked for his advice; Bultmann recommended that he contact me. I accepted, and asked for a leave of absence from the Lutheran Church of Hannover. This put me into an academic career.

---

1. The dissertation was published as *Synoptische Überlieferung bei den Apostolischen Vätern* (TU 65; Berlin: Akademie-Verlag, 1957).

2. Conzelmann became professor of New Testament at the University of Zurich in 1955, later moved to Göttingen in Germany, where he completed his distinguished career; he also served for one semester as visiting professor at Harvard University in 1963.

3. Georgi became my successor when I left Heidelberg for Harvard University, later was visiting professor at Harvard, taught for several years at San Francisco Theological Seminary in San Anselmo, came to Harvard University in 1970 as my colleague, and in 1984 accepted an invitation to a professorship at the University of Frankfurt, where he also became the founding dean of the faculty of theology at that university.

Heidelberg was an entirely new experience. Marburg had provided a somewhat parochial atmosphere (and during the years of my study, 1945–50, it was economically very difficult to move to another university). There were several good and competent teachers, to whom I owe much. I profited among others from Professor Ebbinghaus's (a committed Kantian) lectures on Immanuel Kant and from several courses in modern German literature—almost all works that were not permitted in Nazi Germany. But there was for us only one truly inspiring master, Bultmann. Heidelberg, on the other hand, had assembled the one and only great theological faculty in the first two decades of postwar Germany: Gerhard von Rad in Old Testament studies, Günther Bornkamm in New Testament studies, Hans Freiherr von Campenhausen and Heinrich Bornkamm in church history, Edmund Schlink and Peter Brunner in systematic theology—to name only a few of the most outstanding theologians. There was also Hans-Georg Gadamer teaching philosophy.

This faculty also had attracted an impressive number of younger scholars. My colleague as teaching assistant in Old Testament was Klaus Baltzer,[4] in church history Heinz Kraft,[5] in systematic theology Wolfhart Pannenberg,[6] in pastoral theology Friedemann Merkel.[7] Cooperation with Baltzer and Merkel resulted in a seminar on "Exegesis and Preaching" that we taught jointly as soon as I had achieved the status at Heidelberg that allowed me to offer courses in my own right.[8]

Under Bultmann's guidance, I had learned to be a good exegete and form critic. The work on my dissertation on the Apostolic Fathers, however, also forced me to pay more attention to the world of the second century. In Heidelberg I chose for my next project Justin Martyr.[9] But investigating the Gospel quotations of Justin Martyr forced me to deal also with Justin's quotations from the Septuagint, which involved entering into the complex questions of the revisions of the Septuagint with reference to the Hebrew text.[10] I was, at the same time, immersed in the theological debates of that dis-

---

4. Baltzer later taught at Garrett in Evanston, IL, then briefly at Bethel Theological Seminary in Germany, and finally at Munich. He also spent a term as visiting professor at Harvard University. He would become my closest friend and guide in the study of the Hebrew Scriptures. He became the only European scholar who served from the beginning as a member of the editorial board of the new commentary series "Hermeneia," which Frank M. Cross of Harvard and I had begun in the late sixties and which is still well and alive, published by Fortress Press.

5. Later professor in Kiel, Germany.

6. He later taught for several decades at Munich and became the leading and most discussed scholar in his field.

7. He became professor of pastoral theology at the University of Münster and served there for a number of years as rector of the university.

8. This seminar continued after I had left Heidelberg, with Dieter Georgi taking my place. Many of its proceedings were published in the form of aids to ministers for the preparation of their sermons in the series *Göttinger Predigtmeditationen*. At Harvard I have for many years offered a similar seminar together with Harvard's Preacher to the University, Prof. Dr. Peter Gomes.

9. In order to obtain a full-time teaching position (the *venia legendi*) at a German university, one had to submit a second major piece of scholarship and pass requirements for what is called *Habilitation*.

10. This work resulted in my *Habilitationsschrift* "Septuaginta und Synoptischer Erzählungsstoff bei Justin dem Märtyrer." It was never published because two specialists in LXX studies rejected my thesis about the version of the LXX that Justin had used. Later at Harvard I learned from my colleague Frank Cross and his more recent studies of the revision of the LXX that I was on the right path.

tinguished faculty and its associates from other fields (especially the philosopher Hans-Georg Gadamer, who was actively participating in the monthly meetings of the *Theologische Societät*). The new second professor for New Testament, coming to Heidelberg during my years there, was Karl-Georg Kuhn, who was intensely interested in the newly discovered Dead Sea Scrolls. For several years I participated in what we called the "Qumran Cave," where faculty and doctoral students read and deciphered the new Hebrew texts—no German, English, or French translations were available at the time. As I happened to have a photo lab at my home, I became the one who provided (illegally!) photocopies for all participants. Then there were the annual three-day meetings of the "Old Marburg Students"—scholars who had studied under Bultmann (and Heidegger) in Marburg. It was a most distinguished assembly of several dozen scholars, older and younger, in which worship of our admired teachers, foremost Bultmann, competed with the critical questions of a new generation. Unforgettable are the discussions of the paper that Ernst Käsemann presented to that assembly in 1954, which ignited the new search for the historical Jesus.[11]

All this opened up perspectives that I had not imagined as a Marburg student: learning a new perspective in the study of the Hebrew Bible (mostly mediated through my friend of many years Klaus Baltzer); becoming familiar with the newly discovered Dead Sea Scrolls through Kuhn's working group; being led on a path of a more rigorous understanding of the history of ancient Christianity through Hans von Campenhausen, arguably the most significant historian of the ancient church of the twentieth century; and becoming involved in the renewal of New Testament studies in the circle of doctoral students of Bornkamm, from which emerged a number of important New Testament scholars (Dieter Georgi, Hannes-Odil Steck, Egon Brandenburger, Ulrich Wilckens, H. E. Tödt, Ferdinand Hahn, Dieter Lührmann, and several others). This was the birthplace of a new beginning, after Bultmann, of a fresh understanding of the world of the New Testament in the twentieth century. During my four years at Heidelberg I learned that texts had to be grounded more firmly in their specific historical situations. Hans von Campenhausen: "Don't tell me that you do not believe that Paul wrote 2 Thessalonians; tell me where and why and in what situation that document was produced." Von Campenhausen also told me that I had to write that book on the history and development of early Christian Gospels—a request that I managed to fulfill only much later.[12] But most of all, Günther Bornkamm's careful reevaluation of the theological situation after Bultmann made a great impression. Yes, demythologizing was an important issue. But there are historical questions that demanded attention, foremost the question of the historical Jesus. Bornkamm's reactions and critical evaluations of my publications during the following decades remained as signs of encouragement as I moved further away from my beginning positions.

---

11. "The Historical Jesus and the Christ of the Kerygma" (first publishd in German in *ZThK* 51 [1954] 125–53). I was the assistant of Bornkamm while he was working on his book *Jesus von Nazareth* (Urban Taschenbücher; Stuttgart: Kohlhammer, 1956). This immensely successful book was translated into English (and into several other languages) with a preface by James M. Robinson and later republished in a new edition, for which I wrote the preface: *Jesus of Nazareth* (Minneapolis: Fortress Press, 1995).

12. I was able to publish a comprehensive examination of the development of the Gospels only much later: *Ancient Christian Gospels: Their History and Development* (Philadelphia: Trinity Press International, 1990).

In 1958 I followed an invitation to Harvard University, where I accepted a tenure position in 1959. If Heidelberg was the liberation from Marburg's parochialism, Harvard became a place of unimagined challenges of a new world and a hitherto only very poorly known world of scholarship—much of it represented by refugees from Nazi tyranny.[13] It forced me to realize that German New Testament scholarship had been frozen in a conventional exercise of traditional models of inquiry. My colleagues at Harvard in the New Testament department were Amos Wilder and Krister Stendahl. But there were also G. Ernest Wright and Frank M. Cross in Old Testament; George Hunston Williams (the last universal church historian of the past century) and the Dutch Reformation historian Heiko Oberman in church history; Paul Tillich, Paul Lehmann, and R. Richard Niebuhr (son of H. Richard Niebuhr and nephew of Reinhold Niebuhr) in systematic theology; Werner Jaeger and Ernst Bloch in the Classics department; and most of all Arthur Darby Nock, the great scholar of Greek religion. Encounters with other influential scholars, not teaching at Harvard University, challenged me in the years to come, especially the meetings with Bultmann's and Heidegger's student Hans Jonas and with Bultmann's and Karl Barth's student James M. Robinson. All this introduced me to a world of scholarship and theology for which my German theological training had left me very ill prepared. It taught me to realize that Hitler's pre– and post–World War II intellectual horizon had become unforgivably parochial.

Amos Wilder, older brother of Thornton Wilder and a poet in his own right, was the first American scholar who had challenged the problem of demythologizing from a completely different perspective: the issue was not to rid the New Testament of its mythology but to translate its mythical concepts into the mythology and poetry of the twentieth century. I learned that myth and poetry had long since formed the ideology of the self-understanding of the American soul and that this was the language into which the message of the New Testament must be translated. In order to understand this, it was necessary to become acquainted with American literature: William Faulkner, Thornton Wilder, Walt Whitman, Herman Melville, and others, which I read eagerly during my first years at Harvard.

Krister Stendahl had been a student of Anton Friedrichsen at Uppsala. Many years of the jointly chaired New Testament seminar for doctoral students required intense listening to a different way of handling the historical-critical method. Much of this took roots slowly and is visible only in some of my more recent articles on Paul. When Ernst Käsemann visited Harvard, he offered a very severe criticism of Stendahl's essay on "Paul and the Introspective Conscience of the West." But over the course of time it seems to me that Stendahl's insights are crucial for a better understanding of Paul.

Frank M. Cross, eminent Dead Sea Scroll investigator and specialist in Northwest Semitic epigraphy, like Krister Stendahl a few years older, and the more senior G. Ernest Wright were both students of W. F. Albright, from whom they had learned that Bultmann was probably the antichrist. There was no way to talk about that with Albright himself, whom I happened to meet a few times. But his two students, who

---

13. I recall a meeting of several Jewish scholars at Brandeis University in Waltham, MA, in my early years at Harvard, where the fact that I spoke German fluently was taken as evidence that I was Jewish!

were teaching at Harvard, would become very influential partners of discussion, especially because they stimulated a more active interest in the Dead Sea Scrolls and in biblical archaeology.

Special mention is due to Arthur Darby Nock, then as professor of history of religion a member of the Faculty of Divinity at Harvard University, who became a close advisor for my work for five years until his untimely death. When the question of my tenure at Harvard University arose in 1959, he invited me to his study in order to get to know me better. A glass of strong whiskey and a cigar were part of the discussion. At the end of a two-hour meeting, he told me that he would vote in my favor under the condition that I would submit to him for review everything that I wanted to publish, before I sent the manuscript to the publisher—a request that I fulfilled faithfully. I was working at that time on several articles for the *Theologisches Wörterbuch zum Neuen Testament*.[14] All of these were read critically by Nock and profited immensely from his incredible knowledge of Greek literature and his merciless destruction of any theological fancy.[15]

Hermeneutics and demythologizing, however, still held my attention. There was a circle of American New Testament scholars, among them Robert F. Funk and James M. Robinson, who were strongly influenced by Bultmann. Drew University in New Jersey held several conferences on hermeneutics in the early sixties that drew an impressive number of competent scholars in biblical studies, church history, and theology. To the first of these, Gerhard Ebeling and Ernst Fuchs were invited. For the second conference (1963), Martin Heidegger and Heinrich Ott (Karl Barth's successor in Basel) had agreed to come. But a month or so before the conference, I received a rather urgent phone call from the organizer, Robert Funk: Heidegger's physician had told him that his health was not well enough for the flight across the Atlantic; did I know anyone, who could take his place? Somewhat innocently I suggested Hans Jonas, who accepted and presented his paper on "Heidegger and Theology,"[16] which was published several times.[17] It was fascinating, stunned Heinrich Ott,[18] and in fact terminated for me as well as for others in the United States the belief that Heidegger's anthropological existentialist analysis was a useful tool for the translation of the New Testament into the language of our time.

I had met Jonas, whose work on Gnosticism all of us students at Marburg had once read with great interest, for the first time during my first year in the United States

---

14. "Σπλάγχνον, σπλαγχνίζεσθαι, εὔσπλαγχνος, πολύσπλαγχνος, ἄσπλαγχνος," *ThWNT* 10 (1962) 548–59; "Συνέχω, συνοχή," *ThWNT* 7 (1964) 875–85; "Τέμνω, ἀτομία, ἀπότομος, ἀποτόμως, κατατομή, ὀρθοτομέω," *ThWNT* 8 (1965) 106–13; "Τόπος," *ThWNT* 8 (1966) 106–13; "Ὑπόστασις," *ThWNT* 8 (1969) 571–88; "Φύσις," *ThWNT* 9 (1970/71) 246–71. All of these are now published in English translation in *TDNT.*

15. Nock's immense erudition is most evident in his many articles and countless book reviews, edited by Zeph Stewart, *Essays on Religion and the Ancient World* (2 vols.; Cambridge: Harvard University Press, 1972).

16. Hans Jonas reports this event in his book *Erinnerungen* (Frankfurt am Main: Insel, 2003) 304–6.

17. First in *Review of Metaphysics* 18 (1964) 207–33; then in *The Phenomenon of Life: Toward a Philosophical Biology* (New York: Harper & Row, 1966) 235–61; also in German: "Heidegger und die Theologie," *EvTh* 24 (1964) 621–42.

18. He had published a few years earlier a thorough and fundamentally positive analysis of this question: *Der Weg Martin Heideggers und der Weg der Theologie* (Zurich: Zollikon, 1959).

(1958). I was invited to present a paper to a circle of scholars in New York interested in questions of hermeneutics, and I presented a paper about Paul's Second Letter to the Corinthians; but I was bitterly attacked, especially by Morton Smith (who would later become a close friend). As my English was not fluent enough to defend my position persuasively, one of the participants stood up and gave a brilliant defense of my paper. I had not understood his name when he was recognized; but after the meeting he came over to shake my hand and said, "Ich bin Hans Jonas; wir Bultmann-Studenten müssen doch zusammenhalten" ("I am Hans Jonas; we students of Bultmann have to stick together").

This was the beginning of my personal acquaintance, which became important for me and for others, more than Jonas ever knew. There was another unforgettable meeting in the same year, when Bultmann and his wife visited New York, at which also Hannah Arendt was present.[19] In 1961 Jonas had delivered, upon my recommendation, the Ingersoll Lecture on Immortality at Harvard University Divinity School on "Immortality and the Modern Temper."[20]

Numerous other meetings with Jonas would come in the decades after the conference at Drew University. But these meetings were no longer on questions of hermeneutics and philosophy and theology. What had at that time begun to capture our interest were the Gnostic texts from Nag Hammadi. For many years Jonas participated regularly in annual meetings of a circle of scholars (sometimes we met at his house in New Rochelle, graciously hosted by Lore Jonas), who were interested in a reconsideration of the question of early Christianity and Gnosticism on the basis of the new manuscript discoveries.[21] Jonas also was an important voice in the discussions of the International Conference on Gnosticism at Yale University in 1978.[22]

The leader in the organization of this new interest was James M. Robinson of Claremont Graduate School and the director of the newly founded Institute for Antiquity and Christianity in Claremont, California, which also led the way to publishing the facsimile edition of the Nag Hammadi manuscripts, their preliminary English translation,[23] and finally a critical edition of all these texts. In spite of my limited knowledge of Coptic, I was invited to participate.[24] Several former doctoral students from Harvard

---

19. I cannot help but to note here that this meeting took place in the faculty club of Columbia University in New York and that only the men were allowed to enter through the front door, while Mrs. Bultmann, Hannah Arendt, and my wife had to enter through a back door and use a different elevator at the back of the building!

20. *HTR* 55 (1962) 1–20; repr. in Jonas, *Phenomenon of Life,* 262–84.

21. He had meanwhile become an American authority on Gnosticism through the publication of his book *The Gnostic Religion: The Message of the Alien God and the Beginnings of Christianity* (Boston: Beacon, 1958; rev. ed. 1963).

22. The proceedings were published by Bentley Layton, ed., *The Rediscovery of Gnosticism* (2 vols.; Studies in the History of Religions 41; Leiden: Brill, 1980).

23. James M. Robinson, *The Nag Hammadi Library in English: Translated by Members of the Coptic Gnostic Library Project of the Institute for Antiquity and Christianity* (San Francisco: Harper & Row, 1977), and several updated editions.

24. "The Gospel of Thomas: Introduction," in Bentley Layton, ed., *Nag Hammadi Writings of Codex II, 2–7* (2 vols.; NHS 20; Leiden: Brill, 1989) 1.38–49; with Stephen Emmel and Elaine Pagels, *Nag Hammadi Codex III, 5: The Dialogue of the Savior* (NHS 26; Leiden: Brill, 1984).

University's doctoral program in New Testament and Christian Origins also became members of the publication team for these texts: Harold W. Attridge, Bentley Layton, Elaine H. Pagels, and Birger A. Pearson. Also my new colleague George MacRae, S.J., a distinguished New Testament scholar who had joined the faculty at Harvard Divinity School in the early seventies, was an active participant in these efforts.

My interest in these newly discovered Gnostic texts also brought new international contacts. The late Hans-Martin Schenke invited me to (East) Berlin a number of times, where I met other scholars from his working group in East Germany (at that time the interest in the Nag Hammadi texts was marginal at best in West Germany). My work on the apocryphal Gospels also drew the attention of the scholars in Geneva and Lausanne, especially of François Bovon,[25] who were engaged in the new critical edition of the apocryphal acts of the apostles, which resulted in several invitations to Geneva (two articles included in this and the second volume in English translation are the fruits of those visits). I should not forget here the fruitful exchanges that developed with Tjitze Baarda, now professor emeritus of the Free University of Amsterdam,[26] where I was privileged to spend a semester as a visiting professor.

In view of the discovery of the *Gospel of Thomas,* first published in 1958, it was clear that a comprehensive book on the history of Gospel literature would have to wait. More Gnostic Gospels appeared soon. Foremost the *Dialogue of the Savior* and the *Apocryphon of James* (otherwise known as the *Epistula Jacobi*) demanded attention for the completion of this project. Preliminary work on these matters resulted in the joint publication with my friend James Robinson of *Trajectories Through Early Christianity.*[27] This gave me the general outline for the writing of an introduction to the New Testament, for which I was under contract with the publishing house Walter de Gruyter of Berlin,[28] and it pointed the direction to the long-planned book on ancient Christian Gospels, which had to wait for two more decades before it was ready for publication.[29] But the publication of *Trajectories* also set the stage for an increasing number of international contacts.

Meanwhile, the New Testament faculty at Harvard Divinity School underwent some changes. Amos Wilder had been retired for some time; Krister Stendahl became dean, and, after his resignation, he accepted an appointment as bishop of Stockholm in Sweden. In their place the New Testament was enriched by the addition of the learned English Semitist John Strugnell, who was deeply involved in the publication of the

---

25. Bovon later joined the faculty of Harvard Divinity School, where he is active.

26. He also spent a year as visiting professor at Harvard University.

27. *Trajectories Through Early Christianity* (Philadelphia: Fortress Press, 1971; repr. Eugene, Or.: Wipf and Stock, 2006); it was published in German translation as *Entwicklungslinien durch die Welt des frühen Christentums* (Tübingen: Mohr/Siebeck, 1971); later also a Japanese translation appeared (Tokyo: Shinkyo Suppansha, 1975).

28. *Einführung in das Neue Testament im Rahmen der Religionsgeschichte und Kulturgeschichte der hellenistischen und römischen Zeit* (De Gruyter Lehrbuch; Berlin: de Gruyter, 1980). It appeared two years later in two volumes in a new English version: *Introduction to the New Testament,* vol. 1: *History, Culture, and Religion of the Hellenistic Age* (Philadelphia: Fortress Press; Berlin: de Gruyter, 1982); vol. 2: *History and Literature of Early Christianity* (Philadelphia: Fortress Press; Berlin: de Gruyter, 1982). Second editions of the two volumes were published by de Gruyter in 1995 and 2000, respectively.

29. See n. 12 above.

Dead Sea Scrolls, my old Heidelberg friend Dieter Georgi, and George MacRae, S.J., whose specialty was the investigation of the Coptic Gnostic texts from Nag Hammadi and with whom I had already developed a close friendship, when he was still teaching at the nearby Weston Jesuit School of Theology. It is difficult to describe the excitement and enrichment that resulted from these fifteen years of close cooperation. Every semester we taught jointly a seminar for advanced New Testament students (never more than twelve students) and a second seminar for doctoral students working on their dissertations. We went out for drinks and dinner together every single week and also otherwise shared and discussed our various research projects and the projects our doctoral students pursued. The field of New Testament and Christian origins thus encompassed everything: Old Testament Apocrypha, Pseudepigrapha, and Dead Sea Scrolls to New Testament Apocrypha and the Nag Hammadi Library, of course including New Testament exegesis and theology. The excellent libraries of Harvard University facilitated greatly the work of our doctoral students as well as our own research. Moreover, there was no such thing as "my" doctoral student; all dissertations became the common concerns of the entire team of professors, often aided by our Old Testament colleague Frank Cross and increasingly by colleagues from the classics department, among them Zeph Stewart, Gregory Nagy, and the professors of classical archaeology George Hanfmann and his successor David Mitten. This was an unbelievably enriching environment, in which the teachers were as much challenged as the students.[30] These golden years of my career at Harvard University have formed my scholarly perspectives more than anything else.[31]

There was, however, an additional element that brought a new focus to my scholarly work. In 1970 I was searching for a project that could entice a major foundation to finance a sabbatical leave of absence, which I had planned for the academic year 1971/72. Sponsored by the Guggenheim Foundation, I had enjoyed the liberation from a year of teaching in 1963/64 in order to work on my project on early Christian Gospels. But that project still needed time, and foundations are rarely willing to support an old project that had not brought visible results the first time around. For some time, my colleagues and friends G. Ernest Wright and Frank Cross had complained about the lack of the involvement of critical New Testament scholars in the field of biblical archaeology. Fundamentalist scholars especially were flooding the Holy Land with fanciful archaeological research in the footsteps of Jesus and Peter. Other New Testament scholars were simply piggybacking upon the research of Old Testament excavators without a vision of the contribution of archaeology to the origins of the New

---

30. From this circle of doctoral students emerged several leading scholars. In addition to doctoral students from the sixties like Eldon J. Epp, Birger Pearson, George W. E. Nickelsburg, A. Thomas Kraabel, Demetrius Trakatellis (now Greek Orthodox Archbishop of America), Abraham J. Malherbe, and many others, I should mention especially Harold W. Attridge, Bentley Layton, Elaine Pagels, Adela Yarbro Collins, Bernadette Brooten, and Steven Friesen.

31. All this would change when Dieter Georgi moved back to Germany in 1984 to become the founding dean of the new faculty of theology at the University of Frankfurt, George MacRae died unexpectedly in 1985, and John Strugnell moved to Jerusalem a year later to become director of the project of the Dead Sea Scroll publications.

Testament studies. Although archaeology was despised in the circles in which I had grown up (Ernst Fuchs: "This is just archaeology of the empty tomb!"), I finally decided to take up their suggestions. As far as I knew, however, most writings of the New Testament did not originate from Palestine but from the areas of western Asia Minor, Macedonia, and Greece. Thus I decided to apply for a sabbatical grant from the American Council of Learned Societies for the exploration of archaeological resources for New Testament Studies in Turkey, Macedonia, and Greece, supported by my Old Testament colleagues and by the professor of classical archaeology at Harvard, George Hanfmann, confessing that I knew nothing about it, had never been to an excavation, and knew nothing about the subject matter, but I wanted to learn. Miraculously, I got the necessary financing for this adventure.

I spent one semester in the spring of 1972 at the American School of Classical Studies in Athens.[32] Wherever I went, it was assumed that I was probably "trailing the footsteps of the apostle Paul." It was difficult to get rid of that ominous designation. But armed with a camera and with the help of my former student Dr. Demetrios Trakatellis, then bishop of Athens, I managed to get acquainted with Greek archaeologists at various sites and museums and to get my message across: I wanted to learn more about the archaeological monuments giving witness to the cultural, social, and religious environment that could illuminate the world of early Christianity in the areas in which its characteristic forms of organization and most of its writings were shaped. Lasting friendships and working relationships developed from these beginnings and lasted over many decades, especially with Dr. Judith Binder at the American School of Classical Studies, Dr. Katerina Rhomiopoulou,[33] and Dr. Charalambos Bakirtzis.[34] Later, when I had spent several summers in Turkey, Professor Klaus Nohlen and Dr. Wolfgang Radt of the Pergamon excavations, the old team of the Ephesos excavators, Proferssor Dieter Knibbe, Dr. Stefan Karwiese, Dr. Ulrike Outschar, Dr. Stephan Scherrer, Dr. Maria Aurenhammer, Dr. Hilke Thür, Drs. Heinrich and Susanne Zabehlicki, and others became strong supporters of our project; and at Sardis Professor Crawford Greenwalt was very welcoming. They also were helpful to establish connections to excavators at other sites.

Over the period of thirty years, members of a team of doctoral students and I myself were able to assemble a collection of 8,300 slides from Greece and Turkey (and also some from Rome, Pompey, and Herculaneum) through annual visits to archaeological sites and museums, including visits to many European museums. The results of the close study of these materials, in which many graduate students at Harvard University participated, were first published in hard copy in a two-volume series "Archaeological Resources for New Testament Studies" with slides and a one-page description, interpretation, and bibliography for each slide. This very expensive and cumbersome series has now been replaced by an expanded CD-Rom version, published in 2004, includ-

32. Since they did not know what to do with a NT scholar I was classified as a "Research Fellow 'Other.'"

33. Director of the Archaeological Museum at Thessaloniki, later at the National Museum of Archaeology in Athens, and sometime administrator of archaeological sites and museums of the Greek government.

34. Archaeological Ephoros for Eastern Macedonia and Thrace at Kavala and now Ephoros for Byzantine Archaeology for Central Macedonia in Thessaloniki.

ing 860 slides, a page of interpretation for each slide, indices, glossaries, and cross-references, including materials from Athens, Corinth, Isthmia, Olympia, Delphi, Thessalonike, Philippi, Pergamon, and Ephesos.[35] The entire collection of slides is at this time transferred into electronic format and is now accessible as part of the Harvard University Pictorial Resources. I am at this time continuing to supervise the process of cataloguing.

This result of more than thirty years of the study of archaeological materials from Greece and Turkey has been supplemented since 1979 by regular seminars, including on-site sessions in Greece and Turkey, for graduate students in the study of religion in order to acquaint them with the opportunities and challenges of studying nonliterary materials. These seminars were offered by Harvard Divinity School and the Harvard Faculty of Arts and Sciences and directed by my friend Dr. David Mitten, professor of classical archaeology, and myself. Harvard Divinity School has been fortunate to appoint a very gifted younger New Testament scholar with good training in classical archaeology, Dr. Laura Nasrallah, who is very successful in continuing this venture in early Christianity and archaeology.

In order to facilitate the interaction between archaeologists and students of early Christianity, Harvard Divinity School, together with the Harvard departments of Classics and Fine Arts, has also sponsored several symposia on specific excavations, to which in each case six to eight excavators from abroad have been brought together with American scholars in the study of the New Testament and early Christianity. I published the proceedings of the symposia on Ephesos and on Pergamon in the series Harvard Theological Studies;[36] those of the recent symposium on Corinth have just been published by Harvard University Press;[37] and a symposium on Thessalonike under the leadership of Dr. Laura Nasrallah will take place in May 2007.

The Society of Biblical Literature once had an annual lecture series that was entitled "How My Mind Has Changed."[38] If I ask myself that question right now, I can only answer that it has been a long way from the time when I was an enthusiastic student of Bultmann with the firm belief that demythologizing was the most important issue of New Testament scholarship to a stage in my life where bringing archaeologists and students of early Christianity together would occupy much of my time and seemed to me the most worthwhile thing I could contribute. But that path has not been determined by deliberate design. Rather, it was prompted by the need to respond to new challenges, discovery of new sources, interactions with colleagues, and responding to

---

35. Helmut Koester, ed., *Cities of Paul: Images and Interpretations from the Harvard New Testament Archaeology Project* (Minneapolis: Fortress Press, 2004).

36. *Ephesos: Metropolis of Asia: An Interdisciplinary Approach to its Archaeology, Religion, and Culture* (HTS 41; Valley Forge, Pa.; Trinity Press International, 1995); and *Pergamon, Citadel of the Gods: Archaeological Record, Literary Description, and Religious Development* (HTS 46; Harrisburg: Trinity Press International, 1998). My own contributions to these volumes are included in the present volume as chapters 22 and 13, respectively.

37. Daniel N. Schowalter and Steven Friesen, eds., *Urban Religion in Roman Corinth* (HTS 53; Cambridge: Harvard University Press, 2005).

38. I was at one time invited to present such a lecture at the annual meeting but did not accept because of a number of unfortunate circumstances.

interests brought up by doctoral students. On the other hand, as some essays in this volume show, I have never given up my first love: biblical exegesis and theology.[39] Looking back over fifty years of research and teaching, begun in Heidelberg in 1954, and still continuing, *Deo volente,* as "research professor" at Harvard University, I can only express my gratefulness to the colleagues and numerous doctoral students at Harvard and to the many friends and colleagues at other universities in the United States and abroad, blessed that I received more than I was ever able to return. But it is also fitting to express my gratefulness to Harvard University. It provided the openness that allowed completely free exploration of unorthodox paths of inquiry and teaching, encouraged close cooperation across the lines of disciplines and faculties, and generously made needed resources available.[40]

39. At this time I am working together with my friend of half a century Klaus Baltzer on a monograph in biblical theology. A preview of this work appears in chapter 10 of this volume in the essay "Suffering Servant and Royal Messiah: From Second Isaiah to Paul, Mark, and Matthew."

40. That only rarely included funds for research, travel, or symposia; the university usually expected that professors would find the needed money from sources outside the university, in which the respective development offices of the faculties were willing to assist. I am grateful to many donors, especially to the participants of several Harvard Alumni Tours, to former students, to many friends, and to my one-time student Prentis Tomlinson.

INDEX OF ANCIENT LITERATURE

INDEX OF NAMES AND SUBJECTS

INDEX OF GREEK TERMS

INDEX OF MODERN AUTHORS

From Jesus to the Gospels

Interpreting the New Testament in Its Context

Helmut Koester

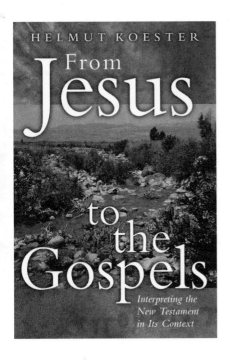

Cloth
320 pages
$39.00
ISBN 978-0-8006-2093-6

Insights into the traditions behind the Gospels—from one of the foremost New Testament scholars of our time. The companion volume to *Paul and His World*.

DATE DUE

5/11/08			